PHILOLOGICAL AND HISTORICAL COMMENTARY
ON AMMIANUS MARCELLINUS XXIV

PHILOLOGICAL AND HISTORICAL COMMENTARY ON AMMIANUS MARCELLINUS XXIV

BY

J. DEN BOEFT
J.W. DRIJVERS
D. DEN HENGST
H.C. TEITLER

BRILL
LEIDEN · BOSTON · KÖLN
2002

This book is printed on acid-free paper.

Library of Congress Cataloging-in-Publication Data

Library of Congress Cataloging-in-Publication Data is also available.

Die Deutsche Bibliothek - CIP-Einheitsaufnahme

Philological and historical commentary on Ammianus Marcellinus XXIV
/ by J. den Boeft, J.W. Drijvers, D. den Hengst and H.C. Teitler.
– Leiden ; Boston ; Köln : Brill, 2002
ISBN 90 04 12335 0

ISBN 90 04 12335 0

© Copyright 2002 by Koninklijke Brill NV, Leiden, The Netherlands

All rights reserved. No part of this publication may be reproduced, translated, stored in
a retrieval system, or transmitted in any form or by any means, electronic,
mechanical, photocopying, recording or otherwise, without prior written
permission from the publisher.

Authorization to photocopy items for internal or personal
use is granted by Brill provided that
the appropriate fees are paid directly to The Copyright
Clearance Center, 222 Rosewood Drive, Suite 910
Danvers MA 01923, USA.
Fees are subject to change.

PRINTED IN THE NETHERLANDS

CONTENTS

Preface	VII
Introduction	IX
A note on chronology	XIII
Legenda	XXV
Maps	XXVIII
Commentary on Chapter 1	1
Commentary on Chapter 2	29
Commentary on Chapter 3	69
Commentary on Chapter 4	99
Commentary on Chapter 5	149
Commentary on Chapter 6	169
Commentary on Chapter 7	201
Commentary on Chapter 8	223
Bibliography	233
Indices	247

PREFACE

The commentary on book 24 is our fifth contribution to the series, which was initiated by P. de Jonge. The geography of southern Mesopotamia and the precise chronology of the events posed considerable problems. We have aimed at plausible solutions, but for some details the available evidence offered only scant assistance.

We thank the friends and colleagues who have helped us with their advice and Ines van de Wetering, who corrected our English. Mrs. F.E. Derksen-Janssens gave our maps of the Euphrates region their final form. Each of us benefited from a period of study at the Fondation Hardt at Vandoeuvres (CH). Thanks are due to the Netherlands Organization for Scientific Research (NWO), which subsidized the correction of the English manuscript.

The series has been taken over by the publishing house Koninklijke Brill NV. We thank Mr. Egbert Forsten for his careful handling of the previous volumes.

J. den Boeft
J.W. Drijvers
D. den Hengst
H.C. Teitler

INTRODUCTION

Book 24 of the *Res Gestae* forms the middle part of the trilogy on the Persian expedition. In book 23 the author dealt with the final preparations and the march up to the border of Persia, adding two digressions concerning artillery and the Persian empire respectively in order to provide the reader with the information which he deemed necessary for him to understand the proportions of the enterprise. He now continues with the description of the progress made by Julian's main force along the Euphrates and the Naarmalcha. However, he fails to inform the reader about the emperor's precise military strategy, let alone his final objective. Even the primary strategic goal which Julian had in mind is implicitly revealed only when its impracticability is convincingly pointed out to him by his staff: a successful siege of Ctesiphon was beyond the power of the expedition to achieve.

Until that embarrassing discovery the balance between successes and setbacks during the anabasis had been decidedly positive. A number of strongholds had been taken and destroyed, among which were the important cities of Pirisabora and Maozamalcha, and near Ctesiphon the only pitched battle against a Persian force had resulted in a resounding victory. The losses which had been suffered during the march were not excessive and cannot have been unexpected by military experts. Suddenly, however, without having suffered a defeat, the expedition ran aground as the staff realized that Ctesiphon was impregnable. One may wonder why this had not been ascertained beforehand through accurate reconnoitring, but even more astonishing is the impression arising from Ammianus' account, that no alternative strategy had been prepared and that the immediate future of the expedition seemed to be decided in a makeshift manner. The decision led to the destruction by fire of the great majority of the ships accompanying the army's anabasis which had sailed down the Euphrates and the Naarmalcha. Possibly the author himself had been on board of one of these ships at least for part of the journey. Although Julian had good reasons for this decision, he clearly failed to convey these to his men, who experienced the burning of the ships as a terrible menace to their safety and who thereupon fell victim to despondency and despair. It is precisely on this note that the book ends.

INTRODUCTION

Book 24 can fruitfully be compared to Zosimus, book 3, chapters 14–26. There are many parallels, and the differences and omissions in the reports of the two historians offer ample material for a thorough comparison between them. Yet the most interesting difference is the fact that Ammianus has so many *visa* to offer: he took part in the expedition and therefore was a first-hand eye-witness. This fact has produced a number of invaluable memories, above all those concerning the behaviour of the protagonist and the general feelings of his men. This is shown especially in the various cases in which the first person plural is explicitly or implicitly present in the description of what was going on: these were not 'their' experiences, but 'ours'! This aspect of Ammianus' report gives the writing its place among the striking autobiographical texts of antiquity. Here one has a rare opportunity to live through a major event with the assistance of an intelligent and sensitive eye-witness, who had the literary talent to depict the feelings of those on the spot. In such a report there is no room for digressions; the brief picture of the fairyland of the large palm plantations in 3.13–14 serves directly to convey an impression of the luxurious surroundings in which the expedition found itself for a brief period of time.

As to the first aspect mentioned, Julian's behaviour, or more specifically, his emotional reactions to the events and his remarkable rashness, is clearly indicated. It is true that Zosimus also refers to the emperor's feelings: οὐκ ἤνεγκε μετρίως ὁ βασιλεύς, ἀλλὰ μετὰ θυμοῦ (3.19.2), but this is a rarity; Ammianus, on the other hand, repeatedly mentions Julian's emotional reactions, such as his optimism: *celso praeter alios spiritu* (1.1), his anger: *concitus ira immani* (3.2 and 5.7), *ira gravi permotus* (5.10), *increpitis optimatibus* (7.3), and finally his gloom: *maerebat…imperator* (7.8). An even more remarkable feature of Julian's behaviour is his propensity to recklessness. This is explicitly mentioned in 6.4: *ut propius temeritatem multa crebro auderet*, but the author had already reported some dangerous examples in 2.14–17, 4.3–5, 5.6. Even if this last passage is a mere duplicate of the episode narrated in 4.3–5, it shows how large Julian's temerity loomed in the author's memory. These episodes function as omens, foreshadowing his death, the more so since omina proper, which dominated the report of events in book 23, are conspicuously absent in the present book, with one telling exception: after the great victory in the battle near Ctesiphon (6.4–13), Julian, expecting a bright future, made a huge sacrifice to the war god in his accustomed manner. This sacrifice resulted in disaster: in fact, none of the sacrificial beasts could be slaughtered in the ritually correct way, a horrifying omen,

INTRODUCTION   XI

to which Julian himself reacted in an even more ominous manner, by omitting Mars from his future veneration. Hubris had expanded to bursting point, marking the peripeteia of the heroic adventure.

Indeed, the author's report also differs from Zosimus' account in its explicit references to historical precedents, which demonstrated the greatness of the enterprise. This was not a merely average military operation, but one which could easily bear comparison with the heroic feats of the past. Hence Julian as a Scipio Aemilianus redivivus in 2.16–17, or using a confident phrase after the example of Trajan (3.9), or proving to be not in the least inferior to Manlius Torquatus or Valerius Corvinus (4.5). And in assessing the quality of the victory near Ctesiphon, the author continues with a short laudatory catalogue of great military heroes and their feats in Greek history, from Hector to the Persian wars, which this glorious day could equal. Such aspects of Ammianus' narrative strategy should not be regarded as mere embellishing exaggerations: in combination with the hidden and overt references to the terrible failure of the expedition and together with the atmosphere of uncertainty and despondency in the final chapters the writing conveys something of the inexplicable and enigmatic character of the course of events through which the author had lived. Even many years later, when he was writing his report, he was unable to come to terms with the fickleness of Fortune and to understand why a majestic and potentially successful expedition had ended so miserably. Precisely this dilemma of the historian, who was an eye-witness, has produced a fascinating, even moving, historical document. At times it lacks precision, its details do not always stand the test of reliability, but it does tell the reader what it was like to be there and to experience success and failure, exultation and sheer despair, which alternated in bewildering fashion. The very last sentence of the book, which describes the effects of an enormous dust cloud, could serve as a *Chiffre* for the entire experience: *nec enim ad usque vesperam aere concreto discerni potuit quidnam esset, quod squalidius videbatur.*

A NOTE ON CHRONOLOGY

Section 23.5.12 is the last of the five passages in book 23 which furnish precise chronological data about Julian's march from Antioch to the east. In the passage in question Amm. tells us that on the second day of the march from Cercusium towards Dura, a distance of approximately fifty kilometers covered in two days (cf. *itinere bidui* in 24.1.5), a soldier named Iovianus was struck by a bolt of lightning. This happened on April 7 363 (*secuto itidem die, qui erat septimum idus Apriles, sole vergente iam in occasum*). It is not before 24.8.5 that we hear of the next precise date: after being deterred from besieging Ctesiphon Julian decided to set off on the journey home on June 16, 363 (*sextum decimum kalendas Iulias*). Taking these data as a starting point, with the help of Zosimus' account and using expressions in Amm. like *postridie, insequenti die, die secuto* etcetera, an attempt at reconstructing the chronological order of events can be made. However, it should constantly be kept in mind that this reconstruction is built on rather shaky foundations, "le résultat de fragiles reconstitutions", to quote Paschoud, speaking of Brok's chronological survey (n. 59; cf. n. 75: "sa chronologie fantaisiste"). Apart from Brok 257–9 one can consult Dodgeon-Lieu, 1991, 231–7.

From Dura, or rather, from the spot opposite Dura, on the left bank of the Euphrates which was reached on April 7, the army marched southwards for four days (*Exin dierum quattuor itinere levi peracto*, 24.1.6; cf. Zos. 3.14.2 σταθμοὺς δ' ἐντεῦθεν διελθὼν τέσσαρας), to arrive (on April 11, apparently) at a place which was to be the point of departure for a surprise attack on the insular fortress of Anatha (today 'Āna), carried out by a flotilla under the command of Lucillianus and started at nightfall (*vespera incedente cum expeditis mille impositis navibus Lucillianus comes… mittitur Anathan munimentum expugnaturus*, ibid.) – Zosimus does not explicitly mention Anatha; he says instead, that the army came to a place called Phathusas, situated opposite an island in the river (εἴς τι χωρίον ἀφίκετο. Φαθούσας ὄνομα τούτῳ. ἦν δὲ ἀντικρὺ ἐν τῷ ποταμῷ νῆσος, ἔχουσα φρούριον, 3.14.2); however, from the rest of his narrative it is clear that the island to which he refers can only be Anatha.

During the night Lucillianus' mission remained undetected (*obsidebatur insula nebulosa nocte obumbrante impetum clandestinum*, ibid.; Zos. 3.14.3 ἕως μὲν ἦν νύξ, ἐλάνθανον οἱ πολιορκοῦντες), but on the

XIV   A NOTE ON CHRONOLOGY

following day (*postquam advenit lux certa*, 24.1.7; Zos. 3.14.3 ἡμέρας δὲ γενομένης), i.e. on April 12, the Romans were spotted by their enemies. After the Persians had surrendered Anatha on the very same day, the fortress was set on fire (*statim munimento omni incenso*, 24.1.9). On the following day (*postridie*, 24.1.11), i.e. on April 13, a tornado created considerable havoc. On that same day (*eodem die*, ibid.) the Euphrates overflowed its banks.

The next point of reference mentioned by Amm. is Thilutha (*ad castra pervenimus nomine Thilutha in medio flumine sita*, 24.2.1; cf. Zos. 3.15.1 Ἐντεῦθεν ὁδόν τινα διαμείψας ἐνέτυχεν ἑτέρᾳ τοῦ ποταμοῦ νήσῳ, Lib. *Or.* 18.219 Φρούριον ἕτερον ἦν ἐν νήσῳ περιεξεσμένῃ), to be identified with the rocky island of Telbes, which is situated 12 km south-east of ʿĀna/Anatha. Thilutha therefore could have been reached in a day's march, that is, if the army departed from Anatha immediately after the tornado had subsided, on April 14. The army passed Thilutha without attempting to capture the fortress by military action, and it likewise refrained from trying to storm Achaiachala (*quo transito cum ad munimentum aliud Achaiachala nomine venissemus fluminis circumitione vallatum arduumque transcensu, refutati pari responso discessimus*, 24.2.2; cf. Zos. 3.15.2 ἕτερα δὲ φρούρια κατέλιπε) – unfortunately the location of Achaiachala is not clear; is it another island fort, to be sought on the island of Bidjân, some 15 km south of Telbes? (so, hesitatingly, Gawlikowski, 1990, 90); if so, it could have been reached also on April 14; or should Achaiachala be identified as modern Haditha, which lies on the right bank of the Euphrates, at a distance of some 60 km from Telbes? (so Musil, 1927, 239, followed by e.g. Brok 108–9 and Fontaine n. 315; note however that on his map Fontaine situates Achaiachala on the left bank of the river); in the latter case (which is preferred here) it would have taken another two days (April 15 and 16) to reach Achaiachala, or rather, to come to a spot on the left bank of the Euphrates which lay at the same level as Achaiachala/Haditha on the right.

The next day (*postridie*, ibid.), i.e. on April 17, Julian and his forces, in passing, set fire to a castle which had been abandoned by its garrison. In the next two days (April 18 and 19) two hundred stadia were covered before they arrived at a place called Baraxmalcha (*postera igitur et insequenti die stadiis ducentis emensis ventum est ad locum Baraxmalcha*, 24.2.3). From there, having crossed the Euphrates, they went to Diacira on the right bank of the river, at a distance of seven miles (*unde amne transito miliario septimo disparata Diacira invaditur*, ibid.; Zos. 3.15.2 σταθμοὺς δέ τινας παραμείψας εἰς Δάκιρα παρεγένετο, πόλιν ἐν δεξιᾷ πλέοντι τὸν Εὐφράτην κειμένην), and entered the city

A NOTE ON CHRONOLOGY   XV

(on April 20, presumably; though the distance from Baraxmalcha to Diacira was only seven miles, the crossing of the Euphrates will have taken some time). Diacira, modern Hît, deserted by its inhabitants, was burnt. Next (on April 21, it would seem) they passed a spring bubbling with bitumen (*traiecto fonte scatenti bitumine*, ibid.) – they apparently had crossed the Euphrates to the left bank once again; Amm. omits to mention this, but Zos. 3.15.3 is explicit: Ἐπὶ δὲ τῆς ἀντικρὺ ᾐόνος, δι' ἧς ὁ στρατὸς ἐποιεῖτο τὴν πορείαν, πηγή τις ἦν ἄσφαλτον ἀνιεῖσα.

After that (but probably still on April 21) they came, according to Amm., to Ozogardana (perhaps modern Sâri al-Hadd), where a tribunal of the emperor Trajan was to be seen (*Ozogardana occupavimus oppidum... in quo principis Traiani tribunal ostendebatur*, ibid.) – in Zosimus' version Ozogardana is called Zaragardia and two villages which the army passed on its way to Zaragardia are mentioned, Sitha and Megia: μεθ' ἣν (i.e. the spring with bitumen) εἰς Σίθα, εἶτα εἰς Μηγίαν ἀφικόμενος, μετ' ἐκείνην εἰς Ζαραγαρδίαν πόλιν ἦλθεν, ἐν ᾗ βῆμα ἦν ὑψηλὸν ἐκ λίθου πεποιημένον, ὃ Τραιανοῦ καλεῖν εἰώθασιν οἱ ἐγχώριοι, 3.15.3.

The city of Ozogardana/Zaragardia was burnt, and a two days' rest (April 22 and 23) was given to the soldiers (*hac quoque exusta biduo ad refectionem corporum dato*, 24.2.4; Zos. 3.15.4 Ταύτην ῥᾷστα τὴν πόλιν οἱ στρατιῶται διαρπάσαντες καὶ ἐμπρήσαντες αὐτήν τε τὴν ἡμέραν καὶ τὴν ὑστεραίαν ἡσυχίαν ἦγον). Towards the end of the second night (*prope extremum noctis, quae secundum diem secuta est*, ibid.) there was an (unsuccessful) attempt by the Surên and a Saracene phylarchus to capture Hormisdas, the Persian prince who served in the Roman army (cf. Zos. 3.15.4–6). The following day at daybreak (*primo lucis exordio*, 24.2.5; Zos. 3.15.6 τῇ ὑστεραίᾳ), i.e. in the morning of April 24, a battle took place, after which the army came to the village of Macepracta (*miles ad vicum Macepracta pervenit*, 24.2.6), where half-destroyed remains of walls could be seen (*in quo semiruta murorum vestigia videbantur*, ibid.) – it would appear that the ruins at Ummu-r-Rûs are identifiable with Macepracta, for it is difficult to see to what other walls Amm.'s description could apply (to assume with Dillemann, 1961, 156 and Fornara, 1991, 8 that Macepracta and Phissenia, mentioned in Zos. 3.19.3, are one and the same city, is far-fetched; see Paschoud n. 50); if so, Macepracta could have been reached on April 25.

According to Amm. 24.2.7 the Euphrates divides near Macepracta, one branch flowing into the interior parts of Babylonia, another, called Naarmalcha, past Ctesiphon (*hinc pars fluminis scindi-*

XVI   A NOTE ON CHRONOLOGY

*tur… ducens ad tractus Babylonos interiores… alia Naarmalcha nomine…
Ctesiphonta praetermeat*). The infantry crossed on bridges the latter
arm of the river, or rather, a canal which Amm. calls a branch of the
river (cf. Zos. 3.16.1 τινα τοῦ Εὐφράτου διώρυχα), while the cavalry
with the pack-animals swam across (24.2.7–8) – Zosimus' account
differs considerably, but nevertheless his words in 3.17.2 seem to
refer to the same event: ὁ βασιλεύς… ἐπεραιοῦτο τὴν διώρυχα… τὴν μὲν
ἵππον τοῖς παρατυχοῦσι πλοίοις, τὴν δὲ πεζὴν ναυσίν… διαβιβάσας. It was,
according to Paschoud, at this point of Amm.'s *Res Gestae* that the
sailing of the fleet on the Euphrates and the march of the army along
this river came to an end. From now on, he argues, it was the canal
called by Amm. Naarmalcha which was followed. In our view, however, Matthews' reconstruction should be followed, which means that
Julian continued its advance along the main stream of the Euphrates
and that the fleet also for the time being stayed on the Euphrates
(see for all this the note ad 24.2.7). Next came, south of Macepracta
and south of Amm.'s Naarmalcha, the city of Pirisabora, present-day
al-Ambâr, surrounded by water on all sides (*ad civitatem Pirisabora
ventum est… ambitu insulari circumvallatam*, 24.2.9; Zos. 3.17.3 Ἐλθὼν
δὲ εἰς πόλιν ᾗ Βηρσαβῶρα ἦν ὄνομα; cf. Lib. *Or.* 18.227 πόλις Ἀσυρίων
μεγάλη τοῦ μὲν τότε βασιλεύοντος ἐπώνυμος). To this city Julian laid
siege. Since Pirisabora/al-Ambâr is at a distance of some 20 km from
Macepracta/Ummu-r-Rûs, the city was presumably reached on April
26.

During the first day of the siege (April 27) fighting with missiles
went on from dawn until nightfall (*a die primo ad usque noctis initium*,
ibid.), while all day long (*diei maxima parte*, 24.2.11) the inhabitants
of Pirisabora tried to provoke Hormisdas. In the first stillness of the
night (*tenebrarum silentio primo*, ibid.) siege engines were brought to
bear and soldiers began to fill up the trenches. These activities were
revealed by the still uncertain light of dawn (*vixdum ambigua luce*,
24.2.12), whereupon (i.e. on April 28) the defenders retreated to
the citadel. The ensuing fight went on from dawn to dusk (*a lucis ortu
ad initium noctis*, 24.2.14) and was continued on the following day (*die
secuto*, ibid.), until the sight of a helepolis induced the Pirisaborans
to surrender. This happened on the third day of the siege (i.e. on
April 29), according to Amm.'s reckoning, which is followed here –
Zos. says that the city was taken in two days: πόλεως μεγάλης… ἐν δύο
μόναις ἡμέραις κατὰ κράτος ἁλούσης, 3.18.6.

After Pirisabora was taken the city was burnt (24.2.22; presumably still on April 29), whereupon (*Incensa… urbe, ut memoratum est*,
24.3.3) the emperor addressed his troops, promised them a donative

A NOTE ON CHRONOLOGY XVII

and, when they grumbled, because they thought the promised sum too small, he spoke to them again. This time the soldiers applauded and returned to their tents for a night's sleep (*quieti nocturnae*, 24.3.9). The day after the burning of Pirisabora (*Postera die, quam haec acta erant*, 24.3.1), i.e. on April 30, news was brought of a surprise attack by the Surên on three scouting squadrons of the cavalry. Julian's reaction was quick and efficient (24.3.2; cf. Zos. 3.19.1–2, Lib. *Or.* 18.229–30).

Next, after a march of fourteen miles (*Post haec decursis milibus passuum quattuordecim*, 24.3.10), they came (on May 1, it would seem) to a place which the Persians had flooded by breaking the dykes (*ad locum quendam est ventum, quo itinere nos ituros Persae praedocti sublatis cataractis undas evagari fusius permiserunt*, ibid.) – Zos. 3.19.3 informs us that the nearest city was called Phissenia (ἦλθεν εἴς τι χωρίον ᾧ πόλις ἐπλησίαζε Φισσηνία προσαγορευομένη), enclosed by a deep canal filled with water derived from the so-called Royal River, i.e. the second Euphrates inlet of the Naarmalcha (ibid.; see the notes ad 24.2.7 and 24.3.10). There the emperor gave the army another day's rest (*altero die militi requie data*, 24.3.11; on May 2, apparently), had bridges made and got his men across (presumably on May 3), though not without difficulty (*exercitum non sine difficultate traduxit* – cf. Zos. 3.19.4 ἐπανελθών τε διῆγε τὴν στρατιὰν μετὰ ῥᾳστώνης and Lib. *Or.* 18.232–4.

In the region now reached there were many fields planted with vineyards and fruit-trees (24.3.12, Zos. 3.20.1). After a night's rest here, the march was continued on the following day (i.e. May 4): ἐν τούτῳ τὴν ἐπελθοῦσαν νύκτα διαγαγὼν ἐπὶ τὰ πρόσω τῇ ὑστεραίᾳ προῆγεν (Zos. ibid.). 'Maozamalcha' was to be the next port of call which Amm. explicitly mentions by name (24.4.2; however, Amm. probably misnames the fortress, hence our use of inverted commas) – Zos. speaks of a town called Bithra (apparently on the route to 'Maozamalcha'), about which Amm. is silent: ἕως εἰς Βίθραν ἐληλύθει πόλιν, ἐν ᾗ βασίλεια ἦν καὶ οἰκήματα βασιλεῖ τε ὁμοῦ πρὸς ὑποδοχὴν ἀρκοῦντα καὶ στρατοπέδῳ, 3.19.4. Before reaching 'Maozamalcha' the army, on its march southwards along the Euphrates, first passed several islands (*exercitus plures praetergressus est insulas*, 24.3.14) and then (on May 5, it would seem) came to a place where the main body of the Euphrates splits into a number of channels (*prope locum venit, ubi pars maior Euphratis in rivos dividitur multifidos*, ibid.). In that area the Romans burnt a city abandoned by its Jewish inhabitants (24.4.1), possibly Neherda/Tall Nihar (May 6). After that both fleet and army turned eastwards, following a canal which connect-

XVIII A NOTE ON CHRONOLOGY

ed the Euphrates with the Tigris, i.e. the third Euphrates inlet of the Naarmalcha (see for this the note ad 24.2.7), into the direction of 'Maozamalcha', which was, according to Zosimus, at a distance of ninety stadia (i.e. some seventeen kilometers) from Ctesiphon (3.21.5 τὴν ὁδὸν τὴν ἐπὶ Κτησιφῶντα, σταδίων οὖσαν ἐνενήκοντα). After they had reached 'Maozamalcha', a large city surrounded by strong walls (*cumque Maozamalcha venisset, urbem magnam et validis circumdatam moenibus*, 24.4.2; cf. Zos. 3.20.2 and 3.21.3), a camp was pitched near the city (*tentoriis fixis*, ibid.; this was on May 8, presumably). Near 'Maozamalcha' Julian fell into an ambush when, attended by only a few soldiers, he wanted to examine the position of the city (on May 8 or 9, it would seem). He barely escaped with his life. The next day (*postridie*, 24.4.6; May 10) bridges were built and the army crossed over the Naarmalcha to occupy a camp in a more advantageous place. Then the infantry began the siege of the town, while the cavalry forces concentrated on repelling attacks of the Surên and supplying the army with food taken from the enemy. The attempt to storm the city ended on the first day (May 11) about noon, when the burning sun forced the assailants to retire (*aestus in meridiem crescens effervescente vaporatius sole... cunctos revocaverat*, 24.4.17). It was resumed the next day (*secuto... die*, 24.4.18; May 12). At first no results followed (*aequis manibus et pari fortuna discedunt*, ibid.), but, when the fighting was already slackening, the collapse of one of 'Maozamalcha''s towers, demolished by the violent blow of a ram, gave fresh heart to the Romans so that they continued fighting till the close of the day (*diei... occasus*, 24.4.20). While this was going on (*Dumque haec luce agerentur ac palam*, 24.4.21), underground passages to the walls of the city were dug by sappers. At night (*cum... noctis plerumque processisset*, 24.4.22; i.e. in the night of 12–13 May) an attack on the walls distracted the attention of the defenders and enabled the sappers to enter the city unobserved (cf. Zos. 3.22.4 ἐφάνησαν οἰκίας ἐν μέσῳ... νυκτὸς οὔσης ἔτι βαθείας; Lib. *Or.* 18.238 ἐν μέσαις νυξὶν and 240 ἐν νυκτὶ). The ensuing fight resulted in the capture and destruction of 'Maozamalcha' (on May 13).

After these glorious deeds (*Post quae tam gloriosa*, 24.4.31) the army crossed a network of streams by a series of bridges and came (on May 14, it would seem) to two forts (*ad munimenta gemina venimus*, ibid.). Continuing their march (*Pergentes itaque protinus*, 24.5.1) presumably on the 15th of May the soldiers came (*venimus*) to woods and fields, where they found a palace built in Roman style (24.5.1; cf. Zos. 3.23.2 βασίλεια... εἰς τὸν Ῥωμαϊκὸν μεγαλοπρεπῶς ἐξῃσκημένα

A NOTE ON CHRONOLOGY XIX

τύπον; Lib. *Or.* 18.243 says that the palace showed not Roman, but Persian elegance) and a large park full of all sorts of animals, many of which they killed (24.5.2, cf. Zos. 3.23.1 and Lib. *Or.* 18.243; on May 16). This was not far from Coche, otherwise known as Seleucia (*quo loco pingui satis et cultu, qui ... bus Coche, quam Seleuciam nominant, haud longius disparatur,* 24.5.3; the text is corrupt). After having pitched an extempore camp, the army rested there for two days (*exercitu omni ... biduo recreato,* 24.5.3; i.e. May 17 and 18), while Julian and some skirmishers went ahead to survey a deserted city destroyed in former days by the emperor Carus (*antegressus cum procursatoribus princeps et civitatem desertam collustrans a Caro principe quondam excisam,* 24.5.3); in it was an ever flowing spring which formed a great pool that emptied in the Tigris (*in qua perpetuus fons stagnum ingens eiectat in Tigridem defluens,* ibid.) – this *civitas deserta* is sometimes identified as being Zosimus' Meinas Sabatha, which lay at a distance of thirty stades from Zochase (=Coche): Ἐντεῦθεν ἡ στρατιὰ φρούριά τινα παραδραμοῦσα εἰς πόλιν ἀφίκετο Μείνας Σαβαθὰ καλουμένην· διέστηκε δὲ αὕτη σταδίοις τριάκοντα τῆς πρότερον μὲν Ζωχάσης νῦν δὲ Σελευκείας ὀνομαζομένης (3.23.3). However, it seems preferable to see it as that part of ancient Seleucia which had not become overgrown by the new city of Coche.

After the two days' rest the army had proceeded some distance (*aliquantum progressi,* 24.5.5; cf. Zos. 3.24.1 προιόντος δὲ περαιτέρω τοῦ στρατοῦ), when a Persian detachment sallied forth from a nearby town and came to blows with three Roman cohorts (on May 19, presumably; the outcome of the fight, not mentioned by Amm., is reported by Zosimus: the Romans were victorious and forced the Persians to flee to a city nearby, 3.24.1). Meanwhile the Roman baggage train was attacked *ex contraria fluminis ripa* (ibid.), i.e. from the other side of the Naarmalcha – Zos. 3.24.1, less convincingly, says that the army train itself was on the other side of the ποταμός (while Amm. is silent about the capture of numerous prisoners by Arintheus, Zosimus mentions this before he speaks of the incident with the baggage train). Leaving the place where he had heard of these events (*unde profectus imperator,* 24.5.6) and already approaching the vicinity of Ctesiphon (*iamque regionibus Ctesiphontis propinquans*), Julian all but met death during the reconnaissance of a high and well-fortified stronghold (ibid.; this incident is not mentioned by Zosimus or Libanius; its date: May 20 presumably). A siege followed (*munimentum disposuit obsidere,* 24.5.7), on May 21, it would seem, and the fortress was taken and burnt (*idem castellum incenditur captum,* 24.5.11). Thereupon the army was given some rest (*post*

XX A NOTE ON CHRONOLOGY

quae... requievit exercitus, 24.5.12; on May 22) in a camp which was carefully strengthened for fear of sudden attacks from nearby Ctesiphon (*vallum... cautius deinde struebatur, cum a vicina iam Ctesiphonte repentini excursus at alia formidarentur occulta*, ibid.).

When they had broken camp again (on May 23 presumably), they came to "Trajan's canal" (wrongly called by Amm. Naarmalcha), which at that time was dry (*Ventum est hinc ad fossile flumen Naarmalcha nomine... tunc aridum*, 24.6.1; cf. Zos. 3.24.2 Ἐντεῦθεν ὁρμήσαντες ἦλθον εἴς τινα διώρυχα μεγίστην), but which in former days had been a connecting channel between the Naarmalcha (called here by Amm. Euphrates) and the Tigris (*id antehac Traianus posteaque Severus egesto solo fodiri in modum canalis amplissimi... curaverat...*, *ut aquis illuc ab Euphrate transfusis naves ad Tigridem commigrarent*, ibid.; cf. Zos. 3.24.2 [διώρυχα μεγίστην] ἣν ἔλεγον οἱ τῇδε παρὰ Τραιανοῦ διώρυχθαι Πέρσαις ἐπιστρατεύσαντος· εἰς ἣν ἐμβαλὼν ὁ Ναρμαλάχης ποταμὸς εἰς τὸν Τίγριν ἐκδίδωσι and Lib. *Or.* 18.245 διώρυχα ναυσίπορον... ἄγουσαν δὲ τὸν Εὐφράτην ἐπὶ τὸν Τίγρητα). This canal had been blocked by the Persians with a great mass of stones, but it was cleared out (this must have taken some time, say May 24–26), so that the Roman fleet could reach the Tigris (on May 27 perhaps), which was at a distance of thirty stadia (*tutissimumque ad omnia visum est eadem loca purgari, quae... Persae... mole saxorum obruere multorum. hacque valle purgata avulsis cataractis undarum magnitudine classis secura stadiis triginta decursis in alveum eiecta est Tigridis*, 24.6.2; cf. Zos. 3.24.2 ταύτην [sc. τὴν διώρυχα] ὁ βασιλεὺς καθῆραί τε ἅμα καὶ ἐρευνᾶν διενοήθη, πόρον... τοῖς πλοίοις ἐπὶ τὸν Τίγρητα παρασκευάζων). In the meantime the army crossed the Naarmalcha by shipbridges: *contextis ilico pontibus transgressus exercitus* (ibid.; *transgressus* is Gelenius' reading; Seyfarth prints V's *congressus*; cf. Zos. 3.24.2 [ἐρευνᾶν διενοήθη] εἴ πῃ παρείκοι, γεφύρας τῇ τοῦ πολλοῦ στρατοῦ διαβάσει), advanced towards Coche (*iter Cochen versus promovit*, ibid.) and encamped for a period of rest in a rich region, in the midst of which was a royal hunting-palace (*utque lassitudini succederet quies opportuna, in agro consedimus opulento... cuius in medio diversorium opacum est et amoenum*, 24.6.3) – it was possibly during this rest (May 28–31 presumably) that Julian offered his army various sorts of entertainment to mark the occasion of his birthday.

After this rest Julian decided to cross the Tigris at night in a combined action of army and fleet in order to take possession of the opposite bank (*Augustus... validiores naves... octogenis implevit armatis retentoque secum classis robore firmiore, quam in tres diviserat partes, unam cum Victore comite quiete prima noctis emitti disposuit, ut flumine raptim trans-*

A NOTE ON CHRONOLOGY   XXI

misso ripae occuparentur hostiles, 24.6.4; the night of 31 May). Although
the undertaking was hazardous and was also fiercely opposed by the
enemy, it was successful (24.6.5–7; cf. Zos. 3.25.1–4, Lib. *Or.* 18.250–
3). There followed a full-scale battle (24.6.8–11; cf. Zos. 3.25.5, Lib.
Or. 18.254; on June 1, it would seem), which ended when the Persians
retreated to Ctesiphon, pursued by the Romans. The Roman soldiers
would have followed their fleeing enemy into the city, had not general Victor restrained them (*laxata... acies prima Persarum... retrorsus
gradiens propinquam urbem petebat, quam sequebatur miles... eiusque occipitiis pertinacius haerens omnem cum Pigrane et Surena et Narseo... ad usque
Ctesiphontis muros egit praecipitem... perrupissetque civitatis aditus lapsorum agminibus mixtus, ni dux Victor nomine... prohibuisset,* 24.6.12–13;
cf. Zos. 3.25.5–6, Lib. *Or.* 18.255). According to Amm. the battle
had taken all day (*ad usque diei finem a lucis ortu,* 24.6.12). Zosimus
3.25.5 reports that it lasted from the middle of the night until noon
next day: ἐκ μέσης νυκτὸς... μέχρι μέσης ἡμέρας (from Lib. *Or.* 18.254
ἐν νυκτὶ καὶ σκότῳ it can also be inferred that the fighting started in
the night, cf. Soz. *HE* 6.1.8 ἐν νυκτὶ).

Immediately after the successful engagement outside Ctesiphon
(on the first of June, according to our estimate) Julian rewarded
some soldiers with crowns (24.6.15), prepared to sacrifice a number
of victims to Mars Ultor (which resulted in a fiasco, 24.6.16), and considered, with the highest ranking officers, the strategy to be followed,
in particular concerning the siege of Ctesiphon (*Digesto itaque consilio
cum primatibus super Ctesiphontis obsidio,* 24.7.1). The better opinion,
viz. not to lay siege to Ctesiphon, prevailed (*vicit sententia melior,*
24.7.2), whereupon Julian sent Arintheus to ravage the surrounding
countryside and to pursue scattered enemies (ibid.). Amm. is silent
about the time it took to do all this (and probably other things as well;
there is undoubtedly a lacuna after *hinc opulenta* in 24.7.3). Zosimus
on the other hand, although he does not refer to any of the events just
mentioned, gives very precise chronological data. According to him it
was on the day following the battle near Ctesiphon that Julian sent his
army across the Tigris (Τῇ δὲ ὑστεραίᾳ τὸν Τίγρητα ποταμὸν ὁ βασιλεὺς
τὸ στράτευμα ἐπὶ πολλῆς ἀδείας διαβιβάσας, 3.26.1), and two days after
the battle that he himself with his bodyguard crossed the river (τρίτῃ
μετὰ τὴν μάχην ἡμέρᾳ καὶ αὐτὸς μετὰ πάσης τῆς ἀμφ' αὐτὸν δορυφορίας
ἐπεραιοῦτο, ibid.). The emperor then, according to Zosimus, went
to a place called Abouzatha and stayed there for five days: καὶ πρός
τι χωρίον ἐλθὼν (Ἀβουζαθὰ τοῦτο Πέρσαι καλοῦσιν) ἡμέρας ἐν τούτῳ
διέμεινε πέντε (ibid.). Zosimus' words about the crossing of the Tigris
are very puzzling and raise doubts as to his chronology. However,

XXII　　　　A NOTE ON CHRONOLOGY

there are no grounds not to believe that the army stayed some time in Abouzatha (its site is unknown). The aftermath of the battle of Ctesiphon and the stay in Abouzatha may therefore have taken the first week of June.

Having abandoned the idea to besiege Ctesiphon Julian decided (about June 8) to leave the Tigris on his left and to invade rapidly the inner parts of the Sasanian empire (*flumine laeva relicto... mediterraneas vias arripere citato proposuit gradu*, 24.7.3; cf. Zos. 3.26.2 ἄμεινον ἔχειν ᾠήθη μηκέτι συμπαραπέμπειν τῇ ὄχθῃ τοῦ ποταμοῦ τὸν στρατόν, ἀνιέναι δὲ ἐπὶ τὴν μεσόγειαν and Lib. *Or.* 18.264). Since there seemed no further need for ships, the fleet was almost totally burnt; the repeal of this decision came too late (24.7.4–5; cf. Zos. 3.26.2–3 and Lib. *Or.* 18.262–3). The march into the interior (*ad interiora tendebat*, 24.7.6; cf. Zos. 3.26.3 ὀλίγον δ' ἀνωτέρω τοῦ ποταμοῦ τὸ λειπόμενον ἔδει ποιήσασθαι τῆς ὁδοῦ; June 9–13 presumably) went through a fertile region which provided food in abundance (*alimenta affatim opulentis suggerentibus locis*, ibid.), but soon the scorched-earth policy of the Persians prevented the Romans from advancing and forced them to stay in a stationary camp until the flames died down (*procedere vetiti stativis castris, dum flammae senescerent, tenebamur*, 24.7.7; June 14). This camp should perhaps be identified as being Zosimus' Noorda (Νοορδᾷ δὲ τῷ τόπῳ προσσχόντες αὐτοῦ που κατέλυον (Zos. 3.26.3), modern Djisr Nahrawan, where the Romans captured and killed many Persians (ἔνθα πολλοὶ πανταχόθεν ἡλίσκοντο Πέρσαι καὶ κατεσφάζοντο (but in Zosimus' version the scorched-earth policy of the Persians only began after the stay in Noorda, when the Romans had crossed the river Douros, the modern Diyala: Ἐλθόντες δὲ εἰς τὸν Δοῦρον ποταμὸν διέβησαν τοῦτον γέφυραν ζεύξαντες, 3.26.4).

It must have been in the *stativa castra* (at Noorda?) that the deliberations took place about the entire situation (*super rerum summa consultabatur*, 24.8.2; June 14–15). This resulted in the decision to return home. In 24.8.4 Amm. says that the gods were consulted, not as to whether or not the army had to turn back, but as to which route it should take (*consulta numinum citabantur, utrum nos per Assyriam reverti censerent an praeter radices montium lenius gradientes Chiliocomum prope Corduenam situm ex improviso vastare*). It was decided to choose the royal road east of the Tigris into the direction of Corduena (*sedit... sententia, ut... Corduenam arriperemus*, 24.8.5) and on 16 June camp was broken (*et sextum decimum kalendas Iulias promotis... signis*, ibid.): the κατάβασις had begun.

A NOTE ON CHRONOLOGY   XXIII

The results of our reconstruction are shown below in a diagram. It suggests a high degree of accuracy, but appearances are deceptive. Once again we want to warn the reader: all dates but the first and the last are no more than reasonable guesses.

April 7	Off Dura
April 8–11	From the neighbourhood of Dura southwards
April 11	Nightly attack on Anatha
April 12	Anatha set on fire
April 13	Tornado; flooding of the Euphrates
April 14–16	From Anatha via Thilutha to Achaichala
April 17–19	From Achaichala to Baraxmalcha
April 20	From Baraxmalcha to Diacira
April 21	From Diacira to Ozogardana
April 22–23	Rest given to the soldiers
April 24–25	From Ozogardana to Macepracta
April 26	From Macepracta to Pirisabora
April 27–29	Siege and capture of Pirisabora. Speech of Julian
April 30	The surprise attack of the Surên reported
May 1–3	Near Phissenia
May 4–6	From Phissenia to a Jewish city (Neherda?)
May 7–8	To 'Maozamalcha', via Bithra
May 9–13	Siege and capture of 'Maozamalcha'
May 14–16	From 'Maozamalcha' to a palace built in Roman style with a park for hunting, not far from Coche
May 17–18	A two days' rest; reconnaissance of a civitas deserta (Meinas Sabatha?)
May 19	Skirmishes and attack on the baggage train
May 20–21	Siege and capture of a fortress
May 22	A day's rest
May 23	Arrival at 'Trajan's canal'
May 24–26	Clearing out of 'Trajan's canal'
May 27	The Roman fleet reaches the Tigris
May 28–31	Period of rest (Julian's birthday?)
May 31	Crossing of the Tigris at night
June 1	Battle before the gates of Ctesiphon
June 2–7	March to and stay at Abouzatha
June 8–13	March inland; burning of the fleet
June 14–15	Stay in a stationary camp (at Noorda?)
June 16	Beginning of the retreat

LEGENDA

1. The lemmata are taken from W. Seyfarth's Teubner-edition (Leipzig 1978), with one alteration: consonantial u is always printed as v (*venit* instead of *uenit*).

2. For references to Greek authors we follow the abbreviations and indications of books and chapters in H.G. Liddell and R. Scott, *A Greek-English Lexicon*. Passages in Latin authors are indicated according to the system of the *Oxford Latin Dictionary*. For later and Christian authors we follow the *Thesaurus Linguae Latinae*.

Some exceptions to these rules:

- In the case of Caesar, Sallust and Tacitus the division of the chapters into sections in the Teubner-editions has also been taken into account.
- Seneca's *Dialogi* are referred to with the title of the individual works.
- For the Panegyrici Latini Mynors' OCT-edition has been used.
- The *Epistulae* of Julian are quoted from Bidez' edition in the Budé-series.
- Eunapius' *History* is quoted from Blockley's edition (*The Fragmentary Classicising Historians of the Later Roman Empire*, vol. II, Liverpool 1983).

3. As to secondary literature the following rules are observed:

- References to the six volumes of De Jonge's commentaries and to our commentaries on Books 20, 21, 22 and 23 are usually given with 'see (the note) ad ...' or 'q.v.'.
- Books or articles are normally referred to with the name of the author(s), the year of publication and the page(s). The full titles can be found in the bibliography; e.g. Hagendahl, 1921, 64 refers to H. Hagendahl, *Studia Ammianea*, Uppsala 1921, page 64.
- Occasionally reference is made to commentaries on other authors, e.g. Austin's on Vergil and Koestermann's on Tacitus, or to well-known editions like those in the Budé-series. As a rule these works are omitted from the bibliography.
- Of the following books, which are referred to regularly, only the name of the author and the page(s) are given:

Bitter	N. Bitter, *Kampfschilderungen bei Ammianus Marcellinus*, Bonn 1976.
Blomgren	S. Blomgren, *De sermone Ammiani Marcellini quaestiones variae*, Diss. Uppsala 1937.
Brok	M.F.A. Brok, *De Perzische expeditie van keizer Julianus volgens Ammianus Marcellinus*, Groningen 1959.
Ehrismann	H. Ehrismann, *De temporum et modorum usu Ammianeo*, Diss. Strasbourg 1886.
Fesser	H. Fesser, *Sprachliche Beobachtungen zu Ammianus Marcellinus*, Diss. Breslau, 1932.
Fontaine	J. Fontaine, *Ammien Marcellin, Histoire, IV (Livres XXIII–XXIV)*, 2 vols., Paris 1977.
Harmon	A.M. Harmon, *The Clausula in Ammianus Marcellinus*, New Haven 1910 (Transactions of the Connecticut Academy of Arts and Sciences 16, 117–245).
Hassenstein	G. Hassenstein, *De syntaxi Ammiani Marcellini*, Diss. Königsberg 1877.
Jones	A.H.M. Jones, *The Later Roman Empire 284–612. A Social, Economic and Administrative Survey*, Oxford 1964 (repr. 1986).
Kühner-Stegmann	R. Kühner and C. Stegmann, *Ausführliche Grammatik der lateinischen Sprache*, II, Satzlehre, 2 vols., Hannover 1955⁴, 1976⁵.
Leumann	M. Leumann, *Lateinische Laut-und Formenlehre*, Munich 1977.
Matthews	J.F. Matthews, *The Roman Empire of Ammianus*, London 1989.
Paschoud	F. Paschoud, *Zosime, Histoire Nouvelle, II, 1 (Livre III)*, Paris 1979.
Sabbah	G. Sabbah, *La méthode d'Ammien Marcellin. Recherches sur la construction du discours historique dans les Res Gestae*, Paris 1978.
Seager	R. Seager, *Ammianus Marcellinus. Seven studies in his Language and Thought*, Columbia 1986.
Szantyr	J.B. Hofmann and A. Szantyr, *Lateinische Syntax und Stilistik*, Munich 1965 (repr. 1972).

LEGENDA   XXVII

Wagner-Erfurdt   J.A. Wagner, *Ammiani Marcellini quae supersunt,*
                 cum notis integris Frid. Lindenbrogii, Henr. et
                 Hadr. Valesiorum et Iac. Gronovii, quibus Thom.
                 Reinesii quasdam et suas adiecit, editionem ab-
                 solvit Car. Gottl. Aug. Erfurdt, 3 vols., Leipzig
                 1808 (repr. in 2 vols, Hildesheim 1975).

The following translations are often referred to with the name of the
translator only:

Caltabiano   M. Caltabiano, *Ammiano Marcellino. Storie,* Milan 1998.
Hamilton   W. Hamilton and A. Wallace-Hadrill, *Ammianus Mar-
             cellinus: the Later Roman Empire (AD 354–378),* Har-
             mondsworth 1986.
Rolfe   J.C. Rolfe, *Ammianus Marcellinus,* with an English trans-
             lation, 3 vols., London-Cambridge Mass. 1935–1939
             (repr. 1971–1972).
Selem   A. Selem, *Le Storie di Ammiano Marcellino. Testo e Traduzi-
             one,* Turin 1965 (repr. 1973)
Seyfarth   W. Seyfarth, *Ammianus Marcellinus, Römische Geschichte.
             Lateinisch und Deutsch und mit einem Kommentar versehen,*
             II, Berlin 1983[5] and III, Berlin 1986[3].
Veh   O. Veh, *Ammianus Marcellinus. Das römische Weltreich vor
             dem Untergang,* übersetzt von Otto Veh, eingeleitet und
             erläutert von G. Wirth, Zurich-Munich 1974.

4. In cases where this is helpful for the reader or relevant for the
interpretation the cursus is indicated as follows:

   – *revocávit in státum*: cursus planus
   – *sublátius éminens*: cursus tardus
   – *fécit et vectigáles*: cursus velox

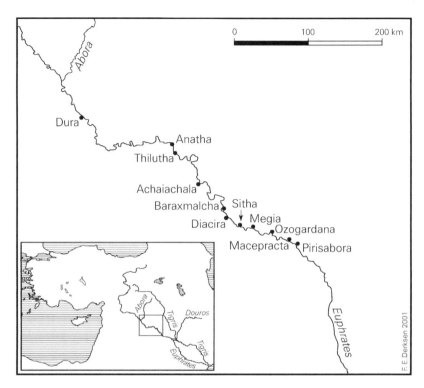

From Dura to Pirisabora

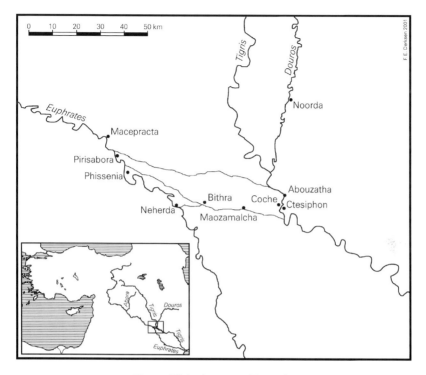

From Pirisabora to Noorda

CHAPTER 1

Introduction

The first chapter of this book describes how Julian crosses the border into Persia. The troops, Amm. tells us, were in excellent spirits, and hailed their leader in an *acclamatio* as invincible. Julian himself is described as diligent and cautious, having prepared every last detail before entering enemy territory and taking great pains to prevent surprise attacks from his wily adversaries. He commands the heart and centre of the army, while his trusted commanders Nevitta, Arintheus, the Persian prince Hormisdas, Dagalaifus, Victor and Secundinus are in charge of the flanks and the rear of the army (§ 1–2). In order to impress the enemy, Julian extends his army in such a way that there is a ten mile stretch between the front and the rear. The fleet on the Euphrates is ordered to stay close to the army (§ 3–4).

The first city they reach on the march is Dura, which turns out to be deserted (§ 5), but military action seems inevitable four days later, when the army finds the fortress Anatha in its path. Lucillianus is sent out to launch a surprise attack, but his troops are seen by one of the inhabitants of the fortress. Before trying to take Anatha by force, Julian enters into negotiations to persuade the garrison to surrender. Thanks to the mediation of Hormisdas, the inhabitants agree to the Roman terms and leave the fortress, which is set on fire. The inhabitants are deported to the Syrian city Chalcis. Among them is a former Roman soldier, almost a hundred years old, who had been left behind during the expedition of Maximianus in 296–297 and now rejoices in the prospect of being buried in Roman soil. The capture of a number of enemy reconnaissance troops by the Saracen auxiliaries, of whose presence we are informed here for the first time, crowns these successes (§ 6–10).

Immediately after this Amm. reports two setbacks. A sudden violent storm causes havoc and one day later the Euphrates floods, which leads to the loss of some ships. Amm. leaves the question unanswered whether this flooding was accidental or caused by the enemy (§ 11).

Still, the troops proceed on their way undismayed. They feel protected by heaven and are full of praise for their commander, whose diligence is emphasized once again (§ 12–13).

2 COMMENTARY

Julian's strategy with regard to provisioning his troops is set out in §13–14. He collects all the food he can use from the land of the enemy, in order to save the food he has brought with him on the ships. After that he burns the fields and the farms. In that way he does damage to the resources of the enemy, while boosting the morale of his own troops, who earn their food by their own valour.

Two anecdotes in this chapter are a sign of the author's personal presence at the events. In §6 Amm. describes how the soldiers caught a large number of deer and feasted on them. In the last section he reports how a drunken soldier, who had swum across the river, fell victim to his Dutch courage.

1.1 *Post exploratam alacritatem exercitus* Amm. resumes his narrative at the point where he had inserted the excursus on Persia, i.e. after the emperor's speech to his troops on crossing the river Abora, the border between Roman and Persian territory (23.5.25). For *explorare*, 'to ascertain' rather than 'to inquire into', cf. 25.1.15 *Exploratum est enim aliquando ab Hasdrubale Hannibalis fratre ita citius vitam huiusmodi adimi beluarum. Alacritas* is the intended effect of Julian's *adhortatio*; cf. 24.6.11 *cum undique solito more conclamaretur virorumque alacritatem sonans classicum iuvaret*, Caes. *Gal.* 1.41.1 *summa... alacritas et cupiditas belli gerendi* and Liv. 7.33.4 *universus exercitus incredibili alacritate adhortationem prosecutus ducis.*

impetrabilem principem superari non posse The same idea is expressed in 17.13.34 (contio) *deum... ex usu testata non posse Constantium vinci* and, even more explicitly, in 26.7.17 (omnes) *testati more militiae Iovem invictum Procopium fore*. For *impetrabilis*, 'successful', cf. 14.8.5 (Nicator Seleucus) *efficaciae impetrabilis rex, ut indicat cognomentum*. As to *principem*, the use of this word to denote Julian is quite frequent in Book 24, as is that of *imperator* (see for these terms the notes ad 20.4.12 and 21.4.4). *Iulianus* is rarer and occurs, apart from in this section, in 24.2.17, 24.3.9, 24.6.11, 24.6.16 and 24.7.6. In 24.2.21 we find *Caesar* and in 24.6.4 *Augustus,* for which titles see the notes ad 20.4.5 and 22.12.8.

deum usitato clamore testati "Calling God to witness" (Hamilton). This is an *acclamatio* which confirms the bond between the emperor and his troops, as observed by Brok 93 and Fontaine n. 283. For comparable situations where soldiers, but also civilians and senators, loudly exclaim their sentiments: 18.6.2, 21.5.9, 21.10.7 (with note), 24.6.15, 28.6.23, 29.5.22 and in general Aldrete, 1999. Cf. also

CHAPTER 1.1

HA *Dd* 1.6–8: *Adclamatum: 'Macrine imperator, di te servent. Antonine Diadumene, di te servent. Antoninum diu vivum omnes rogamus. Iuppiter optime maxime, Macrino et Antonino vitam! tu scis, Iuppiter, Macrinus vinci non potest. tu scis, Iuppiter, Antoninus vinci non potest. Antoninum habemus, omnia habemus. Antoninum nobis di dederunt. puer Antoninus dignus imperio!'* The content of this *acclamatio* is (of course) fictional, but the form is authentic.

Iulianus summae rei finem imponendum maturius credens It is not immediately clear what the phrase *summa res* means. The only other instances in the *Res Gestae* are 15.5.19 *invadendaeque summae rei ... affectator*, where it indicates the supreme power, and 17.4.6 *prosperitatibus summarum rerum elati*, where it refers to ambitious ventures. The latter meaning fits the present context well: Julian wanted 'to bring his ambitious undertaking to completion.'

†*extracta quiete nocturna* The preceding *maturius*, whether it has real comparative force or not, is hardly compatible with prolonging the soldiers' period of rest, which would be the meaning of *extracta* (TLL V 2.2069.13–32). For that reason *extracta* seems untenable, especially since Amm. uses *extrahere* only in its literal sense 'to draw out from'. The simplest remedy is E's *exacta*, which Amm. uses regularly of time, e.g. 16.11.1 (= 18.5.8) *exacta ... hieme*, 16.12.62 *post exactum iam diem occinente liticine revocatus ... miles.*

itinerarium sonare lituos iubet With the meaning "signum proficiscendi" *itinerarium* is found only here (TLL VII 2.567.60). Active *sonare* could be defended by comparing it to Tac. *Ann.* 2.32.3 *cum classicum canere iussissent* (admittedly in a very different context).

praestructis omnibus, quae difficultates arduae belli poscebant Strictly speaking, a coordinator between the main verbs *iubet* and *incendebant* is indispensable, and, moreover, *et* after *iubet* could easily have been lost. Still, it would be just as easy to understand that Amm. himself lost track in this monstrous period (eight participle constructions!). It seems prudent, therefore, to keep V's text. On *praestruere* see the note ad 20.6.2 *cunctisque praestructis*. There is a note on *arduus* ad 20.5.3.

Apart from logistics, the preparations must have included the marching route and the tactics employed, i.e. the marching formation as described in section 2 of this chapter.

4   COMMENTARY

candente iam luce Assyrios fines ingressus I.e. after crossing the Abora, as related in 23.5.5. *Iam* refers back to *praestructis omnibus*. The necessary preparations had taken so long that the army entered Assyria in broad daylight. For the expression cf. 31.7.10 *Candente itaque protinus die signo ad arma capienda... dato*. The variety of ways in which Amm. indicates the beginning of day is discussed by Hagendahl, 1921, 102–3.

The same event is described in Zos. 3.13.3 ὁ βασιλεὺς... προσφωνήσας... τὴν ἐπὶ Πέρσας εἰσβολὴν ἐποιήσατο; 3.14.1 Εἰσβαλόντι τοίνυν εἰς τὰ Περσῶν ὅρια τῷ βασιλεῖ. In Amm. Assyria is either a general designation for the Persian empire or it denotes specifically the region Assyria; in the present case it most probably refers to the Persian empire, as observed in the note ad 23.2.7.

The sequence of events is not very clear in Amm.'s account. In 23.5.5, q.v. and 23.5.15 Amm. had already mentioned the crossing of the Abora, which de facto implied that the Roman army had entered the Sasanid empire (presumably 6 April). The fact that this is repeated here is not easy to explain. Possibly Amm. just wants to recapitulate the narrative where it was broken off (23.5.15) before Julian's speech and the excursus on Persia, or he has conflated his sources. See the introductory note ad 23.5.7 for the scholarly discussion on Amm.'s garbled report from a chronological point of view. Add to the literature cited there Paschoud n. 36 ad Zos. 3.13.4.

celso praeter alios spiritu obequitans ordinibus In 22.12.5 Julian is described as *maioris praeter ceteros spiritus* and in 25.3.8 on his deathbed he was *magno spiritu contra exitium certans*. The verb *obequitare* is found several times with the dative in Livy (TLL IX 2.49.84–50.6). Amm. has it with an accusative in 24.2.9 *cuius* (Pirisabora) *obequitans moenia imperator et situm*, possibly as a result of a misinterpretation of Livy 26.10.3 (Hannibal) *moenia situmque urbis obequitans contemplabatur*. Cf. 24.5.6 *cum paucis obequitans muros*. There is a remarkable similarity both in the setting and in the phrasing with Curt. 3.10.4, about Alexander entering Persian territory after drawing up his troops in marching order: *cumque agmini obequitaret, varia oratione... milites adloquebatur*.

aemulatione sui For a similar use of the gen. obiectivus *sui* cf. 21.2.4 *Utque omnes nullo impediente ad sui favorem illiceret*.

cunctos ad officia fortitudinis incendebat 'To show their bravery in their deeds'. Cf. 27.6.6 *pietatis officium aggrediar*. As Cicero had said in *de*

CHAPTER 1.2

Orat. 2.345 *singularum virtutum sunt certa quaedam officia ac munera.* In *Tusc.* 2.43 he specifies: *fortitudo cuius munera duo sunt maxima, mortis dolorisque contemptio.*

ductor usu et docilitate firmatus Julian is portrayed as a cautious army **1.2** commander from the beginning of his military career, cf. 16.2.11 *erat prouidus et cunctator, quod praecipuum bonum in magnis ductoribus opem ferre solet exercitibus et salutem.* Wagner's explanation of *usu et docilitate* as "peritia experiendo contracta", which is quoted with approval in TLL V 1.1769.82, is inadequate. Of course, Julian had a lot of personal experience as a military commander after his years in Gaul, but Amm. repeatedly stresses the importance of knowledge gained from books: 15.1.4 *id reputasset legens vel audiens,* 17.5.14 *id experiendo legendoque scientes,* 22.8.1 *visa vel lecta.* So *docilitas* is used in its normal meaning 'aptness to learn'. In 21.12.1 Julian, who calls himself *antiquitatum peritus* in 23.5.21, is confident that Aquileia will not be taken *legensque et audiens hanc civitatem… numquam… excisam* and in 24.2.16 he is aware of a historical parallel to his recklessness from his reading of Polybius. It is evident from Lib. *Or.* 18.245 that Julian also made use of books in geographical matters: ἐζήτει διώρυχα ναυσίπορον καὶ ταύτην ἐκ βίβλων. In the note ad 16.12.47 De Jonge gives a slightly different interpretation of *docilis / docilitas.*

It is not known which tactical manuals – of which there were many in the fourth century – Julian had studied, but from references by Amm. to the great generals of the past, Alexander (21.8.3), Pyrrhus (24.1.3) and Scipio (24.2.16), we may surmise that he had studied the tactics employed by these great men. Kaegi, 1981 and Bouffartigue, 1992, 497 suggest that Julian may have studied Constantine's συγγράμματα. In 25.4.7 the emperor is called by Amm. *armatae rei scientissimus.* In spite of his undisputed military skills, it is unlikely that Julian wrote *de rebus bellicis* in Greek, as John Lydus (*Mag.* 1.47) reports.

metuens, ne per locorum insolentiam insidiis caperetur occultis As he had told his men in 23.5.21 *nihil enim praeter dolos et insidias hostium vereor.* See Veg. *mil.* 3.6 on the degree of caution to be observed when an army is marching through enemy territory.

agminibus incedere quadratis exorsus est The *agmen quadratum* was a common marching formation; it provided the army with maximum security against unexpected attacks. It is already described by Hirt. *Gal.* 8.8.4: *Hac ratione paene quadrato agmine instructo in conspectum*

6 COMMENTARY

hostium celerius opinione eorum exercitum adducit. Amm. also mentions the *agmen quadratum* in 25.3.2, 27.2.8, 10.6, 29.5.39, 31.12.4. Nicasie, 1998, 199–202 and figs. 9 + 10 (where the Euphrates is incorrectly situated on the left) explains this marching formation, both in general and in the particular case of Julian's expeditionary force as described by Amm. in this section. The advance guard was formed by light troops which also protected the flanks – Amm.'s 1500 *excursatores (excursatores quidem quingentos et mille sensim praeire)*; when possible, the flanks were also protected by features of the terrain, such as rivers. The heavy infantry and the baggage train formed the heart of the formation – the flank-guard consisting of legions led by Nevitta (*dextra legiones aliquas cum Nevitta*), the main force led by Julian himself (*ipse vero medios pedites regens*), and the cavalry under Arintheus and Hormisdas protecting the other flank (*cornu vero laevum cum equitum copiis Arintheo tradidit et Hormisdae*). The rear consisted of experienced troops; these could be legions or light infantry or cavalry – the troops under Victor and Dagalaifus and the troops from Osdroene led by Secundinus (*agmina vero postrema Dagalaifus cogebat et Victor ultimusque omnium Osdroenae dux Secundinus*). In his description of Julian's marching formation Zosimus confuses the left and right flanks, see 3.14.1 and Paschoud n. 37.

excursatores quidem quingentos et mille Zos. 3.14.1: χιλίους ἔγνω καὶ πεντακοσίους προπέμψαι, κατασκεψομένους εἴ τι πολέμιον ἢ προφανῶς ἢ δι᾽ ἐνέδρας ἐπίοι, Λουκιλλιανὸν αὐτοῖς ἐπιστήσας. Malalas, *Chron.* 13.330: καὶ προηγεῖσθαι αὐτῶν προσκουλκάτορας προσέταξεν ἄνδρας γενναίους ἐκ τοῦ ἀριθμοῦ τῶν λαγκιαρίων καὶ ματτιαρίων χιλίους πεντακοσίους. It is far from certain that the *excursatores* were cavalry as implied by Rolfe ('mounted scouts'), followed by Nicasie, 1998, 162, 200, who adds (p. 201) that they can be assisted by light infantry and archers. It is more likely, as Brok 96 followed by Fontaine n. 288 already noticed, that the *excursatores* were infantry units since Malalas' προσκουλκάτορας are reminiscent of Vegetius' *exculcatores* (*mil.* 2.15.6, 17.1), which are definitely light-armed infantry. Also Amm. 25.1.2, where *excursatores* are mentioned, indicates that these are infantry units; cf. Zos. 3.26.5. Another indication that infantry is meant is Zos. 3.16.2: the 1500 men are ordered to cross marshy territory and a canal, and Zosimus' report implies that to cross these was difficult for horses. Furthermore, Malalas reports that these troops were recruited from the Mattiarii and Lancearii (but Hoffmann, 1970, 139 n. 175 doubts if is he right); both units are also mentioned by Amm. 21.13.16, q.v. and 31.13.8 and are clearly light infantry troops. See

CHAPTER 1.2

for Lancearii and Mattiarii Hoffmann, 1969–1970, Bd. 1, 328–9, especially n. 175. It is likely that the *excursatores* are identical with the *velites* (17.2.1, 13.17, 21.12.9, 24.1.13, 4.3); see also Brok 106–7. Zosimus (3.14.1, 16.3, 17.1), in contrast to Amm. and Malalas (possibly quoting Magnus of Carrhae), reports that the advance guard was commanded by Lucillianus; see for him the note ad 23.3.9 and Woods, 1998, who i.a. thinks that Lucillianus was *comes* of the Mattiarii and Lancearii. It seems that normally Julian himself led the light infantry which went ahead of the main army; 24.1.13, 4.3, 5.3.

sensim The adverb emphasizes the caution with which the army proceeds; it is repeated by *cautius gradientes*. Cf. 21.12.6 *sensim incedentes et caute*. On adverbs in *-im* see the note ad 20.5.3 *perstringere pauca summatim*.

quod erat totius roboris firmamentum 'The heart and the strength of the whole army'. The use of two near synonyms (Liv. 36.18.2 *Macedonum robur... velut firmamentum circa... munitiones constituit* and Cic. *Mur.* 58 *firmamentum ac robur totius accusationis*) suggests that *roboris* must be taken as a gen. identitatis. *Totius*, however, can only refer to the army as a whole, as if Amm. had written *robur exercitus*.

legiones aliquas In spite of the natural protection provided by the river this safety measure was still necessary because the Euphrates could easily be crossed and therefore enemy attacks from across the river could be expected, and actually happened as will become clear from 24.5.5. These legions also had to maintain contact with the fleet. See Brok 97.

Nevitta PLRE I, Nevitta. First mentioned by Amm. in 17.6.3, q.v. as *equestris praepositus turmae* which he became in 358. In 361 he became *magister armorum* (21.8.1, q.v.), i.e. *magister equitum per Gallias* (21.8.3, 10.2, q.v.); Demandt, 1970, 581–2. Also in 361 he was a member of the Chalcedon tribunal (22.3.1, q.v.). In 362 he was consul together with Mamertinus (21.10.8, 12.25, 22.7.1, q.v.); see Bagnall et al., 1987, 258–9. With Dagalaifus he conducted the siege of Maozamalcha; 24.4.13, Zos. 3.21.4. He was most probably of German origin. He wanted a military man like himself to be the successor of Julian: *Nevitta et Dagalaifus proceresque Gallorum virum talem ex commilitio suo quaeritabant* (25.5.2). Except for this quotation Nevitta is not mentioned again in ancient sources after Julian had

8   COMMENTARY

died. According to Amm. he was a brave man (17.6.3) and a loyal
supporter of Julian (21.10.2), but uncultivated, boorish and, worse,
cruel (21.10.8).

supercilia fluminis praestringere iussit Euphratis On *supercilium* 'river-
bank' (cf. ὄφρυς) see the note ad 22.8.8. For *praestringere* see the
note ad 21.7.2.

Arintheo... et Hormisdae PLRE I, Arinthaeus. Like Nevitta, Arintheus
started his military career under the Caesar Julian when, in 355, he
was *tribunus agens vicem armaturarum rectoris*; 15.4.10 with De Jonge's
extensive note on Arintheus' career. Amm. calls him a *lectissimus
dux* (26.8.4). His rank at the time of the expedition is not known,
but he undoubtedly belonged to Julian's best and most loyal generals; the *PLRE* suggests he was *comes rei militaris*, but Demandt, 1970,
583 thinks he was *magister equitum*. In the deliberations about Julian's succession he was on the side of Victor and others who once
belonged to Constantius' entourage (25.5.2). He was among those
who negotiated the peace treaty with the Persians in 363 (25.7.7,
Zos. 3.31.1); later on he was sent on a mission by Jovian to Jovinus in
Gaul (25.10.9). Philost. *HE* 8.8 reports that he supported Valentinian's election as emperor. Amm. mentions his participation as *magister
peditum* in the wars against the Goths in 367 (27.5.4), with whom he
negotiated peace in 369 (27.5.9), and against the Persians in 370/1
(27.12.13, 12.15). He was consul in 372; Bagnall et al., 1987, 278–9.
On his deathbed he was baptised an orthodox Christian (Basil. *Ep.*
269) and seems to have opposed Valens' pro-Arian measures (Thdt.
HE 4.33). He died in 378.

     Hormisdas (*PLRE* I, Hormisdas 2) was the son of the Persian
king Hormisdas II and brother of Sapor II. In 324 he had fled
to the Roman Empire: *regalis Hormisdas, cuius e Perside discessum
supra monstravimus*; 16.10.16, q.v.; cf. Zos. 2.27.1–4; Zon. 13.5. From
Constantius he received a cavalry command; according to Woods,
1997, 289–90 he commanded the *schola scutariorum clibanariorum*.
Julian also gave him a military command (Zos. 3.11.3). During
Julian's campaign he regularly acted as negotiator with the Persians;
24.1.8, 2.11 and 20; Zos. 3.18.1. In 24.2.4 Amm. reports that the
Persians intended to ambush Hormisdas. It is suggested by Lib. *Ep.*
1402 that Julian wanted Hormisdas on the Persian throne instead
of Sapor. In 357 he visited Rome in the entourage of Constantius II.
Woods, 1999, argues that the anonymous Persian of Eunapius *fr.* 68,
who reduced the military success of Constantius II and his soldiers to

CHAPTER 1.2   9

mockery and laughter, is the same as prince Hormisdas. In 26.8.12 Amm. mentions Hormisdas' son, also named Hormisdas, who was nominated proconsul by the usurper Procopius and who later served under Theodosius I (Zos. 4.30.5). See for his name, a doublet of Ohrmazd (Ahura-mazdāh), Justi, 1895, 7–10 and Gignoux, 1986, 98 and 137–8.

per plana camporum et mollia An echo of Sallust, *Hist.* 4.24 *Italiae plana ac mollia.* The gen. inversus is used frequent ly in geographical observations, cf. 27.2.8 *per aperta camporum sequebatur* and 27.5.4 *per plana camporum errantes. Mollia* is brought under the heading "de regionibus paulum declivibus rebusque leniter curvatis" in TLL VIII 1380.13–28. Cf. the description of the Isaurian people in 14.2.5, who were used to mountainous terrain and for that reason *eos* (montes) *ut loca plana persultat et mollia.* The alternative interpretation 'soft', preferred by Rolfe, who translates "fields and meadows" can, however, not be excluded.

agmina vero postrema Dagalaifus cogebat et Victor Cf. Malalas, *Chron.* 13.330 Βίκτορα δὲ καὶ Δαγαλάιφον κατέταξεν ὄπισθεν τῶν λοιπῶν πεζῶν (thus Mendelsohn and *FGrHist* 225 F 1; Dindorf prints πλοίων) εἶναι καὶ φυλάττειν τὰ πλήθη. For Dagalaifus see *PLRE* I, Dagalaifus and the extensive note ad 21.8.1. For his consulship in 366, Bagnall et al., 1987, 266–7. He seems to have had great influence on the nomination of Jovian (25.5.2) as well as on that of Valentinian (Philost. *HE* 8.8); toward the latter he displayed an unusually candid behaviour; 26.4.1.

For Victor, *PLRE* I, Victor 4. Victor was of Sarmatian origin (31.12.6) and a Christian; Greg. Naz. *Ep.* 133, Thdt. *HE* 4.33, Basil. *Ep.* 152. An officer under Constantius (25.5.2), he probably became *magister peditum* in 362 (Zos. 3.11.3, 13.3 τοῦ μὲν πεζοῦ Βίκτορα στρατηγὸν) and in that capacity participated in Julian's expedition, even though Amm. refers to him either as *dux* or *comes*; see Demandt, 1970, 581–2. In the expedition he played an important role; 24.4.13, 31, 6.4, 13; Zos. 3.13.3, 16.3, 17.1, 21.5, 25.7. He was *magister equitum* under Valens; 27.5.1, 9, 30.2.4, 31.7.1, 12.6; Zos. 4.24.3. He participated in the battle of Adrianople (31.12.6, 13.9) and reported the news of the defeat to Gratian (Zos. 4.24.3). He was consul in 369; Bagnall et al., 1987, 272–3. In the deliberations about Julian's succession he was on the side of Arintheus (25.5.2). He was ambassador to Sapor in 363 (Lib. *Or.* 24.20), to the Goths in 366 (27.5.1) and 369 (27.5.9), and once again to the Persians in 377–8

10   COMMENTARY

(30.2.4–7, 31.7.1). According to Amm. 31.12.6 he was a prudent man: *cunctator et cautus.*

Osdroenae dux Secundinus For Osdroene see the note ad 23.2.7. Add to the literature cited there Frakes, 1993. Secundinus is only known from this passage. Apparently the frontier army of Osdroene participated in the Persian campaign. There were seven frontier armies along the eastern border – garrisoned in Palestine, Arabia, Phoenice, Syria, Osdroene, Mesopotamia and Armenia –, all of them commanded by *duces*; Jones 609.

1.3 *laxatis cuneis iumenta dilatavit et homines* See for *cuneus* the note ad 23.5.8. By extending the marching column Julian wanted to give the impression that his army was larger than it actually was. He apparently used this kind of tactical device more often; in 21.8.2–3 Amm. describes how Julian, when marching against Constantius, divided his army to give the impression of a huge force. It was a common tactical device which was also employed by Alexander and many other skilful generals after him. In 25.3.2 the same marching formation is described; in this case the condition of the terrain forced the army to march in an elongated column (*exercitus pro locorum situ quadratis quidem, sed laxis incedit agminibus*). The extended marching column has its dangers. Veg. *mil.* 3.6.22 warns against enemy attacks if the column is thinned out: *illudque vitandum, ne per neglegentiam aliis festinantibus, aliis tardius incedentibus interrumpatur acies aut certe tenuetur; continuo enim hostes interpellata pervadunt.*

Zos. 3.14.1 reports that Julian positioned the cavalry on the left wing accompanied by part of the infantry, while the rest of the army followed some seventy stades behind; in between was the baggage train with the pack animals, carrying heavy armour and other equipment, and their attendants. This description not only differs from that of Amm. but is also very unclear; see Paschoud n. 37. According to Zosimus the length of the marching formation is 70 stades (c. 13 km): σταδίοις διεστῶσα ἑβδομήκοντα; Amm. gives a length of 10 Roman miles (= 14.8 km). The difference may be explained by the fact that Amm. measured from the beginning of the column (*a signiferis primis*), whereas Zosimus gives the distance between the troops in the front and those in the rear; see Dillemann, 1961, 144.

si erupissent usquam Amm. uses *erumpere* often for sudden attacks or incursions into Roman territory (TLL V 2.838.3–27); cf. 21.7.6

CHAPTER 1.4

(Persarum copias) *prope margines tendere Tigridis incertum, quonam erumpere cogitantes,* 29.1.1 (Sapor) *erupturos in nostra catafractos et sagittarios et conductam misit plebem.*

decimo paene lapide… dispararentur A typically, though not exclusively, Ammianean phrase; see TLL VII 2.952.1–8. Cf. e.g. 14.9.8 *ab Antiochia vicensimo et quarto disiungitur lapide.*

Pyrrhus ille rex…Epirotes A similar stratagem is reported in 21.8.3, where Alexander and other experienced army commanders are mentioned as Julian's models. Pyrrhus is often praised as a great tactician. According to Livy 35.14.8–12, Hannibal was of the opinion that Pyrrhus was second only to Alexander. Pyrrhus is said to have written a tactical manual: Cic. *Fam.* 9.25; Fron. *Str.* 2.6.10, Aen. Tact. *fr.* 1; Plut. *Pyrrh.* 8.2. For *dilatare* cf. 27.2.5 *aciem dilatatam arte sollerti.*

opportunis… perquam scientissimus Cf. Liv. 35.14.9: *Pyrrhum dixisse castra metari primum docuisse; ad hoc neminem elegantius loca cepisse, praesidia disposuisse*; cf. Fron. *Str.* 1.4 (*De transducendo exercitu per loca hosti infesta*). Amm. is the only source which mentions Pyrrhus' ability to disguise the strength of his forces. There is a note on *perquam scientissimus* ad 21.16.7.

ubi convenisset V's *venisset* is, pace Fontaine, who defends this reading and translates "à son arrivée", hardly acceptable without a prefix or an adjunct of direction. Valesius suggested *usu venisset*, which is attractive for paleographical reasons. In the two instances of *usu venire* in Amm., however, (20.11.29 *ut in mari solet usu venire* and 26.7.7 *utque in certaminibus intestinis usu venire contingit*), it means 'to happen' rather than 'to be advantageous', which is the required sense here. It seems best, therefore, to accept Heraeus' *convenisset.*

Sarcinas… improtecta Zos. 3.14.1 describes the position of the baggage train as follows: τοῦτο δὲ τὸ μέσον εἶχε τά τε νωτοφόρα ζῷα, τὰ βαρέα τῶν ὅπλων καὶ τὴν ἄλλην παρασκευὴν φέροντα, καὶ ὅσον ἦν ὑπηρετικόν, ὡς ἂν ἐπ' ἀσφαλοῦς εἶεν καὶ οὗτοι, τοῦ στρατοῦ πανταχόθεν αὐτοὺς περιέχοντος. Amm. does not make it wholly clear whether the baggage train was protected on the right flank by Nevitta and on the left by Arintheus and Hormisdas, as *inter utrumque latus* suggests, or whether is was completely surrounded by Julian's troops in the centre, which seems to be implied by Zosimus' phrase τοῦ στρατοῦ πανταχόθεν αὐτοὺς περιέχοντος. In the former case the position of the bag-

12   COMMENTARY

gage train in relation to Julian's troops is left unspecified by Amm. For
the safety of a marching army it was of importance that the column
remained intact, that everyone moved with the same speed and that
no units dropped behind. The words *procedentium ordinatim, ne qua
vi subita raperentur, ut saepe contigit, improtecta*, where *improtecta* refers
to the baggage train, show Amm.'s personal experience as a soldier.

apparitionem imbellem Cf. Zos. 3.14.1 ὅσον ἦν ὑπηρετικόν. For *apparitio*
see the notes ad 23.5.4 *omnes sequellae* and 23.5.6 *apparitoris cuiusdam*.
The word is used already by Cicero for the official staff of a provincial
governor: *Q. fr.* 1.1.12 *quos... in necessariis apparitionibus tecum esse
voluisti, qui quasi ex cohorte praetoris appellari solent.*

inter utrumque latus instituit procedentium ordinatim There is no good
parallel for *instituere* 'to assign a place to', either in the *Res Gestae*
or in other authors, according to TLL VII 1.1991.34–6 ("fere i.q.
collocare"). *Procedentium* depends on *latus* and refers to the soldiers
on the left and right flank, either of the army as a whole or of Julian's
troops. For this use of the present participle in the genitive plural cf.
29.5.22 *secutusque acclamationem rogantium sanguine vindicari eos*. Seyfarth seems to connect the participle with *impedimentorum*: "wo sie in
geregelter Ordnung vorrücken sollten". Apart from the fact that one
would expect *procedentia, ordinatim procedere* better suits regular troops
than non-combatants. The adverb is a hapax in Amm., but cf. 19.7.3
non inordinatim ut antea, sed tubarum sonitu leni ductante... incedebant.

classis... sinebatur For the fleet see 23.3.9, q.v. Because of the many
bends in the Euphrates, the route by river was much longer than
that by land; Brok 101–2. Even though the army marched along
the left bank of the Euphrates – cf. Gawlikowksi, 1990, 88ff. who
argues that Julian's forces marched along the right bank – it is highly
unlikely that it followed all the bends of the river, apart from the
troops commanded by Nevitta whom Julian had ordered to skirt the
banks of the river (*supercilia praestringere iussit*). Nevitta's troops were
to maintain contact between the fleet and the main army. The fleet
was not permitted to lag behind or to get ahead because it would
then be unprotected and could easily be attacked by the Persians.

tortuosum Cf. Liv. 27.47.10 *per tortuosi amnis sinus flexusque.*

1.5 *Emenso itaque itinere bidui prope civitatem venimus Duram* I.e. two
marching days after entering Persian territory. Dura (modern Qal'af

CHAPTER 1.6   13

as Salihiyah) is some 50 km from Cercusium, the last halting place before the Roman army set foot on Persian soil, which means that the army marched about 25 km per day. Dura-Europos was already mentioned in 23.5.8 (*Duram, desertum oppidum*), q.v. Since the army marches on the left bank of the Euphrates and Dura is situated on the right bank, the preposition *prope* is well chosen. For the use of the first person plural see the notes ad 23.5.7 and 24.6.1.

greges cervorum The same story is told with fewer details by Zos. 3.14.2: πλῆθος ἐλάφων φανὲν οἱ στρατιῶται κατατοξεύσαντες ἅλις ἐχρή-σαντο τῇ ἐκ τούτων τροφῇ. *Cervus* is a generic name for deer; see Keller, 1980, 277–9. Dillemann, 1961, 131–2 thinks Amm. was mistaken and that the soldiers hunted gazelles (*dorcades*), not deer; cf. X. *An.* 1.5.2. Gazelles, whose habitat is dry grass woodland, steppe and desert, did indeed occur in Mesopotamia. Fontaine n. 297 contests this view and thinks that Amm. (and Zosimus) must refer to one of the three species of deer – *cervus elaphus* (red deer), *dama dama* (fallow deer) and *capreolus capreolus* (roe deer) – which occurred in the Middle East in ancient times. The latter species can be discounted since it lives solitarily. Amm. thus either refers to the *cervus elaphus* – cf. Zosimus' use of the word ἔλαφος – or to the *dama dama* (of which the *dama Mesopotamica* was a subspecies) which both live in herds. Every kind of deer provides good food. See Cansdale, 1970, 89–94.

alii ponderibus illisi remorum I.e. while swimming across the river, they were killed by the rowers on the fleet. Amm. often has *pondus* followed by a gen. inversus, e.g. – *armorum* (27.10.12, 28.5.10), – *lacernarum* (14.6.9), – *tignorum tegularumque* (23.2.6), even with abstract words like *invidiae* (16.12.29, 26.6.4, 28.1.52).

natatu assueta veloci In classical Latin *assuetus* is found with dative and ablative. In none of the occurrences in Amm. can it be decided which case is meant. For datives in -*u* see De Jonge ad 19.1.6.

alveo penetrato incohibili cursu evasit ad solitudines notas For *penetrare* 'to cross' see the note ad 21.13.2 *nam si permeato* and 24.4.21. There is a note on *incohibilis* ad 21.16.11. The *solitudines* are part of the Syrian desert.

dierum quattuor itinere levi peracto Cf. Zos. 3.14.2: σταθμοὺς δ' ἐντεῦθεν **1.6** διελθὼν τέσσαρας εἴς τι χωρίον ἀφίκετο. Φαθούσας ὄνομα τούτῳ. ἦν δὲ ἀντικρὺ ἐν τῷ ποταμῷ νῆσος, ἔχουσα φρούριον ὑπὸ πλείστων οἰκούμενον.

14   COMMENTARY

See the note on chronology. It is assumed that Zosimus' Phatousa was situated on the bank of the Euphrates opposite Anatha, i.e. Zosimus' φρούριον; see e.g. Matthews 165. From Amm.'s text it does not become clear where the army made a halt at the end of the fourth day. Musil, 1927, 238, followed by Matthews 172, thinks that it halted way before Anatha – some 40 km – since the 130 km from Dura to Anatha led through some rough terrain for which reason he considers it unlikely that the army could cover a distance of 32,5 km a day. Brok 102, however, considers a place 40 km from Anatha too far away to start the attack by night on the fortress of Anatha. He suggests therefore (102–3) that the army did take a short cut by not following one large bend of the Euphrates. This not only shortened the route by some 10 km but also had the advantage that away from the river the route was less heavy going so that the army could march faster; see also Paschoud n. 39. Nevertheless, the army must have stopped several kilometers before Anatha/Phatousa, otherwise it would have been noticed and Julian could not have attacked the fortress by surprise as was clearly his intention. Amm.'s report, as well as that of Zosimus, suggests that soon after the discovery of the fleet with Lucillianus' men at the break of day, Julian and the rest of the army arrived to urge the Persian garrison to surrender; this implies that the army cannot have camped very far away from Anatha. Cf. Matthews 172, who thinks that the fortress was taken by the fleet and the soldiers commanded by Lucillianus, and that only late in the day, after Anatha had surrendered, the main army led by Julian began to arrive.

vespera incedente See the note ad 20.11.24 about Amm.'s predilection for the feminine forms of this noun.

cum expeditis... expugnaturus Cf. Zos. 3.14.3: Τούτῳ Λουκιλλιανὸν ἐπιπέμψας ἅμα τοῖς ὑπ' αὐτὸν κατασκόποις χιλίοις ἐπολιόρκει τὸ φρούριον. For Lucillianus, see the notes ad 23.3.9 and 24.1.2. These 1000 men were in all probability part of the 1500 *excursatores* mentioned in 24.1.2.

imperatu principis Apart from one inscription, CIL 14.74 *imperatu aram fecit dominae*, the ablative *imperatu* is found only in Amm. (TLL VII 1.561.49–52).

Anathan The name of the fortress recurs in the modern village 'Anan which is situated near ancient Anatha. It was already mentioned by

CHAPTER 1.7   15

Isid. Char. 1 (= *GGM* I 249): Ἀναθὼ νῆσος κατὰ τὸν Εὐφράτην. Lib. *Or.* 18.218 καὶ προιόντες φρούριον εἶδον ἐν χερρονήσῳ τοῦ ποταμοῦ κείμενον may refer to Anatha, as supposed by e.g. Brok 102 and Fontaine n. 300 Libanius makes a mistake when he considers Anatha to be a peninsula rather than an island.

The island of Anatha measures some 950 × 200 m and rises in the centre to *c.* 13 m above the river level. There is no conclusive evidence that it was ever under Roman control for an extended period of time. Perhaps only after Trajan's invasion of Mesopotamia was it temporarily occupied by the Romans. The same may be true for a period in the first half of the third century; we know from the *Res Gestae Divi Saporis* that Sapor I captured the fortress from the Romans *c.* 256; see Honigmann-Maricq, 1952, 12, 146. The *Not. Dign. Or.* 33.20 refers to Anatha, but this must be either an anachronism or a reference to a homonymous site since it is well-nigh impossible that the Romans had a military post a long way downstream of the Euphrates after 363. Epigraphical evidence from the second and third centuries shows that Anatha was an important emporium for merchants from Palmyra and that it even garrisoned Palmyrene soldiers to safeguard the trade route. See Musil, 1927, appendix XVI (pp. 345–9); Northedge, 1983; Oppenheimer, 1983, 26–9; Kennedy, 1986 (with all the relevant references to secondary literature); Kennedy-Riley, 1990, 114–5; Isaac, 1992², 150–2.

quod, ut pleraque alia, circumluitur According to Brok 103, there were no fewer than 44 of these islands between Anatha and Diacira (24.2.3). For *circumluere* cf. 22.8.2 about the Aegean *circumluens et Lemnum et Thasum.* The verb is rare in classical authors. Tac. *Hist.* 4.12.2 uses it for the *insula Batavorum: quam... mare Oceanus a fronte, Rhenus amnis tergum ac latera circumluit.*

per opportuna dispersis Cf. Liv. 30.24.11 *per litora portusque dispersas Romanas naves.*

lux certa This expression is found only in Livy, who writes *vixdum luce certa* in several places (TLL VII 2.1906.75). The similarity with Zosimus' account is again striking: ἡμέρας δὲ γενομένης ὑπὸ τῶν ἐν τῷ φρουρίῳ τινὸς ὑδρείας ἕνεκα προελθόντος ὀφθέντες εἰς θόρυβον τοὺς ἔνδον κατέστησαν (3.14.3).   **1.7**

aquatum quidam egressus The same phrase occurs in Sal. *Jug.* 93.2. Brok 103 points to the description of the water reservoirs of Amida

16   COMMENTARY

in 19.5.4, which are at the level of the river Tigris, from which water was brought up along stairs hewn in the rocks. Amm. had seen similar provisions in all fortifications along rivers in the region (*ut in omnibus per eas regiones munimentis, quae contingunt flumina, vidimus*). Veg. *mil.* 4.10 describes extensively what to do to ensure that the besieged suffer no shortage of water.

ululabili clamore sublato excitos tumultuosis vocibus The same expression is used in 20.6.7, q.v. The adjectives vividly express the fright of the Persians at the unexpected appearance of the Romans. The first occurrence of *ululabilis* is in Apul. *Met.* 4.3. *Tumultuosus* occurs already in classical texts. It corresponds with θόρυβος in Zosimus' version of the event.

a specula quadam altissima explorato situ castrorum There is a hill opposite the fortress of Anatha on the right bank of the Euphrates (Brok 104). Rolfe's translation "had been looking for a site for a camp" cannot be right, since Amm. always uses *situs* to describe a geographical spot, cf. e.g. 24.2.9 *cuius* (Pirisabora) *obequitans moenia imperator et situm* and 24.4.3 *civitatis situm diligenti inquisitione exploraturus.*

quam ocissime This expression is very rare, TLL IX 2.416.6–14. It may have been inspired by Sal. *Jug.* 25.5 *quam ocissume ad provinciam adcedat.*

obsidionales machinas For the various siege engines see 23.4 with the notes.

1.8   *cum non absque discriminibus… certandum* For *absque* see the note ad 14.3.4. *Esse certandum* is a good example of a gerundive as a substitute for the passive future infinitive.

sermone cum leni tum aspero… hortabatur ad deditionem defensores As Crump, 1975, 101 notes, "a wise leader considered the potential benefits of surrender worth the effort, even though he risked being fired upon while approaching the battlements." See the note ad 20.6.3 for such attempts to avoid a siege and compare 20.11.7 (Bezabde), 21.12.4 (Aquileia), 24.2.1 (Thilutha), 24.2.9 (Pirisabora), 24.4.11 (Maozamalcha). The Persian king also made use of it: 19.1.3–6 (Amida), 20.6.3 (Singara), 20.7.3 (Bezabde), as did the Goths when laying siege to Adrianople (31.15.5). According to Lib. *Or.* 18.218 the inhabitants of Anatha surrendered out of fright.

CHAPTER 1.9

There are few examples of *cum... tum* in the sense of *non solum, sed etiam* or rather *modo... modo* in Amm. Cf. the note ad 24.4.16. According to Szantyr 626, the coordination is relatively rare in later Latin.

Hormisda For Hormisdas see the note ad 24.1.2.

promissis eius et iuramentis illecti It is not known which promises were made, but one of them was to spare the lives of the inhabitants, as is mentioned by Zos. 3.14.3: ὁ βασιλεὺς... παρενέγυησε τοῖς ἔνδον ἑαυτοὺς τε καὶ τὸ φρούριον παραδοῦσι πρόδηλον ἐκφυγεῖν ὄλεθρον. The tribunate of Pusaeus, the Persian commander of Anatha, also must have helped in the decision to surrender the fortress. The influence of the old Roman soldier should also not be underrated; Amm. calls him *proditionis auctor* (24.1.10). *Iuramentum* is not found before Tertullian and occurs only in prose.

bovem coronatum... susceptae pacis indicium Amm.'s explanation that the crowned ox indicates the acceptance of peace, is not mentioned in any other source. In keeping with Amm., Fontaine n. 303 speaks of a ritual expressing *captatio benevolentiae* and the wish to come to an agreement. Perhaps analogous rituals are meant in Zos. 1.56.1, where the Palmyrenes brought gifts and sacrifices upon their submission to Aurelian, and X. *Cyr.* 5.2.5, where Gobryas as a sign of his surrender to Cyrus presented the Persian king with all kinds of provisions including cattle, goats, sheep and swine. For the ox as sacrificial animal in Zoroastrian rites, see Duchesne-Guillemin, 1962, 102. Amm. often uses *suscipere* instead of *accipere*. See the notes ad 15.5.5, 17.13.23 and 20.2.3.

1.9

descendére suppliciter Short for *(pacem) suppliciter obsecrantes/rogantes*, as e.g. in 16.12.15, 17.11.3 and 17.12.9.

munimento omni incenso The demolition of the fortress is, as Brok 104 and Fontaine n. 304 already noted, in compliance with one of Julian's goals as expressed in the address to his troops (23.5.18), i.e. the vengeance for the disasters inflicted on the Romans by the Persians; see also the burning of e.g. Diacira, Ozogardana (24.2.3–4) and Pirisabora (24.2.22). The demolition is not mentioned by Zosimus and, perhaps more remarkably, there are no archaeological traces of the burning of Anatha; Northedge, 1983, 235.

18 COMMENTARY

Pusaeus eius praefectus, dux Aegypti postea, honore tribunatus affectus est
See *PLRE* I, Pusaeus. Zos. 3.14.4: Πουσαίῳ δὲ τῷ τούτων ἡγουμένῳ δοὺς
ταξιάρχου φροντίδα τὸ λοιπὸν ἐν τοῖς ἐπιτηδείοις εἶχε, πιστοῦ πειραθείς.
Pusai is a common Iranian name; Justi, 1895, 256 mentions six
other men with this name; cf. further Gignoux, 1986, 150, who i.a.
notes that 'pus' comes from old Persian puça, 'son'. Nothing more
is known about him except what Amm. and Zosimus report. Since
the administrative reorganisation by Diocletian, Egypt had a *praefectus
Aegypti* for civil affairs and a *dux Aegypti Thebaidos utrarumque Libyarum*
for military affairs; see the note ad 22.16.6 and Jones 44, 101.
Following Grosse, 1920, 149, Brok 104 suggests that Pusaeus became
tribunus honorarius, but it is more likely that *honore tribunatus affectus est*
means that Pusaeus "was awarded the rank of tribune", as Hamilton
translates. For tribunes, a general term for commanding military
officers, see the notes ad 22.11.2 and 23.3.9. After his surrender
Pusaeus probably joined the Roman army and participated in the
campaign against the Persians; only then does Zosimus' remark, that
Julian considered him one of his closest friends make sense.

reliqui vero... transmissi sunt Zos. 3.14.4: ἄνδρας μὲν σὺν παισὶ καὶ
γυναιξὶν εἰς τὴν ὑπὸ Ῥωμαίων ἐχομένην γῆν ἅμα φυλακῇ στρατιωτῶν
παρέπεμψε; see also Lib. *Or.* 18.218. Deportation of conquered people was a customary feature of warfare in the Ancient Near East.
Under Sapor I and II many inhabitants of the eastern part of the Roman empire were forcibly moved to new or refounded cities in the
Sasanian Empire, such as those who lived in Dura-Europos who in
256 or 257 were deported by Sapor I. As a consequence of this Dura
became a deserted place; cf. 23.5.8, 24.1.5. Amm. mentions several deportations by Sapor II: 19.6.1–2, 9.1–2, 20.6.7–8 (with note),
20.7.15. The Romans also occasionally deported populations from
captured Persian cities. Diocletian carried off prisoners of war from
Asia to colonies in Thrace (*Pan.* 8.21.1) and Constantius II had inhabitants of a large and important Persian city transferred to Thrace
(Lib. *Or.* 59.83–84). A Syriac chronicle mentions that Julian, after
he had devastated the entire region from Nisibis to Ctesiphon, deported a large number of captives; *Chron. Ps.-Dionysianum* a. 674 =
CSCO 91, 179,24–180,2; Latin transl. CSCO 121, 133–4: *Anno 674°,
descendit Iulianus rex in Persidem, et vastavit totam regionem inde a Nisibi
usque Ctesiphontem in Beth-Aramaye. Inde multos homines abduxit quos collocavit in monte Snsu* (the location of this mountain is not known). See
Lieu, 1986 for deportations in this period by Persians and Romans.
Amm. speaks of Chalcis in Syria, modern Qenneshrin, to distinguish

CHAPTER 1.10   19

it from Chalcis in Coelesyria; it is also called Chalcis ad Belum: *Chalcidem cognominatam ad Belum* (Plin. *Nat.* 5.81). It is further mentioned by e.g. Ptol. 5.15.18, Tab. Peut. IX.5 (*Calcida*). App. *Syr.* 57 reports that it was founded by Seleucus Nicator. It was situated some 100 km south-east of Antioch; see Benzinger, 1899; Millar, 1993, 238–9.

cum caritatibus suis Cf. 18.5.2 *cum coniuge, liberis et omni vinculo caritatum* and see the note ad 20.4.10.

humaniore cultu Cf. the scathing remarks on the *cultus humanitatis* offered to foreigners in Rome in the second digression on Rome (28.4.10): *Ex his quidam, cum salutari pectoribus oppositis coeperint, osculanda capita in modum taurorum minacium obliquantes adulatoribus offerunt genua savianda vel manus id illis sufficere ad beate vivendum existimantes et abundare omni cultu humanitatis peregrinum putantes.*

miles quidam This wonderful story about the old soldier is not found in Zosimus. Matthews 172 suggests that Amm. was among those who heard the soldier tell his story in the Roman camp. This is Amm.'s second reference to Maximianus' Persian campaign of 296–297; the first reference is in 23.5.11, q.v. A similar story about a Roman soldier in Persian service is told in 18.6.16.   **1.10**

perrupisset For *perrumpere* 'to invade' see the note ad 21.7.2 *ne Africa.*

prima etiamtum lanugine iuvenis The phrase is traditional, see TLL VII 2.937.5–25. Amm.'s model may well have been Verg. *A.* 10.323 *flaventem prima lanugine malas.* In 31.10.18 Amm. says about the emperor Gratian *dum etiamtum lanugo genis inserperet speciosa.* It seems that normally service could be done from the age of eighteen. Sons of veterans, however, could join the army from about the age of sixteen. A law from 372 (*Cod. Theod.* 7.1.11) indicates that even boys under sixteen were enrolled; see Nicasie, 1998, 88–90. Veg. *mil.* 1.4.1 mentions that those reaching puberty should be enlisted and that adolescents are the ones to recruit; this implies that even boys of fourteen or sixteen could be recruited. It may therefore be that the soldier of this passage had not long been a *iuvenis*, i.e. had passed the age of fourteen, and that his beard was just beginning to grow when he joined the army and took part in Maximianus' campaign against the Persians. In any case in 363 he must have been well over eighty years of age, but that he was nearly a hundred years old is an exaggeration.

20 COMMENTARY

uxores sortitus gentis ritu complures On *sortiri* see the note ad 23.6.54. The polygamy of the Persians is mentioned in 23.6.76.

exsultans proditionísquë aúctor A hysteron proteron. For *proditio* = *deditio* cf. 15.5.33, where it is used of a person.

praedixisse, quod... sepelietur See the note ad 20.8.10 on Amm.'s use of *quod*-clauses instead of the infinitive construction.

Saraceni procursatores partis cuiusdam hostium obtulere The story is mirrored in 24.3.1, where we are told that Julian hears the disastrous news *Surenam... procursatorum partis nostrae tres turmas inopinum aggressum*. Whereas Amm. does write *pars nostra*, here and in 24.4.28, and *pars hostilis* (16.12.41), *Quadorum pars* (17.12.12), he does not have *pars quaedam nostra*, c.q. *hostilis*. It seems prudent therefore to accept Kellerbauer's transposition of V's *quidam* to follow *Saraceni* or, preferably, to read *quosdam*. For the Saracenes see the notes ad 22.15.2 and 23.3.8; for *procursatores* see the note ad 23.3.4.

1.11 The events recorded in this section remind the reader of the gloomy atmosphere surrounding Julian's expedition evoked in the opening chapters of Book 23. The unfavourable *omina* continue to be related here, possibly to put in perspective the enthusiasm of the soldiers described in the next section. The episode about the hurricane and the flooding is not reported by Zosimus.

Acciderat aliud postridie dirum The use of the pluperfect is startling. The adverb *postridie* typically marks a new stage in the narrative, for which in classical Latin the perfect would have been *de rigueur*. Hagendahl, 1921, 122 demonstrated that in a number of cases, where Amm. switches within one sentence from perfect to pluperfect, the creation of a regular cursus was an overriding concern for the author. Hagendahl also points to an instance, where there is no such explanation for a similar switch (27.12.5). In the case of *acciderat*, in contrast with the following *confúderat ómnia*, the choice of the pluperfect cannot be accounted for on metrical grounds. Kroon and Rose, 1996, 87 present as their impression that the use of the pluperfect "does not differ markedly from what we observe in Classical Latin", although, as they admit, the scarcity of the material does not allow for firm conclusions. Instances like those produced by Hagendahl as well as the present passage make it difficult to subscribe to this opinion. The use of *aliud* is equally uncommon, since *dirum* does

CHAPTER 1.11

not belong to the same category as the event mentioned in the last section, which had made Julian happy (*laetissimo principi*). A comparable instance is 25.10.8 *his ita tristibus laetum aliud addebatur.* See further Szantyr 208 and TLL I 1625.75–1626.7. Löfstedt, 1933, 188–90 warns against interpreting all instances of this use of *alius*, which is found from Plautus onwards, as grecisms. In the case of Amm., however, this does seem a plausible explanation.

The date is 13 April; see the note on chronology.

ventorum enim turbo exortus pluresque vertigines concitans Apart from 24.6.10 *excita undique humus rapido turbine portabatur* this is the only occurrence of *turbo* in its literal meaning. For metaphorical *turbo* see the note ad 21.13.14.

Hurricanes and other kinds of storms are characteristic of the climate of this region in the months of March, April and May. The Babylonians were already familiar with these south-western storms and called them *amurru*; Unger, 1970[2], 123–4. Several modern travellers named by Brok 105 also experienced these devastating storms.

ita confuderat omnia, ut tabernacula multa conscinderentur Heraeus' conjecture *ut tabernacula* for Vm3's *tecta bernacula* creates a smooth text. Meurig-Davies' *ut et tabernacula* and Fontaine's *ut tenta tabernacula* are paleographically even closer to Vm3. *Tenta*, however, seems otiose, whereas the repetition of *et* in the text proposed by Meurig-Davies brings out the force of the storm quite effectively. *Tabernaculum* in Amm. often refers to the tent of the emperor (25.2.2, 3.15, 5.5, 6.7) or that of officers (29.4.5). In 16.1.4 it is used in a general sense, meaning a soldier's tent. In 14.4.4 *tabernaculum* is used to designate the dwellings of the Saracens. It is possible that in this passage Amm. refers only to the larger tents of the emperor and officers. There is some corroboration for this argument in Vegetius who uses *tabernaculum* for officers' tents (*mil.* 2.10.2, 3.8.15) and the word *papilio* for the tents of common soldiers (*mil.* 1.3.2, 23.2, 2.13.6, 3.18.6). The tents of the Roman army were made of high-quality leather; Webster, 1981[2], 167–8 with a reconstruction drawing of the *papilio.* See also Van Driel-Murray, 1990. It is obvious from what is related in section 7 above (*explorato situ castrorum*) that the army camped near Anatha.

spiritu stabilitatem vestigii subvertente Amm. uses *spiritus* with the following meanings: 1. '(last) breath', as in 14.6.25 *turpi sono fragosis naribus introrsum reducto spiritu concrepantes* and 25.5.7 *in ultimo rerum*

22 COMMENTARY

spiritu, 2. 'spirit' as in 15.8.5 *uno paene omnium spiritu* and 28.3.4 *Valentinus... superbi spiritus homo*, 3. 'wind', 'air', as here and in the δόξα of Anaximander on earthquakes in 17.7.12: (terram) *vehementi spiritu quassatam cieri propriis sedibus* and 4. as the equivalent of Stoic πνεῦμα in 20.3.12 *in terra spiritus cuiusdam interni motu suspensa* and 21.1.7 *elementorum omnium spiritus... praesentiendi motu semper et ubique vigens*, q.v. *Vestigii* is a gen. inversus: the storm 'blew them off their feet, which were planted firmly on the ground.'

amne enim repente extra margines evagato mersae sunt quaedam frumentariae naves Amm.'s does not connect the storm winds explicitly with the rising water level, as he had done in his description of the impact of the Etesian winds on the Nile in 22.15.7, q.v. The flooding of the Euphrates may have been caused by the melting snow in the Armenian mountains, which leads to a yearly rise of the water level from the middle of March to mid-May of about two metres (Matthews 154 and 24.8.2 *quodque liquentibus iam brumae pruinis* with the note). That, however, would be a gradual process, whereas Amm. speaks of a sudden inundation (*repente*). The storm, mentioned immediately before the flooding, would certainly be the most natural explanation for the event. Tacitus has a very interesting parallel: *Ann.* 6.37.2 *nuntiavere accolae Euphraten nulla imbrium vi sponte et immensum attolli*, but offers no explanation for the phenomenon. As for the supply vessels, see the note ad 23.3.9. Brok 105–6 mentions modern expeditions during which ships were sunk as a consequence of these yearly storms.

cataractis avulsis ad diffundendas reprimendasque aquas rigare suetas The water works in the Euphrates have been of enormous importance for the agricultural and political organisation of Mesopotamia since the third millennium B.C. See Stol, 1976–1980, and Veenhof, 1993. The military importance of the water management is discussed by Veenhof, 1975. The water of the river was let into a system of canals, which were suitable for water transport and irrigation. For an account from classical times see Strabo 16.1.9–10 (740C). In his Persian digression Amm. had mentioned the subject: (Euphrates) *arva cultorum industria diligentius rigans vomeri et gignendis arbustis habilia facit* (23.6.25). A remark in Isid. Char. 1 (= *GGM* 1 247) shows a remarkable similarity to the present section: ἐνταῦθα Σεμιράμιδος ἐστι διῶρυξ, καὶ λίθοις πέφρακται ὁ Εὐφράτης, ἵνα στενοχωρούμενος ὑπερκλύζῃ τὰ πέδια· θέρους μέντοι ναυαγεῖ τὰ πλοῖα. A slightly different account is given by Briant, 1999, who compares Arr. *An.* 7.7.7 and Hld. 8.5,

CHAPTER 1.12

where κατάρράκται are mentioned, with texts from Mari dating from the second millenium B.C. In his opinion these κατάρράκται served to regulate the course of the river.

Pace Briant, the *cataractae* are best understood as weirs which can be opened to let the water into the canals. Amm.'s use of the word *cataracta* is no indication that he was acquainted with Plin. *Ep.* 10.61.4 where the same word, in the meaning of 'weir', is used; Brok 106. He may well have found the word in a Greek source. In fact, there is no evidence at all that Amm. was familiar with the work of the Younger Pliny; Adkin, 1998.

per insidias an magnitudine fluentorum, sciri non potuit As TLL II 1305.55 remarks, "avelluntur res ab hominibus vel vi naturali." In this section Amm. does not choose between the two possibilities. Sabbah 529 subtly remarks about such cases "L'aveu d'ignorance y renforce le prestige de l'historien." In 24.6.2 we find the same expression. There, however, it is clear that the water was let in on purpose. The same is true of 24.3.10: *quo itinere nos ituros Persae praedocti sublatis cataractis undas evagari fusius permiserunt.* Amm.'s wording certainly suggests a connection between the sinking of the supply vessels and the opening of the weirs, but he leaves it to his readers to fill in the details. One can easily imagine the ships being carried away by the current, caused by the opening of the gates and smashed against the weirs. Libanius *Or.* 18.223 has no doubt that the flooding was intentional: τοῦ στρατοῦ τοίνυν ἐπιόντος ἀνέντες πάσας εἰσόδους τῷ ῥεύματι τάς τε διώρυχας ('canals') ἔπλησαν καὶ δι' ἐκείνων τὴν ἄλλην γῆν. It is not absolutely certain, however, that Libanius refers to the same incident, since he does not mention the storms and the flooding immediately after the surrender of Anatha. Still, he probably does refer to it, since in his account, too, the incident precedes the capture of Pirisabora. See also the note ad 24.3.10. The incident is not mentioned in Zosimus. *Diffundere* and *reprimere* are the usual verbs for releasing or holding in check the flow of water, as e.g. in Cic. *Div.* 2.69 *si lacus Albanus redundasset... Romam perituram, si repressus esset, Veios* and Curt. 3.1.3 *Marsyas diffusus circumiectos rigat campos.*

Post perruptam... urbem... et captivos transmissos Amm. recapitulates **1.12** section 9. The use of *perrumpere* "to force a way into" (OLD 2) is found in Tac. *Hist.* 2.15.1 *perrupta castra.* In Amm. cf. 31.15.8 (ut) ... *civitas perrumperetur impropugnata.*

24 COMMENTARY

elatis vocibus in favores principis consurgebant This again refers to an
acclamatio; cf. 24.1.1. *Elatus* has a different meaning from 20.11.9
elatis passim clamoribus ascensus undique temptabatur in that it expresses
confidence and enthusiasm. See the note ad 21.4.7 and cf. 23.5.8
certiore iam spe status prosperioris elatus. Favor has the concrete sense
'expression of sympathy', as often in Livy, e.g. 4.24.7 *cum gratulatione
ac favore ingenti populi.* The plural is found also in 25.5.6 *Iulianum
recreatum arbitrati sunt deduci magnis favoribus, ut solebat.*

For *consurgere* cf. 27.6.15 *Consurrectum est post haec in laudes maioris
principis* and 17.12.12 *ne... in arma repente consurgeret,* which is probably inspired by Verg. *A.* 10.90 *consurgere in arma.*

dei caelestis... cura For *dei caelestis* see the note ad 21.5.3. To the
literature mentioned there may be added Rike, 1987, 31–4. The
reading *deinde caelestem* of BAG, defended by Blomgren, is very close
to V's *deinde caelestes* and for that reason preferable to Seyfarth's *deinde
dei caelestis.* Amm. has the phrase *caelestis cura* in 18.3.1.

1.13 *Et cui... de obscuris erat suspectior cura* The construction of *cura* with
a dative and the preposition *de* is in itself unobjectionable; TLL IV
1455.62–70 quotes Ov. *Tr.* 3.11.70 as an example: *est tibi de rebus
maxima cura meis.* There is, however, a complication, since the dative
also serves as a dative of the agent with *timebatur.* This makes the
sentence very strained. It is clearly preferable to read *et quia,* a
connecting phrase which occurs in Amm. no fewer than 27 times.
Suspectus has an active meaning here 'on his guard', as in 16.12.27
*stetit impavidus suspectiorque de obscuris nec referre gradum nec ulterius ire
temptavit.*

astus gentis et ludificandi varietas This is a standard feature of the
Persians, who have been characterized as *magis artifices quam fortes* in
the Persian digression (23.6.80) and as *fallacissima gens* in 21.13.4,
q.v. In this respect they resemble the Gauls, who were also feared *astu
et ludificandi varietate* (17.13.27). In 23.5.21, q.v., Julian says that he
fears nothing *praeter dolos et insidias hominum.*

nunc antesignanus, nunc agminibus cogendis insistens In this way Julian
kept the army in a close formation; cf. Veg. *mil.* 3.6.22–23. In his
speech at Cercusium he had reminded his soldiers to keep with the
army on its march (23.5.21), obviously to prevent their becoming
an easy prey for the Persians. According to Veg. *mil.* 3.6.3 it was the
responsibility of the commanding general to take all measures to

CHAPTER 1.14   25

make sure that his army would suffer no attack while on the march
and could repel an enemy attack without losing men. For *antesignanus*
see the note ad 23.5.19. *Insistere* "to concentrate attention" (OLD 6)
is found with a gerund also in 24.4.9 *ut… abigundis insisterent praedis.*
It may have been inspired by Tac. *Hist.* 3.77.3 (insistere) *perdomandae
Campaniae,* as Heubner suggests in his commentary ad loc.

cum expeditis velitibus… scrutabatur Thickets and valleys were likely
places for ambushes. It was the general's task to reconnoitre every-
thing in advance and to detect ambushes before the enemy could
inflict damage; Veg. *mil.* 3.6.25–26. Amm. uses the term *velites* or
velitares several times in his *Res Gestae* (16.11.9, 17.2.1, q.v., 13.17,
19.3.1, q.v., 20.1.3, 21.12.9). They are light armed troops who according to Veg. *mil.* 3.16.5, 7 were very swift and equipped with light
shields, swords and javelins. They could be *auxilia* (16.11.9, 20.1.3;
cf. also 24.2.8, 6.9) and are very likely identical with the *excursatores*
of 24.1.2, q.v. For the *velites* in general see Lammert, 1958.

frutecta squalida vallesque For *squalere* and its derivatives see the note
ad 22.15.22.

affabilitate nativa Brok aptly compares 25.4.9 *genuina lenitudine.* The
noun is found already in Cic. *Off.* 2.48 *comitas adfabilitasque sermonis.*

agros omni frugum genere divites The region between Anatha and   **1.14**
Diacira (Hît) is not particularly fertile. See for climate and vegetation,
Adams, 1981, 11 ff. Possibly, Amm. refers to the region near Anatha,
where the islands and river banks were well cultivated (Musil, 1927,
239) or that beyond Diacira; cf. Brok 107 and Wirth, 1962, 101. Lib.
Or. 18.219–221, who calls Assyria a fertile country, reports also on the
pillaging of the fertile fields and the demolition of barns by the Roman army, but only after the events described by Amm. in 24.2.1–9.

tuguriis Primitive peoples live in *tuguria.* The Huns despised even
these humble dwellings: 31.2.23 *Nec templum apud eos visitur aut
delubrum, ne tugurium quidem culmo tectum cerni usquam potest.*

inflammari permisit Amm. shows a marked predilection for passive
forms of *permittere* followed by active infinitives of the type 14.2.7 *nec
exertare lacertos nec crispare permissi tela,* which is found 38 times. Next in
frequency are active forms of the verb followed by passive infinitives,
as in 25.4.16 *emendari se, cum deviaret a fruge bona, permittens,* which is

26   COMMENTARY

found ten times. Infinitives following active verb forms are invariably deponentia or verbs of movement, as in 16.12.16 *Caesare proximo nusquam elabi permittente* or 18.10.3 *vim in se metuentem prope venire permisit.* There is only one instance of a passive infinitive after a passive verb form: 20.2.5 *nec patefieri, quae scientiam eius latebant, permissis.*

sauciabatur salus hostium nesciorum For *sauciare* see the note ad 20.7.6. There is no parallel in Amm. for predicative *nescius* 'without being aware of it'. It is hardly conceivable that the Persians did not know that the scorched earth policy impaired their safety.

1.15   *quaesitis dextris propriis utebantur* Heraeus had good reason to distrust this clumsy phrase, and to propose *quaesito*, the more so since Amm. writes elsewhere (16.11.12) *libentius enim bellatores quaesito dexteris propriis utebantur.*

alia virtutis suae horrea Cf. 29.5.10 *messes et condita hostium virtutis nostrorum horrea esse fiducia memorans speciosa.*

laeti, quod vitae subsidiis affluentes alimenta servabant, quae navigiis vehebantur The food acquired as a result of the pillaging of the fields was an extra and not really needed in this phase of the campaign, in spite of the loss of some grain ships (see section 11 above). Julian's expedition was well prepared with a fleet carrying ample provisions; 23.3.9, q.v., 5.6. Veg. *mil.* 3.3.3 discusses the importance of the provisioning system for the success of a military campaign. Nevertheless, there was always the dread of scarcity (24.3.14) and extra food supplies were therefore welcome (24.1.5, 2.22, 4.9, 5.3). This became different for the Roman army when the fleet was lost and the crops were desperately needed. The Persians of course realised this, and to make troubles worse for the Romans they burnt their own crops (24.7.6–7), as a consequence of which the Roman soldiers were constantly in need of food supplies (cf. 25.2.1) and procured what they could (25.1.4, 10). Dillemann, 1961, 143 has a list of all passages in Amm. on supplies for the Persian campaign.

According to TLL I 1250.8–25 the verb *afluo* was created to translate the Epicurean t.t. ἀπορρεῖν, as in Cic. *N.D.* 1.114 *cum…ex ipso* (deo) *imagines semper afluant.* In all probability *afluentes* is just a writing error in V (cf. affluentes in ESBAG).

1.16   *vino gravis quidam temerarius miles* From this passage it is clear that the Persians also kept an eye on the Roman army from the right bank

CHAPTER 1.16   27

of the Euphrates, unless one supposes with Gawlikowski, 1990, 88 ff. that the Roman army marched along the right bank and thus the Persians were on the left bank. Libanius alludes to this story in *Or.* 18.22 ἤσθιον, ἔπινον, οὐ μὴν μέχρι μέθης, οὐ γὰρ εἴα τοῦ διὰ μέθην ἀρτίως ἀποσφαγέντος ὁ φόβος. Amm. means undoubtedly that the audacity of the soldier was a form of Dutch courage. In classical Latin this would have been made explicit, e.g. by adding *ideoque*. This is the only instance of *temerarius* in Amm.

nullo urgente A slightly defensive remark, lest any reader might think that an officer was responsible for the death of the soldier.

CHAPTER 2

Introduction

Sections 1–8 of this chapter report the capture and destruction of a number of fortifications along the Euphrates – some, however, proved to be impregnable – and the first encounter with a contingent led by a high Persian commander, viz. the Surena. These successful operations function as an overture to a description of the siege of Pirisabora, apart from Ctesiphon the most important town on the invaders' route. The defenders quickly decided that the town itself could not be held and therefore retired into the citadel, which was situated in a wellnigh impregnable position and contained an abundance of arms and food. However, the superiority of the Roman war engines won the day. The mere building up of a 'helepolis' convinced the citadel's defenders that their task was a hopeless one, so they surrendered, adding a glorious victory to the successes of the expedition.

A remarkable episode is reported in § 14–17: accompanied by a band of vigorous warriors, Julian himself ventures out on an attack on the citadel's gate. It is the first example of his perilous rashness, which was to become evident on other occasions during the sequel of the campaign. No doubt, during battles and other military operations a commander must be visible to his men and show his personal courage and skill, but Julian exaggerates this and even endangers his life quite unnecessarily.

Quibus tali casu patratis At first sight, *tali casu* seems to refer to the **2.1** misadventure of the drunken soldier, reported at the end of the preceding chapter, with *casus* either meaning 'mishap' or 'death', as in 25.3.21 *amici casum*. However, this does not really tally with *quibus…patratis*, since the verb means 'to achieve', 'to accomplish', which makes the reference to a mishap difficult to explain; at best it could be regarded as denoting the "begleitende Umstände" (Szantyr 115): 'when this had been brought to completion while such a mishap took place'. It is more feasible to assume that *tali casu* characterizes all the actions reported in ch. 1, so that Rolfe's "after these successful operations" is quite apt. The phrase *quibus patratis* also occurs in 14.5.9, where De Jonge notes: "Archaismus u. gehoben".

30 COMMENTARY

This is not correct, as appears from the lemma in TLL X 1.772.55 ff., where it is noted that the verb is especially used by "rerum scriptores". There are a few examples in Sallust and Livy and many in Tacitus, e.g. *Ann.* 12.26.2 *quibus patratis.* Possibly in Sallust *patrare* was an archaism, but Amm. must have regarded it as belonging to the usual historiographic vocabulary.

ad castra pervenimus nomine Thilutha in medio fluminis sita Amm. is the only source which gives the name of the fortress; cf. Zos. 3.15.1 (Ἐντεῦθεν ὁδόν τινα διαμείψας ἐνέτυχεν ἑτέρᾳ τοῦ ποταμοῦ νήσῳ, καθ' ἣν φρούριον ὀχυρώτατον ἦν) and Lib. *Or.* 18.219 (φρούριον ἕτερον ἦν ἐν νήσῳ περιεξεσμένῃ καὶ τεῖχος περὶ πᾶσαν ἐληλαμένον μηδὲν ἔξω καταλελοιπὸς αὐτοῦ μηδ' ὅσον δοῦναι χώραν ποδί). Thilutha, modern Telbes (Musil, 1927, 239), was like many of these fortresses located on an island in the Euphrates. Chesney, 1868, 76 mentions fourteen islands between Anatha and Diacira, many of which have small towns often built on an ancient site. Musil, 1927, 166 says "in the midst of the river lay the island of Telbes on which stand a number of old buildings, the walls of which are washed by the Euphrates." Isid. Char. 1 (= GGM I 249) speaks of Θιλαβοῦς νῆσος κατὰ τὸν Εὐφράτην and Asinius Quadratus of Θελαμοῦζα (FHG III, 660). Julian's expeditionary force arrived in Thilutha, which is situated some 12 km from Anatha, on the day after the heavy storms (24.1.11), i.e. two days after the capture of Anatha (14 April; see the note on chronology).

locum immenso quodam vertice tumescentem Cf. Zos. 3.15.1 ἄληπτον πανταχόθεν and Lib. *Or.* 18.219 quoted above. According to Libanius, Julian thought the inhabitants of Thilutha lucky because of the natural strength of their fortress: the emperor considered it madness to assault impregnable positions. This is a clear example of *quidam* qualifying an adj. "in steigerndem Sinn" (Szantyr 196; cf. also the note ad 20.4.13). It adds to the hyperbolic expression.

velut manu circumsaeptum humana In other cases man's hand was responsible for the fortifications, e.g. *riparum aggeribus humana manu instructis* (25.6.8).

ad deditionem incolae temptati mollius, ut decebat Zos. 3.15.1 ἐκδοῦναι σφᾶς αὐτοὺς ἀπῄτει καὶ μὴ ἀναμεῖναι τὸν ἐκ τῆς ἁλώσεως κίνδυνον. When attacking Anatha, Julian could permit himself different approaches: *sermone cum leni tum aspero et minaci hortabatur ad deditionem defensores* (24.1.8, q.v.). Here, however, only a gentle and conciliatory tone 'was

CHAPTER 2.2

fitting', since the fortress seems to have been wellnigh impregnable. A siege would undoubtedly have taken a lot of time and would have prevented a swift progress to Ctesiphon. Persuasion belonged to the tactics used to induce the enemy to surrender; see the note ad 24.1.8.

asperitas edita For *asperitas* denoting the rugged shape of the surroundings cf. 27.12.6 *in asperitate montana*, 15.10.2, 31.8.4, 31. 10.15. The opposite of the present expression is *pars... mollius edita* (21.10.4).

sed hactenus responderunt The adv. is used here with a "sensus restrictivus, i.q. 'eatenus tantum'", linked to what follows; see the examples listed in TLL VI 2751.19ff. Tac. *Ann.* 15.60.3 *Natalis et hactenus prompsit, missum se ad aegrotum Senecam, uti viseret* etc. is a clear case. Other examples in Amm. are 14.11.22, 16.5.12, 28.4.16, 30.5.2. See for different meanings of *hactenus* the notes ad 22.8.37 and 22.16.18. Note the use of the perfect tense in *responderunt*. The preceding imperf. *firmabant* describes a state of affairs which passed through several stages, but *responderunt* records a fact.

quod... se quoque utpote regnorum sequellas victoribus accessuros Viansino lists this as Amm.'s only instance of *quod* with acc.c.inf, which occurs often in late Latin (cf. Szantyr 578). This singularity seems to preclude the assumption of a grecism in Amm., as in the cases referred to by Szantyr for which ὅτι with acc.c.inf. in the NT is an example. For *utpote* in explanatory phrases cf. 18.2.17 (q.v.), 18.6.1, 21.1.8. See for *sequellae* the note ad 23.5.4, the only other instance in Amm.; Rolfe's "appendages" suits the the present context well. Zosimus reports the reaction of the besieged in these words: τῶν δὲ τοῦτο ποιήσειν ὅπερ ἂν καὶ τοὺς ἄλλους δρῶντας θεάσαιντο ὑποσχομένων (3.15.1); as Brok notes, the difference is but slight. Zos. 3.15.2 and Lib. *Or.* 18.219 argue that Julian did not want to lose time on operations of no importance, especially since the defenders of fortresses would go over to the Roman side as soon as Julian had defeated Sapor.

praetermeantes moenia ipsa naves nostras In Amm.'s other instances **2.2** *praetermeare* is used about the flow of rivers. Although *ipsa* could be an example of the anaphoric use of *ipse* (Szantyr 190), it might express that the ships passed 'straight by' the walls of the castle. Not before 24.6.1–2 do we hear again of the fleet (see for this the note ad 24.2.7).

32   COMMENTARY

verecunda quiete With this apodictically presented emendation Haupt, 1876, II 388 got rid of all problems linked to *verecundia*. In itself this advantage is no proof of its correctness. There is no other example in Amm. of *quies* being qualified by an adj. expressing the thoughts or feelings of those keeping quiet, in this case the respect the Persians had for the Roman fleet which they watched passing by their fortress, and their refraining from provocative shouts. Apul. *Met.* 7.22 *meum verecundum silentium* seems the nearest parallel. Regarding V's *cundia* as decisive implies the unlikely interpretation of *verecundia* as an abl. causae and *quiete* as an adverb. As to the meaning of *quies*, it could denote 'silence', as in 16.12.8 *indictaque solitis vocibus quiete* and Tac. *Ann.* 1.25.2 *atrox clamor et repente quies*, or 'absence of aggression', as in 24.2.20 (q.v.).

cum ad munimentum aliud Achaiachala nomine venissemus Zosimus does not mention this fortress nor any other until Diacira (3.15.2 ἕτερα δὲ φρούρια κατέλιπε, ταῖς ὁμοίαις πεισθεὶς ὑποσχέσεσιν. ᾤετο γὰρ μὴ περὶ μικρὰ διατρίβειν τὸν χρόνον, ἀλλ᾿ εἰς τὸ κεφάλαιον ἑαυτὸν ἐμβαλεῖν τοῦ πολέμου. σταθμοὺς δέ τινας παραμείψας εἰς Δάκιρα παρεγένετο). According to Musil, 1927, 239, followed by Matthews 146, Achaiachala may be identical with al-Hadîta on the right bank of the Euphrates; but cf. Gawlikowski, 1990, 90 who thinks it corresponds with Bidjân; al-Hadîta is some 60 km from Telbes, which means that it was some 75 km (45 km as the crow flies) south of Anatha. It probably took two days to march from Thilutha to Achaiachala: see Brok 109 and Fontaine n. 315. This means that the Roman army arrived there on 16 April (see the note on chronology).

fluminis circumitione vallatum Musil, 1927, 239 assumes that the town was separated from the mainland by a canal or a branch of the Euphrates, since Amm.'s phrase does not imply that it was situated on an island in the middle of the river.

arduumque transcensu Cf. 19.5.6 *multitudini transcensu scalarum iam propugnacula ipsa prensanti*, of which the present phrase is almost an abbreviated version.

alia postridie castra… praetereuntur incensa Neither name nor location of this stronghold is known; Musil, 1927, 239 thinks it may be identified with "the Sifle ruin". For *postridie*, i.e. 17 April, see the note on chronology. The use of the passive *praetereuntur* is caused by the author's wish for variation in his narrative. It was the Roman army

CHAPTER 2.3

which set these fortifications on fire, a usual measure, as is shown in 24.1.12, 24.2.3, 24.2.22.

postera igitur et insequenti die I.e. 18 and 19 April; see the note **2.3** on chronology. TLL V 1. 1024.5 ff. presents an extensive survey of the frequency with which various authors use fem. and masc. *dies* in the singular. In this survey it is recorded that as opposed to 66 cases of masc. Amm. has only two instances of fem. Judging by TLL V 1.1035.11–2, these two are provided by the present text and by 24.3.1 (29.3.3 *eadem... die* has been overlooked). This is remarkable in that Caesar has *postera die* only once: *Gal.* 5.49.5 (if the v.l. *postero* is not to be preferred) as opposed to many instances of *postero die*. The latter phrase is very frequent in Livy, whose manuscripts have *postera die* only in 2.49.2 (cf. Briscoe, 1981, 396) but even here Ogilvie accepts Drakenborch's *postero*. The classic study of feminine *dies* is Fraenkel, 1917, 24–68. About the original Latin usage he concludes "dass die ganz scharfe Fixierung eines einzelnen Tages, die Bezeichnung eines Datums nur mit Hilfe des Maskulinums von *dies* gegeben worden kann" (29). On p. 55 n. 2 he argues that Amm. borrowed his two instances of *postera die* from Tacitus, in whose oeuvre *postera die* occurs twice as often as *postero die*. Hofmann, 1938, 269–70 agrees with Fraenkel's suggestion that the scarcity of fem. *dies* in such a late Latin author as Amm. is to be explained "aus bewusstem Streben dieses Griechen, eine Genusregel der Schule mechanisch und sklavisch durchzuführen".

stadiis ducentis Amm. uses Greek as well as Roman designations (*lapis, passus, miliarium, milia*) for distances throughout his work without apparent consistency. It seems likely, according to Brok 109, that the use of stades in the geographical digressions goes back to Amm.'s sources, but that the use of stades in his description of Julian's expedition is no indication for a Greek source (pace Klotz, 1916, 483) since he also uses *lapis* (24.1.3, 25.5.6, 7.8, 8.6), *passus* (24.3.10) and *miliarium* (24.2.3). See Brok 109 for all passages in the *Res Gestae* where distances are mentioned. Two hundred stades is approximately 37 km, so that the army covered 18/19 km a day.

Baraxmalcha According to Musil, 1927, 239 this site may be identified with 'Awîre on the left bank of the Euphrates. Chesney, 1868, II 436 cannot be right in mentioning Jibba as the site of Baraxmalcha,

34 COMMENTARY

since it is too far to the south. From 'Awîre a ford leads by way of the island of al-Flêwi to the right bank of the river. The distance of seven miles between Baraxmalcha and Diacira, modern Hît, as given by Amm., as well as the crossing of the river for which a ford is convenient (*unde amne transito miliario septimo disparata Diacira invaditur civitas*), coincides nicely with the 10 km distance between present-day 'Awîre and Hît and the presence of a ford by way of the island al-Flêwi. Musil thinks that "barax" may be a corruption of the Arabic root "farad" of "faraz", meaning ford; hence Baraxmalcha could mean "The Royal Ford".

amne transito miliario septimo disparata Diacira invaditur civitas Diacira (Dacira according to Zosimus) was situated on the western bank of the Euphrates: πόλιν ἐν δεξιᾷ πλέοντι τὸν Εὐφράτην κειμένην (Zos. 3.15.2). It is the modern town of Hît, situated on two hills on the right bank of the Euphrates, pace Streck, 1903. Diacira in Aramaic (dî qîna) means a place where naphta/ bitumen is found; pace Fontaine n. 317. Presumably Isid. Char. 1 (= GGM I 249) refers to it: Ἀείπολις, ἔνθα ἀσφαλτίτιδες πηγαί; Ptol. 5.19.4 Ἰδικάρα may refer to the same place. In ancient times it was also called Is; Hdt. 1.179. D.C. 68.27.1 may refer to the same place, but see Bennett, 1997, 273 n.77. For Diacira see Weissbach, 1914; Musil, 1927, 26, 239, 350–3; Paschoud n. 41 ad Zos. 3.15.2; Oppenheimer, 1983, 164–168. See for the geographic expression *miliario septimo disparata* the notes ad 20.3.7 and 20.4.13.

habitatoribus vacua, frumento et salibus nitidis plena Zos. 3.15.2: ἥν τινα τῶν οἰκούντων ἔρημον εὑρόντες οἱ στρατιῶται σῖτόν τε πολὺν ἐναποκείμενον ἥρπασαν καὶ ἁλῶν (Reitemeister's emendation of mss. ἄλλων) πλῆθος οὐ μέτριον. Diacira was not a deserted town like Dura-Europos or the stronghold mentioned in 24.2.2, but the inhabitants had fled out of fear for the Roman army, like those of Ozogardana (see below). Diacira was obviously not a fortified place as were Thilutha and Achaiachala. Apart from the *salinae* about which Burgundians and Alamanni frequently quarreled (28.5.11), this is the only passage in Amm. in which the importance of salt comes to the fore. Musil, 1927, 28 mentions innumerable springs of salt water near Hît; the salt is obtained through evaporation: "The ground in the vicinity of Hît consists of yellow limestone, from which issue many springs with salt or somewhat bitter water, the latter smelling of sulphur." Brok 110 draws attention to the word *nitidus* indicating that the salt was white and pure.

CHAPTER 2.3   35

in qua templum alti culminis arci vidimus superpositum Amm. probably
refers to a temple of the *iwan* type, a tall vaulted hall with a wide,
arched opening at one end. This type first appeared in the Parthian
period in the second century B.C.; see Hopkins, 1942; Lenzen, 1955;
Schlumberger, 1970, 187–8; Colledge, 1977, 47–8. Brok 110 notes
the fact that in Zosimus' account only a part of the army crossed the
river to deal with Diacira. From *vidimus* he concludes that Amm. must
have taken part in this raid: *in qua* supports this idea. Although *alti
culminis arci…superpositum* could also refer to a view from a distance,
Brok's suggestion is attractive.

qua incensa caesisque mulieribus paucis, quae repertae sunt Zosimus registers the same unedifying spectacle: γυναῖκάς τε τὰς ἐγκαταλειφθείσας
ἀποσφάξαντες (3.15.2). Presumably, both authors wanted to stress
the cowardly flight of the enemy who had left these women behind. As to *incensa*, cf. Zos 3.15.2 οὕτω κατέσφαξαν ὥστε οἴεσθαι τοὺς
ὁρῶντας μηδὲ γεγονέναι πόλιν αὐτόθι.

traiecto fonte scatenti bitumine From Zos. 3.15.3 it is obvious that
this bitumen source was on the left bank of the Euphrates: Ἐπὶ
δὲ τῆς ἀντικρὺ ἠόνος, δι' ἧς ὁ στρατὸς ἐποιεῖτο τὴν πορείαν, πηγή τις
ἦν ἄσφαλτον ἀνιεῖσα. Pace Gawlikowski, 1990, 90 the main force of
Julian's army had apparently remained on this side of the river and
only a small contingent of soldiers crossed the river to Diacira; Brok
110; Paschoud n. 44; Matthews 147–8. Bitumen, also called asphalt,
is a semi-solid or solid substance consisting of oil; see Forbes, 1955,
3 ff. for nomenclature and classification of bituminous materials;
idem, 15 for a picture of a bitumen spring near Hît. In the oldest
literature in which Hît is mentioned, references are made to its
bitumen springs. Forbes, 1955, 37 ff. also relates how the asphalt
was collected at the beginning of the 20th century: it was separated
from the water with which it comes to the earth's surface, the water
being squeezed out by hand-pressure and lumps were formed. It
seems likely that in ancient times bitumen was collected in the same
way. Cf. Musil, 1927, 28: "The bitumen of the surface resembles
dirty scum…The bitumen is scooped up with palm leaves, stored
in large pieces, then diluted with lime and exported by boat." The
applications of bitumen were various, but it was especially used as
a building material (mortar) in Mesopotamia; Forbes, 1955, 67–74.
The walls of Babylon were constructed with bitumen as mortar; see
23.6.23 with the note. To the sources mentioned there may be added
D.C. 68.27.1; cf. also X. *An.* 2.4.12, D.S. 2.12.1 and Zos. 3.17.5. The

36 COMMENTARY

walls of Pirisabora (see 24.4.12) were also constructed with baked bricks and bitumen.

Ozogardana occupavimus oppidum Zos. 3.15.3 is more detailed in his description of the route followed by the Roman army than Amm.: μεθ᾽ ἣν εἰς Σίθα, εἶτα εἰς Μηγίαν ἀφικόμενος, μετ᾽ ἐκείνην εἰς Ζαραγαρδίαν πόλιν ἦλθεν (Zosimus' Σίθα seems to be the same as Diacira; Paschoud n. 42). Ozogardana is, according to Musil, 1927, 240 modern Sari-al-Hadd. Cf. Gawlikowksi, 1990, 90–91.

in quo principis Traiani tribunal ostendebatur Zos. 3.15.3: ἐν ᾗ βῆμα ἦν ὑψηλὸν ἐκ λίθου πεποιημένον, ὃ Τραιανοῦ καλεῖν εἰώθασιν οἱ ἐγχώριοι. This version seems to imply that the inhabitants 'showed' the platform, but according to Amm. they had already fled. Possibly *ostendebatur*, which is the only finite pass. form of the verb used by Amm. himself (21.1.14 is a quotation), has to be taken in a mediopassive sense; cf. TLL IX 2.1124.3–9, where i.a. are listed Sen. *Ot.* 8.5.6 *cogitatio nostra caeli munimenta perrumpit nec contenta est id quod ostenditur scire*, id. *Ep.* 79.2 (Aetna) *aliquanto longius navigantibus solebat ostendi.* D.C. 68.30.3 situates the *tribunal* nearer to Ctesiphon. For Trajan and his expedition against the Parthians (114–117) see the extensive note ad 23.5.17.

2.4 The events of this section are more elaborately described by Zos. 3.15.4–6. According to Zosimus Julian was amazed that his army could progress so far without meeting any hostility from the Persians either by way of an ambush or openly. He therefore sent Hormisdas with a small contingent of soldiers ahead since the Persian prince knew the country best. The Persians, led by the Surên, awaited him on the other side of a canal, which was connected with the Euphrates, with the intention of surprising him and his soldiers. However, Hormisdas could not cross the canal because of a sudden rise of the water level. The following day Hormisdas detected the Persians, attacked them and killed several of them, after which he rejoined the main force. Zosimus makes no mention of Podosaces.

hac quoque exusta Amm.'s *hac* refers to *oppidum*, which at first sight is surprising, but "grammatisch höchst auffällig sind eine Reihe krasser Inkongruenzen, die dadurch entstehen, dass ein Pronomen bzw. Adj. oder Partizip nicht, wie erwartet, auf ein vorhergehendes Wort, sondern auf einen damit synonymen Begriff bezogen wird" (Löfstedt, 1933, 142). This quotation specifically concerns Lucretius, but

CHAPTER 2.4   37

Löfstedt also deals with other authors, e.g. Eutr. 9.9.1 *Mogontiacum
quae* etc. These facts induced Blomgren 50 to reject Petschenig's
confident emendation: "Dass Ammian so geschrieben haben sollte,
ist nicht denkbar, sondern es liegt die in V ganz gewöhnliche Ver-
tauschung des *o* durch *a* vor" (1892, 680). Indeed, after *qua incensa*
(§3), which correctly refers to *civitas*, the fem. is hardly surprising,
even less so since after all the name of the town, Ozogardana, is
fem.

Surena, post regem apud Persas promeritae dignitatis Amm. describes the
status of this dignitary somewhat more precisely in 30.2.5 *potestatis
secundae post regem*. See also 24.3.1 *Surenam Persicum ducem*; 24.4.7
Surena hostium dux; 24.6.12 *cum Pigrane et Surena et Narseo potissimis
ducibus*; 25.7.5 *Surenam et optimatem alium*; and Zos. 3.15.5 σουρήνας
(ἀρχῆς δὲ τοῦτο παρὰ Πέρσαις ὄνομα). Surena or Surên is not only
the personal name of the head of the Surên, one of the seven
great Parthian families (cf. for the name Justi, 1895, 316–7), but
also a title – comparable to that of Caesar or Arsaces, which are
personal names as well as titles – which the head of this family
was allowed to bear by hereditary right. The Surên had certain
hereditary privileges and functions such as the crowning of the king
and the military command in the field. The Surên remained after the
king, Sapor of course in these days (see for him the note ad 20.6.1
truculentus rex ille Persarum), the supreme military commander under
the Sasanids. See Bivar, 1983, 51 ff. and Lukonin, 1983, 703 ff. The
Romans were first confronted with a head of the Surên family in
the battle of Carrhae; Plut. *Crass.* 21; D.C. 40.16.1, 21.1, 26; see
also Tac. *Ann.* 6.42.7; Iust. 41.2.1. Since the authority in question
was hereditary, it seems even less correct to say that it had been
'earned' or 'acquired' (*promeritae*). Translators tend to smoothe over
this puzzling detail.

Malechus Podosacis nomine This Saracen leader is only known from
this passage; *PLRE* I, Podosaces. Zosimus does not refer to this person. Amm.'s detailed information about him may testify to the author's personal involvement. That he called him a bandit (*latro*)
means, according to Matthews 352, "little more than that his people conducted a normal Saracen lifestyle in a context defined by
allegiance to the Persian interest". Malechus, the Latin form of the
Semitic 'malik', is probably a title meaning 'king'. It inspired Seyfarth and Hamilton to render it with 'emir'. It has been suggested
by Altheim-Stiehl, 1965, 325–8 that Malechus, and not Podosaces,

38 COMMENTARY

was the name of this Saracen leader, and that the passage should be translated as 'by the name of Malechus, son of Podosaces'. This is supported by the genitive *Podosacis*, since Amm. uses the nominative before *nomine*, as in Gelenius' Podosaces. Matthews 148, 351–2 also calls him Malechus, but leaves the possibility open that Amm. may have confused the title with the name.

phylarchus Saracenorum Assanitarum Leaders of Arab tribes are normally designated by the title of phylarch in Graeco-Roman texts; cf. Gschnitzer, 1968, 1072–1079 for an elaborate discussion of Arab phylarchs, including many references to the relevant sources. The Saracens fought on the Roman as well as on the Persian side; see the note ad 23.3.8 and Brok 254–5. The name *Assanitae* occurs only here. They may be the same as the Ghassanids, one of the loose federations of nomadic Arabs we know from later sources; Matthews 352. See Bowersock, 1994, 132–3.

famosi nominis latro Despite his impressive titles, this man was no more than "a notorious brigand" (Hamilton) in the eyes of the *miles et Graecus*.

omni saevitia per nostros limites diu grassatus In all its simplicity this carefully composed phrase expresses the author's irritation at the protracted savagery which the barbarian brigand permitted himself in 'our borderland'. See for *limes* in this sense the note ad 23.3.4; the essential word *nostros* was perhaps deliberately placed in the middle. Add to the literature given in the note ad 23.3.4: Zuckermann, 1998 who, in reply to the views of Isaac 1992², argues that a *limes* defended by fortifications, i.e. a defended border, did exist in the eastern part of the Roman empire.

quem ad speculandum exiturum Zos. 3.15.4 explicitly states that Julian assigned this task to him: Ὁρμίσδην εἰς κατασκοπὴν ἐκπέμπει. See for Hormisdas the note ad 24.1.2.

sunt temptamento frustrati Agreeing with Clark's and Seyfarth's rejection of V's *temptamenta*, Fontaine refers to *spe... frustrati* in 22.6.4 and 28.6.7. See for the passive sense of *frustratus* the note ad 22.6.4.

quod angusta... non potuit The parallel report in Zos. 3.15.6 is quite illuminating: εἰ μὴ διῶρυξ ἐν μέσῳ τοῦ Εὐφράτου ('one of the Euphrates' channels between Hormisdas and his waylayers'), πέρα τοῦ

CHAPTER 2.5   39

συνήθους ῥυεῖσα, τῶν περὶ τὸν Ὁρμίσδην ἐκώλυσε τὴν διάβασιν. From Zosimus' report it becomes clear that it was Hormisdas who was prevented from crossing an adjacent channel. The translations of Caltabiano, Fontaine and Seyfarth betray a different assumption, viz. that the attackers could not cross. TLL VII 2222.8–10 shows that the only other instance of *interluvies* is ps.Sol. 22.13; as its meaning "i.q. interiectio aquae" is suggested.

This section should not be regarded as a succinct description of the **2.5** battle in question, but should rather be read as a highly impressionistic sketch of a skirmish *tout court*. Instead of providing precise details of the movements, the author paints a dazzling picture, the individual traits of which flash briefly and brilliantly.

primo lucis exordio I.e. the morning of 24 April; see the note on chronology.

visi tunc primitus corusci galeis et horrentes indutibus rigidis After having captured a number of castles during its southward march, Julian's army now for the first time (*primitus*) stood face to face with a Persian military force. The enemies' glistening helmets immediately caught the eye. The plur. of *indutus*, an infrequently used synonym of *indumentum*, is quite rare, as appears in TLL VII 1280.44 sqq; Amm.'s other instance is 30.7.4. In contrast to Petschenig, who proposed *praerigidis*, Meurig-Davies, 1948, 217–218 took V's *rerigidis* as a case of dittography, referring to similar instances elsewhere in V, e.g. 22.16.15 *homininum*, 19.8.6 *superperarer*. Seyfarth agrees, rejecting Petschenig's *praerigidis* in favour of the cursus tardus. These Persian soldiers were the famous and fearful *catafractarii*, mail-clad cavalry; see the note ad 20.7.2. Add to the literature cited there Michalak, 1987, who is of the opinion that *catafractarii* and *clibanarii* (a term which only occurs in the sources in the fourth century) are synonyms, and Mielczarek, 1993, who distinguishes between the two on tactical grounds. *Catafractarii*, fighting in deployed column order and armed with a spear, were especially employed against infantry whereas *clibanarii*, fighting in wedge-column order and also armed with a spear, were used to fight against mounted opponents. Cf. Nicasie, 1998, 197 n.47 who thinks that there is insufficient knowledge about battle tactics to allow for such a clear differentation between *catafractarii* and *clibanarii*. See in general for Sasanian armies Nicolle, 1996.

40   COMMENTARY

in procinctum impetu veloci tendentes See for the various meanings of *procinctus* the notes ad 16.11.6 and 20.1.3. Here it means 'battle'. In combination with *tendere in* it also occurs in 19.2.6 and 30.5.17. Bitter 135 mentions a number of other instances of *impetu* with adj. For *involare* with acc. cf. Tac. *Hist.* 4.33.1 *improvisi castra involavere.* Other instances in Amm. are 16.12.36 and 19.2.6.

validis viribus This phrase first occurs in Enn. *Ann.* 298 Sk. See Skutsch ad loc. for a number of other cases in Cic., Lucr. and Verg. Amm.'s only other instance is 31.15.3.

ira tamen acuente virtutem "In the field anger may act as a valid inspiration to the troops, but it is sharply criticized in their commanders, Roman or foreign" (Seager 35). As Veg. *mil.* 3.12.6 advocates, *dicenda etiam quibus militum mentes in odium adversariorum ira et indignatione moveantur.* Amm. 21.13.16 is such a case. Here, however, there was neither time nor need for a rousing speech. See also Bitter 137.

clipeorum densitate contecti, ne possint emittere, coegerunt For Amm.'s apparently indiscriminate use of *clipeus, parma* and *scutum* see the note ad 21.2.1, and for his various references to a *testudo* the note ad 20.7.2. By sticking together in a closely knit pack the soldiers neutralized their enemy's most dangerous skill, archery. TLL III 1532.5–6 mentions this as the only pure instance of *cogere*, 'to compel', in combination with a *ne*-clause. But why should the *testudo*-formation as such impede the archers' shooting? Alternatively, *coegerunt* could mean 'they drove together'. In that case the absence of a direct object (e.g. *hostes*) is slightly more surprising. However, *ne... emitterent* is now definitely easier to understand: they drove the archers together, in order to render them unable to shoot (*emittere*) their arrows; see TLL V 2. 505.58–9. Amm. does not explicitly mention the final outcome of the battle; the Roman victory only becomes clear in the next section: *vincendi primitiis.*

2.6 *animatus his vincendi primitiis* For *animare* with the meaning 'to encourage' see the note ad 20.4.12. For *primitiae* merely denoting "quaecumque prima sunt" cf. TLL X 2.1253.60ff. and the note ad 14.1.1. Here the term tallies nicely with *primitus*: the first sight of the enemy developed into the first victory. It is not very likely that Libanius' information (*Ep.* 1402.2) that no less than 6000 Persians were killed while on reconnaissance, refers to the success

CHAPTER 2.7 41

of the Roman soldiers described here, as suggested by Brok 113–4. Libanius' words are more in accordance with 24.6.15, q.v.

Macepracta pervenit, in quo semiruta murorum vestigia videbantur It is tempting to consider these remains as belonging to the Median Wall, also called the Wall of Semiramis, mentioned by X. *An.* 1.7.15, 2.4.12; Str. 2.1.26 (80C), 11.14.8 (529C); Barnett, 1963. The Median Wall, however, should be looked for more to the south along the line Sippar-Seleucia; see Weissbach, 1931. Zosimus does not mention these remains, only the canal (3.16.1) which Amm. refers to in the next section. Macepracta is hard to locate but, basing himself on the mention of a canal nearby, Musil, 1927, 240 situates it near the settlement of Ummu-r-Rûs, which is some 70 km from Hît. Brok 114 and Fontaine n. 323 accept this. Cf. Dillemann, 1961, 156 and Fornara, 1991, 8 who have the unlikely suggestion that Macepracta is the same as Zosimus' Phissenia (3.19.3 with n. 50 of Paschoud). For *semiruta* cf. Sal. *Hist.* 2.64 *semiruta moenia*, Liv. 31.24.3 *spectaculum semirutae… urbis*, Tac. *Ann.* 4.25.1 *castellum semirutum*.

tueri ab externis incursibus Assyriam dicebantur See for the geographical situation and the political status of Assyria the note ad 23.6.15. The verbal form *dicebantur* here denotes information which was available at the time, without naming the informants.

hinc pars fluminis scinditur Although *scindi*, 'to branch off', is not supported by any clear parallels (although Plin. *Nat.* 5.90 quoted below ad *civitatibus circumiectis*, is very similar), "Hier teilt sich ein Flussarm ab" (Seyfarth) and, perhaps more precisely, "si stacca una parte del fiume" (Caltabiano) seem to convey the author's intention quite satisfactorily.

2.7

largis aquarum agminibus ducens ad tractus Babylonos inferiores Cf. for *agmen* "de fluviis, imbre sim." TLL I 1340.34–51, and especially Verg. *G.* 1.322 *venit agmen aquarum.* See for *ducere*, "to lead, bring (of a road or sim.)", OLD s.v. 9; cf. 23.3.1 *duae ducentes Persidem viae regiae*, 25.10.5 (iter) *quod ad Tauri montis angustias ducit*, and see for *tractus* in a geographical sense the note ad 16.3.1. In view of the acc. *Babylona* (23.3.6 and 23.6.2) *Babylonos* should be accepted as a gen.; cf. 26.6.4, 26.8.2, 26.8.3, 31.1.4 *Calchedonos* and see Neue-Wagener I 253–5 and Leumann 262. It denotes the region (*nomen provinciae*) and not the city as in 23.6.2, 6.23 q.v.; see TLL II 1654.54–1655.10.

42   COMMENTARY

civitatibus circumiectis Such as Babylon (for which see the note ad
23.6.23). Cf. Plin. *Nat.* 5.90, who, speaking of the bifurcation of the
Euphrates near Masice (to be identified as Pirisabora, see the note
ad 24.2.9), says that the left branch flowed via Seleucia to the Tigris
and the right branch to Babylon and beyond: *scinditur enim Euphrates
a Zeugmate DLXXXXIIII milia p. circa vicum Masicen et parte laeva in
Mesopotamiam vadit, per ipsam Seleuciam circaque eam praefluenti infusus
Tigri, dexteriore autem alveo Babylonem, quondam Chaldaeae caput, petit
mediamque permeans, item quam Mothrim vocant, distrahitur in paludes.*

*alia Naarmalcha nomine, quod fluvius regum interpretatur, Ctesiphon-
ta praetermeat* These words require close attention, for, to quote
Paschoud, "parmi les nombreux problèmes de géographie historique
que soulève l'expédition perse de Julien, les plus difficiles sont incon-
testablement ceux qui sont en relation avec le tracé du Naarmalcha".
The quotation is taken from the appendix on the Naarmalcha at the
end of vol. 3 of Paschoud's excellent edition of Zosimus (p. 246).
Paschoud tackled the problems concerning the Naarmalcha (Amm.
uses the name twice, here and in 24.6.1 *fossile flumen Naarmalcha
nomine, quod amnis regum interpretatur, tunc aridum*) also in n. 44, 50,
51, 52, 58, 65, 67 and 68 of the same volume, and in an article
in *Syria* 55 (1978) 345–359. Not all of his findings, which are undoubtedly ingenious, received general acceptance. Fontaine agrees,
wholeheartedly in n. 325, hesitantly in n. 368. Van Laere refers to
them in a footnote (1982, 269 n. 1; cf. 276), but completely ignores them in his own argument. According to Oppenheimer, 1983,
228 n. 14 Paschoud is "totally wrong": "These studies were written
in ignorance of the cuneiform and Arabic sources, of research on
them, and of recent archaeological exploration". Matthews in his
magnum opus does not show himself convinced by Paschoud either
(502 n. 54).
    Before we come to the two main matters at issue, viz. the problem
of the location of the Naarmalcha and the question whether or not
Julian's fleet left the Euphrates for the Naarmalcha at this point in
Amm.'s narrative (24.2.7), some preliminary remarks are required.
In the first place, there is, due to environmental and climatic change
on the one hand, and human impact on the land on the other, "after
more than fifty years of survey investigation … still no satisfactory
picture of the network of rivers and canals which coursed across
the lower Mesopotamian plain in antiquity" (Cole-Gasche, 1998, 1;
it is the opening phrase of a volume of articles entitled *Changing
Watercourses in Babylonia*). As to the impact of political conditions

CHAPTER 2.7   43

during the period with which we are concerned, "the scale and complexity of Sasanian irrigation was unrivaled anywhere until the industrial era" (Butzer, 1995, 145).

In the second place, the name Naarmalcha is derived from Aramaic nar, 'river', and malkha, 'royal' (Isid. Char. 1 (= GGM I 249) is the first classical author to mention it: Ἔνθεν, i.e. from Neapolis on the Euphrates, διαβάντων τὸν Εὐφράτην καὶ Ναρμάλχαν ἐπὶ Σελεύκειαν τὴν πρὸς τῷ Τίγριδι, σχοῖνοι θ'). Amm.'s explanation of the name in the present text (*quod fluvius regum interpretatur*) and in 24.6.1 (*quod amnis regum interpretatur*) is therefore perfectly correct. We shall see later that Amm. is mistaken when he calls the watercourse in 24.6.1 Naarmalcha instead of 'Trajan's canal', but that does not detract from his explanation of the name. Earlier Plin. *Nat.* 6.120 had also given the right exegesis, although he confused Assyrian and Aramaic: *ab Assyriis vero universis appellatum Narmalchan, quod significat regium flumen.* Complications arise when one compares 23.6.25 *et Marses et Flumen Regium et Euphrates* (based on Ptol. 5.20.2 Διαρρέουσι δὲ τὴν χώραν ὅ τε Βασίλειος ποταμὸς ... καὶ ὁ καλούμενος Μααρσάρης, ὃς τῷ μὲν Εὐφράτῃ συμβάλλει). If, as seems the natural interpretation, the *Flumen Regium* in that passage should be identified as the *fluvius regum/amnis regum* of the other two texts of Amm. and, accordingly, with the Naarmalcha or 'royal river', what then is the *Marses* supposed to be? The name *Marses* (and Ptolemy's Μααρσάρης) is commonly seen as a rendering of Babylonian nar šarri, which, like Aramaic nar malkha, means 'royal river'. Therefore it would seem that Amm. (like Ptolemy) is mistaken when he distinguishes the *Marses* from the *Flumen Regium.* Or (and this would furnish a solution to many of the problems discussed here) was there perhaps more than one 'royal river'? Indeed, it has often been observed (cf. e.g. Weissbach, 1935, 1441–2; Dillemann, 1961, 153; Chaumont, 1984, 100; Van der Spek, 1992, 237–8; Verhoeven, 1998, 213–4) that in Babylonian as well as in classical sources more than one watercourse was called 'royal river'. This is of course rather confusing and it did confuse Amm., who in 24.2.7 as well as in 24.6.1 uses Naarmalcha as a proper name for watercourses which, as will be argued in the note ad 24.6.1, were definitely not one and the same.

In the third place, it is important to realize that our sources do not always distinguish between rivers and canals. This is not only apparent in Amm. 23.6.25 *perfluunt autem has easdem terras potiores ante alios amnes, hi, quos praediximus, et Marses et Flumen Regium et Euphrates* (see the note ad loc.), but also in the present text: Amm. here calls the Naarmalcha a *fluvius,* but from a comparison with the parallel text

44 COMMENTARY

of Zosimus (εἴς τινα τοῦ Εὐφράτου διώρυχα διῆλθον, ἐκτεινομένην μὲν εἰς μῆκος ἄχρι τῆς Ἀσσυρίων, συμπαρατεινομένην δὲ πάσῃ τῇ μέχρι τοῦ Τίγρητος χώρᾳ, 3.16.1) it is clear that he is talking about a canal (on the other hand, Zosimus in 3.19.3 speaks of βασιλέως ποταμός and in 3.24.2 of ὁ Ναρμαλάχης ποταμός). And in 24.6.1 the words *fossile* and *fodiri in modum canalis* prove that, despite the terms *flumen* and *amnis*, the *fossile flumen Naarmalcha nomine, quod amnis regum interpretatur* must also be a canal. Cf. on the one hand Polybius, who speaks of the 'king's canal' (πρὸς τὴν βασιλικὴν διώρυχα, 5.51.6), and on the other Strabo, who refers to the 'royal river' (μεταξὺ δὲ τοῦ Εὐφράτου καὶ τοῦ Τίγριος ῥεῖ καὶ ἄλλος ποταμός, βασίλειος καλούμενος, 16.1.26 [747C]). More evidence in Van Laere, 1982, 270. This lack of precision (from a modern point of view) was not a new phenomenon, but was already discernable in Babylonian and Assyrian texts, cf. Stol-Nissen, 1976–1980, 356. In other words, in modern parlance one could call the Naarmalcha 'royal river' as well as 'royal canal'.

In the fourth place, whatever the location of this canal, its function is clear: to form a connection between Euphrates and Tigris or, in Amm.'s own words, *ut aquis illuc ab Euphrate transfusis naves ad Tigridem commigrarent* (24.6.1). Note that Herodotus already observed that Mesopotamia was intersected by canals and that the largest of them, which was navigable, ran in an south-easterly direction from the Euphrates to the Tigris: ἡ γὰρ Βαβυλωνίη χώρη πᾶσα ... κατατέτμηται ἐς διώρυχας· καὶ ἡ μεγίστη τῶν διωρύχων ἐστὶ νηυσιπέρητος, πρὸς ἥλιον τετραμμένη τὸν χειμερινόν, ἐσέχει δὲ ἐς ἄλλον ποταμὸν ἐκ τοῦ Εὐφρήτεω, ἐς τὸν Τίγρην (1.193.2).

It is beyond dispute that such a navigable canal must have been used by Julian's fleet, which at first sailed on the Euphrates (cf. e.g. 23.3.9, 24.1.4 and 24.2.2) but later was found on the Tigris (24.6.2). Cf. Malalas *Chron.* 13.330 καὶ κατῆλθεν ὁ βασιλεὺς μετὰ τοῦ στρατοῦ παντὸς διὰ τῆς μεγάλης διόρυγος τοῦ Εὐφράτου τῆς μισγούσης τῷ Τίγρητι ποταμῷ. Curiously, however, it is not before 24.6.1–2 that Amm. relates that the fleet had left the Euphrates and was now near the Tigris. When and where precisely Julian's fleet left the Euphrates for the canal leading to the Tigris is nowhere explicitly stated. In 24.2.6–7 Amm. only says that the Naarmalcha branched off from the main course of the Euphrates (somewhere south of Macepracta and north of Pirisabora, cf. 24.2.9, q.v.), that the infantry crossed this branch on carefully constructed bridges and that the cavalry swam across. Not a word of the fleet. There is not a word of the fleet either in Zosimus' account (3.16.1–3). Nevertheless, according to Paschoud, it was at this point (24.2.7) of Amm.'s *Res Gestae* that

CHAPTER 2.7   45

the sailing of the fleet on the Euphrates and the march of the army along this river came to an end. From now on it was the canal, called by Amm. Naarmalcha, which was followed ("ce canal, au moins dans son premier tronçon, doit être identique avec l'actuel Saklâwîja", n. 44). See for Paschoud's arguments in the first place n. 44 and 50. Note that he himself in n. 50 admits that the evidence is not overwhelming: "Il peut paraître audacieux de déduire tout cela de l'expression maladroite de Zosime" (sc. 3.19.3). Paschoud's map 3 conveniently shows the consequences of his interpretation.

Paschoud's suggestion is ingenious, but Amm. says in 24.3.14 that the army *prope locum venit, ubi pars maior Euphratis in rivos dividitur multifidos.* The obvious interpretation of *pars maior Euphratis* is: 'the main stream of the Euphrates', that is, that part of the Euphrates which after the bifurcation mentioned in 24.2.7 flowed into the direction of Babylon (*hinc pars fluminis scinditur largis aquarum agminibus ducens ad tractus Babylonos interiores*). That this is the right interpretation is admitted by Paschoud n. 51 ("Il doit s'agir du cours proprement dit l'Euphrate"). However, apparently aware of the fact that this would demolish his theory, he then resorts to a less than ideal attempt to save it: "Mais nous avons vu ... que l'armée de Julien a certainement dû suivre le Naarmalcha ... Le *prope locum* doit donc être entendu d'une manière nuancée, 'à la hauteur de' ... Une autre possibilité est qu'Ammien nomme Euphrate ce qui serait en réalité le Naarmalcha". Neither solution is very convincing.

Matthews' reconstruction of the route of Julian (149 ff., with map 5 on p. 150), which does not conflict with the wording of Amm. in 24.3.14, seems more attractive. It is based on the supposition that there was not just one Euphrates inlet of the Naarmalcha, but that there were at least three: 1) the one mentioned in the present text, "at least in its earlier sections the ancient predecessor of the Saqlawiyah canal" (149), 2) the βασιλέως ποταμός of Zos. 3.19.3 (quoted in full ad 24.3.10), "possibly on the alignment of the later Radwaniyah canal" (151) and 3) the inlet located by Ptolemy 5.18.7–8 and a text in the Babylonian Talmud, Qiddushin 70b (= Oppenheimer, 1983, 279 nr. 12), near the Jewish city of Neherda, at the same latitude as Sippar and Seleucia. "The source of the ambiguity in locating the Euphrates inlets of the Naarmalcha may well be that the original 'King's river' (nâr šarri of Babylonian texts) had run from Sippar to the Tigris at the time when Sippar lay on the Euphrates, and that all three later inlets which connected the Euphrates with the ancient canal as the bed of the river shifted westwards came to share its name" (151). In what follows we adopt the outlines of Matthews' reconstruction,

46   COMMENTARY

whilst adding some details which he left out. Needless to say, our sketch does not pretend to be the truth and nothing but the truth. It is the best we can make of the evidence at our disposal. The fact remains that on crucial points the sources are silent.

It would seem then that Julian's army crossed the inlet of what Amm. in 24.2.7 calls the Naarmalcha, that it continued its advance along the left bank of the main stream of the Euphrates and that the fleet also for the time being stayed on the Euphrates. After the siege and capture of Pirisabora (24.2.9f.) the army reached the second of the three inlets just mentioned, not far from Zosimus' Phissenia (3.19.3). Was this the spot where the fleet left the Euphrates? We think not, in view of 24.3.14. Having passed this inlet of the Naarmalcha (24.3.10), the army now marched for a while through the plain between this channel and the Euphrates. On its march southwards it passed several islands situated in the Euphrates (24.3.14). It then came to a place where the main body of the Euphrates divided into a number of channels (*in rivos... multifidos*, ibid.; cf. for such *rivi* 23.6.25 *Euphrates... qui tripertitus navigabilis per omnes est rivos*). One of these was 'the royal river' as Ptolemy and the talmudic text, cited above, knew it (in the area nearby the Romans burned a city abandoned by its Jewish inhabitants, 24.4.1, possibly Neherda/Tall Nihar, as in Ptolemy and Qiddushin 70b). Here both army and fleet turned eastwards and from now on followed this Naarmalcha.

cuius in exordio turris in modum Phari celsior surgit I.e. where the Naarmalcha is drawn off from the Euphrates near Pirisabora. For the Alexandrian Pharos, see the note ad 22.16.9. See for *exordium* in a topographical sense the note ad 22.8.38. The Alexandrinian Pharos had become the common designation for all lighthouses; cf. Juv. 13.76 *Tyrrhenamque Pharon*. The comparative *celsior* creates a cursus planus.

pontibus caute digestis According to De Jonge ad 15.4.1 *digerere* here means "to construct". 'To arrange in due order' may be more in accordance with its usual meanings, especially since it probably concerns ships' bridges, as De Jonge notes ad 17.1.1. See also the notes ad 23.2.7 and 23.5.4. However, TLL V 1.1118.42 has a different suggestion for *digestis*: "*id est distributis*". This is less easy to understand, since 'distribution' implies a number of bridges in different places. See for the positive meaning of *cautus* the note ad 23.5.5. The reason why it is used here only becomes clear in the next sentence: the

CHAPTER 2.8   47

cavalry crossed at a spot where the river flowed more gently. Here the force of its stream called for cautious proceedings.

equites vero cum iumentis armati clementiores gurgites fluminis obliquati **2.8** *transnarunt* Being impeded in their movements by their armour, the horsemen could only cross where the water was calmer. TLL III 1333.26ff. lists this as one of the texts in which *clemens* is "i.q. quietus"; cf. Ov. *Met.* 9.116–7 *qua sit clementissimus amnis, / quaerit.* Bömer notes ad loc.: "*clemens* ist in dieser Verbindung singulär". Predicative *obliquati* is shorthand for *obliquatis meatibus* (16.12.57, 30.1.9): the horsemen swam across 'diagonally', "transversalmente" (Caltabiano); this probably implies that the cavalry swam across with the help of the river's current which was not very strong here; *obliquati* should not be combined with *fluminis*, as the translations of Seyfarth and Hamilton imply. Brok's (115) reasoning that the cavalry did not cross the river at the same spot as the infantry, but probably more to the east, since the cavalry was situated on the left (eastern) wing of the marching army (see 24.1.2), is convincing.

... alia multitudine subita petiti telorum hostilium If *alia* is regarded as a nom. sing., it is necessary to assume a lacuna, which Heraeus tentatively filled with *pars flumine absumpti interierunt*. Češka, 1974, 93 argues that this assumption is superfluous, if *alia* is taken with *multitudine*: after the Persian archers referred to in §5, here again a mass of arrows threatens the Romans. Fontaine n. 326 also opposes the lacuna, following some early editions in reading *alii*, which he explains in these terms: "une corrélation *equites* (ss. entendu *alii*) ... *alii*...". From this results his rendering: "une partie d'entre eux furent brusquement harcelés par une volée nourrie de projectiles ennemies". None of the three solutions offered is fully satisfactory: Češka's is the least likely, Fontaine's the most economical, if *petiti* is interpreted as *petiti sunt*. Unfortunately, there does not seem to be a parallel for his bold idea about *alii*. Assuming a lacuna is inevitable and the fact that Zosimus' report suggests a far more complicated turn of events than Amm. could be an added reason for this assumption.

Zosimus' account (for which see Paschoud n. 44, Buck, 1990, 114 and Woods, 1998, 244) takes up one page and a half in the Budé edition. In it he relates that at first the crossing of the canal (τινα τοῦ Εὐφράτου διώρυχα, 3.16.1) was prevented by the mud, the depth of the water and the fact that the opposite bank was guarded by the enemy. Thanks to Julian's shrewdness and experience, however,

48 COMMENTARY

these difficulties were overcome. The emperor ordered Lucillianus (see for him the notes ad 24.1.2 and 24.1.6) to fall upon the Persians' rear with the 1500 men assigned to him for scouting (how and when Lucillianus was to reach the other side of the canal, is not stated). Victor (cf. 24.1.2 q.v.) was ordered to cross the canal under cover of darkness and then to make contact with Lucillianus. Together these generals succeeded in beating the Persians and thus made possible an unhindered crossing of the canal.

quos egressi auxiliares ad cursum levissimi Cf. 24.6.9 *cum levis armaturae auxiliis.* These troops were probably the same as the *velites* mentioned in 24.1.13 q.v. After having crossed the boatbridge, these swift troops very quickly arrived at the spot where Sasanian archers (*quos*, referring to *hostes*, implied in *hostilium*) were attacking the Roman cavalry. The latter, while crossing the river, were an easy target. The Roman footsoldiers were able to chase the Persians away and to kill (several of) them. It does not become clear from Amm.'s text if only some or all enemies were killed. Fontaine n. 327 goes to considerable lengths to defend the early editions' *cursuram* for V's *cursurum.* However, TLL IV 1529.5–16 shows its rarity. Most occurrences are in Plautus, and in Amm. it would be a hapax. It is more likely that V committed dittography. For *levis ad* cf. 31.2.8 *ad pernicitatem sunt leves.*

laniatu avium prostraverunt Cornelissen's plea for *laniatu* as a dat. (1886, 276: "prostraverunt eos ut lanianda auibus rapacibus corpora permitterentur") convinced Seyfarth: "als Beute für Raubvögel", but most translators follow Wagner's "haud secus atque aves rapaces", where *laniatu* is regarded as an abl. modi. Fontaine n. 327 adds that *cervicibus insistentes* points to a "métaphore filée des oiseaux de proie": *laniatu avium* is to be interpreted as "ut aves laniantes". Cf. also 29.2.21 *coetus furiarum horrificus… cervicibus Asiae totius insedit.*

2.9 *Quo negotio itidem gloriose perfecto ad civitatem Pirisabora ventum est, ambitu insulari circumvallatam* Zos. 3.17.3 Ἐλθὼν δὲ εἰς πόλιν ᾗ Βηρσαβῶρα ἦν ὄνομα. Zos. 3.17.2 reports that after the encounter with the enemy while crossing the river, Julian and his army where not troubled further by Persian soldiers before arriving at Pirisabora. The adverb *gloriose* provides one more reason to assume a lacuna before *alia multitidine* in §8, since it is more in accordance with Zosimus' extensive account than with Amm.'s short version (cf. Klein, 1914, 93 and Klotz, 1916, 484). The name Pirisabora is a corruption of Peroz-Shapur, meaning the victorious Sapor (cf. Gignoux, 1986, 148). In

CHAPTER 2.9   49

former days it was called Mesichise (cf. the note ad 23.5.7) or Misiche: καὶ ἡμεῖς Μισιχην διὰ τοῦτο Πηρωσσαβουρ ἐπωνομάσαμεν (*Res Gestae Divi Saporis*, l. 10), to be identified with Masice in Plin. *Nat.* 5.90 ("la Misiche de Sapor est certainement la Masicen de Pline", Paschoud, 1978, 348), quoted ad 24.2.7. There are two versions of the construction of Pirisabora; it was either founded by Sapor I to commemorate his triumph over Gordian in 243, or it was (re)constructed by Sapor II; Oppenheimer, 1983, 363 n.62. After Ctesiphon it was the most important city of the Sasanid empire; Zos. 3.18.6. Zosimus also reports about the great supplies of arms which were kept in Pirisabora which may explain its later Arab name al-Anbâr, meaning 'the Arsenal'. See Musil, 1927, 240, 353–7; Maricq, 1958, 353–356; Maricq, 1965, 95 ff., photographs on pp. 147–56; Oppenheimer, 1983, 363–4. Zos. 3.17.3–5 presents a far more elaborate description of the strong fortifications of Pirisabora than Amm. Lib. *Or.* 18.227 also refers to Pirisabora: πόλις Ἀσυρίων μεγάλη τοῦ μὲν τότε βασιλεύοντος ἐπώνυμος, τεῖχος δὲ εἴσω τοῦ τείχους ἔχουσα δεύτερον ὥστ᾿ εἶναι πόλιν ἐν πόλει βραχυτέραν ἐν μείζονι κατὰ τοὺς κάδους τοὺς ἐν ἀλλήλοις κειμένους. The words *amplam et populosam* contrast with the small and more than once deserted places the expedition had encountered until then. Cf. for *ambitu insulari circumvallatum* 15.11.3 about Lutecia: *circumclausum ambitu insulari*. In Amm.'s other three instances (17.2.2, 18.6.10, 31.10.15) *circumvallare* has its primary meaning "to surround with siegeworks" (OLD s.v. 1). In TLL III 1177.38–43 the present text is listed among a small group of instances in which a natural enclosure is described ("de rebus naturae vel corpore inclusis aliqua re"). As was noted ad 22.8.10, "*insularis* hardly occurs outside Amm.". From Zosimus' more elaborate description of the city and Amm.'s own report of the siege it becomes clear that, strictly speaking, Pirisabora, though surrounded by water, was not situated on an island.

obequitans moenia imperator et situm Amm. mentions several times that Roman emperors as well as the Persian sovereign personally reconnoitre the strength of a city or stronghold: 19.1.5, 20.7.2 Sapor at Amida and Bezabde; 20.11.6 Constantius at Bezabde; 24.4.3, 5.6 Julian at Maozamalcha and a fortress near Ctesiphon. Cornelissen's *iustum* was prompted by his understandable surprise at *situm* in combination with *obequitare*. However, he overlooked the probable example in Liv. 26.10.3, which is mentioned in the note ad 24.1.1; cf. also Zos. 3.17.3 τὸ μέγεθος ἐσκόπει τῆς πόλεως καὶ τὸ τῆς θέσεως ὀχυρόν.

50 COMMENTARY

obsidium omni cautela coeptabat Having inspected the city's defences, Julian now proceeds with the utmost prudence, which in warfare is a praiseworthy virtue, as other instances of *cautela* in Amm. illustrate: 14.2.7, 16.12.20, 26.7.12, 29.1.18. Vegetius also commends *cautela* in a number of passages, with *mil.* 4.38.3 as a fixed rule: *sicut providos cautela tutatur, ita neglegentes exstinguit incuria.*

a propugnandi studio summoturus Cf. 19.8.2 *a studio propugnandi removebatur.*

quibus per colloquia saepe temptatis For the attempt to persuade the enemy to surrender before siege was laid, see the note at 24.1.8.

armatorum triplici corona circumdatis muris This was done to isolate the town and to ward off sorties by the besieged. It was a normal feature of a siege – so normal that Vegetius does not even mention it in his chapters on siege warfare – but the number of lines may differ. Sapor used a fivefold line in his siege of Amida (19.2.2), Jovinus only a double line when he besieged Aquileia (21.12.4). In his siege of 'Maozamalcha' Julian also surrounded the town, with a triple line of soldiers (24.4.10).

a die primo ad usque noctis initium Basing himself on a number of comparable expressions in Amm., Günther, 1891, 68 added *a* to V's text. Some examples he adduced are 14.6.10 *a primo ad ultimum solem,* 20.3.1 *a primo aurorae exortu ad usque meridiem,* 24.6.12 *ad usque diei finem a lucis ortu.* Baehrens, 1912, 299ff. regarded the present text as one example among many in various authors of the omission of a preposition where it is "für das Verständnis des Satzes...nicht ganz notwendig". However, in 1925, 63 he left the "äusserst konservativen Standpunkt, den ich dort einnahm" and bowed to Günther's *a.* This was rejected by Fontaine n. 331, on different grounds: "Cet ablatif de durée limitée est parfaitement classique". So he renders: "le premier jour" (i.e. 27 April; see the note on chronology). This cannot be dismissed offhand, yet the parallel phrases and the fact, that on the second day too hostilities took place *a lucis ortu ad initium noctis* (24.2.14), definitely point to Günther's *a.*

2.10   *animo praestantes et viribus* This expresses the high esteem in which Amm., as a professional soldier, holds his enemy, and thus emphasizes what the Romans achieved in capturing Pirisabora.

CHAPTER 2.10 51

per propugnacula ciliciis undique laxius pansis See the note ad 20.6.4 on the ramparts (*propugnacula*) and ad 20.11.9 about the Cilician rugs and their functions. These were hung from the walls in order to protect the defenders as well as to hide them from view. Hides, sails, curtains and other similar materials were regularly used in sieges: Th. 2.75.5; Liv. 38.7.10; Sisenna, *Hist.* 107; Aen. Tact. 32.1.9–10; Philo Byz. *Polior* 95.34; Dexippus *Scyth. fr.* 29.3 = *FGrHist.* IIA, 474; J. *BJ* 3.172–3.

obtecti scutis vimine firmissimo textis Cf. *cratesque vimineas* (19.7.3, q.v.) and the note ad 20.7.2 *densitate operum*. Wagner refers to Eun. *fr.* 27.2: οἱ δὲ τῶν Πάρθων οἰσυίνας ('of wicker work') ἀσπίδας ἔχοντες καὶ κράνη οἰσυίνα πλοκήν τινα πάτριον πεπλεγμένα. Fontaine may well be right in preferring V's *obiectis scutis* to Gelenius' *obtecti scutis*, though not on the grounds he adduces in n. 333. Quoting Verg. *A.* 2.443–4 *clipeos…obiciunt* and 12.377 *clipeo obiecto*, he concludes that "le geste d' *obicere* est plus héroïque que celui d' *obtegi*", which makes it more apt in the present text. There are, however, more matter-of-fact arguments: *obtegere* occurs only once more in Amm. and in a transferred sense; *obicere* is more frequent: cf. e.g. 22.12.2 *obiectus efferatarum gentium armis*; cf. also 20.6.3 *obiectu vinearum*; the following phrases in Livy could be regarded as decisive: 2.10.3 *in obiecto…scuto*, 4.38.4 *obiectis parmis*, 22.6.4 *obiectis scutis*.

ferrea nimirum facie omni…hominis speciem contegebant Cf. 19.1.2 *ferreus equitatus*. Amm. was obviously fascinated by the coats of mail, which gave warriors 'a completely iron appearance'. About the heavy-armoured on the battlefield Veg. *mil.* 2.17.3 uses a comparable expression: *tamquam murus, ut ita dicam, ferreus stabat.* Cf. for a similar description of armour fitting the lines and movements of the body 16.10.8 *quos lamminarum circuli tenues apti corporis flexibus ambiebant per omnia membra diducti, ut, quocumque artus necessitas commovisset, vestitus congrueret iunctura cohaerenter aptata* (In Rolfe's translation: "Thin circles of iron plates, fitted to the curves of their bodies, completely covered their limbs; so that whichever way they had to move their members, their garments fitted, so skilfully were the joinings made".). Further examples of the author's fascination with the fact that 'a human shape' (*hominis speciem*) could be turned into a *ferrea facies* are 24.4.15, where he compares the ringlets of the cuirass with the feathers of a bird, 24.6.8 and 25.1.12. Cf. also Sal. *Hist.* 4.66 (*ferrea omni specie*); Claud. *in Ruf.* 2.355 (*simulacra ferrea*), de VI cons. Hon. 569 (*ferrati viri*). These 'iron men' apparently were not only cavalry

52 COMMENTARY

(*catafractarii*), but also helped to defend besieged cities; cf. 24.4.15 *hostem undique lamminis ferreis in modum tenuis plumae contectum*. As was stated in the note ad *insulse nimirum et leviter* (21.10.8), *nimirum* here emphatically introduces an explanatory addition to what had been reported in the preceding text.

2.11 *Hormisdae ut indigenae et regalis colloquia petentes obnixe* Cf. 24.1.8 *ad colloquium petito Hormisda*. In this case Amm. explicitly mentions the reason, which was 'officially' given by the besieged, in order to contrast it with their real purpose, which was provoking and insulting Hormisdas. Cf. Zos. 3.18.1 νῦν μὲν Ὁρμίσδην αὐτοῖς πεμφϑῆναι διαλεχϑησόμενον περὶ σπονδῶν ἐξαιτοῦντες, νῦν δὲ ὕβρεσιν αὐτὸν περιβάλλοντες ὡς αὐτόμολον καὶ φυγάδα καὶ τῆς πατρίδος προδότην. The adv. *obnixe*, a synonym of *pertinaciter*, also occurs in 29.2.14, where it is an adjunct with the verb *rogare*.

die maxima parte exempta TLL V 2.1502.32 lists this as an instance of *eximere* with a period of time as Patiens being used as a synonym of *consumere*. The parallel in 30.1.5 *pleraque die parte emensa* suggests that *die* has to be taken as a gen.; see for this form Leumann 270. CIL 3.12036 *eius die* is a clear example.

probris atque conviciis ut male fidum incessebant et desertorem Cf. *probrosis conviciis* (20.4.17, 30.1.16); *incessere* denotes attacking with missiles, e.g. *lapidibus subiectos incessebant et telis* (20.11.9), or with abuse: *ut segnem incessentes et timidum* (17.11.1), *quos incessens delatoresque appellans* (22.7.5), *verbis turpibus incessebant ut perfidos* (25.6.6). Zosimus' report, quoted above in the first note of this section, is similar.

hac lenta cavillatione See the note ad 22.8.33 *per cavillationem* for Amm.'s use of this word. Here it denotes sarcastic jeering, which went on and on (*lenta*).

multiformes admotae sunt machinae coeptaque altitudo complanari fossarum For the various siege-engines see the digression 23.4 with the notes. The trenches had to be filled for the siege-engines to be moved close to the walls. It appears that this was done rather quickly and that these trenches were not a great obstacle for the Roman besiegers. Cf. Veg. *mil.* 4.5.1, according to whom ditches before cities should be made as wide and deep as possible, so that they could not easily be filled in and levelled by besiegers. As was noted ad 20.11.6 *fossarumque altitudine*, the phrase *altitudo fossarum* can best be taken as

CHAPTER 2.12   53

a gen. inversus: "die tiefen Gräben" (Seyfarth). In 17.7.13, 26.10.17, 29.5.25 *complanare*, 'to level', concerns the pulling down of buildings, in 27.8.6 *complanari* denotes the flat surface of a calm sea. The present case can be compared with 19.8.2 *complanatum spatium, quod … hiabat.* The ditches are filled and the resulting surface is made level.

vixdum ambigua luce I.e. 28 April; see the note on chronology. The **2.12** expression is curious and seems to be a contamination of *ambigua luce*, 'when the morning light was still uncertain' and *vixdum luce certa* (Liv. 9.42.7).

arietis For the *aries*, a battering-ram, see the notes ad 23.4.8–9.

relictis civitatis duplicibus muris These double walls have not been mentioned before; cf. Zos. 3.17.3 (Pirisabora) δύο μὲν γὰρ κυκλοτερέσι περιείληπτο τείχεσιν. Zosimus adds that the citadel in the middle was defended by its own walls. Perhaps Amm. implies that the besiegers had only noticed it during their preparations of the siege. Also Lib. *Or.* 18.227 mentions the double line of defences: τεῖχος δὲ εἴσω τοῦ τείχους ἔχουσα δεύτερον, ὥστ᾽ εἶναι πόλιν ἐν πόλει βραχυτέραν ἐν μείζονι.

continentem occupant arcem asperi montis interrupta planitie superpositam Lib. *Or.* 18.228 tells that the inhabitants withdrew out of fear into the smaller fortification, which they considered stronger. Similarly, Zos. 3.18.2 reports that the inhabitants thought they would not be able to defend the town and for that reason withdrew to the acropolis. See for *continens* as a synonym of *coniunctus* or *contiguus* TLL IV 709.79ff. This does not pose any problem, but *interrupta* does. Translators dispose rather easily of this word: "on a precipitous plateau" (Rolfe), "auf der zerklüfteten Oberflache" (Seyfarth), "sul pianoro accidentato" (Caltabiano): these and comparable renderings are attractive except for the fact that there are no parallels for such a meaning of *interruptus*, which here can only express a natural discontinuity which does not tally with *continentem*. One wonders whether V's *interapta* does not hide *intersaepta*, which would refer to a barrier made by man's hand, viz. the *minae murorum* in this same section; see also Zos. 3.17.3 ἀκρόπολις δ᾽ ἦν ἐν μέσῳ τεῖχος ἔχουσα καὶ αὐτή. Cf. Liv. 24.23.4 *murique ea pars quae ab cetera urbe nimis firmo munimento intersaepiebat Insulam*, 31.46.9 *muro intersaepta urbs est*. In 14.2.4 *intersaepientes*, printed by Clark and Seyfarth, is a plausible correction

54 COMMENTARY

of V, but in 29.5.30 *intersaeptos* is V's reading. Forcellini's lexicon s.v. *superpono* quotes the present text as the only example of the verb with an abl. The dat. is more usual, as in Liv. 1.34.9 *humano superpositum capiti decus* and the only example in Tac.: *Ann.* 15.37.2. Amm. has three clear instances of the dat.: 17.4.15 (q.v.), 20.11.26, 24.2.3.

Argolici scuti speciem As Henr. Valesius already noted, this description of a round shape (*rotunditati*) harks back to Verg. *A.* 3.637 *Argolici clipei... instar.* Zosimus phrases it in more sober terms: τμήματι κύκλου τρόπον τινὰ ἐμφερές (3.17.3). See also Sabbah 535 n. 76 and Daremberg-Saglio I, 1249, 1253.

in qua excellebant minae murorum The fem. relative pronoun refers to *arcem, planitie* – which is most likely – or *medietas*. Since all three in fact belong to the same topographical situation, this is not of vital importance. What does merit attention is the fact that the plateau or the citadel was in fact walled, which could be expressed by *intersaepta*; see above the note ad *continentem occupant arcem.* The *minae murorum* are reminiscent of Verg. *A.* 4.88; see the note ad 20.6.2. Vergilian commentators do not agree about the precise meaning of the phrase. Does *minae* denote "something projecting, like *pinnae*, 'battlements'" (Austin) or is *minae murorum* the equivalent of "muri alti, quasi altitudine sua minantes" (Heyne)? In Amm.'s case only the latter interpretation can be regarded as feasible: surely not merely the battlements, but the walls as such had been constructed (*fabricatae*) with pitch and brickwork; see the next note.

bitumine et coctilibus laterculis fabricatae Cf. 23.6.23 *Babylon, cuius moenia bitumine Semiramis struxit* (with the note ad loc.), 24.4.19 *turris latere coctili firmissime structa* and Curt. 5.1.25 *murus instructus laterculo coctili bitumine interlitus.* For the frequent use of bitumen as a building material in this part of the world, see Forbes, 1955, 67–74, and the note ad 24.2.3. Cf. Zos. 3.17.5 πύργοι δὲ εἱστήκεσαν περὶ τὴν τάφρον μεγάλοι, τὰ μὲν ἀπὸ γῆς μέχρι μέσου δι' ὀπτῆς πλίνθου δεδεμένης ἀσφάλτῳ, τὰ δὲ μετὰ τὸ μέσον πλίνθῳ τε ὁμοίᾳ καὶ γύψῳ δεδομημένα. Lib. *Or.* 18.235 mentions that the walls of the fortress were constructed with baked bricks and bitumen.

quo aedificii genere nihil esse tutius constat Here and in comparable passages, like 23.5.14, "*constare* exprime l'évidence objective, la règle établie scientifiquement, par l'observation ou l'expérience, donc indiscutable" (Sabbah 398 n. 108). Structures built with bricks

CHAPTER 2.13   55

combined with bitumen are extremely strong and hence safe. D.C.
68.27.1 remarks that bitumen in combination with baked bricks af-
fords great security and is stronger than any rock or iron.

miles pervasa urbe, quam viderat vacuam Of course this operation **2.13**
had been commanded by Julian: ὁ βασιλεὺς ἐπαφῆκε τῇ πόλει τῶν
οἰκούντων ἐρημωθείσῃ τὴν δύναμιν (Zos. 3.18.2).

multimoda tela fundentes Cf. λίθοις τε καὶ βέλεσι συνεχέσιν (Zos. 3.18.2).
In contrast to *multiformis* and *multiplex*, the late Latin adj. *multimodus* is very rare in Amm. In fact, the only other occurrence,
31.2.12, is a conjecture by Petschenig, not accepted by Seyfarth.
Veg. *mil.* 4.8 mentions suppplies which the besieged should have
available for the defence of the walls; among them bitumen, sulphur, liquid pitch, 'burning oil' (*incendarium oleum*), iron and wood
to make arms, and stones of various sizes for throwing and sling-
ing.

cum enim idem prohibitores catapultis nostrorum urgerentur atque ballistis
As was noted ad 21.12.9, *prohibitor* is a rare word for 'defender'. It
occurs seven times in Amm., four of which in the present book: cf.
24.2.19, 24.4.23 and 24.5.7. See for the anaphoric use of *idem* TLL
VII 1.204–6, De Jonge ad 15.5.19,20, Szantyr 188. Brok 120 supposes that the combination of *catapultae* and *ballistae* is reminiscent
of Livy, who in several cases combines the two: 21.11.7, 21.11.10,
24.40.15, 26.21.7, 31.46.10, 32.10.11, 39.5.16. The only other instance of *catapulta* in Amm. is 15.12.1. It is remarkably absent in
23.4, the chapter devoted to the various types of artillery; its absence
is explained in the note ad 23.4.2. The *ballista* is described in 23.4.2–
3; see the notes ad loc. and the drawing after p. 80. For catapults
see the collected studies on these stone-throwing machines by Baatz,
1994.

ex edito arcus erigebant fortiter tensos Although presented without any
argument, Cornelissen's *dirigebant* deserves attention. A few examples of *dirigere* (or *derigere*) *arcum* are mentioned in TLL V 1.1242.27–
29: Pers. 3.60, Man. 2.171, Stat. *Ach.* 1.632. The emendation would
create a picture of volleys discharged from above. However, the verb
is normally used of arrows; cf. Hor. *Carm.* 4.9.17–18 *tela Cydonio /
direxit arcu*, and *erigebant* could express that the defenders raised
their mighty bows high, for all to see. Cf. also TLL V 2.778.28–9. As
to the high position (*ex edito*), Vegetius' observation deserves to be

56 COMMENTARY

mentioned: *Sagittae quoque arcubus missae et saxa manibus, fundis sive fustibalis directa, quanto de excelsiore loco exeunt, tanto longius penetrant* (*mil.* 4.29.2).

quibus panda utrimque surgentia cornua See for the specific form of the Scythian or Parthian bow the note ad 22.8.37 *circumductis utrimque.* Ghirshman, 1962, especially with the plates on 207–13, gives a clear impression of this bow.

ita lentius flectebantur The comparative is perhaps partly chosen to create a cursus velox, but 'quite slowly' is by no means out of tune here. Translators tend to combine *ita* with *lentius*, rendering the latter adverb in imaginative ways: "so pliably" (Rolfe), "così agilmente" (Caltabiano), and even "avec une souplesse remarkable" (Fontaine). As was discussed in the note ad 22.9.3 *ita magnis*, *ita* can be combined with an adj. (or adv.), but *ita* + comparative seems unlikely. Moreover, a far better sense is created, if *ita* concerns the (skilful) *manner* of handling the bow and *lentius* the (laborious) *slowness* of this action: 'the bow's curves were quite slowly bent in such a manner that etc.'. Strictly speaking, in view of the author's own description in 22.8.37, *flectere* is not the correct term for this type of bow.

ut nervi… harundines ferratas emitterent A more detailed description of the shooting action is given in 25.1.13, with specific attention to the expert skill (*summaque peritia*) shown by the left hand fingers of the archers, which provided the arrows with their lethal precision.

letaliter figebantur Cf. *harundines… vulnera perniciosa portantes* (25.1. 13). Cf. Zos. 3.18.2: ἐγίνετό τε πολὺς ἑκατέρωθεν φόνος. Lib. *Or.* 18.228: οἱ δὲ τὸ μὲν ἔχοντες, τῷ δὲ προσιόντες βάλλονται μὲν ὑπὸ τῶν ἄνωθεν τοξοτῶν καὶ ἀπέθανόν τινες.

2.14 *dimicabatur nihilo minus utrubique saxorum manualium nimbis* See Szantyr 497 for the meaning of *nihilo minus* here: "Häufiger ist im Spätlatein die … rein anknüpfende Bedeutung"; see also the note ad 21.6.6. See for *saxa manualia* the note ad 20.7.10. Brok 120 may be right in supposing that these are the same as the *saxa muralia* mentioned in 20.11.15, 21.12.13, q.v. These were most likely huge stones which were dropped down from the wall of the besieged town to crush the besiegers as well as their siege engines; cf. Veg. *mil.* 4.8.4 *maxima* [saxa] *vero pondere formaque volubili in propugnaculis digerentur, ut demissa per praeceps non solum hostes obruant subeuntes, sed etiam*

CHAPTER 2.14

machinamenta confringant, 24.4.16: *alii quin etiam saxa volventes ingentia.* Stones were a common weapon used in sieges: 14.2.18, 20.6.4, 11.9; Veg. *mil.* 4.8.3–4. Cf. further 20.7.6 *sagittarum... nimbi.* This metaphor is not new; cf. e.g. *telorum nimbo peritura* (Luc. 4.776).

neutrubi inclinato momento In Amm.'s other two instances of *neutrubi* (19.2.13 [q.v.] and 21.1.12) the adverb is also combined with *inclinatus.* TLL VIII 1392.23 regards the present instance of *momentum* as denoting the weight which by its impact tips the scales. Like Blomgren 42, Seyfarth prefers an asyndeton to Gelenius' *et* before *neutrubi*, which is printed by Clark. In the case of an asyndeton punctuation is indispensable, after either *nimbis* (Blomgren) or *momento* (Fontaine).

destinatione magna protractum pari sorte diremptum est See for *destinatio*, 'determination', the note ad 20.11.7 and for *pari sorte* the note ad 23.5.6.

die secuto I.e. 29 April; see the note on chronology. It is to be noted that, according to Amm., the siege of the citadel had already been going on for more than two days, when Julian, on the third day, undertook his hazardous action (after the failure of which he ordered to construct the helepolis), whereas according to Zos. 3.18.6 the siege only took two days.

et aequi vigores gesta librarent Clark also accepted Cornelissen's neat emendation of *viores.* The subst. is frequent in Amm. and the resulting phrase is acceptable: "die gleiche Kraftsanstrengung hielt den Kampf in der Waage" (Seyfarth). Fontaine, however, conjectures *aequiores*, regarding V's fault as a dittography of *ui*, but his rendering is very puzzling: "à tel point égaux que leurs exploits s'équilibraient". With *librare* the image of a balance is continued.

Amm. now begins his report of an astonishing episode, during which Julian took enormous risks by taking part in a perilous attack on the citadel's gate. The contents of this report are absent in Zosimus, possibly because he or his source(s) found it embarrassing to mention the emperor's hazardous action, which, moreover, ended in failure. There is no reason to distrust Amm., who was an eye-witness, the less so since he explicitly defends the action in § 16–7.

omnes aleae casus inter mutuas clades experiri festinans Cf. 26.6.12 *aleam periculorum omnium iecit abrupte.* "War was proverbially a gamble"

58 COMMENTARY

(Nisbet-Hubbard ad Hor. *Carm.* 2.1.6, quoting various Greek and Latin parallels). Amm.'s careful phrase retains the image of a die, which, having been cast, can fall in all possible ways and directions (*omnes casus*). Eager to experience this himself amidst the massacre, Julian is in danger of becoming a gambler. During his Persian campaign he took considerable risks, not only here (cf. §15 *non ante discessit, quam telorum congerie, quae superiaciebantur, se iam cerneret obruendum*), but also later on (cf. 24.4.3 *in perniciosas praecipitatus insidias ex ipso vitae discrimine tandem emersit*, 24.5.6 *oppetisset tormento murali, ni vulnerato armigero, qui lateri eius haerebat, ipse scutorum densitate contectus evitato magno discrimine discessisset* and 24.6.15 *ignoratus ubique dux esset an miles*; cf. Brandt, 1999, 387: "Dieser Herrscher...zeigt von Anfang bis Ende seiner militärischen Karriere immer wieder Unvorsichtigkeit"). In this he resembles Alexander, who, according to Arrian, was so reckless that he got himself wounded several times (Arr. *An.*2.27.2, 3.30.11, 4.3.3, 4.23.3, 4.26.4, 6.10.1, 7.10.2; Alexander is chided for his irresponsible temerity in 6.10.3 and 6.13.4). But if Amm. had read Polybius (see for this the note ad §16 *legerat enim Aemilianum Scipionem*), he would have known that the historian from Megalopolis more than once stressed the general's duty to avoid unnecessary risks (cf. 10.3.7, 10.13.1–2, 10.24.2–3, 10.32.9–11, 10.33.4–5). For an echo of Polybius' advice see ch. 33 of Onasander's *The General.*

cuneatim stipatus densetisque clipeis ab ictu sagittarum defensus Brok 121 notes that *cuneus* does not necessarily denote a wedge formation. This tallies with TLL IV 1404.39: "posterioribus temporibus i.q. caterva, ala, vexillatio"; see also the note ad 23.5.8 *militarem cuneum.* For this reason *cuneatim stipatus* is best rendered by 'surrounded by a closely-packed formation' (see OLD s.v. *cuneatim*). Cf. also *cuneatim circumsistentes* (16.12.8) and *multitudine stipatus armorum* (21.13.6, q.v.). See the note ad 22.6.2 *denseti* for Amm.'s use of *densare* and *densere*, and consult especially Hagendahl, 1921, 62–3.

veloci saltu comitantibus promptis Viansino s.v. *saltus* provides an interesting reference to Sal. *Hist.* 2.19. This fragment can be found in Veg. *mil.* 1.9: *De exercitio Gnaei Pompei Magni Sallustius memorat 'cum alacribus saltu, cum velocibus cursu, cum validis vecte certabat'.* Now in §16 Amm. reports that Julian was imitating an outstanding general from republican times. The present text may be an allusion to another great general who vied with his soldiers, as Julian was in fact doing now. In any case, Amm.'s only other instance of *saltus* with the

CHAPTER 2.15   59

meaning 'leap', 'jump' is 21.16.19 about Constantius' physical skills
(q.v.). In his final thrust Julian was accompanied by those who were
'keen to attack'; cf. 31.8.10 about the officer Barzimeres: *prorupit
cum promptis accinctis ad proelium.*

crasso ferro crustatum The citadel's gate was 'covered by a thick layer
of iron'. The only other occurrence of *crustare* in Amm. is *humus
crustata frigoribus* (15.10.5).

saxis et glande ceterisque telis See the note ad 20.6.6, in which i.a. the   **2.15**
use of the collective singular of *glans* is explained. Here the singular
is remarkable, since the present text is clearly reminiscent of Tac.
Hist. 5.17.3 *saxis glandibusque et ceteris missilibus. Glandes* are bullets
(often of lead) hurled from a sling; 20.6.6, q.v., 26.8.8, 31.7.14. For
saxa see the note ad 24.2.14 above.

fodicare tamen paratos valvarum latera ... vocibus increpans crebris In the
other two instances of *fodicare latera* in Amm. (26.10.13, 29.1.28)
the phrase expresses torture: Julian is urging his men 'to give the
doors a sound flogging'. Amm.'s other instances of *increpare* usually
occur in a context of reproach, e.g. 18.8.5 *obiurgatorio sonu vocis in-
crepitus,* 21.16.13 *crudelitatis increpans Caesarem,* 28.6.19 *Romanumque
ut desidem increpans.* This is not surprising, since in the vast majority
of the cases dealt with in TLL VII 1 the verb is used "vituperandi
causa" (1052.13 ff.). The present case could be "adhortandi causa"
(1056.23 ff.), as in Verg. *A.* 10.830–1 *increpat ultro / cunctantis socios,* but even in these cases there is usually a connotation of scold-
ing.

quam telorum congerie, quae superiaciebantur, se iam cerneret obruendum
See for Amm.'s use of *congeries* the note ad 20.1.1. The besieged
obviously had a considerable supply of projectiles at their disposal.
They had prepared themselves after the manner advised in Veg. *mil.*
4.8.2–4. *Obruendum* is one of Amm.'s many instances in which the
gerundive substitutes the inf. or part.fut.pass.

evasit cum omnibus tamen paucis levius vulneratis, ipse innoxius Amm.'s   **2.16**
apologetic handling of the episode, which had clearly begun at the
end of the preceding section ('only the danger of being crushed by
the sheer mass of projectiles made withdrawal necessary') is firmly
continued here: hardly any damage had been suffered during the
hazardous action.

60 COMMENTARY

verecundo rubore suffusus This is a remarkable echo of Ovid. When Daphne was urged by her father to marry, she hated the idea and *pulchra verecundo subfuderat ora rubore* (*Met.* 1.484), which in its turn could be an imitation of Verg. *G.* 1.430–1 about the moon: *at si virgineum suffuderit ore ruborem, ventus erit.* Bömer ad loc. mentions some comparable expressions, but none of these is so close to Ovid that another model of Amm.'s phrase can be envisaged. In their translations Rolfe, Seyfarth and Caltabiano explicitly add shame as the cause of Julian's blushing. In this they are no doubt right, as the context shows. Julian felt badly for not having been able to live up to his model.

legerat enim Aemilianum Scipionem cum historiarum conditore Polybio, Megalopolitano Arcade, et triginta militibus portam Carthaginis impetu simili suffodisse Zon. 9.29 is the only other author who tells the story about Scipio Aemilianus forcing the gate of Carthage; see for a different version App. *Pun.* 117. Scipio Aemilianus had succeeded where Julian had failed. In his speech to the soldiers immediately after the invasion into Persian territory Julian had adduced many a historical parallel *ut antiquitatum peritus* (23.5.21, q.v.). The present text is the most notable of Amm.'s references to his fondness for histor(iograph)y. It has also induced Büttner-Wobst to include Amm. 24.2.14 (from *imperator omnes*)-17 as *fr.* 19a 1–4 of book 38 in his edition of Polybius; cf. Walbank ad loc. Scipio Aemilianus is also mentioned in 17.11.3 (q.v.), 23.5.20 (q.v.) and 25.10.13. According to Polybius himself (38.19.1) he belonged to the entourage of Scipio during the third Punic War; cf. D.S. 32.8. In view of the fact that Polybius is more than once introduced in scholarly literature on Amm., it is a sobering thought that this is the only place in the *Res Gestae* where he is mentioned. Moreover, the author does not even state explicitly that Julian had read about the episode in Polybius. However, this is not unlikely, although Bouffartigue, 1992, 318 notes: "La source directe de Julien a quelques chances d'être une anthologie d'exploits militaires, ou encore un traité de poliorcétique". See for examples of *conditor* in the meaning 'author' TLL IV 146.70 ff., e.g. Plin. *Nat.* 7.111 (about Thucydides) *rerum conditorem.* Whatever the precise reason for the detailed information in *Megalopolitano Arcade* (see on this Sabbah 69), it presumably implies that the historian was thought to be a relatively unknown person. For *suffodere*, 'to undermine', cf. *murorum ima suffodere* (21.12.6, q.v.).

sed fides recepta scriptorum veterum recens factum defendit The very same report on the historical episode, which he had so unsuccessfully

CHAPTER 2.17   61

chosen as a model, exonerates Julian from all blame. Cf. the expression *monumentorum veterum … fides* in 22.16.13 (q.v.) and Symm. *epist.* 1.95.3 *priscorum voluminum fides*, in which *fides* denotes the reliable report of events in the past. OLD s.v. *recipio* 8 provides a number of instances of *receptus* with the meaning "approved" or "established"; cf. 18.4.5 *receptissima … lege*, 21.10.8 *moris antiquitus recepti* (q.v.). TLL V 1.297.44 registers the present instance of *defendere* as an example of "i.q. male facta excusare". Cf. Sen. *De ira* 4.10.6 *vitium natura defendit, Ep.* 116.8 *vitia nostra quia amamus, defendimus*, Suet. *Cal.* 30 *defensaque Tiberi saevitia quasi necessaria.*

testudine lapidea tectam Here *testudo* is used in its architectural sense; **2.17**
cf. Verg. *A.* 1.505 *media testudine templi*, where the word means "'saddleback'; not 'vault'" (Austin ad loc.). Seyfarth's "mit einem steinernen Schirmdach" is quite clear.

moles saxeas detegunt TLL V 1.792.80–1 curiously lists this phrase as an instance of *detegere* with the meaning "tecto privare". Hamilton seems right in assuming that the "massive stones of the arch" (*testudo*) are meant here. By taking these away, the defenders tried to deprive Scipio of his cover. If this is correct, the phrase is a contamination of *Aemilianum detegunt* and *moles saxeas demunt.*

urbem nudatam irrupit The city had been left undefended by its inhabitants, so that in this respect too, forcing an entry was made easier.

obumbrata caeli facie See for other instances of *caeli facies* TLL VI 1.50.32–7. As Fontaine n. 342 notes, *fragmentis montium* is reminiscent of Vergil: *A.* 9.569 and 10.698 *ingenti fragmine montis*. With this phrase *telorum congerie* (§15) is upgraded to such an extent that Julian's plight assumes wellnigh heroic proportions: "the face of heaven was darkened by fragments torn from mountains" (Hamilton).

aegre repulsus abscessit With this detail Amm. puts the finishing touch to his apology. The enemy succeeded in driving back Julian and thus forcing his withdrawal, but with difficulty (*aegre*).

His raptim ac tumultuarie agitatis Whether this refers to the episode **2.18**
reported in §14–17 or to the whole of the siege of Pirisabora up to that moment, it is clear that the phrase expresses the common sense judgment of a military expert: the actions mentioned had taken place

62   COMMENTARY

in a haphazard and hurried way. One is reminded of the final words
of 21.5 (q.v.): after an extensive report on Julian's moral and material
preparations for his eastward march against Constantius, the author
coolly winds up this report with *temere se fortunae commisit ambiguae.*
For all his sympathy for Julian, Amm. from time to time could not
refrain from expressing some doubts about his military expertise.
See the note ad 21.12.18 for the use of *agitari* as a rare synonym of
agi or *fieri.*

cum operositas vinearum et aggerum impeditissima ceteris urgentibus cernere-
tur TLL IX 2.698.55 ff. lists this as an instance of *operositas* with
the meaning "confectio operosa" (698.48). The rare superlative
impeditissima occurs only here in Amm.; it should be combined
with *cerneretur*: 'when it was clearly perceived (*cerneretur*) that the
painstaking preparation (*operositas*) of siege-works was being hindered greatly (*impeditissima*) by the other urgent tasks'. A *vinea* was
meant to protect the besiegers from stones and missiles thrown and
shot down by the beleaguered; cf. the note ad 19.5.1. For *aggeres* see
the note ad 20.11.12; cf. also 19.5.1. Cf. Lib. *Or.* 18.228: χώματα δὲ
αἴροντες ὑπὲρ τὸ τεῖχος παρεστήσαντο τοὺς συνειλημμένους ὁμολογίᾳ. See
for *urg(u)entia* as a noun the note ad 21.1.3. It is not clear which other pressing matters are meant. Mark the difference between *cerneret*
(24.2.15), where Julian is the Agens, and *cerneretur*, the Agens of
which is not expressed, because in this case the Patiens is the primary topic; see the note ad *concursu maximo* (24.7.5).

machinam, quae cognominatur helepolis See Amm.'s detailed description in 23.4.10–13 and the notes ad loc., which show its most unsatisfactory character.

iussit expeditius fabricari Zos. 3.18.2 ascribes Julian's decision to con-
truct a helepolis to either the emperor's ingenuity to adapt himself
to the town's situation, or his considerable experience. The materials
for constructing the helepolis had been transported by the fleet; cf.
23.3.9. The comparative is needed to contrive a *cursus velox*; the
word denotes the efficient speed with which the machine needed to
be constructed.

qua, ut supra docuimus, rex usus Demetrius…Poliorcetes appellatus est
Cf. the notes ad 23.4.10 *cuius opera…est appellatus,* of which the
present phrase is a variation. Amm.'s words create a difficult problem.
Zos. 3.18.3 describes the *machina* as πύργου σχῆμα τετραγώνου,

CHAPTER 2.19   63

which reached to the full height of the walls and accommodated archers and other ballistic experts. This seems to tally with the fear of the besieged that the 'vast structure would rise above their bulwarks', as Amm. reports in § 19. It is inevitable to conclude that the description of the helepolis in 23.4.10–13 does not correspond with the apparatus of the present text.

superaturam celsarum turrium minas Within the structure of the entire **2.19** period this also expresses the expectation of the defenders that the vast machine would rise above the merlons on the high towers; *minas,* however, could also be interpreted as discussed in the note ad 24.2.12 on *minae murorum.*

prohibitores oculorum aciem intentius conferentes Cf. *intentius contemplati* (§ 12). Once more Amm. stresses that their mere perception of the hard facts induced the defenders to draw their lucid conclusions. Cf. for the phrase 'the sight of their eyes' 18.6.21 *nisi oculorum deficeret acies* (q.v.). See for *prohibitores* the note ad 24.2.13.

instantiam obsidentium perpensantes Like the more frequent *perpendere,* the verb *perpensare,* which also occurs in 16.4.1 and 19.11.9, express-es a careful weighing of facts, in the present case the obvious de-termination of the besiegers. This is precisely the main difference with Zosimus' report. Amm. focusses strongly on the psychology of the besieged, who were prudent enough to accept the mental and technological superiority of their attackers. It is a minor example of the well-known Graeco-Roman conceit concerning the awe felt by barbarians for modern accomplishments.

subito verterentur ad preces The defenders must have realised that they were defeated – they were only a small contingent (2500, cf. § 22) in comparison with the huge numbers of Roman soldiers – the moment the Romans set foot on their walls, and subsequently decided to give up their resistance. Zos. 3.18.3 reports that the Persians resisted for a while longer before they finally surrendered.

fidem Romanam pansis manibus protestantes The expression *fides Ro-mana* is less common than one would have expected. Livy has a number of instances of *fides populi Romani* or *Romanorum,* but *fides Romana* can only be found in Liv. 8.25.11, 21.19.10 and 33.2.5. For *pansis manibus* cf. Caes. *Gal.* 1.51.3 *passis manibus,* Verg. *A.* 3.263 *pan-sis… palmis;* cf. also Skutsch ad Enn. *Ann.* 490 and see for an illustrat-

64 COMMENTARY

ed catalogue of the varieties and functions of this gesture Demisch, 1984. Cf. for the rare verb *protestari* Apul. *Met.* 10.28 *uxor medici… magnoque fidem eius protestata clamore*, "the doctor's wife…appealing with a loud cry for his protection" (Hanson).

2.20 *cessasse operam* Gelenius' *opera*, printed by Clark and Fontaine, fits the context well. TLL IX 2.848.54 ff. lists a number of instances of *opus* (sing. and plur.) in which "significantur varia instrumenta muris admota". Petschenig, 1891, 352 defends V's *operam* in these terms: "Denn nur von der Arbeit an dieser Maschine (viz. the helepolis), nicht aber von Belagerungswerken im allgemeinen ist die Rede". This has obviously convinced Seyfarth, who in his bilingual edition had printed *opera*, and in his app. crit. Fontaine concedes: "fortasse legendum". If anything, it is the lectio difficilior, and in opposition to Petschenig's restriction it could express the exertions of the besiegers in general. According to Zos. 3.18.3 the siege tower was finished and used.

munitores See the note ad 21.12.8 for Amm.'s use of this term to denote the besiegers.

quod quietis erat indicium certum In 15.10.7, 17.12.15, 20.1.1 (q.v.), 24.3.4 *quies* denotes 'peace'. The present case, however, rather belongs to the category "absence of violence or aggression" (OLD s.v. 5a), e.g. exemplified by Vell. 2.25.1 *tanta cum quiete exercitum per Calabriam Apuliamque…perduxit*. The use of *indicium*, 'sign', is not surprising, but *certum* is remarkable in that it is even stronger than *plenum* in 15.8.15 and *magnum* (Clark's emendation) in 21.16.12. The besieged were sure that the inactivity of the besiegers could only signify a deliberate suspension of hostilities.

conferendi sermonis This expression can already be found in Plautus, e.g. *Cur.* 290 *conferunt sermones inter sese*, and it occurs in many authors. The present text is Amm.'s only instance.

2.21 Comparing Zos. 3.18.4–6 with Amm. 24.2.21 ff., Paschoud n. 48 notes: "Nous avons ici un bon exemple de narrations parallèles très voisines, et où pourtant chaque témoin fournit des détails que l'autre ignore ou passe sous silence". Concerning the present section, this is an amazing understatement. Amm.'s report of the successful negotiations develops into the description of a full-blown *adventus*. There is not the slightest hint of this in Zosimus, who regards the

CHAPTER 2.21

quick success at Pirisabora as a fine feat which enhanced Roman prestige, but leaves it at that.

hocque impetrato This can only mean that a preliminary interview with Hormisdas took place, as a result of which a meeting with Julian himself was arranged.

Mamersides praesidiorum praefectus demissus per funem This picturesque detail is absent from Zosimus' report. One cannot very well imagine Amm. inventing this scene. It is quite understandable that the gate was not opened as long as there was no official agreement about the terms of the surrender, so that the commander, whom Zosimus calls Μομόσειρος (3.18.4), had to come down from the citadel in a different manner. The man is only known from Amm. and Zosimus. He is not mentioned in the *PLRE*; see Baldwin, 1976, 120. In 24.5.3 it is reported that near Seleucia Julian saw the bodies of kinsmen of Mamersides: *corpora vidit suffixa patibulis multa necessitudinum eius, quem prodidisse civitatem Pirisaboram rettulimus supra.* They were definitely killed in revenge for Mamersides' surrender to Julian. See TLL X 2.631.7–13 for some instances of *praefectus praesidii* (e.g. Liv. 21.48.9) or *praesidiorum* (CIL 9. 3083).

vita cum impunitate sibi consortibusque suis firmiter pacta Cf. Zos. 3.18.4: Καὶ συνεδόκει τῶν ἔνδον Περσῶν ἕκαστον διὰ μέσου τοῦ στρατεύματος ἀσφαλῶς διαβῆναι, ῥητὸν ἀργύριον καὶ ἱμάτιον ἔχοντα, παραδοθῆναι ⟨δὲ⟩ τῷ βασιλεῖ τὴν ἀκρόπολιν. Lib. *Or.* 18.228 reports that one of the terms of surrender was that the inhabitants of Pirisabora should never be restored to the Persians, because they knew that they would then be flayed alive. Mark the use of *impunitas*. Whereas in §20 the besieged asked *vitam cum venia*, 'the victors' gracious refraining from the usual consequences of their success', they now receive 'exemption from punishment' as if they were guilty of a crime. TLL VI 1.820.74 lists the present case of *firmiter* in a section of instances where the adv. means "fere i.q. tuto". For *vitam pacisci* cf. Sal. *Jug.* 26.1.

plebs omnis utriusque sexus... patefactis egreditur portis Cf. what happened, when the citizens of Constantinople learned that Julian was approaching their city: 22.2.4 *effundebatur aetas omnis et sexus.* See the note ad loc. on scenes of *adventus* in general. See also the description of Julian's arrival at Sirmium (21.10.1) and Antioch (22.9.14) with the relevant notes.

66   COMMENTARY

pace foederata cum religionum consecrationibus fidis The verb *foederare* does not occur in classical Latin. Amm. also combines it with *pacem* in 25.7.14, 27.5.9 and 30.2.3. The first case is a variation of the present text: *foederataque itaque pace annorum triginta eaque iuris iurandi religionibus consecrata.* Cf. also *obstricto religionum consecratione colloquio* (15.5.30, q.v.), *sub consecratione iuris iurandi* (26.6.13). As these parallels show, the present text refers to an oath sanctioned in a sacred way. Peace (as the Roman euphemism goes) was sealed with the hallowed sanctions (*consecrationibus*) of sacred ritual (*religionum*), which deserved to be trusted (*fidis*).

salutarem genium affulsisse sibi clamitans Caesarem magnum et lenem Six years before at Argentoratum, when the soldiers had been inspired by a rousing speech of Julian, they urged him to lead them against the Alaman adversaries, *atque, ut exitus docuit, salutaris quidam genius praesens ad dimicandum eos, dum adesse potuit, incitabat* (16.12.13). Thus again what Amm. had said in retrospect about Julian's virtues became true: people in Gaul rejoiced *tamquam solem sibi serenum post squalentes tenebras affulsisse* (16.5.14). Small wonder that Sirmium and its neighbouring towns (21.10.2, q.v.) and Antioch (22.9.14, q.v.) greeted him *ut sidus salutare.* In view of these parallels it is not surprising that the people of Pirisabora are said to have experienced the same feelings as those in Vienne in 355: *salutarem quendam genium affulsisse* (15.8.21). Yet it is legitimate to ask whether the indigenous inhabitants of a Persian stronghold on the Euphrates really could have expressed themselves in such terms. Is it not likely that the author, who was present at the event, clothed his report about the understandably great relief felt by the besieged that they had escaped with their lives, in the terms of a Graeco-Roman *adventus*? See further the note ad 21.10.1 *cum lumine multo* on this ritual. Add to the literature cited there Dufraigne, 1992 and Lehnen, 1997. Remarkably, this is the only place in book 24 where Julian is called *Caesar.*

2.22   *nam cetera multitudo obsidium ante suspectans navigiis parvis permeato amne discessit* With *nam* the author introduces a note in which he polemicizes against other war reports. He reckons that the number of those who had surrendered was 2500 and not 5000, as the tradition, preserved in Zos. 3.18.4, has it. However, that author had also detracted those who had fled beforehand: δίχα τῶν πλοίοις μικροῖς διὰ τῆς διώρυχος οἵων τε γενομένων διαφυγεῖν. The parallel with Amm. is obvious, but his arithmetic has a different outcome. The use of

CHAPTER 2.22

the perfect tense in *discessit* instead of the pluperfect is the more remarkable in that it occurs in a main clause, which is not frequent in Amm., in contrast to instances in secondary clauses. See Ehrismann 31–3.

in hac arce...exussere victores The report in Zos. 3.18.5–6 is quite similar, the most notable difference being that Zosimus does not explicitly mention the burning of the town itself. Moreover, his account is more elaborate: in the citadel a great quantity of corn was found, as well as every kind of arms and engines, and a large amount of furniture and other baggage. Most of the corn was loaded onto the ships and the soldiers divided the rest of it among themselves. The arms which were useful for Roman warfare were kept, but the typical Persian arms were either burned or thrown into the river.

CHAPTER 3

Introduction

In the first part of this chapter the bright colours of the success at Pirisabora (ch. 2) are followed by the report of two gloomy episodes. First an unexpected Persian attack exposes the vulnerability of Julian's forces. Then the soldiers protest against the unsatisfactory amount of their financial rewards. Julian is not in a position to improve on his *donativum*, but he does hint at the opportunities offered by Persia's riches. Gradually, the gloom lifts: first the soldiers' morale is restored and next, Julian is proved more than right: the expedition reaches a region full of palm-trees and other types of food, described by Amm. in terms remininiscent of Hellenistic novels. In this land of Cocaigne the army's condition is completely transformed: instead of shortage it is now sheer abundance which endangers the soldiers' physique: *ubi formidabatur inopia, ibi timor saginae gravis incessit* (§ 14).

The composition of the chapter's first sections is rather surprising. The burning of Pirisabora, mentioned in 24.2.22 (*reliqua cum loco ipso exussere victores*), is followed by the attack of the Surena and its aftermath (24.3.1–2), which is in fact ahead of events. The chronological order can be found in Zos. 3.18.6–19.2: viz. Julian's coping with his soldiers' discontent (Amm.'s § 3–9) and next the attack of the Surena. Amm., however, begins with the last mentioned episode (§ 1–2), which enables him to return in § 3 (q.v.) to the moment of glory, where he had interrupted his narrative: *Incensa denique urbe, ut memoratum est.*

Postera die, quam haec acta erant On April 30 (see the note on chronology). Cf. for fem. *die* the note ad 24.2.3. The structure of the phrase is normal, as is shown by the following instances: *postero igitur die, quam illa erant acta* (Cic. *de Orat.* 2.12), *postero die quam hostem vidit* (Liv. 22.14.11), *Baias, quas postero die quam attigeram reliqui* (Sen. *Ep.* 51.1). **3.1**

perfertur ad imperatorem cibos per otium capientem nuntius gravis Cf. for the motif of an interruption caused by grave news *Augusto inter*

70 COMMENTARY

haec quiescenti per hiemem apud Sirmium indicabant nuntii graves et crebri (17.12.1), *Constantium Sirmi etiamtum hiberna quiete curantem permovebant nuntii metuendi et graves* (19.11.1). We find the content of this report also mentioned by Zos. 3.19.1. There are slight differences between Amm. and Zosimus, but on the whole the two passages are quite similar. Cf. also Lib. *Or.* 18.229. In military contexts *otium* often has a negative connotation, the most condensed form of which can be found in one of Vegetius' *regulae bellorum generales*: *Exercitus labore proficit, otio consenescit* (*mil.* 3.26.13). Cf. 24.7.3 *ob inertiam otiique desiderium*. But *otium* can also denote the much needed rest after strenuous operations: *brevi... otio cum milite recreatus* (16.2.6), *otio communi assensu post aerumnas multiplices attributo* (20.7.7). In combination with *cibus* it occurs in 16.12.11 *post otium cibique refectionem et potus*, 31.7.8 *capto per otium cibo*, which is directly reminiscent of Liv. 21.55.1 *cibo per otium capto*. See for a wholly different meaning of *otium*, viz. 'retirement', the note ad 20.2.5 *digredi iussit ad otium*. The specific detail (*cibos per otium capientem*) is only mentioned by Amm.

Surenam, Persicum ducem Cf. for *Surena* the note ad 24.2.4. Zosimus gives as additional information that the forces of the Persians were not inconsiderable and that the attack was launched from one of the cities of Assyria: ὁ σουρήνας δὲ μετὰ δυνάμεως οὐκ ὀλίγης ἔκ τινος τῶν ἐν Ἀσσυρίᾳ πόλεων...ἐπελθών (3.19.1). In 3.19.2 he informs us that Julian afterwards had the city taken and burnt.

procursatorum partis nostrae tres turmas inopinum aggressum Cf. Zos. 3.19.1 τοῖς προηγουμένοις τοῦ Ῥωμαίων στρατοπέδου κατασκοπῆς ἕνεκεν ἐπελθών, οὐ προϊδομένοις τὸ ἐσόμενον. It would seem that the mounted *procursatores* of the present text (see for the term the note ad 23.3.4 and also Austin and Rankov, 1995, 40–2) are to be distinguished from the *excursatores* of 24.1.2 (q.v). The three *turmae* will have numbered about 1050 cavalrymen (a single *turma* in Amm.'s time seems to have comprised circa 350 men, cf. 18.8.2 *duarum turmarum equites circiter septingenti ad subsidium... missi* and see the note ad 23.3.4). For unit sizes in the late Roman army in general see now Coello, 1995: the author discusses passages in Amm. on p. 60–6. The adj. *inopinus* occurs often in Amm., used predicatively e.g. in 19.8.11 *inopini... visebantur*, 27.2.1 *inopinus maiorem barbarorum plebem... exstinxit.*

paucissimos trucidasse, inter quos strato tribuno Cf. Zos. 3.19.1 ἕνα μὲν τῶν ἡγουμένων τριῶν ὄντων ἀνεῖλεν (sc. the Surena) ἅμα τισὶ τῶν ὑπ᾿

CHAPTER 3.1   71

αὐτῷ τεταγμένων and Lib. *Or.* 18.229 τῶν τοίνυν προβεβλημένων τῆς προνομῆς τῶν ἱππέων κακῶς ἠγωνισμένων ὥστε αὐτοῖς καὶ τὸν ἵππαρχον ἀποθανεῖν. For *paucissimos* cf. the note ad 20.6.7 *caesisque promisce paucissimis.* In the present text it adds to the picture of Julian's alert reaction in § 2: although the losses as such were inconsiderable (apart from the ignominious disappearance of a standard), he acted swiftly and safely. For *tribunus* see the note ad 23.3.9 and Vogler, 1995, 394–9, who notes on p. 394: "Les tribuns sont les officiers les plus couramment cités, et ils le sont surtout pour les campagnes qu' Ammien a personnellement connues... Ils apparaissent moins dans les derniers livres".

unum rapuisse vexillum From Zos. 3.19.1 Brok 124 infers that Amm. here uses *vexillum* in a general meaning ('standard') and that in fact Amm. was thinking of the same *draco* as the one which Zosimus mentions: ἐγκρατὴς ἐγένετο στρατιωτικοῦ σημείου, δράκοντος ἐκτύπωμα φέροντος. Note, however, that Amm. distinguishes *vexilla* from *dracones* in 15.5.16 (*cultu purpureo a draconum et vexillorum insignibus... abstracto*), as does e.g. Veg. *mil.* 3.5, which does not make Brok's suggestion very convincing.

A *vexillum* was a square piece of cloth, hung from a crossbar carried on a pole (cf. Seston, 1969, 695–7, Webster, 1981², 139–40 and Southern-Dixon, 1996, 125–6, with figs. 21, 59 and pl. 13). It was gleaming (27.2.6) and most often purple or red (15.5.16, 20.6.3). Sometimes it was lettered (Suet. *Vesp.* 6.3, D.C. 40.18.3, Veg. *mil.* 2.13) or embroidered with gold (16.10.2). It most closely resembled the modern flag (cf. 20.6.3, 24.6.5, 27.10.9 and Dennis, 1982). The only preserved example of a *vexillum,* dyed scarlet and bearing an image in gold of a Victory standing on a globe (cf. 16.12.12 *vexilla victricia*), was found in Egypt (cf. Rostovtzeff, 1942).

Dracones i.e. hollow, open-mouthed dragon's masks, behind which "flowed a long tapered streamer, the shape of a modern windsock which gives the direction of the wind on an airfield" (Webster, 1981², 136), are described in 16.10.7: *purpureis subtegminibus texti... dracones hastarum aureis gemmatisque summitatibus illigati hiatu vasto perflabiles et ideo velut ira perciti sibilantes caudarumque volumina relinquentes in ventum* (cf. 16.12.39 *purpureum signum draconis summitati hastae longioris aptatum,* Nemes. *Cyn.* 85–8, Greg. Naz. *Or.* 4.66, Them. *Or.* 1.2 a, Claud. *III Cons. Hon.* 138–41 and Sidon. *carm.* 5.402–7). According to Arr. *Tact.* 35.3 such standards were Scythian in origin, Lucianus *Hist. Conscr.* 29 speaks of Parthian dragons. A third-century Roman example was found near the fort of Niederbieber (Southern-

72 COMMENTARY

Dixon, 1996, 126 with pl. 19). For more information and many pictures see Coulston, 1991.

3.2 *concitus ira immani cum armigera manu festinatione ipsa tutissimus pervolavit* The first words are an imitation of Vergil *A.* 9.694 *immani concitus ira.* Cf. 24.5.7 and Hagendahl, 1921, 10. Zos. 3.19.2 also stresses the emperor's rage: Τοῦτο μαθὼν οὐκ ἤνεγκε μετρίως ὁ βασιλεύς, ἀλλὰ μετὰ θυμοῦ τοῖς ἀμφὶ τὸν σουρήναν ὡς εἶχεν ἐπιπεσὼν κτλ. It is the first sign of his loss of composure, which increased in the course of the campaign. See especially ch. 5 of this book. Cf. for Julian's anger Seager 33–6 and for the *cupiditas irascendi* in Amm. Brandt, 1999, 167 ff. In itself it is understandable that Julian was worried by the setback, the more so because the incident could be seen as an unpropitious *omen*, like the one which Dio reports in 40.18.3: during Crassus' ill-fated expedition against the Parthians one of the standards, apparently a *vexillum* (σημεῖον δέ τι τῶν μεγάλων, τῶν τοῖς ἱστίοις ἐοικότων καὶ φοινικᾶ γράμματα... ἐχόντων), fell into the Euphrates in the midst of a violent storm and was lost. The phrase *cum armigera manu* also occurs in 23.3.8 (q.v.). Although the verb *festinare* is quite frequently used by Amm., this is his only instance of the noun. See for a different instance of the combination of speed and safety 21.4.1 *eum vi incautum rapere festinabat, ut securitatem suam provinciarumque locaret in tuto,* and for Julian's reliance on speed in general the introduction to the commentary on 21.9.

grassatoribus foeda consternatione depulsis Amm. is terser than Zosimus, who reports that Julian not only put the Surena's men to flight, but recaptured the lost standard and took the city from where the Persians had launched their attack: τοῖς ἀμφὶ τὸν σουρήναν ὡς εἶχεν ἐπιπεσὼν τούτων μὲν εἰς φυγὴν ἔτρεψεν ὅσοι διαφυγεῖν ἠδυνήθησαν, τὸ δὲ σημεῖον ἀναλαβὼν τὸ παρὰ τῶν πολεμίων ἀφαιρεθὲν ἐπῆλθε παραχρῆμα τῇ πόλει καθ᾽ ἣν ὁ σουρήνας ἀποκρύπτων τὸν λόχον τοῖς κατασκόποις ἐπῆλθε, εἷλέ τε κατὰ κράτος καὶ ἐπυρπόλησε (3.19.2). As TLL VI 2198.48 notes, *grassatores* are men "qui praedandi causa vagantur"; the word could have been used to characterize the Saracen commander Podosaces, *famosi nominis latro... diu grassatus* (24.2.4). Such men lacked real courage and could be 'driven off in disgraceful confusion'. The term occurs in a similar context in 24.5.10.

residuos duo tribunos sacramento solvit ut desides et ignavos For *residuus* as a synonym of *reliquus* see the note ad 20.4.6. As to the two

CHAPTER 3.2　　　　73

surviving tribunes (their colleague had been killed, cf. *strato tribuno* in the preceding section), Amm. is more precise than Zosimus, who, although he also had said that there were three Roman commanders, omits to mention the fate of the third. Zosimus only says that the Surena killed one of the three officers (3.19.1, quoted above) and that another was degraded by Julian because he had lost his standard and had preferred his own safety to the greatness of Rome (τὸν δὲ τῶν κατασκόπων ἡγεμόνα, διότι τοῖς πολεμίοις τὸ σημεῖον ἀπέλιπε, τὴν σωτηρίαν τῆς Ῥωμαϊκῆς μεγαλοφροσύνης ἔμπροσθεν ποιησάμενος, παρέλυσέ τε τῆς ζώνης καὶ ἐν ἀτιμίᾳ τὸ λοιπὸν εἶχεν, 3.19.2).

On the other hand, Zosimus may be right in adding the words καὶ ἐν ἀτιμίᾳ τὸ λοιπὸν εἶχεν as a clarification to παρέλυσέ τε τῆς ζώνης. Zosimus thus suggests that the punished officer was degraded rather than dismissed from the service, which does not seem illogical, in view of the fact that the army had penetrated deeply into Persian territory, that to go home would be rather difficult for an individual and that an emperor could make use of degraded soldiers in other ways (we know from 25.1.8 that Julian forced some cavalrymen, who had been charged with running away in action, to march among the baggage-train with the prisoners; cf. 29.5.20 *omnes contrusit ad infimum militiae gradum*).

Amm.'s *sacramento solvit* at first sight is less clear than what Zosimus reports. Nevertheless, he probably means the same, for in most other passages where Amm. mentions someone 'released' from his oath', he explicitly adds that such a person was sent (or went) home. So in 16.7.1 *eum sacramento solutum abire iussit in larem*, 28.2.9 *sententia principis sacramento exutus abiit ad lares* and 28.6.25 *solutus sacramento Palladius... discessit ad otium*; 30.7.3 is a different case: there the person in question was *honeste sacramento solutus* before he went home. Here such an addition is missing. Moreover, Libanius, who in *Or.* 18.229 refers to the same incident, also speaks of degrading (καταβιβάζων) the culprits, not of sending them home.

For a discussion of the term *sacramentum*, the oath soldiers had to swear on their enlistment (*milites... cum matriculis inseruntur, iurare solent; et ideo militiae sacramenta dicuntur*, Veg. *mil.* 2.5), see Campbell, 1984, 19–32. Cf. also the note ad 21.5.10. For *ut desides et ignavos* cf. Arrius Menander in *Dig.* 49.16.6 pr. *Omne delictum est militis, quod aliter, quam disciplina communis exigit, committitur: veluti segnitiae crimen vel contumaciae vel desidiae.*

decem vero milites ex his, qui fugerant, exauctoratos capitali addixit supplicio secutus veteres leges Corbulo punished the soldiers who had fled

74 COMMENTARY

far less severely (Tac. *Ann.* 13.36.2–3). The verb *addicere* is often used as a t.t. for condemning someone to be punished. Amm. has a number of instances, e.g. *poenae letali* (22.3.12), *perenni servitio* (23.6.83). The present phrase also occurs in 15.3.2 (in the plural) and 15.7.5. " Decimationis supplicium haud dubie intellegit". So Wagner-Erfurdt, followed by e.g. Fiebiger, 1901 and Klotz, 1916, 487. Other scholars (e.g. Brok 124–5 and Fontaine in n. 349) are less sure of this interpretation. Ernesti, quoted by Wagner, even suggested that Amm.'s Greek origin played him false: "lege aut decimos aut error est Graeculi decimationem non intelligentis".

There is no need to doubt that Amm., a military historian and a *miles quondam* himself, was aware of the meaning of decimation, the time-honoured punishment for army units which, as in the present case, had disgraced themselves (Plb. 6.38.1 points to the expediency of the measure, which spared commanders the difficult task of inflicting the death penalty on all soldiers). Neither is there any need to doubt that Amm.'s wording in itself can refer to this practice, pace Brok 124. It is perhaps true that to modern readers Amm. would have been easier to understand, if instead of *decem ... milites* he had written *decimum ... quemque* (as Tac. does in *Ann.* 3.21.1; cf. Liv. 2.59.11 *decumus quisque* and Tac. *Ann.* 14.44.4), but a comparison with Polybius (the oldest and most explicit authority we have on the practice of decimation) shows that, if the context is clear, the use of a distributive is not absolutely necessary. When a commanding officer, as Polybius says in 6.38.2, considers decimation necessary, he assembles the soldiers, brings up those guilty of leaving the ranks, reproaches them sharply "and finally chooses by lot sometimes five, sometimes eight, sometimes twenty of the offenders, so adjusting the number thus chosen that they form as near as possible the tenth part of those guilty of cowardice" (καὶ τὸ τέλος ποτὲ μὲν πέντε, ποτὲ δ' ὀκτώ, ποτὲ δ' εἴκοσι, τὸ δ' ὅλον πρὸς τὸ πλῆθος αἰεὶ στοχαζόμενος, ὥστε δέκατον μάλιστα γίνεσθαι τῶν ἡμαρτηκότων, τοσούτους ἐκ πάντων κληροῦται τῶν ἀποδεδειλιακότων, transl. Paton). The problem, however, is that in the case under discussion those *qui fugerant* numbered about 1050 (cf. the note ad § 1 *procursatorum partis nostrae tres turmas*). Amm.'s *decem ... milites* therefore is only one percent of the total, which rules out that he refers here to decimation in its strict sense.

In executing the ten soldiers Julian followed ancient laws: *secutus veteres leges*. Decimation was the traditional punishment for those who deserted their post or yielded their standards (Plb. 6.38, already quoted, D.H. 9.50.7; Fiebiger, 1901). Julius Caesar (D.C. 41.35.5), Domitius Calvinus (D.C. 48.42.2), Marcus Antonius (D.C. 49.27.1;

CHAPTER 3.3   75

Fron. *Str.* 4.1.37) and Gaius Octavianus (D.C. 49.38.4; Suet. *Aug.* 24.2) are among those whose use of decimation is recorded. But this is not to say that there were no measures other than decimation which a commander could take. Cf. e.g. Arrius Menander in *Dig.* 49.16.6.3: *Qui in acie prior fugam fecit, spectantibus militibus propter exemplum capite puniendus est.*

Zosimus is silent about any punishment, apart from that inflicted on the officer who had lost the standard (3.19.2, quoted above), but Lib. in *Or.* 18.229, praising Julian's firm behaviour, is in accordance with Amm. in mentioning the execution of some of the soldiers. Other passages in Amm., which refer to the death penalty inflicted on soldiers, are quoted by Müller, 1905, 618–20 (in his paper on the death penalty Arce, 1974 does not pay attention to specifically military matters; see for this subject Sander, 1960 and Brand, 1968). They include cases of mutiny (29.5.22, where it is said that the general Theodosius turned some soldiers of the Constantiniani over to their colleagues to be slain in the old-fashioned way, *eos…prisco more militibus dedit occidendos,* had the hands of the officers of a *cohors sagittariorum* cut off and the rest of this cohort slain) and desertion (29.5.24, 29.5.31 and 29.5.49). Julian himself wrote in a letter to Oribasius (*Ep.* 14, 385 c) that soldiers who deserted their post should be put to death and denied burial, but 25.1.8–9 shows that he sometimes was more lenient than his letter would suggest or than he was in the present case (*hoc enim correctionis moderamine leniori…contentus est imperator,* 25.1.9). It is impossible to decide whether Amm. here approves of Julian's ruthless heeding of 'ancient laws'. He uses a neutral adj. to denote their antiquity and not one which expresses awe and respect like *priscus*; cf. his disparagement of Constantine, *novatoris turbatorisque priscarum legum* (21.10.8), and *priscis…vetita legibus* (27.9.10). In 29.5.22, quoted above, on the other hand, he fully agrees with the strong measures taken by Theodosius. He does not merely use the word *priscus,* but also explicitly defends the general against *obtrectatores malivoli,* reminding them of the fact that the cohort in question had behaved badly and had set a bad example: *admonemus hanc cohortem et facto fuisse et exemplo adversam* (29.5.23).

Incensa denique urbe, ut memoratum est As was noted above in the introduction, with *ut memoratum est* Amm. resumes the narrative which he had interrupted in 24.3.1 for the story of the attack of the Surena and its consequences (the burning of Pirisabora had been mentioned in 24.2.22: *reliqua cum loco ipso exussere victores*). See

76 COMMENTARY

for such cross references Woodman-Martin ad Tac. *Ann.* 3.18.1 *ut saepe memoravi.* Zosimus' report on the sequence of events is more straightforward. After having spoken of the capture of Pirisabora (3.18.6), Zosimus subsequently refers to Julian's speech and the donative to the soldiers (ibid.; his words, quoted below, correspond to Amm.'s sections 3–9), and concludes with the Surena episode (3.19.1–2).

The way in which Amm. arranges the events has bewildered some scholars. Klotz, for example, states "dass Ammian nicht im Stande gewesen ist, zwei Vorlagen zu einer Einheit zu verschmelzen" (1916, 488; he follows Klein, 1914, 98). Brok 123 on the other hand praises our historian and indeed, by arranging the material in the way he does, Amm., perhaps better than Zosimus, prepares his readers for Julian's speech (in §4–7). Otherwise the effect of this speech would have been spoilt. The problems concerning the sequence of events have been overlooked by Williams, 1997, 68–71, which unsettles her entire interpretation of the soldiers' protest and Julian's reaction.

constructo tribunali insistens Cf. the comparable phrases in 15.8.4 (if Valesius' emendation is accepted), 17.13.25, 21.5.1, 21.13.9 (q.v.), 23.5.15 (q.v.). See also the introductory note on book 20, ch. 5.

actis gratiis exercitui convocato… argenteos nummos centenos viritim pollicitus Cf. Zos. 3.18.6 ἐφ᾽ οἷς ὁ βασιλεὺς φιλοφρονούμενος τὸ στράτευμα λόγοις τε καθήκουσιν ἐτίμα καὶ ἕκαστον ἀργυροῖς ἑκατὸν νομίσμασιν ἐδωρεῖτο. As to the pieces of silver, it is difficult to assess their worth, i.a. because it is doubtful whether or not Amm. uses the word *nummus* in a technical sense (for the introduction of the silver *nummus* as equivalent of 25, later 100 *denarii* see Callu, 1978; see further Paschoud n. 36). Against it speaks the fact that in 24.4.26 and 26.7.11 *nummus* is used for gold coins.

For the first time in his report of the Persian campaign Amm. mentions a donative to the soldiers. Zos. 3.13.3 concerns an earlier occasion, viz. soon after the crossing of the river Abora (cf. the note ad 23.5.24), when Julian gave each soldier one hundred and thirty pieces of silver (ἀργυρῶν τε νομισμάτων τριάκοντα καὶ ἑκατὸν τῶν στρατιωτῶν ἕκαστον δόσει τιμήσας). See Delmaire, 1989, 552–4 for other examples (i.a. 17.9.5–6) of *donativa* or *dona* given to or withheld from soldiers before or after a battle.

cum eos parvitate promissi percitos tumultuare sensisset The alliteration emphasizes the soldiers' potentially dangerous emotional reaction.

CHAPTER 3.4–7   77

Although *parvitas* is only firmly attested in 22.15.13, the present
emendation of V is reliable, since *parcitas*, the only real alternative,
does not occur in Amm. and, moreover, as TLL X 1.327.44 notes, usually concerns the "habitus animantium parcorum". Amm.'s predilection for *percitus* is discussed in the notes ad 20.11.5 and 21.3.1. The
verb *tumultuare* denotes the potentially dangerous rioting and dis-
turbing of the order by masses of civilians or soldiers. In the present
case the soldiers were making a noisy scene; see the note ad 22.10.5.
Zosimus is silent on this. Whatever the worth of the *nummi* (see
above), they apparently were far below the soldiers' expectations.

ad indignationem plenam gravitatis erectus A similar expression about
Julian occurs in 17.10.8 *ad indignationem iustam… erectus* (q.v.) and
25.1.8. The contrast with Constantius is evident: *ultra modum solitae
indignationis excanduit imperator* (20.9.2, q.v.). See for *indignatio* as "a
powerful weapon in the orator's armoury" Woodman ad Vell. 2.66.3.

The tone and contents of Julian's speech contrast rather sharply   **3.4–7**
with his earlier speeches to his soldiers in the *Res Gestae*. In 16.12.9–
12, before the battle at Argentoratum, he aims to canalize their
enthusiastic fighting spirit into a safe and prudent course. When
addressing them after the pronunciamiento at Lutecia (20.5.3–7)
he could refer to their loyal support and protection. On the eve
of the adventurous eastward march against Constantius he again
appealed to their loyal service, stressing the need for disciplined
action (21.5.2–8). Finally, after the invasion into Persian territory,
he used the lessons of history in his appeal to destroy the historic
enemy once and for all (23.5.16–23). In all these cases Julian could
count on the soldiers' enthusiasm and their devotion to his person.
This time, however, he is entirely on the defensive. The soldiers have
made their demands quite clear: they want more material rewards,
and he is unable to satisfy this claim. The treasury is empty as the
result, so he says, of the ill-considered and faint-hearted policies of
the preceding administration. So he has to step down from all high-
flown appeals to their courage and spirit and has to adopt a more
down-to-earth argument, which essentially consists in sketching the
possibilities of enriching themselves by plunder. The absence of all
laudatory appellativa is in accordance with this. He does not address
them with words like *commilitones mei* (16.12.9), *propugnatores mei
reique publicae fortes et fidi* (20.5.3) or *fortissimi milites* (23.5.16). It
is surely to the author's credit that unlike the tradition preserved
by Zosimus, he does not attempt to hide the ugly realities of a

78 COMMENTARY

discontented army and the emperor's shortage of financial resources. He only endeavours to uphold Julian's dignity by his lofty references to the prime importance of inner freedom and the training of the mind.

3.4 *"En", inquit, "Persae circumfluentes rerum omnium copiis…"* Right at the beginning of the speech, *en* draws attention to the visual perception of Persian wealth. One of Amm.'s purposes in writing the digression on the Persian provinces in 23.6 was to give a description of the natural resources of the Persian empire, as is argued in the introduction to ch. 6 of the commentary on book 23. Cf. especially 23.6.15, 29, 31, 41, 45, 48, 51, 56 and 85–8 (on pearls). The phrase seems to have been inspired by Cic. *Amic.* 52 *circumfluere omnibus copiis atque in omnium rerum abundantia vivere*; see Fletcher, 1937, 380. Cf. for *circumfluere*, "to be abundantly supplied with" (OLD s.v. 4), *alimentorum uberi copia circumfluere* (22.16.7).

ditare vos poterit opimitas gentis Mark the vast difference with *abolenda nobis natio molestissima* (23.5.19, q.v.). In 16.11.9, 17.2.1 (q.v.) and 19.11.2 the comparatively rare word *opimitas* also occurs within a context of plundering.

unum spirantibus animis The same phrase occurs in 27.10.9 and 29.5.28, passages from which it may be tentatively surmised that it denotes practical consensus in a given situation rather than the true harmony which Julian had asked in an earlier speech to his soldiers: *concordiam spondete mansuram et fidem* (21.5.7), and which was manifest at the moment of the invasion into Persian territory: *favorabilis studio concordi cunctorum* (23.5.15).

ex immensis opibus egentissima est, tandem credite, Romana res publica For *ex* denoting a previous situation which has been changed cf. TLL V 2.1101.26 ff. A fine instance is Andromache's lament *Ex opibus summis opis egens, Hector, tuae* (Enn. *scen.* 85, quoted in Cic. *Tusc.* 3.44; see Jocelyn's note ad loc. [= *fr.* 80 in his edition of Ennius' tragedies]). See for *tandem* in directives expressing the "feeling that the state of affairs involved 'should have already been realized'" Risselada, 1999, 104.

per eos, qui, ut augerent divitias, docuerunt principes auro quietem a barbaris redemptare Continuing in the track of Kellerbauer and Cornelissen, Günther, 1891, 70 proceeded to his convincing emendation of V's

CHAPTER 3.5   79

text. The only other occurrence of *redemptare* is Tac. *Hist.* 3.34.3: prisoners of war *a propinquis adfinibusque occulte redemptabantur*. For *quies* see the note ad 24.2.20. Amm. more than once gives expression to resentment against courtiers and other officials who increased their private means at the expense of the public interest: 16.5.15, 18.1.1 *quorum patrimonia publicae clades augebant*, 31.14.3. Cf. Thompson, 1947, 128 and Demandt, 1965, 44f.

To bribe satellite kings and other barbarians with money and gifts was an old custom of the Romans, already attested in Tac. *Ger.* 42.2 and Plin. *Pan.* 12.2 (cf. Gordon, 1949). It did not become obsolete in Late Antiquity (cf. Blockley, 1985 and Demandt, 1989, 270). According to Orosius 5.1.10ff. it was quite reasonable to pay a fair price in order to achieve peace and happiness (*Tributum pretium pacis est. Nos tributa dependimus, ne bella patiamur*), but other authors rejected this solution as disgraceful, cf. e.g. Priscus *fr.* 9.3 (Blockley), Priscianus *Anast.* 201–3 (V p. 271 Baehrens), Procop. *Pers.* 1.19.32–3 and Julian himself, who chided Constantine (*Caes.* 329 a), Constantius (*Ep. ad Ath.* 280 a-b, 286 a) and Silvanus (*On Kingship* 98 c-d) for having given subsidies to barbarians. In Amm. we find the practice mentioned in 21.6.8 and 26.5.7. The facile prejudice, which springs from a faulty analysis of the political situation created by the migrations and other developments directly across the borders of the Empire, is not without reason put into the mouth of the emperor.

direptum aerarium est, urbes exinanitae, populatae provinciae Julian coolly enumerates the disastrous results of the preceding administration's policies. See for *diripere* as a synonym of *despoliare* TLL V 1.1261.68ff., especially Curt. 10.6.23 *ad diripiendos thesauros*, Flor. *Epit.* 4.1.2. Cf. also 29.1.43 *ut opimum aerarium eius diriperetur*. Originally the *aerarium (Saturni)* was the senate's treasury, as opposed to the imperial *fiscus*. However, "*aerarium* désigne le trésor impérial dès les années 320 et, à partir du milieu du IV^c siècle, les deux composantes de l'*aerarium* sont les Largesses Sacrées et la *res privata*" (Delmaire, 1989, 6). Cf. the notes ad 20.11.5 and 22.11.6.

In the speech to the soldiers after the crossing of the Abora Julian had also spoken of the ruin caused by the Persians, i.a. mentioning *miseranda recens captarum urbium* (23.5.18). See the note ad loc., with its reference to 25.4.24 (*urbes excisae... provinciae gravibus impensis exhaustae*). For *exinanire* in a context of plunder cf. 26.8.13 *Arbitionis domum... iussit exinaniri*, Cic. *Pis.* 96 *laceratae Athenae, Dyrrachium et Apollonia exinanita*.

3.5

80 COMMENTARY

*mihi nec facultates nec propinquitas generis suppetit, quamvis ortu sim no-
bilis* For *facultates*, 'resources', cf. e.g. Caes. *Gal.* 2.1.4 *qui ad con-
ducendos homines facultates habebant.* As it stands, the text quoted in
the lemma means: 'I have neither resources nor relatives (who might
provide them), although I admit to be of noble birth'. In this case
propinquitas would denote Julian's 'kin' (cf. 14.11.7 *in propinquitatis
perniciem inclinatior*), with *generis* added as a gen. explicativus, identitatis or inversus. In his *Letter to the Athenians* Julian himself also refers
to his noble birth, stating that on his father's side he was descended
from the same stock as Constantius II (Καὶ ὅτι μὲν τὰ πρὸς πατρὸς ἡμῖν
ἐντεῦθεν ὅθενπερ καὶ Κωνσταντίῳ τὰ πρὸς πατρὸς ὥρμηται, φανερόν. τὼ
γὰρ ἡμετέρω πατέρε γεγόνατον ἀδελφὼ πατρόθεν, 270 c; cf. Jul. *Caes.*
315 a and, for Julian's maternal side, 25.3.23 *Basilina matre iam inde a
maioribus nobili*). However, Julian adds sarcastically that the relation-
ship with the emperor had done him no good, and he even blames
Constantius for the death of numerous relatives (six cousins, Julian's
own father and his two brothers, 270 c – 271 a) – this reads as a commentary on Amm.'s *nec propinquitas generis suppetit.* Yet one wonders
whether an adj. denoting wealth or status which qualified *generis* has
been lost; cf. 14.1.1 *propinquitate... regiae stirpis*, 26.6.18 *stirpis propin-
quitatem imperatoriae.* This would make the concessive clause easier to
understand: 'in spite of my high birth, I am not closely connected
with wealthy relatives.' As to the lack of *facultates*, for this, too, we may
adduce the *Ep. ad Ath.* In 273 b Julian accuses Constantius of having
robbed him of his paternal inheritance, so that not even a trifle was
left: πατρῷον γὰρ οὐδὲν ὑπῆρχέ μοι οὐδὲ ἐκεκτήμην ἐκ τοσούτων, ὅσων
εἰκὸς ἦν πατέρα κεκτῆσθαι τὸν ἐμόν, οὐκ ἐλαχίστην βῶλον ('not the
smallest clod of earth'), οὐκ ἀνδράποδον, οὐκ οἰκίαν. ὁ γάρ τοι καλὸς
Κωνστάντιος ἐκληρονόμησεν ἀντ᾽ ἐμοῦ τὴν πατρῴαν οὐσίαν ἅπασαν, ἐμοί
τε, ὅπερ ἔφην, οὐδὲ γρῦ ('not a morsel') μετέδωκεν αὐτῆς.

The adj. *nobilis* here does not seem to refer specifically to sena-
torial birth as in the cases dealt with in the note ad 21.10.7 *eminuit
nobilitatis.*

praeter pectus omni liberum metu Cf. 16.8.7 about the comes sacrarum
largitionum Ursulus, who, having forced his way into the consisto-
rium without any fear, *ore et pectore libero docuit gesta*, and 20.8.9 in a
speech of Julian: *libero pectoris muro, ut ita dixerim, saeptus* (cf. the note
ad loc.).

*nec pudebit imperatorem cuncta bona in animi cultu ponentem profiteri
paupertatem honestam* Julian now contrives an elegant example of *de*

CHAPTER 3.5   81

necessitate virtutem facere. His slender means appear to be an asset, not a cause for shame. For *ponere in*, "to place in a category", cf. OLD s.v. 22b. See Cic. *Fin.* 5.54 about Demetrius of Phalerum: *animi cultus ille erat ei quasi quidam humanitatis cibus.* The metaphoric use of 'cultivation' is explained in Cic. *Tusc.* 2.14: *ut ager quamvis fertilis sine cultura fructuosus esse non potest, sic sine doctrina animus; ita est utraque res sine altera debilis. cultura autem animi philosophia est; haec extrahit vitia radicitus* etc. See further on this subject Partoens, 1999, 173–182.

Whereas Philemon and Baucis 'admitted' their poverty (Ov. *Met.* 8.633 *paupertatemque fatendo*) and Acilius Buta 'confessed' it to Tiberius (Sen. *Ep.* 122.10 *paupertatem confitenti*), Julian went so far as to 'avow' it (*profiteri*). But then this poverty is, of course, "worthy of respect". Cf. in a different context Vell. 2.129.3 (ut) *neque honestam paupertatem pateretur dignitate destitui* (with Woodman's note) and Tac. *Ann.* 2.48.3 *honestam innocentium paupertatem levavit* (with Goodyear's note). Woodman suggests that *honestam paupertatem* could be a phrase used by Tiberius in an actual speech. A more or less similar thought is expressed in 14.6.10–11, where Amm. turns against rich snobs, and argues that their forefathers had contributed to the greatness of Rome not by riches, but by valour in war and a simple lifestyle (*maiores suos, per quos ita magnitudo Romana porrigitur, non divitiis eluxisse, sed per bella saevissima nec opibus nec victu nec indumentorum vilitate gregariis militibus discrepantes opposita cuncta superasse virtute*). He there points to the 'honourable poverty' of Valerius Publicola, Regulus and Scipio.

nam et Fabricii familiari re pauperes rexere bella gravissima, gloria locupletes Julian adapts a time-hallowed exemplum to his purpose (see for the use of exempla in Amm. Blockley, 1994; on p. 61 he notes: "His use of *exempla* is in scale and range unprecedented in the Latin historical writing that survives"; cf. also Brandt, 1999, 96 and Wittchow, 2001). Usually C. Fabricius Luscinus, consul in 282 and 278, censor in 275, serves as a model of frugality and incorruptible integrity. Amm. refers to him in the latter sense in 30.1.22 (he is also mentioned in 24.4.24 *extimabatur Mars ipse... affuisse castra Lucanorum invadenti Luscino*). Fabricius, however, was also renowned for his military prowess, having been twice honoured with a triumphus. He could rightly be called 'rich in glory', in contrast to his material poverty (cf. Münzer, 1909, Broughton, 1951, 189, 193–4 and Broughton, 1984, 89). As Brok 128 suggests, the plural *Fabricii* implies that the name is used "als Vertreter der Gattung" (Szantyr 19): 'men like Fabricius' (cf. Cic. *de Orat.* 2.290 *tu Fabricios mihi auctores... protulisti*, Luc. 10.152 *Fabricios*

82 COMMENTARY

Curiosque graves). None of the examples of *bellum regere* listed in TLL II 1839.52–7 provides a real parallel for the present phrase which denotes the actual command during wars. Possibly, it is a Grecism. In a glossary *regere* is mentioned as Latin for διέπειν; cf. Hom. *Il.* 1.165–6, A. *Pers.* 105–6 πολέμους πυργοδαίκτους διέπειν. Fontaine has tried to keep as close as possible to V's *gravissimae* by printing *e gloria locupletes*, translating this by "riches de gloire", which is not possible. If the preposition is rightly added, the phrase can only be rendered by 'rich as a result of glory', whatever that may mean precisely. The mere abl., however, is definitely preferable, because of the parallel with *familiari re pauperes* and in view of the normal construction, the metaphoric use of which can be illustrated by V. Max. 4.8 *ext.* 2 about Gillias from Agrigentum: *erat opibus excellens, sed multo etiam animo quam divitiis locupletior.* Alternatively, one might conjecture *gravissime*, but it would be Amm.'s only instance of this form. Moreover, the adj. *gravis* is combined with *bellum* in 14.2.1, 26.6.20, 30.8.5: *gravissima* is indeed a plausible emendation.

3.6 *haec vobis cuncta poterunt abundare* If *haec…cuncta* is not to be regarded as deliberately vague, it refers back to the beginning of the speech: *En Persae* etc., with *haec* in a deictic sense, supported by an opportune gesture of the orator.

si imperterriti deo meque, quantum humana ratio patitur, caute ductante mitius egeritis Possibly, the rare adj. *imperterritus* is a creation of Vergil (*A.* 10.770). Other references to the cooperation of god and man in Julian's speeches are *deo vobisque fautoribus* (21.5.5), *adero ubique vobis adiumento numinis sempiterni* (23.5.19). Julian's own leadership is limited by the possibilities of a human being: *ratio* either denotes "faculty of reason" (OLD s.v. 7b) or something like "constitution" (OLD s.v. 12); cf. also 15.4.1 *quantum ratio patitur*, 23.6.10 *quantum ratio sinit*, in both cases concerning the restrictions implied in the author's 'plan of action'. See for the positive meaning of *cautus* the note ad 23.5.5. TLL VIII 1159.27 interprets the present case of *mitius* as a synonym of *moderatius*; cf. also Fontaine's "assez docilement".

sin resistitis ad seditionum revoluti dedecora pristinarum, pergite! Rebellion would mean relapsing into the ugly, mutinous practices of the past. The adj. *pristinus* is a 'vox media', which can be used in a negative context: *in vobis resident mores pristini* (Pl. *Truc.* 7, about the Romans' notorious miserliness). Brok 128 surmises that Julian refers to

CHAPTER 3.7

recent cases of usurpation, but he may well have the whole of Roman military history in mind. In order to solve Clark's problem 'cursus causa' with *pergite*, Fletcher, 1930, 196 suggests *iam pergite*, which is not unattractive from a paleographic point of view. More important, however, is, that the insertion of *iam* would tally well with the findings of recent linguistic research on this particle. It "focuses on the element in its scope as something which runs counter to a particular standard or expectation" (Kroon and Risselada, 1998, 444); in the present case the soldiers could not expect Julian to say such a thing (cf. Caltabiano's rendering "proseguite pure!"). Moreover, the pattern, *si... iam* is quite usual (see *ib.* 442). For *pergere*, "to go on" (OLD s.v. 3), often in the imperative, cf. Cic. *de Orat.* 1.34 *pergite, ut facitis.* In any case, an impatiently used abrupt imperative fits the context well, but Clark's tentative *perite* would be far too aggressive; *pergite* could even imply a sarcastic paradox: by 'moving on' they would in fact return to their bad old ways.

confecto tantorum munerum cursu moriar stando For *cursus*, 'career', **3.7** see the relevant note ad 22.10.6, and cf. especially 25.3.19 *in medio cursu florentium gloriarum*, "au milieu d'un carrière florissante et glorieuse" (Fontaine). The idea that an emperor ought to die standing originates in Vespasian's famous words *'imperatorem' ait' 'stantem mori oportere'* (Suet. *Vesp.* 24), repeated in D.C. 66.17.2 'τὸν αὐτοκράτορα' ἔφη 'ἑστῶτα δεῖ ἀποθνήσκειν' and *epit.* 9.18 *'stantem', ait, 'imperatorem excedere terris decet'.* Later Turbo, prefect of Hadrian's praetorian guard, took a leaf out of Vespasian's book: when the emperor advised him to take things somewhat easier, he reacted with τὸν ἔπαρχον ἑστῶτα ἀποθνήσκειν δεῖ (D.C. 69.18.4).

contempturus animam, quam mihi febricula eripiet una Cf. Hier. *in Ps.* 93 (CC 78.145.111–3) *Cum omnia cogitaverint per annos triginta, una febricula venit, et tollit omnes cogitationes*, and August. *de catech. rud.* 25 (CC 46.150.66). These parallels show that Amm.'s phrase is a variation of a current saying. Cf. also the comparable phrases in Sal. *Jug.* 106.3 and Tac. *Ann.* 14.59.1.

aut certe discedam For *discedere* denoting retirement cf. the phrase with which Amm. alludes to the present text in his elogium of Julian: (ut) *allocutusque tumentes armatos discessurum ad vitam minaretur privatam, ni tumultuare desistent* (25.4.12). See for his threat to retire during the hectic days of the pronunciamiento at Lutetia 20.4.8 and the note ad loc.

84   COMMENTARY

nec enim ita vixi, ut non possim aliquando esse privatus He might have added that this was the status he had once held: ἐτύγχανον δὲ ἰδιώτης ἔτι (Jul. *Mis.* 351 b). See the last note ad 22.9.9. As Lindenbrog already pointed out, there is a close parallel in D.C. 68.3.1 concerning the emperor Nerva: Νέρουας δὲ οὕτως ἦρχε καλῶς ὥστε ποτὲ εἰπεῖν "οὐδὲν τοιοῦτον πεποίηκα ὥστε μὴ δύνασθαι τὴν ἀρχήν τε καταθέσθαι καὶ ἀσφαλῶς ἰδιωτεῦσαι." Cf. also Cic. *Tusc.* 5.62 and *Q. fr.* 1.1.21–3.

praeque me fero… doctrinarum Among translators and commentators only Fontaine n. 358 appears puzzled by this remarkable finish to Julian's speech. What is its function within the train of thought? Presumably, the emperor wants to stress that his eventual (or imaginary) retirement would not be an ugly case of desertion; he proudly rejoices that there are enough competent military authorities under whose leadership the expedition could successfully continue. The great project of Persia's subjugation is not merely dependent on Julian's personal accomplishments: others could complete it just as well. Cf. for *spectatissimus* expressing a person's high degree of distinction Tac. *Ann.* 4.6.3 *res suas Caesar spectatissimo cuique… mandabat,* 29.5.8 (about Theodosius sr.) *spectatissimi ducis adventu.* In 22.7.7 Amm. had said that Julian put in command of the army *rectores… diu exploratos.* In 24.1.2 the following generals are listed: Nevitta, Arintheus, Hormisdas, Dagalaifus, Victor and Secundinus. Lucillianus, the commander of the fleet, is mentioned i.a. in 24.1.6. As to *perfunctos,* the third hand's correction of *perfectos* in V, this would be the only instance of *perfungi* in Amm. It could stress the distinguished commanders' past experience, but this tallies less well with *doctrinarum.* Moreover, as appears in the list of examples in OLD s.v. 3b, *perfectus* can express that a person's accomplishments in a certain field leave nothing to be desired, e.g. Cic. *de Orat.* 1.58 *perfectos iam homines in dicendo.* Cf. 27.7.2 *omni ex parte perfectus.* Other expressions used by Amm. to denote a systematic knowledge of military matters are *bellicis… studiis eruditus* (31.14.5) and *militaris rei scientia* (22.7.9, cf. also 25.4.1 and 27.8.10). See for this last expression Brandt, 1999, 335–9, who does not refer to the present text.

3.8 *Hac modesta imperatoris oratione* Unless Heraeus' conjecture in 14.5.6 is accepted, this is the only instance of the adj. *modestus* in Amm. It is a curious echo of a phrase in the speech which Constantius addressed to Julian at his elevation to the rank of Caesar: *modesteque increpans desides* (15.8.13). The precise meaning which Amm. attaches to *modestus* will become clear in the immediate sequel to the present text.

CHAPTER 3.8   85

inter secunda et aspera medii The translators do not agree about the meaning of these words, choosing two divergent solutions. Fontaine's rendering may serve as an example of one of these: "qui gardait un juste milieu dans le succès comme dans les échecs". No doubt *secunda* can denote success, as in 15.5.23 and 16.12.61, where it contrasts with *tristia* and *adversa* respectively. For *asper* denoting adversity see the list in TLL II 812.43–60; a very clear example is provided by *casus secundet asperos* (*Ambr. Hymn.* 2.15 Fontaine). Since 'amid' is one of the normal meanings of *inter*, Rolfe's "amid prosperity and adversity" seems commendable. However, *medii* poses a problem in this case. There are no convincing instances of *medius* being used absolutely in the sense '(mentally) balanced' (cf. Caltabiano's "equilibrato"). When it concerns a person, the extremes avoided are usually implied, as in the case of 14.9.2 about Constantius: *cetera medium principem* (see, however, the note ad 21.16.8 *aliis principibus mediis comparandus*), or explicitly added, often with a phrase including *inter*, as in 30.7.4 (concerning Valens) *inter probra medium et praecipua*, or the well-known formula about Valentinian's stance in religious matters: *inter religionum diversitates medius stetit* (30.9.5); cf. also Tac. *Hist.* 1.49.2 *ipsi medium ingenium, magis extra vitia quam cum virtutibus.* In the present text, too, it is rather strained not to combine *inter* and *medii* in a comparable way. Now *asper* is an apt term to express a person's harshness, specifically in his treatment of others: 18.6.18 *suopte ingenio irritabilis et asperrimus*, 27.6.3 *licet asper esset et formidatus.* In the present context *lenis* cannot serve as a contrast, since this denotes a praiseworthy quality, which cannot characterize behaviour which in the given situation would deserve reproach. In itself *secundus* is not a negative term; it occurs in phrases expressing approval, as in 17.13.25 *militarique consensu secundo*, 21.13.10 *accipite, quaeso, aequis auribus et secundis*, 26.2.2 *voluntate praesentium secundissima.* Being confronted with his soldiers' discontent, Julian would have acted imprudently by addressing really harsh words to them. It would, however, have been equally wrong to comply gracefully with their complaints. Any sort of indulgent approval of their thoughts was out of the question, and thus Julian steered a middle course between two possible reactions: "der sich in der Mitte zwischen Freundlichkeit und Strenge hielt" (Seyfarth, followed by Hamilton, whose "indulgence" for *secunda* is an improvement). See for substantivated adjectives in the neutr. plur. Szantyr 153–4.

With the second interpretation the phrase quoted in the lemma can be regarded as an explanation of *modesta*: in choosing the middle

86   COMMENTARY

course, Julian demonstrated *moderatio*; see for the importance of this virtue Seager 13–4.

pro tempore delenitus In their various languages translators agree about the meaning of *pro tempore*: Hamilton's "for the time being" may serve as an illustration of this curious agreement. In fact, this phrase definitely has another meaning, as may become clear from these examples: (ut) *consiliumque pro tempore et pro re caperet* (Caes. *Gal.* 5.8.1), *rebus turbidis pro tempore ut consuleret* (Tac. *Ann.* 12.49.2). Obviously, *pro tempore* means 'as circumstances allowed', 'in accordance with the situation'. In Amm. the phrase occurs ten times. Some examples: 14.10.10 *imperator pro tempore pauca dicturus* means that Constantius intends to speak "a few words appropriate to the occasion" (Rolfe); when he was the object of the Antiochenes' jests, Julian was *coactus dissimulare pro tempore* (22.14.2), "contraint de n'en pas tenir compte en raison des circonstances" (Fontaine). For *delenire*, 'to quiet down', cf. *efferatamque diu plebem aegre postea delenitam* (27.3.13).

cum meliorum exspectatione This contrasts the future with the present situation (*pro tempore*).

cunctorum aspirante consensu TLL II 841.70–2 assumes that *aspirare* here is the equivalent of *adniti*. It rather seems to be a synonym of *favere*, as in Curt. 4.4.19 *licet felicitas adspirare videatur*. Perhaps Amm. chose the word as an echo of *unum spirantibus animis* (§4).

auctoritatem eius sublimitatemque cordis extollebat in caelum "die wesentliche Leistung der *auctoritas* ist es, die Soldaten zu einer Sinnesänderung zu bewegen" (Brandt, 1999, 351). Presumably, *sublimitas cordis* is a flowery variation of *magnanimitas*, a virtue ascribed to Julian *in re civili* in 16.5.9. The verb has been chosen with care: the soldiers speak highly of Julian's lofty character.

vere atque ex animo Cf. Ter. *Eun.* 175 *utinam istuc verbum ex animo ac vere diceres*, alluded to by Cat. 109.3–4. In the present text *ex animo* seems to specify the adverb: 'truly and sincerely'. Amm.'s only other instance of *ex animo* is 30.5.9: "ehrlichen Herzens" (Seyfarth).

solet armorum crepitu leni monstrari Amm.'s information about the soldiers' reactions by way of noises produced by their shields and spears lacks precision. See the notes ad 15.8.15, 20.5.8, 21.5.9, 23.5.24. In 21.5.9 the soldiers' approval of Julian's words is i.a.

CHAPTER 3.9   87

expressed by *immani scutorum fragore*. In the present situation they produced only a soft sound. According to the author this was not a bad sign, but rather proved the sincerity of their feelings.

repetitis post haec tentoriis The fact that the soldiers repair to their tents is also explicitly reported in 17.13.34, 19.5.8, 20.7.15 and 31.15.15. Here it is not superfluous, but expresses that the emotions had died down and things now returned to normal. For Roman army tents see Van Driel-Murray, 1990. **3.9**

victui se recreavit et quieti nocturnae V's *victuise creavit* etc. has been dealt with in different ways. Walter, 1914, 702 proposed to keep the dativi and to emend the verb to ⟨*se*⟩ *secrevit*: "sie trennten sich … um zu essen und ruhen". Tac. *Ann.* 2.12.3 *secreti et incustoditi inter militaris cibos* is one of the texts he adduces, but in the quoted phrase the author wanted to emphasize the fact that the soldiers were among themselves, without their officers. Baehrens, 1925, 61 rejected this solution offhand. It can be added that Amm.'s two instances of a finite form of *secernere* concern entirely different situations: in 22.8.25 it is a geographical term and in 25.3.15 the separation of body and soul at death is discussed. The other solution, *victu se recreavit*, is well supported by 14.2.12 *victu recreati et quiete* and 27.2.5 *suisque pro temporis copia cibo recreatis et somno*, but implies the emendation of V's dativi. In his bilingual edition Seyfarth accepted this, printing *victu se recreavit et quiete nocturna*. The Teubneriana, however, presents a hybrid text, which seems impossible to explain: 'they refreshed themselves in order to enjoy some food and sleep'?

cum non per caritates, sed per inchoatas negotiorum magnitudines deieraret assidue See for *caritates*, 'loved ones', the note ad 20.4.10. Amm. has a liking for *magnitudo* with a gen.; the present case is best explained as a gen. inversus: 'the great projects which had been started'. According to the TLL s.v., *deierare*, which occurs only here in Amm., is a synonym of *iurare*. Julian obviously made a habit of it: *assidue* indicates that the oath quoted was not a unique or occasional expression.

sic sub iugum mitteret Persas, ita quassatum recrearet orbem Romanum As appears from the imperfect tense, Amm. reports Julian's oath in the *oratio obliqua*. In such formulae *ita* and *sic* denote the wish for a success, which in its turn will be the condition of the vow or oath in question. See for this Appel, 1909, 152, Fordyce ad Cat. 17.5, Nisbet-Hubbard ad Hor. *Carm.* 1.2.1. Whereas in the

88   COMMENTARY

first part a characteristic phrase from Roman military history is used (it also occurs in 14.8.4, 14.10.14, 21.16.14 [as a metaphor], 23.6.83, 25.9.11), the second contains a personification; *quassare* more than once occurs in phrases denoting disease or ill health: 14.5.2 *aegrum corpus quassari etiam levibus solet offensis*, 31.4.5 *quassatus morbo letali*, Cat. 33.13–4 *hic me gravedo frigida et frequens tussis / quassavit* (see Fordyce ad loc.), Suet. *Aug.* 81.2 *quassato corpore*; *recreare* can denote physical recovery: *remediis multiplicibus recreatus* (27.6.4), (Piso Germanicum) *recreatum accepit* (Tac. *Ann.* 2.69.2). The Roman empire is a patient in need of medical treatment. See OLD s.v. *recreare* 3 for other examples concerning a political entity, e.g. *illam tu provinciam adflictam et perditam erexisti atque recreasti* (Cic. *Ver.* 3.212). For Amm.'s use of *orbis Romanus* see the notes ad 21.13.13, 22.9.1, 23.5.19.

ut Traianus fertur aliquotiens iurando dicta consuesse firmare Trajan is referred to fifteen times in Amm.; see the relevant note ad 23.5.17. His words quoted here are not attested elsewehere, nor are the *similia plurima* to which Amm. refers at the end of this section.

Mary, 1992, 610 n. 96 suggests, not very convincingly, that the reference to Trajan is possibly a hidden polemic concerning the question who really was a second Trajan, Constantine the Great or Julian the Apostate. Pointing 1) to the fact that Constantine, when he aimed at restoring Roman authority in Dacia in 328, issued a contorniate with a picture of a bridge (RIC 7 [1966] nr. 298) – this would indicate that Constantine tried to surpass Trajan in glory – and 2) to Jul. *Caes.* 329 c, where Constantine is depicted as pretending to be Trajan's equal, Mary suggests that "le passage d'Ammien pourrait être un écho subtil de cette polémique, et permettrait à l'historien de suggérer discrètement qui, de Constantin ou Julien, est le véritable émule de Trajan". Interestingly, *epit.* 48.8 regards Theodosius as a second Trajan: *Fuit autem Theodosius moribus et corpore Traiano similis.*

The pleonasm *aliquotiens…consuesse* is the counterpart of *assidue*. Cf. for (*con*)*firmare*, 'to vouch for', 16.12.64 *iurando confirmans*, 27.6.14 *His dictis sollemnitate omni firmatis.*

sic in provinciarum speciem…Aufidum superem Trajan's words have been thoroughly dealt with by Hartke, 1975. Referring to 14.8.12 (Palaestinam) *in provinciae speciem…formavit*, he argues that *species* instead of *forma* (cf. Suet. *Jul.* 25.1 *Omnem Galliam…in provinciae formam redegit*) denotes a special status different from the normal status of a province. However, *species*, 'outward appearance', does not

CHAPTER 3.10   89

necessarily imply a contrast with 'essence'. See for the plur. *Dacias*, which sounds somewhat anachronistically from Trajan's lips before the conquest of this territory, the note ad 21.5.6 and Szidat, 1996, 40–1, who remarks: "Das Problem bedürfte einer neuen generellen Untersuchung". As to *Hister*, it was noted ad 21.8.2 and 22.8.44 that the Danube is called by Amm. now *Hister* and now *Danubius*, without a difference in meaning (both names are found in one and the same section in 17.13.4, q.v.). Trajan's famous bridge over the Danube, built by Apollodorus of Damascus (Procop. *Aed.* 4.6.13), was situated just below the Iron Gates gorges near Drobeta (modern Turnu Severin). See Austin-Rankov, 1995, 176–7 with n. 8. The bridge filled Dio with awe, although in his days only the piers were still standing (D.C. 68.13.1–6). Pictures of it can be seen on Trajan's Column in Rome.

As to the second phrase, Brok 130 had already defended V's *aufidum*, which had caused the suspicion of many. How could the great river of Middle Europe be put on the same level as Apulia's regional stream? Even the fact that Horace was born near its borders could not allay the doubts. Brok, however, pointed to the construction of the via Traiana from Beneventum to Brundisium as one of the great projects of Trajan's reign. This road i.a. had to cross the Aufidus, now called Ofanto, which made the building of a permanent bridge necessary. Cf. CIL 9.6.5 *viam et pontes [a] Benevento Brundisium pecunia su[a fecit]*, sc. Traianus, and Bennett, 1997, 139. Hartke, 1975, 190 quotes ASS Febr. II, 310ff., the early medieval *vita Sabini* (see BHL 7443): *pons, qui a Traiano Augusto constructus super fluenta est Aufidi.* Hartke argues that "die beiden ungefähr um die gleiche Zeit in Gang befindliche Bauten, die berühmte Donaubrücke von Dobreta und die Aufidusbrücke an dem markantesten Punkt der berühmten *via Traiana*" (201) are totally equivalent. The explanations of Brok and Hartke are convincing, so that *et Aufidum* can be regarded as correct. Even Clark's tentative *ut Aufidum*, accepted by Fontaine, is not necessary and even wrong, since the bridge at Dobreta seems to have been completed before the one across the Aufidus. Moreover, in such oaths comparative sentences with *ut* are unusual (cf. Nisbet-Hubbard ad Hor. *Carm.* 1.3.1).

Post haec decursis milibus passuum quattuordecim ad locum quendam est **3.10** *ventum arva aquis abundantibus fecundantem* Musil, 1927, 240 observes: "Fourteen miles from al-Ambâr (Pirisaboras) brings us to the inlet of the present Daffâr canal. The low plain to the southeast is even now occasionally flooded by the Euphrates, forming a lake or

90 COMMENTARY

slough over fifteen kilometers long and one kilometer wide". In the meaning "to cover (a distance)" (OLD s.v. 8a) *decurrere* is rare; *septingenta milia passuum vis esse decursa biduo?* (Cic. *Quinct.* 81) is another instance. See also TLL V1.229.9ff. Normally the Agens of *fecundare* (of which verb this is Amm.'s only instance) in an 'agricultural' sense is water: *cum… Nilus… fecundet arva* (Sol. 1.51), (Hiberus) *locos fecundat unda* (Avien. *ora* 249). However, in the present case the 'certain spot' (or 'region') contains a system of water supply for irrigation. Amm.'s other instances of *arvum* are 14.4.3, 23.6.25 and 31.3.8. No doubt it is a predominantly poetic word, but it also occurs twice in Livy, three times in (ps.) Sallust and nine in Tacitus.

Amm. does not mention the name of the *locus* the army reached (on May 1, it would seem; see the note on chronology), but from the parallel account of Zosimus we know that it was near a city called Phissenia: Προελθὼν δὲ ἐπέκεινα, διά τε τοῦ ποταμοῦ τὴν πορείαν ποιούμενος ('along the river', not 'crossing the river', see Paschoud n. 50) ἦλθεν εἴς τι χωρίον ᾧ πόλις ἐπλησίαζε Φισσηνία προσαγορευομένη, 3.19.3. The ποταμός here must be the Euphrates (but Paschoud n. 50, in accordance with his theory referred to in the note ad 24.2.7, opts for the Naarmalcha). This city was enclosed by a deep canal filled with water obtained from the so-called Royal River: ταύτης τῷ τείχει συμπαρέθεε τάφρος, ἣν βαθυτάτην οὖσαν ἐπλήρωσαν ὕδατος οἱ Πέρσαι, μέρος εἰς ταύτην οὐκ ὀλίγον τοῦ πλησιάζοντος μετοχετεύσαντες ποταμοῦ· βασιλέως ποταμὸς ἦν ὄνομα τούτῳ. See for this βασιλέως ποταμός, "possibly on the alignment of the later Radwaniyah canal" (Matthews 151), the note ad 24.2.7. Since there were no hostilities to be feared from the inhabitants, Julian's army passed Phissenia without trying to capture it: ταύτην διαδραμόντες τὴν πόλιν (οὐδὲν γὰρ ἦν ἐκ ταύτης εὐλαβεῖσθαι πολέμιον).

Musil, 1927, 240 proposes to identify Phissenia with "the small ʿAkar an-Naʿêli ruin, lying about two kilometers from the Euphrates on the left bank of an ancient canal", but Paschoud n. 50 is sceptical: "J'estime pour ma part qu'il est vain de vouloir identifier Phissénia et Bithra soit avec des lieux mentionnés par Ammien, soit avec des ruines aujourd'hui visibles".

quo itinere nos ituros Persae praedocti sublatis cataractis undas evagari fusius permiserunt As to *itinere… ituros*, Szantyr 124–5 has a long list of instances of "einem etymologischen bzw. 'ausmalenden' Instrumental" in the style of Verg. *A.* 1.669 *nostro doluisti saepe dolore*. As appears from TLL X 2.586.43–56, most instances of *praedocere* are forms of the perfect participle; cf. 14.2.15 *horum adventum praedocti*, 22.1.2 *inspectu*

CHAPTER 3.11

iecoris, ut aiebat ipse, praedoctus (q.v.). Cf. Zos. 3.19.3 ὁδὸν διῄεσαν τέλματι χειροποιήτῳ διάβροχον. οἱ γὰρ Πέρσαι τήν τε διώρυχα τῇ χώρᾳ καὶ τὸν ποταμὸν αὐτὸν ἐπαφέντες ἀδύνατον κατά γε τὴν αὐτῶν οἴησιν πεποιήκασι τῷ στρατῷ τὴν διάβασιν ('they went by a road which deliberately was made swampy and wet; by diverting the water of the canal and the river itself over the land the Persians had made passing impossible; or so they thought'). Lib. *Or.* 18.223–227, also speaking of the opening of weirs etc., seemingly refers to the same episode. However, as Paschoud n. 50 points out, in Libanius' version this took place before the capture of Pirisabora. See for *cataracta*, 'weir', the note ad 24.1.11.

altero die militi requie data May 2 (see the note on chronology). Cf. **3.11**
Zos. 3.19.4 ἡλίου δὲ ἤδη δύντος ὁ μὲν στρατὸς ἐπὶ τῶν τόπων ηὐλίζετο τούτων.

imperator ipse praegressus This is one of the instances in Amm.'s report on the Persian expedition which show that Julian's prominent personal role loomed large in the author's memory. Zos. 3.19.4 also focusses on the emperor's leadership in the present situation and his precise orders to the sappers who had to solve the problems posed by the inundation.

constratis ponticulis… traduxit There are two problems in V's text: *periculis* and *procia*. Mommsen's wish to keep the former – which would make *non sine difficultate* superfluous – entailed the emendation *constructis* (to go with *navibus*) and *cortice* for *procia*: 'when ships had been constructed from bladders and bark'. This solution seems rather strained, i.a. because in adverbial phrases with *periculum* "longe praestat sing." (TLL X 1.1468.10), as in *magno cum periculo suo* (Liv. 2.23.9), *ingenti periculo* (Liv. 21.57.3). However, Amm. does have *cum periculis ultimis evadebant* (20.11.10). On the other hand, *pontibus constratis* (17.1.2, q.v.), *ponte constrato* (18.2.14), *iniectis ponticulis* (21.12.9), *constratis… pontibus* (24.4.6, q.v.) make the variant or conjecture *ponticulis* quite plausible. After the catastrophic failure of the expedition (inflated) leather bags were used to build temporary bridges across the Tigris: *utribus e caesorum animalium coriis coagmentare pontes architecti promittebant* (25.6.15). For a detailed draft of such a bridge cf. Anon. *de mach. bell.* 16. A not dissimilar floating bridge, made of wooden wine barrels, was made by some engineers (τινες τῶν τεχνιτῶν) of the emperor Maximinus, according to Hdn. 8.4.4 (cf. HA *Max.* 22.4 *ponte itaque cupis facto Maximinus fluvium transivit*). Cf. Mary, 1992, 597.

92   COMMENTARY

For the remaining problem *procia* Fontaine boldly conjectures *parvis*, which implies a paleographically difficult case of corruption. Heraeus' *pro copia*, accepted by Thörnell, 1927, 14, is less problematical in this respect. Moreover, Thörnell's rendering of the whole phrase is persuasive: "er schlug viele Brücken aus Schläuchen und nach Möglichkeit aus Schiffen ebenso wie aus abgesägten Palmenstämmen und führte so nicht ohne Schwierigkeit das Heer über". For the bridges emergency materials, such as bags and beams were used in addition to the normally employed ships, 'as far as these were available' at the time. The added advantage is the absence of any need to emend the perfectly explicable *consectis* to *confectis* (Heraeus) or *contectis* (Fontaine). The resulting text essentially tallies with the first half of Zosimus' report on the measures which were taken: βασιλεὺς δὲ στρατιώτας ἑαυτῷ καὶ τεχνίτας ἀκολουθεῖν ἐπιτάξας δένδρα ἐκτέμνων καὶ ξύλα διωρύχας τε ἐζεύγνυε, τοῖς τέλμασί τε γῆν ἐπετίθει, καὶ τὰ βαθέα τῶν ὁδῶν ἀπεπλήρου, καὶ ταῖς στενοχωρίαις εὖρος ἐνεποίει τὸ μέτριον ἔχον (3.19.4). In contrast to this report and the parallel in Libanius (καὶ αὐτίκα πλείους μὲν ἐπὶ γῆς οἱ φοίνικες, συχναὶ δὲ ἀπὸ τούτων αἱ γέφυραι, *Or.* 18.234) Amm. especially remembered the leather bags; Zosimus or his source was also impressed by the painstaking work of filling swamps and widening roads with earth. *Utres,* leather bags inflated or filled with hay (Arr. *An.* 5.12.3: ἐπληροῦντο τῆς νυκτὸς αἱ διφθέραι τῆς κάρφης), were sometimes used to keep a person or a thing afloat in water and to transport him (or it) across a stream. See e.g. Caes. *Civ.* 1.48.7, Sal. *Hist.* 3.37, Liv. 21.27.5, Suet. *Jul.* 57 and Curt. 7.8.6 (*super utres iubet nare levius armatos*). In Amm. the word is found in this sense in 25.8.2 (soldiers crossed the Tigris *supersidentes utribus*). In 30.1.9 we find a slight variant: the Armenian king Pap crossed the Euphrates on beds fastened upon two *utres* . He had had no problem in finding them, since there was an abundant supply in the country where he then was (*quorum erat abundans prope in agris vinariis copia*, 30.1.9). Neither had Julian, it would seem, for he too had *vineae* at hand: *agri...plures consiti vineis* (24.3.12). Otherwise animals had to be killed, as in the case of the Rhodian in Xenophon's *Anabasis*, who said he needed two thousand skin bags to transport the Greeks across the Tigris: Ἀσκῶν, ἔφη, δισχιλίων δεήσομαι. πολλὰ δ᾽ ὁρῶ πρόβατα καὶ αἶγας καὶ βοῦς καὶ ὄνους, ἃ ἀποδαρέντα καὶ φυσηθέντα ῥαδίως ἂν παρέχοι τὴν διάβασιν (X. *An.* 3.5.9). Whether there was in the army a special corps of *utricularii*, as Rolfe suggests, is doubtful. They are nowhere attested (the *utric(u)larii* of southern Gaul, mentioned in CIL 12.187, 12.7. and 12.4107, were civilians).

CHAPTER 3.12–3   93

During their northward march from Cynaxa the 'Ten Thousand' had also used palm trees to cross inundated land: ἀλλ᾽ ἐποιοῦντο διαβάσεις ἐκ τῶν φοινίκων οἳ ἦσαν ἐκπεπτωκότες, τοὺς δὲ καὶ ἐξέκοπτον (X. *An.* 2.3.10).

non sine difficultate traduxit This differs from διῆγε τὴν στρατιὰν μετὰ ῥᾳστώνης (Zos. 3.19.4). However, in the eyes of Klotz, 1916, 488–9, *non sine* is here "ein ungeschickter Pleonasmus der Negation", an explanation for which the relevant discussion in Szantyr 802–7 offers no parallel. One should either assume that *non* wrongly crept into the textual tradition (*non sine* occurs a dozen times in Amm.) or simply accept the difference from Zosimus, which after all should not be exaggerated by assuming that *non sine difficultate* is necessarily a litotes.

Amm. interrupts his report on the progress of Julian's invasion for a delightful short digression, which is caused by his wish to explain the phrase *consectis palmarum trabibus* in § 11. Both *visa* and *lecta* contribute to the digression, which conveys something of the impression which the huge plantations of date palms must have made on those partaking in the expedition. Apart from dates these palms produced timber and fibres. Valesius refers to Plutarch's report that the natives ascribed an impressive range of advantages to the palm trees: Βαβυλώνιοι μὲν γὰρ ὑμνοῦσι καὶ ᾄδουσιν ὡς ἑξήκοντα καὶ τριακόσια χρειῶν γένη παρέχον αὐτοῖς τὸ δένδρον (Plut. *Quaest. conv.* 8.4.5 = *Mor.* 724e). The corresponding passages in Zosimus and Libanius are 3.20.1 and *Or.* 18.234, respectively.   **3.12–3**

consiti vineis varioque pomorum genere Cf. the similar phrase about a place in Mesopotamia in 18.6.16 *locum vineis arbustisque pomiferis consitum.* The presence of vines deserves attention. In Herodotus' time the Mesopotamian soil produced οὔτε συκέην οὔτε ἄμπελον οὔτε ἐλαίην (1.193), but Zosimus also explicitly mentions the vines in this region: ἄμπελοι παραπεφύκεσαν ἄχρι τῆς τῶν φοινίκων κόμης τοῖς κλήμασιν ἀνατρέχουσαι (3.20.1). Seyfarth seems right in rejecting the attempt of Walter, 1925, 438 to allay Clark's doubts c.c. by adding *uberes* after *genere.* The haplography which is presumably assumed is indeed not entirely impossible, but there is no parallel for this emendation in Amm. and *arbor ibi niveis uberrima pomis* (Ov. *Met.* 4.89) only proves that *uber* can occur with *poma* as its complement.   **3.12**

ubi oriri… nemorum Mark *assuetae*: this detail alone indicates that being an eye-witness was not the author's only source of information.

94 COMMENTARY

Moreover, the expedition did not reach Mesene, the region where the Euphrates and the Tigris entered the Persian Gulf, which, presumably as part of the Indian Ocean, must be meant by *mare… magnum*. This does not seem to have been a standard name for one particular sea only. It is used to denote the Atlantic in *illo mari quod Atlanticum, quod magnum, quem Oceanum appellatis* (Cic. *Rep.* 6.21) and *In eo* (viz. Europe's first great gulf) *maria nuncupantur: unde inrumpit, Atlanticum, ab aliis Magnum* (Plin. *Nat.* 3.74), but in Plin. *Nat.* 9.47 *intrant e magno mari Pontum* it obviously denotes the Mediterranean. Mesene, also called Characene, the southern part of modern Iraq, stretched from the head of the Persian Gulf to the confluence of Euphrates and Tigris and had as its chief city Charax Spasinu, formerly called Alexandria (Plin. *Nat.* 6.138). For quotations of classical and talmudic sources mentioning Mesene and a short history of the country see Oppenheimer, 1983, 241–56 (note, however, that Amm. 23.6.23 and 43, cited in Oppenheimer's list, are irrelevant, for the *Mesene* and *Charax* mentioned in these passages are to be sought elsewhere; see our notes ad loc.). Cf. also Potts, 1988 and Bowersock, 1989.

termites et spadica The specific meaning of the rare word *spadix* is provided by Gel. 3.9.9 *palmae termes ex arbore cum fructu avulsus spadix dicitur.* Amm.'s alternative *spadicum* is unique.

ex fructu mellis et vini conficitur abundantia TLL VIII 610.45 ff. lists a number of instances in which *mel* does not denote honey, but another sweet substance. The present one is "une sorte de liqueur qu'on obtenait en faisant bouillir les dates (φοίνικες) légèrement fermentées" (G. Lafaye in Daremberg-Saglio III 2.1704b). It was a well-known product: *mellis foenicini* (*Edict. Imp. Diocl.* 3.12 Lauffer). Cf. Hdt. 1.193 (date-palms) ἐκ τῶν καὶ σιτία καὶ οἶνον καὶ μέλι ποιεῦνται. Plin. *Nat.* 14.102 gives a very short description of the way in which palm wine was produced: *mitiorum quas vocant chydaeas modio in aquae congiis tribus macerato expressoque*, "a peck of the rather soft dates called in Greek 'common dates' being soaked in two and a quarter gallons of water and then pressed" (tr. Rackham). Pliny does not advise drinking it: *palmeum capiti noxium* (*Nat.* 23.52). The 'Ten Thousand', however, had not spurned it, taking οἶνον τε ἐκ τῆς βαλάνου ('date') πεποιημένον τῆς ἀπὸ τοῦ φοίνικος (X. *An.* 1.5.10); cf. also X. *An.* 2.3.15 ἐνῆν δὲ σῖτος πολὺς καὶ οἶνος φοινίκων καὶ ὄξος ἑψητὸν ἀπο τῶν αὐτῶν.

CHAPTER 3.13

et maritari palmae ipsae dicuntur See TLL VIII 402.79 ff. for the 'agricultural' use of *maritare*. Most often it is one of the "vivid terms of the countryman for the 'marrying up' of the vine and its supporting tree" (Fordyce ad Cat. 62.49). In the present text all the emphasis is on *ipsae*: the process was a perfectly natural one. In such a way *ipse* occurs in passages describing the Golden Age: Verg. *Buc.* 4.21–2 *ipsae lacte domum referent distenta capellae / ubera*, Tib. 1.3.45 *ipsae mella dabunt quercus.*

The phoenix dactylifera is dioecious: the feminine trees have to be pollinated by hanging male inflorescences between a crop of trees. This is already mentioned by Hdt. 1.193.5, and, more correctly and precisely, by Thphr. *HP* 2.8.4 ὅταν ἀνθῇ τὸ ἄρρεν, ἀποτέμνουσι τὴν σπάθην ἐφ' ἧς τὸ ἄνθος εὐθὺς ὥσπερ ἔχει, τόν τε χνοῦν ('bloom') καὶ τὸ ἄνθος καὶ τὸν κονιορτὸν κατασείουσι κατὰ τοῦ καρποῦ τῆς θηλείας· κἂν τοῦτο πάθῃ, διατηρεῖ καὶ οὐκ ἀποβάλλει. In Pliny's description a slightly romantic tinge is introduced: *circaque singulos plures nutare in eum pronas blandioribus comis* (*Nat.* 13.34). Small wonder that this chapter of phytography drew the attention of authors of fiction and rhetoricians, who readily enlarged on the theme. Ach. Tat. 1.17.3–5 mentions the love of palm trees as a specific instance of a widespread phenomenon: ἄλλο μὲν ἄλλου φυτὸν ἐρᾶν, τῷ δὲ φοινίκι τὸν ἔρωτα μᾶλλον ἐνοχλεῖν ('causes pain'). He then proceeds with a vivid description, which he ends with: καὶ τοῦτό ἐστι γάμος φυτοῦ. Philostr. *Im.* 1.9.6 describes that part of a painting in which the embraces of the trees were depicted. Men. Rh. 402.7 advises to make use of it in praising marriage: περὶ δὲ δένδρων ἐρεῖς, ὅτι κἀκεῖνα οὐκ ἄμοιρα γάμων. See for further examples of the humanization of trees Anderson, 1976, 27–8. Some of Amm.'s contemporaries were also acquainted with the phenomenon: Lindenbrog aptly refers to Basilius *Hex.* 5.47B as a clear parallel of Amm.'s description, e.g. τῆς συμπλοκῆς ἐφιεμένην τοῦ ἄρρενος. See also Ambrose's adaptation of this section in *hex.* 3.55: *concupiscentiae atque amplexus speciem praetendentem* and Claudianus, *Epith. dict. Hon. Aug. et Mar.* 66–7 *nutant ad mutua palmae / foedera*. Such parallels clearly suggest that Amm. found his information in *lecta*, viz. those also studied by his contemporaries.

generare feminas seminibus illitas marum For *femina* and *mas* denoting trees of different gender cf. Plin. *Nat.* 13.34 ff. See TLL VI 1795.47–55 for *generare* as a function of plants.

96   COMMENTARY

feruntque eas… avertuntur This is a very clear indication that Amm. derived his information from *lecta* or personal briefings by local experts. The latter possibility is, however, improbable: surely these experts knew better than what is offered to the reader here. As Brok 134 notes, Plin. *Nat.* 13.35 uses some comparable terms, but clearly mentions human intervention (*ab homine*) as responsible for starting the process.

abortus vitio fetus amittit intempestivos This is Amm.'s only instance of *abortus*; the genitive can be explained as subjective or as a gen. of definition. Cf. also *certe vitiis diffluunt abortivis* (23.8.86). TLL VI 1.639.7 ff. lists a large number of cases where *fetus* denotes the produce or fruit of a plant or a tree. In the present text, however, it rather continues the terminology of human (or animal) procreation.

et si qua femina, cuius arboris amore perculsa sit, ignoretur Obviously, from what he heard or read, Amm. concluded that the staff of the plantations could recognize a lovesick female tree and, in case they were in the dark as to the object of her (secret) love, were able to stimulate the natural process by a technical intervention. See for this type of sentence Kühner-Stegmann 2.581–2. The nearest parallel to the present text is Var. *L.* 7.3 (cum) *Teucer Livii* (= 'in the play of Livius Andronicus') *post XV annos ab suis qui sit ignoretur.* TLL X 1.1198.11 lists the present text as the only specimen of *perculsus amore* in a sexual sense. August. *c. acad.* 3.1.1 *at Licentius fingendis versibus vacavit, quorum amore ita perculsus est, ut…*, which could be an echo of Verg. *G.* 2.476 about love for the Muses: *ingenti percussus amore*, is a different case. The participles *percussus* and *perculsus* are often confused in the textual tradition: see e.g. Mankin ad Hor. *Epod.* 11.2, and consult Seyfarth's app. crit. ad 17.10.7, 17.13.34, 23.4.6, 29.2.28.

hisque indiciis velut coeundi quaedam proditur fides This is a difficult phrase. Sabbah 20 interprets *fides* as one of the cases in which it denotes "une vérité d'apparence, d'une 'vraisemblance' capable de convaincre, dont ne saurait pour autant se contenter un historien". His explanation of *indiciis* tallies with this: here and in other "contextes didactiques" (391) it denotes the outward signs from which something can be concluded about the object in question; cf. e.g. *hisque indiciis hoc proditum ait, quod pisces et herbae et beluae similes per eas paludes gignuntur* (22.15.8). The various translations are on these lines, e.g. "de tels indices sont à l'origine d'une certaine croyance à

CHAPTER 3.14 97

une sorte d'accouplement" (Fontaine). At first sight all this is persuasive, but then some questions arise: can the gerund *coeundi* really be construed in this way? What is the reason for adding *quaedam* (which, for that matter, is only taken account of in Fontaine's rendering)? Moreover, the signs can be said to 'indicate' a state of affairs, as in the words just quoted from 22.15.8, but *fides* in Sabbah's sense is a less likely Patiens of *prodere*. It seems at least worthwhile to attempt an alternative explanation. Amm.'s description implies that a female tree is evidently lovesick; next, its trunk is smeared with its own perfume, the sweet odour of which then attracts a male tree. The 'signs' produced by both trees betray 'as it were' a pledge to a copulation 'of sorts'. Both *coeundi* and *fides* are accompanied by a term which is apt to tone down the somewhat bold phrase, in which the 'human' colouring of the entire description reaches its climax. Cf. also 23.6.85 about the pearls: *cupientes enim velut coitum quendam*. For *fides*, 'pledge', cf. 27.12.6 *fide non amittendae salutis accepta*, 31.15.5 *fide retinendae salutis accepta*. Amm.'s use of *coire* about trees is a rarity. The only other passage noted in TLL III 1418.64–6 is Plin. *Nat.* 17.134 on *terrae ac satorum omnium libido*, which particularly manifests itself in grafts, *cum sit mutua cupiditas coeundi*.

Qua cibi copia satur Amm.'s preoccupation with palm tree erotics **3.14** obviously caused him to overlook that he had failed to mention the 'food' offered by the trees which occurs in other descriptions: the relative lacks a point of reference. See for comparable cases the note ad 23.4.2 *et hac multiplici chorda*.

plures praetergressus est insulas Zosimus is silent about these islands. Instead he says that the emperor reached a town called Bithra, where he found a royal palace and some other buildings: ἕως εἰς Βίθραν ἐληλύθει πόλιν, ἐν ᾗ βασίλεια ἦν καὶ οἰκήματα βασιλεῖ τε ὁμοῦ πρὸς ὑποδοχὴν ἀρκοῦντα καὶ στρατοπέδῳ (3.19.4). According to Musil, 1927, 240–1 the name of this town "is preserved to this day in a group of ruins (Bitra) stretching over a distance of six kilometers from 22 to 28 kilometers south-east of ʿAkar an-Naʿêli (Phissenia) on both the right and left banks of the Euphrates", but Paschoud n. 50 (quoted above ad § 10) is sceptical about this identification. See for Bithra also below, ad 24.4.1.

ubi formidabatur inopia, ibi timor saginae gravis incessit In his edition of Zosimus Paschoud n. 51, following in the track of Thompson, 1947, 134–5 and Dillemann, 1961, 148–9, refers to Eunapius *fr.* 27.5

98 COMMENTARY

Ὅτι τοσαύτη ἐν τοῖς προαστείοις Κτησιφῶντος ἀφθονία τῶν ἐπιτηδείων ἦν ὥστε τὴν περίουσιαν κίνδυνον τοῖς στρατιώταις φέρειν μήποτε ὑπὸ τρυφῆς διαφθαρῶσιν ("The great abundance of supplies in the suburbs of Ctesiphon raised the danger that the soldiers would be ruined by excess", tr. Blockley). The place differs (Eunapius refers this circumstance to the approaches to Ctesiphon instead of to those to Maozamalcha), but the problem is similar. For *incedere*, 'to arise' (of mental states, OLD s.v. 6b), cf. Caes. *Civ.* 3.44.6 *magnusque incesserat timor sagittarum*. Sagina figures in passages of overeating: *saginisque distenti marcebant* (21.12.15, q.v.), 22.12.6, 28.4.34. Vitellius was *medio diei temulentus et sagina gravis* (Tac. *Hist.* 1.62.2).

impetu latenti temptatus neque inultus The abl. *impetu* occurs frequently in Amm. and is accompanied by various adjectives, e.g. *repentino* (seven times), *veloci* (three). This is the only instance of *latenti*. Cf. *impetu clandestino* (31.11.4). Julian's army did not refrain from such secret attacks either: *nocte obumbrante impetum clandestinum* (24.1.6). *Inultus* occurs regularly in the report of battles: *conabantur modis omnibus vitam impendere non inultam* (31.13.6), *cavete inulti animam amittatis* (Sal. *Cat.* 58.21), *pauci gladiatorum resistentes neque inulti cecidere* (Tac. *Hist.* 3.77.2, with Heubner's note). See also the note ad 23.5.17 *nec erravere diu manes eius inulti*.

in rivos dividitur multifidos The meaning of *pars maior Euphratis* must be: 'the main stream of the Euphrates', that is, that part of the Euphrates which after the bifurcation mentioned in 24.2.7 flowed into the direction of Babylon (Paschoud's alternative interpretation is cited in the note ad 24.2.7). One of the *rivi multifidi* seems to have been what Ptolemy 5.18.8 (Ἡ τοῦ Εὐφράτου θέσις, καθ᾽ ἣν σχίζεται εἴς τε τὸν διὰ Βαβυλῶνος ῥέοντα καὶ τὸν διὰ Σελευκείας, ὧν ὁ μεταξὺ καλεῖται Βασίλειος ποταμός) and a text in the Babylonian Talmud, Qiddushin 70b (= Oppenheimer, 1983, 279 nr. 12), knew as the 'royal river' (cf. for *rivus* 23.6.25: *Euphrates ... qui tripertitus navigabilis per omnes est rivos*). It was this 'royal river' or Naarmalcha that Julian's army and fleet from now on followed (see for this the note ad 24.2.7).

For *multifidus* see the note ad 23.4.14 *sagitta est cannea*.

CHAPTER 4

Introduction

After burning down a deserted Jewish settlement (§1), the army, full of confidence, reaches 'Maozamalcha' (§2; see for the inverted commas the note ad 24.4.2). The siege and capture of this important and well defended city is the central event in this long chapter (§2–30). We may safely assume that Amm. witnessed the siege, but his description contains extended passages which are entirely conventional and interchangeable with accounts of other sieges. This blend of personal experience and historical topoi is typical of Amm.'s manner.

The following stages in the siege may be distinguished:

2   The Romans pitch a provisional camp near 'Maozamalcha'.

3–4   During a reconnaissance patrol Julian and his small retinue are attacked from the city. The emperor shows great courage and personally kills one of the attackers. There is a remarkable similarity between this incident and the risk run by Julian when he inspected the *celsum castellum* near Ctesiphon (24.5.6, q.v.). Sapor, too, had almost lost his life in a similar situation, when he explored Amida (19.1.5).

5   The fact that Julian took the *spolia* off two of the attackers prompts a comparison between his bravery and the feat of Torquatus who killed a giant Gaul. The comparison serves to underline the bravery of Julian, who is shown to be in no way inferior to the heroes of Rome's ancient history. The comparisons with Fabricius Luscinus in §24 and Hector in 24.6.14 serve the same purpose.

6   The Romans build a safe camp on the other side of the river. Julian begins the siege of 'Maozamalcha', because he does not want to have enemies in his back on his march toward Ctesiphon.

7–9   An attack by the Surên is repelled. The inhabitants of two cities, whose names are not mentioned by Ammianus, flee partly to Ctesiphon and partly further inland. Julian sees to it that the barbarians bear the burden of the war on their territory and that the provincials do not suffer from it.

100 COMMENTARY

10–12   'Maozamalcha' is described as well-nigh impregnable. Its defenders are courageous and willing to give their lives for the city.

13–14   The technical superiority of the Romans and their methodical approach finally ensure their victory. The general Victor reports that the roads to Ctesiphon are open.

15–17   The warring parties are described. The fighting on the first day remains undecided.

18–20   A first success is booked on the second day, when a battering ram destroys a wall tower, but the resistance of the garrison remains unbroken.

21–23   A second breakthrough is forced by the sappers who have dug a tunnel and emerge within the walls of the city.

24   A comparison with Fabricius Luscinus, who was helped by Mars himself. The god did not give the Romans the opportunity to thank him. The brave men who had dug their way into the city did get their traditional rewards.

25–27   The city is taken and set on fire. The inhabitants are killed. The commander Nabdates is spared by Julian. When the booty is divided Julian is content with a small share. He behaves impeccably towards the captive Persian women.

28   A military engineer is killed when a scorpio backfires.

29–30   A last threat to the victorious army is averted.

31   A son of Sapor rides out to stop Victor from crossing a river, but draws back on seeing the size of the Roman army.

4.1   *civitas ob muros humiles ab incolis Iudaeis deserta* The town is perhaps to be identified with Neherda, Josephus' Νέερδα (*AJ* 18.379), and modern Tall Nihar on the left bank of the Euphrates (so e.g. Brok 135 and Oppenheimer, 1983, 286). Mannert and others, cited by Paschoud and Klein, proposed to identify the city mentioned here with Zosimus' Bithra (3.19.4; cf. the note ad 24.3.14), but Klein (1914, 101), Musil (1927, 241) and Paschoud (n. 50) are, without doubt wisely, sceptical. The date of the burning of this Jewish city will have been May, 6 (see the note on chronology).

    This is the fourth (and last) time in his extant work that Amm. refers to Jews (the other passages are 14.8.12, 22.5.5; 23.1.2–3 is about the temple in Jerusalem). It is the only time that he refers to Jews outside *Palaestina* (see for this province the note ad 22.5.5). As to Mesopotamian Jewry, ever since the Babylonian captivity of the sixth century B.C., Jews have been attested in the land between Euphrates and Tigris, where they lived first under Babylonian, and subsequent-

CHAPTER 4.1

ly Achaemenid, Seleucid, Parthian and Sasanian rule. According to Josephus they totaled in his days 'countless myriads, whose number cannot be ascertained' (μυριάδες ἄπειροι καὶ ἀριθμῷ γνωρισθῆναι μὴ δυνάμεναι, *AJ* 11.133; cf. Ph. *Leg. ad Gaium* 216, 245 and 282). The destruction of the temple in Jerusalem under Vespasian and, in the second century, the suppression of the Jewish revolt during Trajan's reign and the defeat of Bar Kokhba under Hadrian, set in motion a new wave of migration from Palestine to the trans-Euphrates regions, while under the Sasanians Babylonia had superseded even Palestine as the leading Jewish center (cf. Oppenheimer, 1983, 15 and see in general for the Sasanian period Neusner, 1986; Theophylactus Simocatta *Hist.* 5.6 refers to the time of Vespasian: τῶν γὰρ Ἱεροσολύμων ὑπὸ Οὐεσπασιανοῦ τοῦ αὐτοκράτορος ἁλόντων, τοῦ τε ναοῦ ἐμπεπραμένου, ὀρρωδοῦντες πολλοὶ τῶν Ἰουδαίων τὴν Ῥωμαίων ἀλκὴν ἐκ τῆς Παλαιστίνης ὡς τοὺς Μήδους καὶ πρὸς τὴν ἀρχέγονον τιθήνην μεταναστεύουσιν, ἐξ ἧς ὁ προπάτωρ ἐτύγχανεν ὢν Ἀβραάμ). Neherda, Sura, Pumbedita and Mahoza (see for the last mentioned city the note ad § 2) had the most important Jewish communities in Mesopotamia, but there were many more. Dura Europos for instance, mentioned by Amm. in 23.5.8 and 24.1.5, had a synagogue, noted for the murals on its inside walls (now to be seen in the museum of Damascus).

In its literal meaning *humilis* is rare in Amm.; 20.7.1 *ubi loca suspecta sunt et humilia, duplici muro vallatum.* Normally *humilis* refers to social position. Cf. the note ad 22.9.9.

iratorum manu militum conflagravit Cf. 24.2.2 *alia postridie castra… praetereuntur incensa.* The reason for the soldiers' anger is not indicated. Fontaine n. 369 plausibly suggests that they were frustrated because the inhabitants had taken their belongings with them when they left the city. In other cases the anger of the soldiers is provoked by the stubborn resistance of the defenders, as in Bezabde: *magna denique mole ancipiti diu exitio renitentes obsessi postremo plebis immensae ponderibus effuse disiecti sunt. et post haec iratorum hostium gladii, quidquid inveniri poterat, concidebant* (20.7.15). When 'Maozamalcha' is finally taken, *quidquid impetus repperit, potestas iratorum absumpsit* (24.4.25).

placida ope numinis, ut arbitrabatur, erectior A similar remark is made about the army as a whole after the capture of the fortress Anatha: 24.1.12 *affore sibi etiam deinde dei caelestis existimans curam.* See also the note ad 24.6.16. The cautious authorial comment *ut arbitrabatur* has prospective force. See also Wittchow, 2.1, 199. For the comparative

102 COMMENTARY

erectior cf. 26.8.4 *spe prosperorum erectior.* In both cases the comparative may have its full force, as recent events had made the emperors more confident than they were before.

4.2 *cumque Maozamalcha venisset, urbem magnam et validis circumdatam moenibus* It will have taken two days, i.e. May 7–8, to reach 'Maozamalcha' – this, *Maozamalcha*, is the spelling of the Fuldensis adopted by Seyfarth (Gelenius has *Maiozamalcham*, while in 25.8.18 both V and G read *Maiozamalchae*). Fontaine has coined *Mahozamalcha*, which is, however, not attested in the manuscripts, but refers to Aramaic mahoza malkha, 'royal capital'.

The name Maozamalcha raises yet another problem, as Matthews 155–6 observes. Mahoza ('market' or 'town') was the Aramaic name for one of the most important Jewish centres of Babylonia, but, as Talmudic sources make absolutely clear, Mahoza was situated on the banks of the Tigris; therefore it cannot be identical with Amm.'s Maozamalcha, which was situated some 18 kilometers west of the Tigris (Zos. 3.21.5, quoted ad § 13; for talmudic and other sources with regard to the Mahoza area see Oppenheimer, 1983, 179–193; cf. also Stern, 1980, 611). Mahoza is Coche-Ctesiphon, the twin city formed when Coche, or Vēh-Ardašīr, was built in the third century A.D. to replace Hellenistic Seleucia. The Aramaic placename Maozamalcha (malkha meaning 'royal') apparently also refers to Coche-Ctesiphon, "for it would be strange if unadorned 'Mahoza' meant Coche-Ctesiphon while '*royal* Mahoza' were some other place than the Persian capital. It looks as if Ammianus has misnamed the fortress besieged by Julian, either by simple error or possibly by confusing the name of the district in which the fortress stood with that of the fortress itself. A Greek source called the district round Ctesiphon the 'land of the people called the Mauzanitai' – that is, of Mahoza – and some such description as this may be the source of Ammianus' confusion" (Matthews 156) – the Greek source referred to is Malalas (*Chron.* 13.330) καὶ κατῆλθεν ὁ βασιλεὺς μετὰ τοῦ στρατοῦ παντὸς διὰ τῆς μεγάλης διόρυγος τοῦ Εὐφράτου τῆς μισγούσης τῷ Τίγρητι ποταμῷ· καὶ εἰσῆλθεν εἰς τὸν αὐτὸν Τίγρητα ποταμόν· ὅπου μίγνυνται οἱ δύο ποταμοὶ καὶ ἀποτελοῦσι λίμνην μεγάλην. καὶ παρέβαλεν εἰς τὰ Περσικὰ ἐν τῇ χώρᾳ τῶν λεγομένων Μαυζανιτῶν, πλησίον Κτησιφῶντος πόλεως, ἔνθα ὑπῆρχε τὸ Περσικὸν βασίλειον.

The siege and capture of the fortress called Maozamalcha by Amm. will have taken five days (May 9–13; see the note on chronology). In the end the city was totally destroyed (*civitas ampla et populosa virtute roboris excisa Romani in pulverem concidit et ruinas,* 24.4.30). The

CHAPTER 4.2   103

fortress lay undoubtedly near the Naarmalcha, but where its ruins
are to be sought is not altogether clear (in this Paschoud n. 52 and
Matthews 155 concur; they disagree as to the location of the Naarmalcha, as we have seen in the note ad 24.2.7). However, Musil,
1927, 241 confidently believes the heap of ruins at the present Hân
az-Zâd, eighteen kilometers west of Ctesiphon, to be the remains of
the city which Amm. calls Maozamalcha.

Neither Zosimus nor Libanius mention Amm.'s Maozamalcha by
name, but there can be no doubt that the φϱούϱιον of Zos. 3.20.2 ff.
and Lib. *Or.* 18.235 ff. is identical with Amm.'s Maozamalcha. It was,
as Zosimus says, situated on a hill, had two walls (cf. *muris duplicibus* in
24.4.10) and sixteen towers, while a deep canal surrounded the place
(Τοῦ δὲ φϱουϱίου κειμένου μὲν ἐπὶ λόφου, τείχεσι δὲ δύο καὶ πύϱγοις
ἐκκαίδεκα μεγάλοις ὠχυϱωμένου, πέϱιξ τε τάφϱῳ πεϱιειλημμένου βαθείᾳ,
3.21.3). In its neighbourhood were situated a town called Besouchis
and some other forts (Πόλις τε γὰϱ ἐπλησίαζεν αὐτῷ Βησουχὶς ὄνομα,
πολυάνθϱωπος, καὶ ἄλλα φϱούϱια πλεῖστα, 3.20.5).

Libanius (*Or.* 18.235) gives the following description: ἦν γάϱ
τι φϱούϱιον καϱτεϱὸν καὶ τοῦτο ἐν νήσῳ ὄχθου τε καὶ τείχους μέτϱῳ
πϱὸς ἀέϱα ἀνεστηκός, τοσοῦτον ἦν ἑκατέϱου τὸ ὕψος. τὸ μὲν οὖν κάτω
πλὴν κομιδῇ τινος μικϱοῦ πεϱιέζωστο δονάκων πυκνότητι κϱυπτούσῃ
τοὺς ὑδϱευομένους οἳ διὰ καταβάσεως ἀδήλου τοῖς ἔξω κατὰ πολλὴν
ἐξουσίαν ὑπὸ ταῖς τῶν δονάκων κόμαις ἐχϱῶντο τῷ ποταμῷ, τὸ τεῖχος
δὲ κϱεῖττον ἦν μηχανημάτων, τοῦτο μὲν ἐπὶ νήσου πεποιημένον ἦν εἴσω
πᾶσαν εἶχεν αὐτοῦ, τοῦτο δὲ ἐφ᾽ οὕτως ὑψηλῆς, καὶ πϱοσῆν τὸ πλίνθον
ὀπτὴν πϱὸς ἑαυτὴν ἀσφάλτῳ δεδέσθαι ("There was a strong fortress,
this too situated on an island, and because of the combination of
bank and wall, both of them being so high, it soared up to the sky. At
its foot, except for a very small area, there was an encircling growth
of dense reeds that concealed the water carriers who, by means of a
pathway down, invisible to anyone outside, made full use of the river
under cover of the reed-bed. The wall was too high to be attacked
by engines, first because it was built on an island and encircled it
completely, and again, because the island was so sheer; finally, the
baked bricks of which it was composed were bound together by
bitumen", tr. Norman).

There is an interesting statement concerning the site of 'Maozamalcha' in Zosimus' account which is missing in both Amm. and
Libanius, viz. that the city was at a distance of ninety stadia (i.e. some
17 km) from Ctesiphon (3.21.5; see below ad 24.4.13). This is a very
valuable piece of information indeed, for it implies, if correct, that
Julian's army, after having followed the course of the Euphrates up

104   COMMENTARY

to the Jewish city mentioned in 24.4.1, finally had turned eastwards
into the direction of Ctesiphon on the Tigris (along the Naarmalcha,
it would seem; cf. the note ad 24.2.7).

tentoriis fixis providit sollicite, ne This was on May 8, presumably. For
tentoria figere see the notes ad 20.11.6 and 24.3.9. Amm. repeatedly
stresses the caution and the diligence of Julian as an army commander. These characteristics, together with the examples of his personal
valour, prepare the reader for the comparison with the heroes of the
past in section 5.

equitatus Persici... accursu The noun *accursus* is normally, but not
exclusively, used of cavalry. Cf. 17.1.7 *hinc equitum nostrorum accursu,
inde... militum impetu repentino perterrefacti*; TLL I 345.4–21.

cuius fortitudo See for the Persian cavalry the note ad 24.2.5. In
23.6.80 the Persians in general were characterised as *acerrimi bellatores, sed magis artifices quam fortes eminusque terribiles*, so that *fortitudo*
refers to the effectiveness of the cavalry rather than to their "valour"
(Rolfe). Seyfarth's "Schlagkraft" is exactly right. Cf. Brandt, 1999,
319.

immane quantum gentibus est formidata There is a note on *immane
quantum* and similar expressions ad 23.6.78. For *gentes* 'the whole
world' see the note ad 21.5.9 *fortunatum dominatorem gentium.*

4.3   *et hoc disposito* A transitional phrase, in which *et* has only connective
force, cf. 16.12.23 *Hoc itaque disposito,* 17.1.5 *quo ita disposito* and
21.12.3 *Hisque dispositis.*

*stipatus velitibus paucis ipse quoque pedes civitatis situm diligenti inqui-
sitione exploraturus* On May 9, it would seem. Cf. Zos. 3.20.3 ὁ
βασιλεὺς...τὸ φρούριον ἀνεσκόπει, καὶ ὅπου ἁλώσιμον εἴη περιιὼν ἐθεώ-
ρει. Note, however, that in Zosimus' version the emperor was wounded before he explored the position of the city, not while he was
doing so, as Amm., more logically, states. What the emperor was in-
vestigating is stated more fully in 21.12.14 *diligenter inquirens, qua
vi vel machinis posset patefactam irrumpere civitatem.* The role of the
velites has been discussed ad 24.1.13. The small number of the
guards and the vulnerability of the emperor on foot creates suspense.

CHAPTER 4.4   105

praecipitatus Intransitive *praecipitare* is found also in 15.10.5 *incessum praecipitantem*, of a fall into an abyss, and in 22.15.9 of the Nile *e quibus praecipitans ruit potiusquam fluit*; TLL X 2.465.3–70.

ex ipso vitae discrimine tandem emersit Cf. Lib. *Or*. 18.236 καὶ μικρὸν ἀποσχεῖν τοῦ καὶ τὸν βασιλέα τρῶσαι. For similar incidents in Amm. see the introduction to this chapter. For some examples elsewhere of generals whose personal reconnaissance of the enemy's position exposed them to extreme danger see Austin-Rankov, 1995, 63–4. Both *ipse* and *tandem* emphasize the risk Julian had run. Cf. the note ad 24.2.14 *omnes aleae*. For the 'expressive' use of *tandem*, by which an event is deemed to be beyond the speaker's expectations, see Risselada 1998, 107–9. The expression as a whole seems to have been taken from V. Max. 2.10.6 *Marius... ex ipso vitae discrimine... emersit*.

namque per latentem oppidi portam Amm. uses *namque* "to introduce an   **4.4**
example or an illustration" (OLD). For that reason it is less appropriate for *namque* to open a new section, as here and in 16.8.12, 17.11.2 and 23.5.3. The division of the text into sections, which was introduced by Wagner (see Erfurdt's preface p. v) is sometimes inconsistent, cf. 23.1.6 *praecesserat aliud saevum; namque kalendis ipsis* e.q.s. and 22.4.2. *Per latentem oppidi portam* causes suspicion. A city gate could hardly be hidden from view and *oppidi* is otiose. *Oppidi portam* may, however, have been intended as an explanation of *posticam*, which is the word Amm. always uses in similar circumstances, cf. 14.1.6 *latenter intromissi per posticas in regiam*, 19.8.5 *in abstrusa quadam parte oppidi... postica... evado*, 20.11.22 *reserata latenter postica*, 21.12.13 *qui erumpebant clanculo per posticas*, 27.12.3 *iussit ad latentem trahi posticam*.

degressi imaque clivorum pervadentes poplitibus subsidendo In the parallel descriptions of the siege of 'Maozamalcha' by Libanius and Zosimus it is stated explicitly that the fortress was situated on a hill: Lib. *Or*. 18.235 φρούριον... ὄχθου τε καὶ τείχους μέτρῳ πρὸς ἀέρα ἀνεστηκός; Zos. 3.21.3 Τοῦ δὲ φρουρίου κειμένου... ἐπὶ λόφου, which explains both *degressi* and *ima clivorum*. Libanius adds that the foot of the hill was covered with reeds, which probably hid the Persians from view: τὸ μὲν οὖν κάτω... περιέζωστο δονάκων πυκνότητι. *Poplitibus subsidendo* is taken from Verg. *A*. 12.491–2 *se collegit in arma / poplite subsidens* of Aeneas crouching behind his shield. A slightly different posture is described in 16.12.48 *laevum reflectens poplitem barbarus subsidebat*, where it is used of an Alaman, who continues to fight whilst supporting himself on his left knee. Here it must mean that the Persian

106 COMMENTARY

soldiers crossed the ground at the foot of the hill whilst crouching down. The abl. gerundii, for which see the note ad 23.6.79 *nec stando mingens*, offers a welcome alternative for the present participle.

conspectiorem habitu principem The reader is reminded of a similar attack on Sapor described in 19.7.8 *rex... quia conspectior tegentium multitudine procul speculantibus visebatur, petitus crebritate telorum*. For the imperial dress Alföldi, 1980³, 175 starts from Amm.'s description of the proclamation of Procopius in 26.6.15, where we find the purple mantle (*paludamentum*), the *tunica auro distincta*, the purple breeches (*purpureis opertus tegminibus pedum*), the *hasta* and the *mappa*, (*purpureum... pannulum laeva manu gestabat*). In the field the *paludamentum* will have been conspicuous.

erectum altius scutum This puzzling detail is explained by the account in Zosimus, who tells us that the Persian soldier went for Julian's head: κεφαλῇ τὸ ξίφος ἐπήλασεν· ὃ δὲ προιδόμενος ἐπέθηκε τὴν ἀσπίδα τῇ κεφάλῃ (3.20.2). See for *scutum* the note ad 21.2.1.

magna elataque fiducia For *elatus* see the note ad 21.4.7.

unius lateri ferrum infixit The incident is differently related by Libanius and Zosimus. Libanius tells us only that the emperor nearly got wounded (*Or.* 18.236 μίκρον ἀποσχεῖν τοῦ καὶ τὸν βασιλέα τρῶσαι). According to Zos. 3.20.3 the soldier who attacked Julian was killed by the guardsmen: οἱ στρατιῶται συμπεσόντες κατέσφαξαν, which resembles the fate of the second soldier in Amm.'s version, whom *stipatores multiplicatis ictibus occiderunt*.

alterum stipatores multiplicatis ictibus occiderunt As De Jonge notes ad 16.10.2 and 17.13.6, *stipator* is not a t.t. See further the note ad 20.8.14. As to *multiplicatis ictibus*, the same expression occurs in 19.11.15. In 29.6.14 we find *geminatis ictibus*.

residuis There is a note on *residuus* as the equivalent of *reliquus* ad 20.4.6.

spoliatisque ambobus Although the rank of the two victims is not indicated, the context evokes the *spolia opima* of ancient times; cf. e.g. Liv. 1.10.6. The association with the heroic feats of Torquatus and Valerius may have been triggered by the mention of the *spolia*, which figure in the descriptions by Livy (7.10.11, 26.7), although

CHAPTER 4.5   107

Gellius (9.11.13) does not mention the *spolia* explicitly. The two
heroes are, as in the present text, often mentioned in one breath,
cf. e.g. Liv. 9.17.12 (*Manlius Torquatus aut Valerius Corvus*), Ov. *Fast.*
1.601–2, V. Max. 3.2.6 and Flor. *Epit.* 1.8 [01.13]. Cf. for Amm.'s use
of such *exempla* Blockley, 1994 (esp. p. 57: "The range and selection
of the *exempla* locate Julian firmly in the Roman historical tradition").
See now also Wittchow, 2.1.

cum exuviis Amm. uses *exuviae* in its literal meaning 'hide' in 20.7.13
umectis taurinis copertus exuviis and 16.12.39 *velut senectutis pandentis
exuvias*, "like the slough of a serpent" (Rolfe). In 25.1.6 *cuius exuviis
interfector Iuliano oblatis* and 28.2.14 *exuviis referti multorum*, as here,
the *exuviae* are the spoils. Finally, in 14.8.15 *velut hostiles eius exuviae*
and 15.13.4 *Romanis ductoribus ad colligendas oboedientium exuvias
occupatis* they refer to stolen riches.

susceptus For *suscipere* = *accipere* or *recipere* see the notes ad 17.13.23,
20.2.3 and 22.14.1 *nulla probabili.*

sustulit in hoste prostrato aureum colli monile Cf. Liv. 7.10.11 *iacentis*   **4.5**
inde corpus... torque spoliavit. For T. Manlius Imperiosus Torquatus see
Münzer, 1930, Broughton, 1951, 119–20 and Oakley, 1985, 393–4.
The main source for the story of Manlius' duel with the Gaul which
earned him the cognomen Torquatus (it is variously dated to 367,
361, 358 and 357 B.C.) is, apart from Liv. 7.9.6–10.14, Gel. 9.13.

*fudit confidentissimum Gallum alitis propugnatione Valerius, postea cogno-
mento Corvinus* The wording suggests that Amm. is quoting Gellius
9.11.1 *De Marco Valerio, qui Corvinus appellatus est ob auxilium propug-
nationemque corvi alitis* and 9.11.8 *opera alitis propugnatus*; see Hertz,
1874, 279. *Propugnatio* is a hapax in Amm. For *confidens* see the
note ad 20.4.18 *capiti Iuliani.* The form *Corvinus* is e.g. found in
Gel. 9.11.1, Flor. *Epit.* 1.8 [01.13], V. Max. 8.13.1 and D.H. 15.1.4
(ἐπωνυμίαν...Κορβῖνου). The manuscripts of Livy most often have
Corvus (cf. e.g. 7.26.12 *M. Valerium Corvum – id enim illi deinde cog-
nominis fuit*), which is also found in e.g. CIL I² p. 20.44 and Tac.
Ann. 1.9.2. With *alitis propugnatione* Amm. of course refers to the traditional Roman explanation that Valerius adopted this cognomen
because he had received assistance from a raven when he fought
in single combat against a Gaul in 349 B.C. Modern interpretations
differ. Some scholars suggest that the capture of a Gallic helmet
with a raven on top may have led to the cognomen, others that an

108   COMMENTARY

old theme from Italian legend has been associated with the exploits
of Valerius. See for this Oakley, 1985, 394 and Köves-Zulauf, 1985;
for M. Valerius Corvus in general Volkmann, 1948 and Broughton,
1951, 129–30.

hacque gloria posteritati sunt commendati Cf. 16.10.3 *ut glorias suas poster-
itatis celebri memoriae commendarent* and Cic. *de Orat.* 2.36 *historia… qua
voce alia nisi oratoris immortalitati commendatur?*

accedat hoc quoque monumentis veteribus Just like the tale of Valerius:
est in libris annalibus memorata (Gel. 9.11.2) and that of Torquatus,
as recorded by Quadrigarius (Gel. 9.13). Amm. may also have had
Vergil in mind: *A.* 3.102 *veterum volvens monumenta virorum.*

4.6 *Constratis postridie pontibus exercituque travecto* On May 10 (see the
note on chronology). Bliembach, 1976, 169 and Paschoud n. 52
would have it that Lib. *Or.* 18.237 ἔπειτα γεφύρᾳ τὴν νῆσον πρὸς τὴν
ἤπειρον συνῆψεν corresponds to Amm.'s words here. However, see
the note ad 24.4.12.
        For the expression cf. 17.1.2 *flumine pontibus constratis transmisso.*
Pontem consternere means either 'to make a bridge', as in Plin. *Nat.* 4.75
constrato in navibus ponte or 'to cover with planks', as in Hirt. *Gal.* 8.9.3
pontibus traiectis constratisque, where *pons* means 'gangway' (between
two towers). It is not immediately clear which interpretation Amm.
has in mind in 17.1.2 quoted above, where *pontibus constratis* is either
abl. abs. or abl. instrumenti. The present phrase can only be taken
as an abl. abs. Amm. speaks about a real ship bridge here, as e.g.
in 23.2.7 *Euphrate navali ponte transmisso*, q.v., used for crossing the
Naarmalcha. Although in 24.3.11 the text is uncertain, it is evident
that *constratis ponticulis* there refers to duckboards used to cross an
area inundated by the Persians.
        Travectus is found nowhere else in Amm., who writes *transvectus*
in 25.8.3 *Imperator ipse brevibus lembis… transvectus.* For *traiecto*, the
reading of EA, there is only one parallel, viz. 24.2.3 *traiecto fonte*,
where *traicere* means 'to pass by'.

metatis alibi salubrius castris Julian chooses a new location for his
camp, which is safer than the encampment mentioned in § 2 (*tentoriis
fixis*). *Metatus* is also used in a passive sense in 24.8.7 *metatis tutius
quievimus castris.* For *salubrius* cf. 25.4.11 where *salubriter et caute
castra metata* are mentioned as evidence of Julian's qualities as a
military commander. As Crump, 1975, 76 observes, to surround the

CHAPTER 4.7 109

campsite with a double wall was rather unusual. It is a sure sign that Julian wanted to take the utmost precautions against sudden attacks. In a similar case, described in 24.5.12, the emperor resorted to a more traditional design, a single line of stakes reinforced by a deep ditch.

ut diximus Cf. § 2 *cuius fortitudo in locis patentibus immane quantum gentibus est formidata.*

periculosum fore existimans, si gradiens prorsus a tergo relinqueret, quos timeret Fear for an attack in the back apparently (and understandably) was more real now than it had been during earlier phases of the march on enemy territory, when for instance Thilutha and Achaiachala were passed without an attempt to lay siege to these cities (24.2.1–2). Zosimus 3.20.3 and Libanius *Or.* 18.236 give Julian's anger about the attack on his person from 'Maozamalcha' (§ 3–4) as the motive for his decision to lay siege to the city. See Paschoud n. 52, who also compares a similar incident described in 24.5.6, q.v. For Amm.'s use of *gradi* "speciatim de militibus" (TLL VI 2139.71) see the note ad 21.8.4. The varia lectio *prosus* printed by Fontaine was corrected by Vm3 and is found nowhere else in V.

Haec dum magno molimine comparantur As TLL VIII 1356.59 ff. shows, **4.7** *molimen* is predominantly, though not exclusively, found in late authors. Amm. has *ingenti molimine* in 18.5.2 and 29.1.6.

Surena hostium dux iumenta adortus, quae in lucis palmaribus vescebantur See for the Surên the note ad 24.2.4. According to Zosimus, who reports this attack in 3.20.4, the Surên hoped to divert Julian from the siege by stealing his baggage animals and his equipment: τῶν τε ὑποζυγίων καὶ τῆς ἀποσκευῆς κρατήσειν ἤλπισε, καὶ ἅμα τὸν βασιλέα τοῦτο μαθόντα πάντως ἀποστήσειν τῆς τοῦ φρουρίου πολιορκίας. Such palmwoods have been described in 24.3.12–13.

a cohortibus nostris repulsoriis As was noted ad 21.11.2, the word *cohors* in Amm. can be used for units of infantry as well as of cavalry (see also the note ad 14.2.12). It would seem that the latter meaning is to be preferred here. The adjective is a hapax, although the noun *repulsorium* does occur in Heges. 3.5.2, Ps. Cypr. *singul. cler.* 36 and Ambr. *in psalm. 118 serm.* 4.15.2 with the meaning 'fortress', 'defence'. The term suggests that the task of these cohorts was to

110   COMMENTARY

ward off surprise attacks on the train. The soldiers mentioned by Zos. 3.20.5 οἱ δὲ ἀπολυθέντες ἐκ τῆς στρατίας εἰς τὸ κατασκοπεῖν καὶ βοηθεῖν, εἴ πού τι φανείη πολέμιον, οὐκ ἀπεκρούσαντο (*reppulerunt*) μόνον e.q.s. are probably identical to these *cohortes repulsoriae*.

cum paucorum exitio habitus frustra discessit The losses are not sustained by the Surên, as the translations of Rolfe, Fontaine and Hamilton suggest, but by the Romans (so Seyfarth), who are the Agens of *habitus frustra*. For this expression cf. 18.6.6 and 31.12.9.

4.8   In his parallel report in 3.20.5 Zosimus mentions one town, Βησουχίς, as well as a great number of fortresses, from which the inhabitants fled, either to ' Maozamalcha' (εἰς τὸ παρὰ τοῦ βασιλέως πολιορκούμενον) or to Ctesiphon, while others took refuge in the forests (πλὴν τῶν εἰς Κτησιφῶντα διαφυγόντων ἢ κατὰ τὸ δασύτατον τοῦ ἄλσους ἀποκρυβέντων). Despite these minor differences in the factual information, the similarities in phrasing make it very unlikely that the two reports are independent from one another.

quas amnes amplexi faciunt insulas This detail is missing in Zosimus. *Amplecti* with a river as Agens is not found elsewhere in the *Res Gestae*, but cf. e.g. Liv. 21.31.4 (amnes) *agri aliquantum amplexi… mediis campis Insulae nomen inditum.*

parva sui fiducia trepidi Zos. 3.20.5 ἀπολιπόντας τὰ σφέτερα ὡς οὐκ ἀρκοῦντα πρὸς σωτηρίαν. For *sui* cf. the note ad 23.5.15.

ad Ctesiphontis moenia se contulerunt Note that in Amm.'s account nobody seeks refuge in 'Maozamalcha'. As we know from Zos. 3.21.5, quoted ad § 13, Ctesiphon was at a distance of ninety stadia (i.e. some 17 km) from the city which Amm. calls Maozamalcha. Brok 136–7 is wrong in stating that Zosimus referred to Besouchis (for which see above, ad 24.4.2) and the two forts mentioned in this section (*duarum… civitatum*), when he spoke of this distance (but since these forts were near Amm.'s Maozamalcha, the difference is marginal). See for Ctesiphon the note ad 24.2.7.

pars per silvarum densa, alii per paludes vicinas The reading *pars per silvarum* for V's *parsilvarum* seems to impose itself on account of the following *alii per paludes*. At first sight, it seems most natural to interpret *pars… alii* as a subdivision of the subject *incolae*. In that case there should be a full stop after *invecti*, which would then be followed

CHAPTER 4.9   111

by a startling asyndeton. For that reason it is preferable to have a full stop or a colon after *se contulerunt*, as Petschenig, 1891, 352 already postulated. The next sentence, with *dilabuntur* as its main verb, does not describe the different routes to Ctesiphon taken by the refugees from the two cities, but rather a flight further inland, just as Zosimus, in the passage quoted at the beginning of this section, distinguishes between those who went to Ctesiphon and those who hid in the woods. Amm. adds the marshes as their hiding place. This is how Fontaine interprets the successive clauses. It is to be noted that the woods and the marshes are mentioned together (albeit in a different context) by Zosimus who speaks in 3.20.5 about Persians hiding in them: ἐπεὶ δὲ τῶν φευγόντων τινὲς καὶ ἐν τοῖς ὑπὸ τὸ ἄλσος ἕλεσιν ἦσαν.

alveis arborum cavatarum invecti Cf. the description of the fateful crossing of the Danube by the Goths in 31.4.5 *transfretabantur in dies et noctes navibus ratibusque et cavatis arborum alveis agminatim impositi.*

ad unicum auxilium et potissimum itineris longi, quod supererat, dilabuntur In view of expressions like 19.2.14 *exiguas, quae supererant, vires* and 29.5.54 *unum remedium superesse contemplans* it seems best to take *auxilium* as the antecedent of the relative clause. The expression as a whole is far from clear and depends on the interpretation of the genitive *itineris*, which may be taken as possessive 'the only hope on their long journey', or as epexegetic, implying that a long journey was the only hope for the refugees. In the former case *auxilium* would be a reference to Ctesiphon itself, so that *pars* and *alii* would denote two groups among those who betook themselves to Ctesiphon, as an intermediate station on their flight. *Auxilium*, however, is not used by Amm. in the sense of 'refuge'; it seems therefore necessary to opt for the latter possibility. For *dilabuntur* cf. 26.7.1 *nonnulli omnia tutiora praesentibus rati e civitate occulte dilapsi.*

ulteriora petituri terrarum For *ulteriora* 'further inland' cf. 24.7.3 *sed ille avidae semper ad ulteriora cupiditatis... mediterraneas vias arripere citato proposuit gradu.*

resistentes aliquos Brok's interpretation 'stragglers' gives better sense than Rolfe's "who offered resistance".   **4.9**

lintribus et cumbis per varia discurrentes Petschenig, 1891, 353 defended V's *itineribus* against Gelenius' *lintribus*, pointing out that, as the Persians fled through the woods and the marshes, so the soldiers

112   COMMENTARY

(*ipsi quoque*) pursued them along the roads and in boats. Amm.'s usage, however, does not allow for this interpretation, since he always has an attribute with *itineribus* (*lentis, celeratis, magnis* and the like). For 'overland', as opposed to 'by boat', he writes *pedestri itinere* (31.11.6). For *per varia* cf. 16.3.3 *ne alimenta deessent exercitui per varia discursuro*.

subinde perducebant For *subinde* 'repeatedly' see the note ad 23.1.7. *Perducebant* sc. *ad imperatorem*, cf. 14.5.6 (Paulus) *in Britanniam missus, ut militares quosdam perduceret ausos conspirasse Magnentio*, 18.5.6 *Antoninus ad regis hiberna perductus aventer suscipitur*; TLL X 1.1283.22–51.

librata ratione 'After careful deliberation'. On *librare* see De Jonge's notes ad 16.10.21 and 18.2.18.

equestres turmae divisae per globos abigundis insisterent praedis See for *turma* above, ad 24.3.1, for *globus* the notes ad 16.12.49 and 20.5.1. See also Bitter 124–5. As *abigundis* would be the only instance of a gerundive in -*undus* in Amm., it seems appropriate to read *abigendis* (AG). For *insistere* "to set to work on" (OLD 6) see the note ad 24.1.13.

hocque proviso nullo provincialium damno miles visceribus hostium pascebatur The abl. abs. resumes *id enim erat... dispositum*; cf. 17.4.14 *quibus ita provisis* and 20.11.21 *his satis provisis*. Julian's policy, to make the barbarians bear the burden of warfare and to spare the provincials, is emphasized by Amm. In his speech to the troops in 21.5.8, q.v., he had proclaimed *indemnitas provinciarum et salus* as one of his objectives, whereas in the elogium of Constantius in 21.16.17 we read *nec provinciarum indemnitati prospexit, cum multiplicatis tributis et vectigalibus vexarentur*. For the expression cf. 17.1.11 *ex barbarorum visceribus alimenta congesta sunt*. "Sympathy for the long-suffering provincials", as White, 1967, 116 calls it, is one of the *Leitmotive* in the HA, sometimes expressed in terms that show a marked similarity to those used by Amm., e.g. *AC* 14.8 *audisti praefectum praetorii... subito divitem factum. unde, quaeso, nisi de visceribus rei publicae provincialiumque fortunis?* *AS* 15.3 *malum publicum esse imperatorem, qui ex visceribus provincialium homines non necessarios nec rei publicae utiles pasceret* and *A* 7.5 *de praeda hostis, non de lacrimis provincialium habeat*.

Interestingly, Zosimus speaks of a different objective. In his version part of the soldiers had to protect their colleagues, so that those who actually besieged the city under the command of the emper-

CHAPTER 4.10   113

or could do their job undisturbed: ὁ μὲν οὖν βασιλεὺς ἐνίστατο τῇ πολιορκίᾳ κατὰ τὸ καρτερὸν (cf. *imperator... oppidum... maximis viribus oppugnabat* in the next section), οἱ δὲ ἀπολυθέντες ἐκ τῆς στρατιᾶς εἰς τὸ κατασκοπεῖν καὶ βοηθεῖν, εἴ πού τι φανείη πολέμιον, οὐκ ἀπεκρούσαντο μόνον τοὺς ἐπελθόντας αὐτοῖς, ἀλλὰ τοὺς μὲν ἀνελόντες τοὺς δὲ προτροπάδην διώξαντες ἐν ἀσφαλεῖ τῷ βασιλεῖ τὰ τῆς πολιορκίας ἐποίησαν (Zos. 3.20.5).

Iamque imperator muris duplicibus oppidum... maximis viribus oppugnabat **4.10** As to *muris duplicibus*, see Zos. 3.21.3, quoted ad § 2 *cumque Maozamalcha*. Most modern editors have accepted Petschenig's *munitum* before *muris*, which is missing in V. Seyfarth, who had adopted *munitum* in his bilingual edition, follows V in his Teubneriana. Fontaine tries to defend *muris duplicibus* without *munitum* as an abl. qualitatis, but Petschenig was right in observing that Amm. elsewhere writes *muro (muris) vallatum* (20.7.1), – *circumdatum* (20.7.17), (Aquileia) *Ordine... scutorum gemino circumsaepta* (21.12.4).

spe patrandi incepti For *patrare* see the note ad 24.2.1.

ut erat necessarius appetitus, ita effectu res difficillima According to TLL II 282.60–3, *appetitus* is here the equivalent of *impetus*, a usage that is said to be peculiar to Amm. and for which 30.5.2 *e statione proxima reprimebat barbaricos appetitus* is quoted as a parallel. The opposition *appetitus – effectus*, however, rather suggests that the word means 'intention', 'plan' as opposed to its realisation.

accessus undique rupibus amfractu celsiore discissis flexuosisque excessibus ob periculum anceps 'The approach on all sides was perilous because of the danger arising from the fact that the cliffs (on which the fortress was built) were interrupted by steep recesses and winding projections.' In other words, the cliffs were not in a straight line, but curved inwards (*amfractu*) and outwards (*excessibus*). *Celsiore* qualifies *rupibus* rather than *amfractu*. *Excessus* in its spatial meaning is rare; TLL V 2.1228.76–82. Both Amm. 18.6.15 and Solinus 9.2 have the expression *montani excessus*. Why a city wall of such a shape poses difficulties to the besieger is explained by Veg. *mil.* 4.2.2: *si quis ad murum tali ordinatione constructum vel scalas vel machinas voluerit admovere, non solum a fronte sed etiam a lateribus et prope a tergo in sinu circumclusus opprimitur.* As Brok 138 rightly observes, in view of the geographical situation of the area in which 'Maozamalcha' was situated, Amm.'s use of *rupes* here, *saxeus* below and *saxa ingentia* in section 16 must

114 COMMENTARY

be hyperbolical and stereotypical for siege descriptions. The same holds good for Lib. *Or.* 18.235, quoted ad 24.4.2.

turres celebritate et altitudine formidandae There were, according to Zosimus 3.21.3, quoted ad § 2 *cumque Maozamalcha*, sixteen such towers. V's *celebritate* may be defended as referring to the large number of defenders crowded together in the tower, but one would rather expect the word to be used of cities or regions, as in 23.6.15 *Assyria, celebritate et magnitudine et multiformi feracitate ditissima*. The passage quoted from Vegetius shows that BAG's *crebritate* deserves serious consideration. Note that Zosimus in his description of the fortress (3.21.3) mentions sixteen high towers. In his bilingual edition Seyfarth writes *celebritate*, but translates: "die vielen Türme"; likewise, Fontaine prints *celebritate*, and translates "redoutable par leur densité".

proclivis planities flumini imminens Cf. *imaque clivorum* in §4.

propugnaculorum firmitate muniebatur For *propugnaculum* 'bulwark' see the note ad 20.6.4. The gen. inversus is a regular feature of Amm.'s style, in particular in his descriptions; see the note ad 21.10.3.

4.11 *lecta manus et copiosa, quae obsidebatur* It is better not to divide this phrase into two cola, as Seyfarth does, but to take it as one, *quae obsidebatur* being the equivalent of *obsessorum*, and qualifying *manus*. Amm. stresses the valour of the Persian garrison, as he had done in the case of Pirisabora (24.2.10 *defensores animo praestantes et viribus*).

Copiosus refers either to the number of the defenders, or to their equipment. The former alternative seems preferable in view of 28.2.2 (Valentinian plans to divert the course of the Nicer): *quaesitis artificibus peritis aquariae rei copiosaque militis manu arduum est opus aggressus*. Cf. also 31.7.16 *in numero longe minore Romanos cum copiosa multitudine colluctatos*. In 23.6.49 *licet numero paucae victu tamen et cultu perquam copiosae* Amm. uses the abl. limitationis to bring out the meaning 'prosperous'.

nullis ad deditionem illecebris flectebatur Amm. refers to the usual overtures before the actual siege begins. At Anatha the Romans had had more luck, in that the town had surrendered rather quickly (24.1.8–9). At Pirisabora (24.2.19) it had cost more of an effort, but there, too, the Romans had ultimately succeeded in persuad-

CHAPTER 4.11   115

ing the inhabitants to surrender their city. Here there was no way (*nullis*) to achieve this result (neither had there been at Thilutha and Achaiachala, 24.2.1–2).

tamquam superatura vel devota cineribus   In the frequent instances of *tamquam* + participle in Amm. three shades of meaning may be distinguished. The phrase serves a) as a comparison, as e.g. in 30.5.7 *Valentinianus vero tamquam auribus cera illitis ignorabat*, or b) it describes the impression made on observers, as in 15.10.5 *humus crustata frigoribus et tamquam levigata*, or c) it expresses the feelings or intentions of the characters involved, as in 22.2.4 *effundebatur aetas omnis et sexus tamquam demissum aliquem visura de caelo*. At times it is difficult to distinguish between the impression made on observers and the feelings of the characters, as in 16.10.6 on the *adventus* of Constantius in Rome *tamquam Euphraten armorum specie territurus aut Rhenum altrinsecus praeeuntibus signis insidebat aureo solus ipse carpento*. In the present case the phrase conveys the impression made on the Romans. *Devota cineribus patriae* is a striking brachylogy for *devotum patriae vel periturae*. For *cineres* cf. 16.12.61 *cineribus Galliarum insultans* and 28.6.19 *luctuosis provinciae cineribus*. Brok adduces some parallels from prose writers, i.a. Cic. *Sul.* 19 *cum cinis patriae versari ante oculos... coeperat*, but, as Fontaine saw (n. 381), it is more likely that Amm. had Vergil in mind: *A.* 10.59–60 *non satius cineres patriae insedisse supremos / atque solum quo Troia fuit?*

aegre retentabatur inferens se protervius miles   The sentence evokes a picture of dogs straining at the leash. On *aegre* see the note ad 23.6.76. *Protervus* is a hapax in Amm. Surprisingly, there are no parallels for *protervus* in connection with soldiers anywhere. The comparative is used for euphonic and metrical reasons. *Se inferre* is also found in 31.16.4 *quos inferentes sese immodice*. It is a favourite phrase for a violent attack in Vergil, e.g. *A.* 9.4.-1 *an sese medios... in hostes inferat*, 11.742 *Venulo adversum se turbidus infert*. Cf. also Tac. *Ann.* 1.64.1 *Barbari, perfringere stationes seque inferri munitoribus nisi.*

pugnam vel aequo campo iustoque proelio poscens   It seems odd that soldiers express their desire to fight *even* in the open field and in a pitched battle, as if such a merely hypothetical alternative would be more difficult than to fight against enemies defended by high walls and towers. Still, there seems to be no other way to interpret *vel* here. Cf. 14.6.23 *morborum acerbitates celsius dominantur, ad quos vel sedandos omnis professio medendi torpescit*, 16.12.70 *ni fama res maximas vel obum-*

116 COMMENTARY

brantibus plurimis silere nesciret, 21.1.9 *nec enim hoc vel insipiens quisquam dicet.* For *iusto proelio* cf. 15.4.11 *non iusto proelio, sed discursionibus.*

assidue animosis hostem urgendi conatibus urebatur Metaphorical *urere* refers to emotions, such as jealousy (20.4.1 *Constantium… urebant Iuliani virtutes*), suspense (20.11.31 *super his urebat eius anxiam mentem, quod*), anger (30.5.10 *urente irarum nutrimenta tunc officiorum magistro Leone*) or, as here, pugnacity (31.5.8 *urebatur dimicandi studio Thervingorum natio omnis.* Therefore *animosis conatibus* must be interpreted as '⟨the wish to⟩ try valiantly' to put pressure on the enemy. For *animosus* 'confident', 'courageous' cf. 16.12.28 and 27.8.3.

4.12 *Vicit tamen nostrorum consilium contentionem virium maximam* The opposition seems to be between *consilium* and *contentio*. As was said in the preceding section, both parties were eager to fight (which is expressed here by the phrase *contentio virium maximam;* see the note ad 20.4.17), but it was the intelligent and disciplined approach of the Romans that won the day. For a similar pregnant use of *consilium* cf. 16.12.18 *tandem per te virtutem et consilia militare sentimus* and the opposition *ferocientes magis quam consultius* in 21.12.5. Zos. 3.21.2 says: Ἀλλ᾽ οὐδὲ οἱ τῶν Ῥωμαίων στρατιῶται…παρῆκαν εἶδος ἀνδρείας καὶ πολεμικῆς ἐπιστήμης 'fell short of them in the display of courage and military expertise'. Amm.'s text gives the impression of being an imprecise imitation of Zosimus' source, in which *vicit* renders οὐ παρῆκαν.

divisisque operibus Amm. first says that 'the duties were assigned' (*divisisque operibus*) and then, in this and the next section, specifies the task of each commander (*officia quisque distributa capessit ocissime. hinc… inde… Nevitta et Dagalaifus… Victor… offendisse*). In Zosimus' account it is the other way around. He first informs his readers about the tasks of Nevitta and others (3.21.3–5) and then concludes with Ταύτῃ διελὼν τοῖς ἡγεμόσι τὴν ἐπιμέλειαν (3.22.1).

hinc enim ardui suggestus erigebantur, inde fossarum altitudines alii complanabant Zosimus gives more or less the same information, but note that he uses a singular (τάφρῳ) where Amm. has a plural (*fossarum*), and that he once again gives the information in the reverse order: χῶμα ἐπιχέειν ὁ βασιλεὺς τῇ τάφρῳ τοὺς στρατιώτας ἐκέλευσεν, ἕτερόν τε ἐπὶ τούτῳ πρὸς ὕψος ἀνιστάμενον ἐξισωθῆναι τῷ πύργῳ (3.21.3). Libanius in *Or.* 18.237 differs from both Amm. and Zosimus in that he speaks of the building of a bridge to link the island on which

CHAPTER 4.12 117

'Maozamalcha' was situated to the mainland, if indeed his words correspond to Amm.'s words here, rather than to *Constratis...pontibus* in section 6, as Bliembach, 1976, 169 and Paschoud n. 52 assume. Libanius clearly refers to a siege, which is in favour of the connection proposed here: ὁ δὲ πρῶτον μὲν καὶ αὐτὸς πέτραις καὶ βέλεσι τῶν ἐπὶ τοῦ τείχους ἥψατο, καί τις φέρων τὸ βέλος ἐν τῷ σώματι κατέπιπτεν, ἔπειτα γεφύρᾳ τὴν νῆσον πρὸς τὴν ἤπειρον συνῆψεν, οἱ δὲ ἐργαζόμενοι φυλακὴν εἶχον τὰ σκύτινα τῶν πλοίων ("the engineers using the hides of the boats as protection", tr. Norman).

The use of *suggestus* for *aggeres*, the gen. inversus *fossarum altitudines*, for which see the note ad 20.11.6, and the periphrasis *terrarum latibula concava* for *cuniculi* are typical of Amm.'s elevated style in this introduction to the actual fighting.

TLL V 2.588.3ff. labels *enim* as we find it here "inceptivum" or "inchoativum", OLD s.v. 7 calls it "expository". Kroon, 1995, 2. interprets it as an appeal to empathy on the part of the reader ('Imagine...'), which can be understood on the basis of the overall meaning of *enim* as a particle expressing interactional consensus, and is well-suited to "vivid eyewitness accounts". It is not rare in Amm.; cf. e.g. 15.7.2 *prima igitur causa seditionis in eum concitandae vilissima fuit et levis. Philoromum enim...*, 17.7.13 *Fiunt autem terrarum motus modis quattuor: aut enim brasmatiae sunt...*, 17.9.3 *longe autem aliter accidit. frugibus enim nondum etiam maturis* e.q.s.

In Amm. *suggestus* normally refers to the tribunal from which the emperor addresses his troops, as in 21.5.1 *classico ad contionem exercitu convocato saxeo suggestu insistens*, or to mountain ranges, as in 15.10.1 *ob suggestus montium arduos*. Amm. seems to be unique in using *suggestus* with the meaning 'dam'.

terrarum latibula concava oblongis tramitibus alibi struebantur This was done by *legionarii milites*, as we learn from 24.4.21, q.v. Zosimus refers to the mining operation in 3.21.4 (Κατὰ δὲ μέρος ἕτερον τὴν ὑπὸ τὰ τείχη γῆν ὀρύττειν ἐγνώκει, κατὰ τὸ μέσον τοῦ ἐνδοτέρου τείχους, διὰ τοῦ ὀρύγματος ἐπιθήσεσθαι τοῖς πολεμίοις πραγματευόμενος), Libanius mentions it in *Or.* 18.238, where he says that the Persians knew that their enemy was mining (εἰδότες μὲν ὀρύττοντας τοὺς πολεμίους).

As Crump, 1975, 109 observes, Amm. mentions more than once efforts to undermine a city's fortifications (cf. 20.6.3, 20.11.8, 21.12.6). They usually failed, because artillery fire drove the sappers away despite their attempts to protect themselves under *vineae* and *plutei*. At 'Maozamalcha' the mining operation was a success, for a change.

118 COMMENTARY

Amm. goes out of his way to avoid the t.t. *cuniculi*, which he uses in the more factual account in the next section. In § 21 he substitutes the more straightforward *tramitibus subterraneis* for *terrarum latibula*. The adjective *oblongus* causes suspicion. Amm. uses it quite correctly of the island of Proconnesus (22.8.6 *Proconesus insula est oblonga*, q.v.) and in the description of a type of shield (24.6.8 *scutis oblongis et curvis*), but it seems totally otiose to describe a mine shaft as being "longior quam latior" (TLL IX 2.114.74). As an alternative, *obliquus* would be very attractive. Amm. uses it in combination with *trames* in 16.2.10 *tramite obliquo discurso*, 29.5.50 *per tramites adortus obliquos*. Livy has *obliquis tramitibus* in 5.16.5. The reason for approaching the walls sideways or in a zigzag line might be that this makes it more difficult to locate the mines and to take countermeasures.

locabant etiam artifices tormenta muralia in funestos sonitus proruptura For *artifex* 'marksman' cf. 23.4.2 *artifex contemplabilis*, q.v. The *tormenta muralia*, i.e. the stone throwing *scorpio* and the *ballista*, an arrow-shooting engine, are described in detail in 23.4.2–7, q.v. The frightening sound made by these engines is mentioned several times, e.g. 19.5.6 *alii machinarum metu stridentium praecipites acti*. In 19.6.10 they are even fired without missiles, just to intimidate the adversaries: *tormentorumque machinae stridebant sine iaculatione ulla telorum*. Cf. also 24.4.16 *ballistae flexus stridore torquebantur*.

4.13 *et cuniculos quidem cum vineis Nevitta et Dagalaifus curabant* See for *cuniculus* the note ad 21.12.8, for *vinea* ad 24.2.18. As to Nevitta and Dagalaifus, both had been mentioned in 24.1.2, q.v.

There is a slight difference with Amm. in Zosimus' account regarding the tasks attributed to the generals. According to Zos. 3.21.4 Nevitta and Dagalaifus were not in charge of the mines and mantlets, but of the mines and the raising of dams: Νευίττᾳ δὲ καὶ Δαγαλαίφῳ τά τε ὀρύγματα καὶ τὰς τῶν χωμάτων ἐγέρσεις ἐπέτρεψεν. In his next chapter Zosimus (and he alone) adds to this an interesting detail, viz. that those in charge of the mining operation performed so badly that the emperor discharged them and had them replaced: τοὺς δὲ ἐπὶ τῶν ὀρυγμάτων τεταγμένους ἐκμελῶς ἰδὼν τῷ ἔργῳ χρωμένους ἐκείνους μὲν ἀπέστησε, ταύτην αὐτοῖς ὑπὲρ τῆς ἐκμελείας τὴν ἀτιμίαν ἐπαγαγών, ἑτέρους δὲ ἀντεκατέστησεν (3.22.1).

The preposition *cum* is used because the mantlets are indispensable for the protection of the sappers when they start digging.

CHAPTER 4.14 119

ineundis autem conflictibus et defendendis ab incendio vel eruptionibus machinis praeerat imperator In Zos. 3.21.4 too the emperor has this task: τῶν δὲ πολεμίων τοὺς ἐγείροντας τὸ χῶμα βολαῖς συνεχέσιν εἰργόντων, τὴν μὲν ἐν τῷ προφανεῖ μάχην ὁ βασιλεὺς ἀνεδέξατο, πολυειδέσιν ἀμυντηρίοις κατὰ τῶν βαλλομένων εἴτε βελῶν εἴτε πυρσῶν χρώμενος. The noun *conflictus* is post-classical. Amm. uses it seven times. See De Jonge's note ad 19.5.2.

apparatu omni exscindendae urbis labore multiplici consummato Cf. 19.7.2 *apparatu cunctorum alacritate perfecto exsiliente lucifero operum variae species cum turribus ferratis admovebantur*, where, as here, *apparatus* is used specifically of siege engines. See the note ad 20.8.1 *limitem instruebat*. *Labore multiplici* recapitulates the different activities described in the preceding section. For *multiplex* see the note ad 21.6.6.

Victor nomine dux reversus est ad usque Ctesiphonta itineribus exploratis nulla obstacula nuntians offendisse Zosimus' account in 3.21.5 of the action of Victor (see for this general the note ad 24.1.2; "the use of 'dux' by Ammianus here is not technical", PLRE I, Victor 4), is more extensive than that of Amm. Firstly, Zosimus gives more information about Victor's troops and the reason why he was sent on his mission (Βίκτορι δὲ παραδοὺς ὁπλίτας τε καὶ ἱππέας τὰ μέχρι Κτησιφῶντος αὐτῷ διερευνᾶσθαι προσέταξεν, ὥστε, εἴ πού τι φανείη πολέμιον ἀφελκύσαι τὸν βασιλέα τῆς πολιορκίας πειρώμενον, τούτου διὰ τῶν ὑπ' αὐτῷ τεταγμένων κωλυθῆναι τὴν ἐπιχείρησιν). Secondly, he adds the precious information that the distance between ' Maozamalcha' and Ctesiphon was ninety stadia, i.e. about seventeen kilometers (ἅμα δὲ τὴν ὁδὸν τὴν ἐπὶ Κτησιφῶντα, σταδίων οὖσαν ἐνενήκοντα. See for Ctesiphon the note ad 24.2.7). Thirdly, he informs us that Victor's task had consisted not only of exploring the country, but of facilitating in advance the army's march towards Ctesiphon (γεφυρῶν τε κατασκευαῖς καὶ ζευγμάτων αὐτῷ καὶ τῷ στρατῷ ῥᾷονα καταστῆσαι). Zosimus does not explicitly say that Victor returned to 'Maozamalcha', as does Amm. (*reversus est*). But to conclude from this silence that Amm. is not telling the truth, seems unwarranted, pace Brok 139 and Paschoud n. 58 ("il ne pouvait guère revenir vers Maiozamalcha, comme le prétend Ammien").

quo efferati gaudio Amm. uses strong language indeed to describe   **4.14**
the fanaticism of the legionaries. As in *protervius* (§ 11) one senses
some reservation on the part of the author. As Seager 56 observes,

120   COMMENTARY

efferatus is more common of foreigners than of Romans. On closer inspection, even in the few instances mentioned by Seager, where is it allegedly used of Romans, it refers twice to Gallic troops (19.6.4, 20.8.8), once to the rabble of Alexandria (22.11.5) and once to the rioting Roman plebs (27.3.13).

elatique firmioribus animis ad certandum signum opperiebantur armati Translators are unanimous in connecting *ad certandum* with *signum*, but it seems preferable for the end of the colon to coincide with the end of a syntactical unit and to make the gerund dependent on the preceding clause: 'eager to fight and full of confidence they awaited the signal'. *Armati* is best taken predicatively "under arms" (Rolfe). *Signum* is usually followed, as one would expect, by a genitive: 16.12.33 *pugnae signum inconsulte poscentes*, 17.12.10 *orandi signum exspectantibus*, 25.8.2 *transeundi amnis aperte signum dedere bucinae concrepantes*. The abl. abs. *dato signo* is followed by a prepositional phrase with *ad* or *in*: 16.12.36 *Dato igitur aeneatorum accentu sollemniter signo ad pugnandum*, 21.12.11 *datoque signo in receptum*. For *firmus* with *ad* cf. Caes. *Gal.* 7.60.2 *cohortes, quas minime firmas ad dimicandum esse existimabat* and see TLL VI 814.43–8.

4.15   *clangore Martio sonantibus tubis* This sounds like an echo of Vergil's playful description of bees going to war in *G.* 4.70–2: *namque morantis / Martius ille aeris rauci canor increpat et vox / auditur fractos sonitus imitata tubarum*. For the musical instruments used in the army see the note *ad* 20.7.6 and add to the literature quoted there Wille, 1967. The *tuba* is the instrument par excellence for the beginning and ending of battles: 16.12.7 *Iamque solis radiis rutilantibus tubarumque concinente clangore pedestres copiae lentis incessibus educuntur*, 19.6.9 *tubarum perciti clangore castrensium discedebant*. The *lituus*, for which see the note *ad* 23.5.15 fulfills the same function in Amm.: 19.11.15 *in receptum canentibus lituis*, 31.7.10 *signo ad arma capienda ex utraque parte per lituos dato*. The *bucina* is primarily used to wake the soldiers, as in 21.12.5 *aurora iam surgente concrepante sonitu bucinarum partes accensae in clades mutuas* e.q.s., but it also signals the beginning of special manoeuvres, as in 25.8.2 *ubi vero transeundi amnis aperte signum dedere bucinae* and 24.5.9 (ubi) *exercitus cantu concitus bucinarum cum minaci murmure festinaret*. Amm. mentions *tubicines, cornicines, liticines* and uses the general term *aeneatores* ("eine Kollektivbezeichnung für die im Heere dienenden Metallbläser", Wille, 1967, 101). See further the note on *classicum ad* 24.6.11.

CHAPTER 4.15

hostem undique lamminis ferreis in modum tenuis plumae contectum The comparison of the iron corselet to a bird's plumage goes back to Sallust's description of armour-clad horses in *Hist.* 4.65 *paria operimenta erant* (sc. atque equitibus) *namque linteo ferreas laminas in modum plumae adnexuerant*, preserved in Servius' note ad Verg. *A.* 11.770–1, the description of a warhorse: *quem pellis aenis / in plumam squamis auro conserta tegebat.* The comparison brings out the smoothness and the flexibility of the corselet. Both aspects are combined in Amm.'s description of *clibanarii* in 16.10.8 *ut Praxitelis manu polita crederes simulacra* and *quocumque artus necessitas commovisset, vestitus congrueret iunctura cohaererent aptata.* The Sarmates and Quadi used horn corselets for the same purpose: 17.12.2 *loricae ex cornibus rasis et levigatis plumarum specie linteis indumentis innexae.* Cf. also 24.2.10 *ferrea nimirum facie omni, quia lamminae... hominis speciem contegebant*, with the note.

fidentemque For *fidens* (*-nter*), 'full of confidence' see the note ad 20.8.19 *et super ordine.*

tela rigentis ferri lapsibus impacta TLL VII 2.955.63–6 rightly lists this phrase among the "loci dubii". There is no parallel to be found that helps to explain it. Translators take *lapsus* to refer either to the smoothness of the mail ("durch die Glätte", Seyfarth) or to the iron plates sliding over each other ("the folds", Rolfe). The alternatives proposed by the anonymous "viri docti" mentioned by TLL, viz. *cratibus* and *cassibus*, fail to carry conviction, since these terms refer to networks or webs with openings between the wickerwork or the threads, which is exactly what we do not need here. A crux seems to be unavoidable.

crebris procursationibus et minaci murmure Apart from Livy (e.g. 5.19.9 *a procursatoribus quae multa temere inter murum ac vallum fiebant*), Amm. is the only author to use *procursatio*, here and in 26.7.15 *quasi procursatione hostem lacessens* according to TLL X 2.1590.64–70. *Minaci murmure* recurs in 24.5.9. Lucr. 1.276 uses it of roaring stormwinds: *saevitque minaci murmure ventus* (so Markland; the mss. have *pontus*). In Hor. *Carm.* 2.1.17 it is applied to the sound of the *cornu* . See Nisbet-Hubbard ad loc.

nonnumquam compage scutorum... laxius dehiscente The gaps between the shields which the Roman soldiers hold above their heads contrast with the impenetrable protection of the Persians. The shields func-

122 COMMENTARY

tion as a roof (*testudo*) to protect the soldiers as they approach the walls, cf. 14.2.10 *denseta scutorum compage semet scientissime praestruebant* and 16.12.44 *nexamque scutorum compagem, quae nostros in modum testudinis tuebatur*. In *laxius dehiscente* the adverb reinforces the meaning of *dehiscere* as in the following *obstinatius adhaerentes*; for similar qualifications compare the note ad 23.4.2 *eique cochleae*.

qua velut testudine infigurabilium fornicum operiebantur aptissime "with which our men skilfully covered themselves as if by the protection of irregularly shaped arches" (Rolfe). The adj. *infigurabilis* is found only once, as an attribute of God (=ἄμορφος), in Rustic. Conc. I 4 p. 221.10 (TLL VII 1.1422.44–6). It is plainly untenable here. Among the conjectures made, Petschenig's ingenious *in figuram mobilium fornicum* is the most attractive. Cf. 27.2.8 *in agminis quadrati figuram*.

muris obstinatius adhaerentes For *adhaerere* i.q. "non moveri" see TLL I 634.69ff.

eludere et frustrari 'To avoid and to render vain'. Amm. may have borrowed the phrase from V. Max. 3.8.2 *frustrari et eludere*.

4.16 *ubi vimineas crates prae se ferentes…perurgerent* During the siege of Amida, the Persians advanced in the same way *cratesque vimineas praetendentes* (19.7.3); see De Jonge's note ad loc., who quotes Verg. *G.* 1.95 *vimineasque trahit crates* ('harrows'). See also the notes ad 20.7.6 and 21.12.6. *Perurgerent* is an iterative subjunctive.

cum sagittariis funditores…propulsabant Cf. Zos. 3.21.1 and note that Amm.'s *saxa ingentia* and Zosimus' λίθοι represent different kinds of stone: Οἱ δὲ ἐν τῷ φρουρίῳ πολιορκούμενοι βελῶν παντοίων ἀφέσει τοὺς ἐναντίους ἠμύνοντο, λίθων δὲ οὐκ ὄντων αὐτοῖς ἔνδον ἀσφάλτῳ βώλους πεπυρωμένους ἠκόντιζον· ἐτύγχανον δὲ τῶν πεμπομένων αἱ βολαὶ ῥαδίως οἷα καὶ ἐξ ὑπερδεξίου καὶ κατὰ πλήθους πεμπόμεναι ('the besieged in the fortress defended themselves against their attackers by throwing all kinds of missiles; when they were confronted by a lack of stones in the city, they threw instead clods of earth set on fire with asphalt; this proved to be rather successful, since they threw from a higher position and those below were bunched up'). There is a note on *saxa* ad 24.2.14. Amm. distinguishes *sagittarii, funditores* and soldiers who rolled stones from the walls. Therefore *cum sagittariis* is a prepositional phrase. *Cum* preceding *facibus* corresponds with *tum* before *aptatae*. This is one of the rare instances of *cum…tum* in Amm., for

CHAPTER 4.17   123

which see the note ad 24.1.8. Rolfe wrongly interprets *cum* before *facibus* as a preposition. Translate: 'not only did they keep them at a distance with torches and firedarts, also *ballistae* were fired.' For a description of the *malleolus* see 23.4.14, q.v.

tum aptatae ligneis sagittis ballistae... evibrabant According to Libanius the wall of the fortress was too high to be attacked by engines (*Or.* 18.235, quoted ad 24.2.2). Zosimus was better informed: λίθοις γὰρ χειροπλήθεσιν ἔβαλλον, βέλεσί τε οὐκ ἐκ τόξων μόνον ἀφιεμένοις ἀλλὰ καὶ ἐκ μηχανημάτων (3.21.2). For *ballistae* and *scorpiones* see the notes ad 23.4.2 and 23.4.4, respectively. Normally *aptare* in connection with *ballistae* or *arietes* refers to the positioning of the engines, e.g. 19.7.2 *in verticibus celsis aptatae ballistae* and 20.7.10 *aptatique arietes aegre promovebantur*. For the meaning 'to provide with' cf. 24.6.8 *lamminis cohaerenter aptati corporum flexus* and Liv. 9.31.9 *ut quisque liberaverat se onere aptaveratque armis*.

flexus stridore torquebantur "Then there was screeching of ballistas being wound up" (Hamilton). The fearful sound of the siege engines has already been remarked upon above, §12. Cf. also 19.5.6 *alii machinarum metu stridentium praecipites acti*. From 19.6.10 it appears that the *ballistae* were used incidentally for their intimidating sound only: *tormentorumque machinae stridebant sine iaculatione ulla telorum, ut stationibus praesidentes post interemptos socios pone agerentur*. *Flectere* and its derivatives are used for drawing a bow in 24.2.5 *quamvis arcus validis viribus flecterentur*. It is also used in connection with the *ballista*, in 23.4.2 *hinc inde validi iuvenes versant agiliter rotabilem flexum*, 'strong men energetically turn a rotating winch', i.e. to strain the bowstring. *Stridor flexus* indicates the accompanying sound.

quocumque manus peritae duxissent The expertise needed to handle these lethal weapons safely is illustrated by the accident described in §28 below. *Duxissent* is again an iterative subjunctive.

iterum deinde ac saepe geminatis congressibus Cf. 30.6.5 *iterum saepiusque* **4.17** and for similar pleonastic expressions see TLL VII 2.559.22–30. The adverbs prove that *geminare* here means 'to repeat' (TLL VI 1739.54) rather than 'to join together' (TLL VI 1738.83).

aestus in meridiem crescens effervescente vaporatius sole I.e. on the 11th of May (see the note on chronology). According to TLL V 2.154.2 this is the only instance of *effervescere* with *sol* as its subject. Elsewhere the

124 COMMENTARY

verb is used of emotions: 14.5.5 *effervescebat obstinatum eius propositum* and 27.7.4 *ira acerbius effervescens*. For *vaporatus* 'hot' cf. 17.7.12 *vaporatis temporibus*, 18.9.2 *vaporatis aestibus*.

apparatu operum... intentos In classical Latin *intentus* 'intent on' is used with *ad* or *in* + acc., or dative, as in Tac. *Ann*. 2.5.2 *celerandae victoriae intentior*. The same constructions are found in Amm. Cf. 20.9.1 *intentique ad viandum*, 21.4.1 *in unum omni cogitatione intenta*. He has one unambiguous instance of the dative: 21.2.4 *haruspicinae auguriisque intentus*. It seems therefore best to take *apparatu* as a dative. For this ending of the dative of u-stems cf. 19.1.6 *eruendae urbis apparatu nisibus magnis instabat* with De Jonge's note.

cunctos revocáverat fatigátos The use of the pluperfect may be understood as setting the scene for the prolonged fighting on the following day. More probably, the cursus dictated the choice.

4.18 *Eodem mentis proposito* I.e. with the same doggedness. For *propositum* see the note ad 20.5.4 *numquam a proposito*.

secuto quoque die May 12, it would seem. For the expression cf. 15.4.9 *secuto die*, 20.7.7, 21.15.2, 23.5.12. Remarkably, the only author apart from Amm. to use this phrase is the Elder Pliny: *Nat.* 13.126.

controversae partes The use of *controversus* = *oppositus* is idiomatic in Amm. All instances in TLL IV 788.40–54, with the exception of Sol. 27.1, are taken from him. He uses the adjective both of position, e.g. 14.2.3 *quae Isauriae scopulis sunt controversa* and of opposing parties, as here and in 21.12.23 *litesque audiens controversas*. It is used absolutely of the Egyptians in 22.16.23 *controversi et reposcones acerrimi* ("quarrelsome and most persistent duns", Rolfe).

dimicantes instanter The adverb varies *eodem mentis proposito* above. For its meaning cf. Don. *Ter. Ad.* 363.1 *'quaeritare' instanter quaerere*. The action expressed by the present participle is anterior to the main verb *discedunt*. See the note ad 22.8.14 *cedentesque retrorsus*.

aequis manibus The expression is found only here in the *Res Gestae*. Amm. probably came across it in the historians: Sal. *Cat.* 39.4 *si... Catilina superior aut aequa manu discessisset*, Liv. 27.13.5 *aequis manibus... diremistis pugnam*, Tac. *Ann.* 1.63.4 *manibus aequis absces-*

CHAPTER 4.19   125

sum. It goes back to Ennius *Ann.* 167 Sk. *bellum aequis manibus nox intempesta diremit.*

in omne discrimen armatis proximus princeps It is a characteristic of the good commander to stand beside his men 'to brave all dangers'. This quality of Julian is praised several times by Amm., e.g. in the *elogium* 25.4.10 *in pulvere vaporato Persidis augebat fiduciam militis dimicans inter primos.* Occasionally, however, Julian crossed the line between bravery and recklessness, for which he is criticized by the historian. See the introduction to ch. 2. On *princeps* see the note ad 20.4.8 *proiceret insignia.*

civitatis urgebat excidium This meaning of *urgere* "to pursue with vigour" (OLD s.v. 12) is also found in classical authors, e.g. Hor. *S.* 2.7.6–7 *urget propositum*, and Tac. *Hist.* 4.28.3 *Civilis obsidium legionum urgebat.*

ne circa muros diu excubans omitteret maiora, quae temptabat A similar reflection is mentioned by Zosimus: ᾤετο γὰρ μὴ περὶ μικρὰ διατρίβειν τὸν χρόνον, ἀλλ᾽ εἰς τὸ κεφάλαιον ἑαυτὸν ἐμβαλεῖν τοῦ πολέμου (3.15.2), not, however, in his description of the siege of ' Maozamalcha', but with regard to an earlier phase of the expedition, viz. when Julian's army passed Thilutha and Achaiachala (24.2.1–2). The only other instance of *excubare* in Amm. is in the first digression on Rome, used of a layabout, *qui pro domibus excubat aurigarum* (14.6.14).

in destrictis necessitatibus The figurative use of *destrictus*, 'inexorable', 'ruthless' is found e.g. in Tac. *Ann.* 4.36.3 *ut quis destrictior accusator, velut sacrosanctus erat* and V. Max. 8.2.2 *ex amica obsequenti subito destrictam feneratricem agere coepit.* There are no parallels for the present phrase.   **4.19**

nihil tam leve est, quod non interdum etiam contra sperata rerum afferat momenta magnarum The most succinct wording of this commonplace is Cic. *Phil.* 5.26 *minimis momentis... maximae inclinationes temporum fiunt.* Amm. must have modelled himself directly on Liv. 25.18.3 *sed in bello nihil tam leve est, quod non magnae interdum rei momentum faciat.* For *contra sperata*, 'against all expectations', which is found only here, cf. the note ad 20.4.14 *insperata res.*

cum enim ut saepe discessurae partes levius concertarent It seems best to take *ut saepe* with *levius concertarent*, indicating that this long drawn-

126 COMMENTARY

out siege was interrupted several times. *Levius* must mean that the soldiers, just before their temporary withdrawal, fought less fiercely than in the beginning of the day.

abusive incusso ariete In his note on *abusive* in *ALL* 7, 1892, 423–4 Wölfflin offers two paraphrases. The first is "vehementius solito", which is accepted in TLL I 239.8–9. The alternative interpretation, given i.a. by Forcellini s.v.: "perfunctorie, extra usum vel ordinem scilicet legitimum", suits the context much better. The decisive turn in the siege is brought about not by a final effort, but more or less casually, thus illustrating the maxim that small events have momentous consequences. The normal meaning of *abusive* is 'metaphorically', as in Quint. *Inst.* 8.6.35 *nam poetae solent abusive etiam in his rebus, quibus nomina sua sunt, vicinis potius uti, quod rarum in prorsa est.* This is the only instance in Amm. of *incutere* with its literal meaning 'to dash against', for which cf. Liv. 31.46.15 *muri quoque pars ariete incusso... prociderat.* The usual object of the verb is 'fear'.

According to Zosimus 3.22.1 it was the emperor himself who successfully threw a battering-ram into the fray (see for the *aries* the note ad 23.4.8–9): αὐτὸς μὲν διὰ τῶν σὺν αὐτῷ κριὸν μιᾷ πύλῃ προσαγαγὼν οὐ κατέσεισε μόνον αὐτὴν ἀλλὰ καὶ ἔλυσε.

latere coctili firmissime structa In 24.2.12, q.v., it is said that this is the strongest construction of a wall: *quo aedificii genere nihil esse tutius constat.*

4.20 *ibi tum* It is far from evident that this is an instance of what Szantyr 525 calls "abundante konjunktionale Verbindungen", as Fontaine n. 394 asserts. Both here and in 29.1.32 *ibi tum* follows a local adjunct. The same holds for the three instances of *ibi tunc* (20.11.5, 25.8.18, 29.2.14).

facinoribus speciosis inclaruit Amm. uses *inclarescere* once with its literal meaning (*dies inclaruit*, 25.1.1) and several times in the sense of 'to distinguish oneself', for which cf. Tac. *Ann.* 12.37.3 *neque mea fortuna neque tua gloria inclaruisset* with Koestermann's note.

nihil enim asperum ira et dolore succenso militi videbatur The phrase possibly harks back to Sal. *Cat.* 40.4 *nihil tam asperum neque tam difficile esse quod non cupidissume facturi essent.* Cf. also Liv. 25.6.23, where the survivors of Cannae ask Marcellus for the most awkward assignments: *asperrima quaeque ad laborem periculumque deposcimus.*

CHAPTER 4.21   127

After the report of Julian's death the mood of the Roman soldiers was equally embittered: 25.3.10 *miles ad vindictam ira et dolore ferventior involabat.* Bitter 137 n. 416, following Fesser, traces the association of *ira* and *dolor* to epic poetry and Tacitus.

munitoribus...pro salute currentibus There can be no doubt that the *munitores* are the defenders. This poses a problem, since elsewhere in Amm. (21.12.8, 21.12.12, 26.8.3) *munitores* means 'the besiegers'. As was remarked ad 21.12.8, Amm. may be less consistent than philologists think fitting. In the present context *munitores* may be accepted as referring to those defenders who try to repair the breach made by the battering-ram. Fletcher, 1937, 396 ingeniously and convincingly defends *currentibus* by comparing it with the Greek expression τρέχειν περὶ τῆς ψυχῆς, found in e.g. Hdt. 9.37. Cf. also Pl. *Tht.* 172 e πολλάκις δὲ καὶ περὶ ψυχῆς ὁ δρόμος. It must be admitted that Damsté's *certantibus* gives excellent Latin. Cf. e.g. Sal. *Jug.* 94.5 *pro gloria atque imperio his, illos pro salute certantibus.* Liv. 6.18.6 *acrius crederem vos pro libertate quam illos pro dominatione certaturos* with Kraus' note, but to substitute *currere* for *certare* would be just the kind of 'Fehlleistung' one might expect from a bilingual person like Amm.

cum anceps pugna...diei finisset occasus An ungrammatical sentence. The easiest way out is to substitute *proelium* for *pugna* with Heraeus, which, however, leaves the corruption unexplained. Another simple remedy would be to read *occasu* with G, but that would make *finire* intransitive, which it never is in Amm. Perhaps we should just accept the slight irregularity, which may have been caused by the intervening participles *fervens* and *fuso*. In an author who writes periods of such complexity one would expect more mistakes of this kind than in fact there are. For the date see the note ad *secuto quoque die* in section 18.

tum fatigationi consulitur Here again the text is not beyond suspicion. If the phrase is meant to illustrate the grimness of the fight, *tum* would have to be equivalent to *tum demum,* for which there are no parallels in Amm., who writes *ita demum* in such cases, cf. 24.1.14. *Fatigatio* is a hapax in Amm. For the idea cf. 16.2.8 *paulisper moratus, dum fatigato consulit militi.*

Dumque haec luce agerentur ac palam For the coni. after *dum* ("ganz gewöhnlich...in der spätlat. Prosa", Szantyr 614) see the note ad 20.6.1. In 14.1.9 Amm. has the classical asyndeton *luce palam,* which is found e.g. in Cic. *Off.* 3.93 *ut...luce palam in foro saltet* and Verg.   **4.21**

128 COMMENTARY

A. 9.153 *luce palam certum est igni circumdare muros.* The hyperbaton together with the insertion of *ac* produces a cursus planus.

nuntiatur imperatori… legionarios milites… evasuros Zosimus' account in 3.22.2 begins thus: Αὐτὸς δὲ κριὸν ἕτερον (cf. above, ad section 19) ἄλλῃ προσέφερε πύλῃ· καὶ ταύτης δὲ τὴν προσβολὴν οὐκ ἐνεγκούσης, ἧκεν ἀγγέλλων τις ὡς οἱ ταχθέντες τὰ ἀπὸ τῆς τάφρου μέχρι τῆς πόλεως αὐτῆς διορύττειν ἤδη πρὸς τέλος ἀφίκοντο τοῦ ἔργου καὶ πρὸς τὸ ἀναδῦναι γεγόνασιν εὐτρεπεῖς. He then continues with a specification of the units to which the soldiers, charged with the tunnelling, belonged (Amm. merely refers to them with the generic term *legionarii milites*): ἧσαν δὲ οὗτοι τρεῖς λόχοι, ματτιάριοι καὶ λακκιάριοι καὶ βίκτορες. Amm. speaks of Lancearii and Mattiarii in 21.13.16, q.v. and 31.13.8. See for them also the note ad 24.1.2 *excursatores quidem quingentos.* As to the Victores, they are mentioned by Amm. in section 23 of this chapter and further, together with the Iovii, in 25.6.3, 26.7.13 and 27.8.7. The legions of Victores and Iovii, like those of Lancearii and Mattiarii, apparently often operated as a team (see for the Victores in the first place Hoffmann, 1969, I 157 and 324–5).

pervigili cura distento Restless activity characterises the good commander. Fontaine n. 397 aptly refers to Constantius' speech when he made Julian a Caesar: *"Ad summam i, propera sociis omnium votis velut assignatam tibi ab ipsa re publica stationem cura pervigili defensurus"* (15.8.14). *Distento* is probably best taken from *distinere* (TLL V 1.1523.82) and must be distinguished from *distentus* in phrases like 22.12.6 *milites carnis distentiore sagina victitantes,* q.v., 25.10.13 *ex colluvione ciborum avida cruditate distentus* or 30.3.4 *immane quo quantoque flatu distentus,* where the participle belongs to the verb *distendere* . There is room for doubt in instances like 21.16.9 *suspicionesque in huiusmodi cuncta distentae,* q.v. and 30.4.13 *inter sollicitudines iudicum per multa distentas* (TLL V 1.1513.71).

quibus cuniculorum erant fodinae mandatae These are the soldiers under the command of Nevitta and Dagalaifus, mentioned in §13. For the rare *fodina* (= "actus fodiendi", TLL VI 991.69–72) see the note ad 22.15.30 *penitus operosis.*

cavatis tramitibus subterraneis sublicibusque suspensis Cf. § 12 *terrarum latibula concava.* The heteroclite *sublicibus* from *sublica* 'pile' is borrowed from Sal. *Hist.* 4.85 *ne inrumpendi p(ontis)… sublicibus cavata… (es)sent.* As Fordyce remarks ad Verg. *A.* 8.190 *saxis suspensam*

CHAPTER 4.22 129

hanc aspice rupem, suspendere is "the builder's technical term for vaulting." *Sublicibus* is an instrumental ablative.

ima penetrasse fundamentorum This phrase is misunderstood by Rolfe ("had made their way to the bottom of the foundations of the walls") and Seyfarth ("bis an den untersten Rand von Mauerfundamenten vorgedrungen"). As in 21.13.2, q.v., the verb means 'to pass', in this case below the foundations. A similar use is found in 18.3.9 (anseres) *cum montem penetrare coeperint Taurum*: the geese fly over, not through, the Taurus ridge; TLL X 1.1066.71 ff.

cum itaque noctis plerúmquë processísset... ad arma concursum est et consulto murorum invaduntur utrimque frontes Another Sallustianism: *Jug.* 21.2 *ubi plerumque noctis processit*. The change in word order and mood produces a cursus velox. The event will have taken place in the night of 12–13 May. Zosimus in 3.22.3 also speaks of diversionary tactics: Ὁ βασιλεὺς δὲ ταύτην μὲν τέως ἐπέσχεν αὐτῶν τὴν ὁρμήν (sc. of the Mattiarii, Lancearii and Victores, mentioned in 3.22.2 quoted ad § 21), πύλῃ δὲ ἑτέρᾳ θᾶττον ἐκέλευσεν εὐτρεπίζεσθαι μηχανήν, καὶ τὴν στρατιὰν αὐτῇ πᾶσαν ἐφίστη, πείθων τοὺς πολεμίους ὡς τῇ ὑστεραίᾳ ταύτην προσαγαγὼν ἐγκρατὴς τοῦ φρουρίου γενήσεται. In descriptions of battles and sieges *utrimque* normally refers to the two parties involved. That is impossible here. As it is the intention that the defenders *ultro citroque discurrunt, utrimque* must mean 'on both sides (of the spot, where the sappers were digging)'. The phrase seems to have been misunderstood ("de utraque parte") in TLL VI 1362.37–8.

4.22

aeneatorum accentu signo dato Amm. uses the rare word *aeneator* (TLL I 981.43) also in the practically identical opening phrases 16.12.36 and in 19.2.5. See further the note ad 24.4.15 *clangore Martio*.

ut... nec... audiretur ferri tinnitus nec For similar final clauses introduced by *ut... nec... nec* cf. e.g. 17.13.23 *ut nec bellis vexari nec mutari seditionibus possint*. They are also found in classical authors, cf. Cic. *Rep.* 2.23 *ut, quoad certus rex declaratus esset, nec sine rege civitas nec diuturno rege esset uno*. The phrase *ferri tinnitus* ("the clink of the iron tools", Rolfe) suggests that the sappers worked with chisels.

nec quodam intrinsecus obsistente In *ALL* 6, 1889, 268–9 Petschenig shows that the distinction between *quidam* and *quisquam* is lost sight of in Later Latin. He quotes as an example from Amm. 25.1.1 *nec sedere quodam auso nec flectere in quietem lumina*.

130 COMMENTARY

ut… cuniculariorum subita manus emergat In Zosimus' account the goal of the diversionary action is explained in the following words: ἐποίει δὲ τοῦτο (sc. Julian) πᾶσαν ἔννοιαν τοῖς Πέρσαις τῆς διὰ τοῦ ὀρύγματος ἀναιρῶν πολιορκίας (3.22.3). There is no parallel for V's *subitum* in the *Res Gestae*. Compared to *subito* (Em2S), Gelenius' *subita* is the lectio difficilior.

4.23 *quibus ita, ut convenerat, ordinatis et occupatis prohibitoribus* In view of the parallels quoted ad 23.1.5 *quibus ut convenerat ordinatis* it seems best to attribute to *convenerat* the meaning 'as was fitting', rather than 'as they had agreed beforehand'. Cf. Zos. 3.22.4 Τῶν ἀπὸ τοῦ φρουρίου τοίνυν ἁπάντων εἰς τὸ τὴν μηχανὴν ἀποκρούσασθαι συστραφέντων, διορύξαντες τὸν ὑπόνομον ('the underground passage') οἱ ταύτῃ ταχθέντες. For *prohibitor* 'defender' see the note ad 24.2.13.

patefactisque latebris evolat Exsuperius, de Victorum numero miles The verb is well chosen to express the sudden appearance of the sappers from the tunnel; TLL V 2.1066.1–10. The similarities between Amm. and Zosimus are striking, some minor differences notwithstanding. While Amm. simply states that the mine was opened and that Exsuperius, a soldier belonging to a *numerus* of *Victores*, came out first (see for *Victores* and *numerus* the notes ad 24.4.21 and 20.1.3, respectively), Zosimus tells us that the sappers emerged precisely in the middle of a house, where they came across a woman grinding corn. The woman, Zosimus continues, was killed by Superantius, a well-known soldier of the *Victores* and the first man to come out of the tunnel: εἶτα τὴν ἐπικειμένην ἄχρι τῆς ἐπιφανείας γῆν διατρήσαντες, ἐφάνησαν οἰκίας ἐν μέσῳ καθ᾽ ἣν ἔτυχέ τις ἀλετρὶς γυνὴ νυκτὸς οὔσης ἔτι βαθείας σῖτον ἄλευρα εἶναι ἐργαζομένη· ταύτην μὲν οὖν ὁ πρῶτος ἀναδὺς ἐκβοᾶν μέλλουσαν παίσας ἀνεῖλεν· ἦν δὲ Σουπεράντιος, ἐν τῷ λόχῳ τῶν βικτόρων οὐκ ἄσημος (3.22.4) – it would seem that the Exsuperius and the Superantius of Zosimus are one and the same man. The name Exsuperius is more common, as Lindenbrog already pointed out, but the name Exuperantius is also attested, cf. e.g. *PLRE* I s.v. The name Superantius does not occur in *PLRE*. Note further that in Amm.'s version the house (but not the woman) referred to by Zosimus, is mentioned later on in the sentence: *in aede, per quam in lucem prodierant*.

Libanius *Or.* 18.238 is silent about the name of the man who came out of the mine first: καὶ ὁ πρῶτος ἀναρριχώμενος ἐν μέσαις νυξὶν εἰς μέσα πύργου τινὸς διαδὺς ἔλαθε. He does speak, however, of a woman, although in other terms than Zosimus: γραῦν δ᾽ αὐτοῦ μόνην

CHAPTER 4.23   131

σὺν παιδίῳ κατακειμένην, ἐπειδὴ ᾔσθετο, σιγᾶν ἀναγκάσαντες etc. (*Or.* 18.239).

Apart from Amm., Zosimus and Libanius, there is another source which apparently deals with the decisive phase of the siege of ‘ Maozamalcha’, viz. the Suda s.v. ἀνασχοῦσα (A 2094 Adler): ὁ δὲ πρῶτος ἀνασχὼν ἐκ τοῦ ὀρύγματος ἦν Μάγνος, ἀνδρώδης τε καὶ διαφερόντως τολμητής. Unfortunately, while it is very likely that this fragment is concerned with the siege of ‘Maozamalcha’ by Julian’s army, its content contradicts the information given by Zosimus and Amm., in that it makes Magnus, not Exsuperius/Superantius, the first soldier to leap out of the tunnel – in Amm. and Zosimus. Magnus comes second (see below).

It was Norman, 1957 who first called attention to the passage in the *Suda*. He argued i.a. that the “authorship of the fragment should, almost certainly, be attributed to Eunapius” (p. 130), and drew some far-reaching conclusions from this attribution. These conclusions were accepted by e.g. Chalmers, 1960, but, rightly, it would seem, rejected by Cameron, 1963, whose final remark on p. 236 is worth quoting: “Since then Eunapius cannot be claimed as the only candidate for the authorship of this fragment – the attribution to him seems indeed to raise more problems than it solves – and since it is quite possible that *Suidas* (or one of the excerptors) has abbreviated or confused the original, it is rash to claim that his quotation can shed new light on the tangled problem of the interrelationship of the various accounts of Julian’s Persian expedition”. Blockley, 1981–1983, did not accept the passage as belonging to the fragments of Eunapius.

post quem Magnus tribunus et Iovianus notarius Zosimus mentions these men (*PLRE* I, Magnus 2 and Iovianus 1) in the same order: ἐπὶ τούτῳ δὲ Μάγνος, καὶ τρίτος Ἰοβιανὸς ὁ τοῦ τάγματος τῶν ὑπογραφέων προτεταγμένος (3.22.4), but he omits Magnus’ rank of tribune (for *tribunus* see ad 24.3.1). On the other hand, while Amm. describes Iovianus as merely a *notarius* (see for these officials the note ad 20.4.2), Zosimus gives him a fuller title (ὁ τοῦ τάγματος τῶν ὑπογραφέων προτεταγμένος). The Greek words correspond to the designation given to Iovianus by Amm. in 25.8.18: *Iovianus, primus inter notarios omnes, quem in obsidione civitatis Maozamalchae per cuniculum docuimus evasisse cum aliis* (the t.t. for the first man of the *schola notariorum*, not found in Amm., is *primicerius notariorum*, cf. Teitler, 1985, 58–60). Either Amm. did not bother to be precise in the present text, or Iovianus had been promoted in the meantime.

132 COMMENTARY

Libanius does not give any name (neither did he do so in the case of the first man out, see above): τῷ δὲ εἵπετο δεύτερος, καὶ τρίτος ἐκείνῳ (*Or.* 18.238). However, in the *Suda* s.v. ἀνασχοῦσα (A 2094 Adler), quoted above, a man called Magnus is mentioned, not, unfortunately, as the second man to leave the tunnel, but as the first. Although the *Suda* is wrong about the order, it nevertheless would seem that the same Magnus is meant.

The *tribunus* Magnus (together with Exsuperius and Iovianus) earned an *obsidionalis corona* for bravery, according to Amm. in the next section. Nothing more is known of him. His identification with Magnus of Carrhae (so e.g. Klein, 1914, 106; cf. *PLRE* I, Magnus 2 "He could be identical with the historian Magnus 3 of Carrhae"), rejected by Thompson, 1947, 31 and others (cf. Matthews 163 with n. 73), is defended by Fornara, 1991, 14–5.

quos audax multitudo secuta Cf. Zos. 3.22.4 ἔπειτα δὲ πλείους, Lib. *Or.* 18.238 καὶ πᾶς ἐβούλετο τῶν ἀναβαινόντων εἶναι ("and all the sappers were eager to be members of the party completing the climb", tr. Norman).

his prius confossis, quos in aede, per quam in lucem prodierant, invenerunt Cf. Zos. 3.22.4 and Lib. *Or.* 18.238, quoted above (*patefactisque latebris*).

suspensis gradibus procedentes 'On tiptoe'; cf. the description of Isaurian brigands stealing into merchant ships at night: 14.2.2 *per ancoralia quadripedo gradu repentes seseque suspensis passibus iniectantes in scaphas.*

obtruncarunt vigiles omnes ex usu moris gentici iustitiam felicitatemque regis sui canoris vocibus extollentes In a similar fashion both the Romans and the Persians sang the praise of their leaders during the siege of Amida, 19.2.11 *nostris virtutes Constanti Caesaris extollentibus ut domini rerum et mundi, Persis Saporem saansaan appellantibus et pi rosen, quod rex regibus imperans et bellorum victor interpretatur.* The adjective *canorus* is found nowhere else in the *Res Gestae*, although the expression is not uncommon; TLL III 277.17–41.

In Zosimus' version the Persians not only praised the justice and good fortune of Sapor (see for him the note ad 20.6.1 *truculentus rex ille Persarum*), but jeered at Julian and abused him, saying that it would be easier for the Roman emperor to capture the palace of Zeus than their fortress: τότε δὴ λοιπὸν ἐπὶ τὸ τεῖχος ἐλάσαντες ἐπέστησαν παρὰ πᾶσαν ἐλπίδα τοῖς Πέρσαις ᾄσματα λέγουσιν ἐπιχώρια, τὴν μὲν τοῦ

CHAPTER 4.24   133

σφῶν βασιλέως ἀνδρείαν ὑμνοῦντα, διαβάλλοντες δὲ τὴν τοῦ Ῥωμαίων βασιλέως ἀνέφικτον ἐπιχείρησιν· ῥᾷον γὰρ ἔφασκον αὐτὸν τὴν τοῦ Διὸς αἱρήσειν αὐλὴν ἢ τὸ φρούριον (3.22.5). Cf. Lib. *Or.* 18.236 (speaking, however, of the first stage of the siege): Πέρσαι δὲ ἄνωθεν ἐγέλων, ἐτώθαζον (were mocking), ὕβριζον, ἐτόξευον, ἐτύγχανον· ἴσον αὐτοὺς ἡγοῦντο ποιεῖν ὥσπερ ἂν εἰ καὶ τὸν οὐρανὸν ἐπεχείρουν ἑλεῖν and 238: νύκτα καὶ ἡμέραν ἐκώμαζον (were feasting).

The very rare *genticus* instead of *gentilis* is probably borrowed from Tacitus: *Ann.* 3.43.2 *more gentico* (= 6.33.2); TLL VI 1865.61–71.

extimabatur Mars ipse For this alternative form of *existimare* see TLL   **4.24** V 2.1518.18–26. It is found in authors like Cicero and Tacitus, so Seyfarth is certainly right in keeping it. In the note ad 23.5.20 *perplexo et diuturno Marte* it is remarked that Amm. often uses *Mars* as a worn-out metonymy for warfare (cf. e.g. *glorioso Marte* in 14.8.13 and *Marte acerrimo* in 19.1.9). This is not to deny, however, that Mars in the *Res Gestae* can also be a cultic reality (cf. 24.6.16 *complures hostias Marti parabat Ultori* and Rike, 1987, 25–6, Meulder, 1991, 473).

si misceri hominibus numina maiestatis iura permittunt This is a so-called pseudo-conditional sentence of the type *si iustum est credi* (23.6.34); see Pinkster, 1990, 35. Amm. refers to the Platonic tenet θεὸς δὲ ἀνθρώπῳ οὐ μείγνυται (*Symp.* 203 a 2), echoed in Apul. *Soc.* 127 as follows: *Habetis interim bina animalia: deos ab hominibus plurimum differentis loci sublimitate, vitae perpetuitate, naturae perfectione, nullo inter se propinquo communicatu*, which helps to understand the present phrase. In Plato, as in Apuleius, this is the starting point for a discussion of the role of δαίμονες as mediators between gods and men. The same idea is found in Amm.'s digression on the genius in 21.14.5: *sempiternis Homeri carminibus intellegi datur non deos caelestes cum viris fortibus collocutos nec affuisse pugnantibus vel iuvisse, sed familiares genios cum isdem versatos.* In stressing their importance for the contacts between the human and the divine world a compromise was reached between the belief in the unattainable majesty of the gods on the one hand and that in the reality of superhuman intervention in human affairs on the other. Lane Fox, 1986, 102–67 in his long chapter 'Seeing the Gods', offers a wealth of evidence to show how strong and widespread the belief in the active participation of the gods in human affairs was throughout antiquity. See especially p. 148–9 on Julian and Libanius, who in *Or.* 18.172 tells about Julian being advised by Zeus in person on mount Casius: εἰ μὲν οὖν οἷόν τ' ἦν ἀνθρώπῳ

134   COMMENTARY

οὐρανοῦ κοινωνῆσαι θεοῖς, μετ᾽ ἐκείνων ἂν ἦν αὐτῷ τῆς ἑαυτῶν μεταδι-
δόντων χώρας, τοῦ σώματος δὲ ταῦτα οὐκ ἐῶντος αὐτοὶ παρ᾽ ἐκεῖνον
ᾔεσαν διδάσκαλοι τοῦ τί δεῖ ποιεῖν καὶ τί μὴ ποιεῖν γιγνόμενοι.

castra Lucanorum invadenti Luscino For the second time in this book
Amm. refers to C. Fabricius Luscinus. See for the first time 24.3.5
nam et Fabricii… locupletes and the note ad loc. The miracle mentioned
here took place, according to V. Max. 1.8.6, when Luscinus fought
near Thurii against the Lucani, who had chosen the side of Pyrrhus.

hocque ideo creditum est Note the contrast between the imperfect
extimabatur, describing the prevailing opinion at a certain time, and
the perfect *creditum est*, indicating the moment at which this opinion
arose.

in congressu flagranti The participle is found in the same sense in Liv.
31.11.10 *flagrante bello* and Tac. *Ann.* 2.59.1.

*scalas vehens visus formidandae vastitatis armatus… quaesitus… repperiri
non potuit* A typical 'Partizipienhäufung', although *armatus* is a
noun, see the note ad 20.4.22. *Vehens visus* may be interpreted as
the passive rendering of the accusative cum participio *viderunt ve-
hentem.* The extraordinary size of the soldier betrays his superhuman
status; see the note ad 21.2.2 *imago quaedam.* The gen. qualitatis is
also used in the description of the German king Chnodomarius in
16.12.24 *immanis equo spumante sublimior erectus in iaculum formidandae
vastitatis.*

cum recenseretur exercitus For *recensere*, 'to review troops', cf. e.g. Liv.
1.16.1 *cum ad exercitum recensendum contionem… haberet*, 2.39.9, Suet.
Cal. 44.1 and in Amm. 18.6.23, 29.5.9, 31.4.7. For a Greek equivalent
see e.g. Theophylactus Simocatta *Hist.* 2.6 ὁ στρατηγὸς ἐξέτασιν τοῦ
ὁπλιτικοῦ ἐπεποίητο.

cum se ultro offerret, si miles fuisset Adversative *cum* expresses the
contrast between the god's absence and the desire for recognition
which a normal soldier would have shown. Amm. regularly uses the
imperfect in an irrealis of the past, e.g. in his praise of the eunuch
Eutherius 16.7.4: *si Numa Pompilius vel Socrates bona quaedam dicerent
de spadone… a veritate descivisse arguebantur* and a few sentences later
16.7.5 *quem si Constans imperator… audiret honesta suadentem et recta,
nulla vel venia certe digna peccasset.*

CHAPTER 4.24   135

sed ut tunc... ita nunc It is only here that the reason why Amm. mentioned the anecdote about Luscinus becomes clear. It is used for the sake of contrast: after the fall of ' Maozamalcha' the bravest soldiers did receive their rewards. For contrastive use of *ut... ita* cf. e.g. in §10 *ut erat necessarius appetitus, ita effectu res difficillima* and 25.3.16 *dolores omnes, ut insultant ignavis, ita persistentibus cedunt.*

enituerunt hi, qui fecere fortissime In the first place undoubtedly Exsuperius, Magnus and Iovianus (cf. §23). So, rightly, Chalmers, 1960, 153. See Hagendahl, 1923, 29–46 for the way in which Amm. uses the endings *-ere* and *-erunt*. For the rare *enite(sc)o* cf. 21.14.5 *Pythagoras enituisse dicitur* and Tac. *Ann.* 14.53.5 *inter nobiles et longa ⟨de⟩cora praeferentes novitas mea enituit? Fortiter facere* has the specific sense of 'to distinguish oneself in battle'; TLL VI 1163.82–1164.13.

obsidionalibus coronis donati Ever since Gibbon, already quoted by Wagner, Amm. has been taken to task for what he says here (cf. e.g. Klein, 1914, 31: "niemand wird Ammian diese Nachricht glauben"; Den Hengst, *AntTard* 6 (1998) 419: "Ammianus was certainly wrong in mentioning this crown"). Amm., it is argued, mistakenly mentions the *corona obsidionalis*, which used to be given only to a general who had relieved a beleaguered city (cf. Gel. 5.6.8 *Obsidionalis est, quam ii qui liberati obsidione sunt, dant ei duci qui liberavit*; Plin. *Nat.* 22.7 *Eadem vocatur obsidionalis liberatis obsidione abominandoque exitu totis castris*; Fest. p. 190M), while he should have spoken of the *corona muralis*, the reward for the first man to mount the wall of an enemy city (cf. Plb. 6.39.5 Τοῖς δὲ πόλεως καταλαμβανομένης πρώτοις ἐπὶ τὸ τεῖχος ἀναβᾶσιν χρυσοῦν δίδωσι στέφανον; Gel. 5.6.16 *Muralis est corona, qua donatur ab imperatore qui primus murum subiit inque oppidum hostium per vim ascendit; idcirco quasi muri pinnis decorata est*).

It is questionable, however, whether one should adduce as evidence only passages of antiquarians like Gellius and Pliny or the historian Polybius, authors who wrote several centuries before Amm. Polybius, Gellius and Pliny may be right as to the original meaning of the various crowns, but to assume that their words are canonical and represent historical reality throughout the Roman period, is a rather static point of view. Tempora mutantur and, to quote the most recent study of military decorations, based inter alia on epigraphical evidence, "with the exception of the *corona civica*, the crowns lost all connection with the deeds which they were originally designed to commemorate" (Maxfield, 1981, 64; cf. already Steiner, 1906, 33). If in imperial times "no naval encounter was necessary for an

136   COMMENTARY

ex-consul to win a *corona navalis*, no capture of town or camp for a
centurion to receive a *corona muralis*" (Maxfield, ibid.), then it is at
least conceivable that the *corona obsidionalis* also had lost its original
meaning.

Furthermore, are Amm.'s critics right in aiming their criticism
at Ammianus? Should it not rather be Julian who is to blame for
the supposed error? Or are we to assume that the emperor correctly
awarded the appropriate crowns to the qualified soldiers, but that
Amm. in his report of this event made a mess of it, either by mistake
or on purpose (for instance, because "es Ammian häufig weniger
auf die historische Genauigkeit ankommt, als auf die eindrucksvolle
und packende Darstellung", Klein, 1914, 31)? If so, then what about
24.6.15, where Amm. also speaks of crowns given by Julian (*qui
appellans plerosque nominatim, quos stabili mente aliquid clarum fecisse
ipse arbiter perspexit, navalibus donavit coronis et civicis et castrensibus*)?
Is Amm. not to be trusted there either? All this seems rather unfair
to a historian who certainly had read about military decorations in
former times (cf. 25.3.13 *Sicinium Dentatum adiciat ornatum militarium
multitudine coronarum*), and who was also an experienced army officer
(as Tränkle, 1962, 25 n. 14 rightly observes in this respect) as well as
a witness to the events which he describes. If anyone is to be accused
of a mistake, it should be Julian, not Ammianus.

However, it does not seem necessary to assume that either Julian
or Amm. was wrong. The text can be interpreted quite satisfactorily,
if the following considerations are taken into account. Firstly, both
ancient and modern authorities agree that the *corona obsidionalis*
(or *graminea*, Gel. 5.6.9, Plin. *Nat.* 22.6–7) was pre-eminent among
Roman military decorations (Plin. *Nat.* 22.6 ff., Fest. p. 190M, Steiner,
1906, 44, Maxfield, 1981, 67; cf. in general Fiebiger, 1901). Secondly,
modern research has shown that "award-giving on a regular basis
came to an end in the early third century A.D., though sporadic
examples do occur to the very end of the Roman Empire in the
West and into the Byzantine era" (Maxfield, 1981, 19; see for Late
Antiquity also Delmaire, 1989, 547–8). In other words, the giving of
crowns and other decorations instead of donatives in cash (see for
the latter 24.3.3), had become extremely rare and was apparently
restricted to special occasions. Thirdly, the soldiers *qui fecere fortissime*
had, by their masterly example of endurance and bravery, ended a
most difficult and laborious siege and therefore seemed entitled to
the highest possible reward. Under these circumstances the emperor,
wanting to thank them in a special way for their extraordinary
behaviour, conferred on them the crown which in days of old was

CHAPTER 4.25   137

the hardest of all to win, viz. the *corona obsidionalis*, thus reviving an ancient custom in a slightly adapted form.

pro contione laudati veterum more It was a time-honoured custom to praise deserving soldiers in front of the troops. Cf. e.g. Plb. 6.39.2 συναγαγὼν ὁ στρατηγὸς ἐκκλησίαν τοῦ στρατοπέδου, καὶ παραστησά-μενος τοὺς δόξαντας τι πεπραχέναι διαφέρον, πρῶτον μὲν ἐγκώμιον ὑπὲρ ἑκάστου λέγει περί τε τῆς ἀνδραγαθίας, κἄν τι κατὰ τὸν βίον αὐτοῖς ἄλλο συνυπάρχῃ τῆς ἐπ' ἀγαθῷ μνήμης ἄξιον, Cic. *Ver.* 3.185, Sal. *Jug.* 8.2, Liv. 7.7.3, 7.10.14 (with Oakley ad loc.), 26.48.4 and HA *Pr.* 5.1. See also 24.6.15.

Tandem nudata reseratis aditibus multis lapsura invaditur civitas The   **4.25**
participle *nudata* is subordinated to *lapsura*: 'doomed to fall, because it had been laid open'. *Nudare* may be called a standard term for the end of a siege; see the note ad 23.4.9. The same applies to *reserare aditus*. Cf. e.g. 21.12.9 (ut) *aedificii parte convulsa aditus in penetralia... reserarent*. For the attributive use of the future participle see Szantyr 390.

sine sexus discrimine vel aetatis Again a standard element in the description of the capture of a town. Bitter 53 n. 159 has a long list of parallels. Cf. Zos. 3.22.6 Ἐπιθέμενοι δὲ τοὺς ἐν χερσὶν ἔπαιόν τε καὶ ἐκ τοῦ τείχους ὠθοῦντες διέφθειρον, τοὺς δὲ καὶ διώκοντες παντοδαποῖς θανάτου τρόποις ἀνῄρουν, οὔτε γυναικῶν οὔτε παίδων ἀπεχόμενοι and Lib. *Or.* 18.239 οὐδὲν ἔδει ἢ τοὺς ἐπιστάντας σφίσι φονεύειν ἅπαντας ("all they had to do then was to kill any they came across", tr. Norman).

quidquid impetus repperit, potestas iratorum absumpsit The twofold personificatio emphasizes well the irresistible advance and the overwhelming superiority of the invading Roman army. *Potestas* has the same meaning 'superior force' in 26.10.10 *Martiae virtutis potestas aut absumit, quod occupat, aut nobilitat.*

ultimum flentes Cf. 31.8.8 *post quae adulta virginitas castitasque nuptarum ore abiecto flens ultima ducebatur.* It is difficult to decide whether in these striking phrases *ultimum, -a* is a direct object ("en pleurant leur dernière heure venue", Fontaine) or an adverbial accusative ("shedding their last tears", Rolfe). TLL VI 900.33–4 prefers the latter interpretation, but 21.15.2 *ultimum spirans deflebat exitium* is decidedly in favour of the former.

138   COMMENTARY

e muris acti sua sponte praecipites Cf. Lib. *Or.* 18.239 οἱ γὰρ δὴ πλείους αὐτοὺς ἀπώλλυσαν ταῖς ἀπὸ τοῦ τείχους ῥίψεσι.

4.26   *extractus est autem vivus cum satellitibus octoginta Nabdates, praesidiorum magister, quem… servari iussit intactum serenus imperator et clemens* Zos. 3.22.6 also relates that the commander of the fortress (he calls him Anabdates) and his eighty companions were brought before the emperor: (Most inhabitants were killed) πλὴν εἰ μή πού γέ τινας αἰχμαλώτους αὐτοῖς ἔδοξεν ἔχειν· Ἀναβδάτης δὲ ὁ ἀρχιφρούραρχος ἐν τῷ διαδρᾶναι τὸ φρούριον ἁλοὺς ἅμα τοῖς ἀμφ᾽ αὐτόν, ὀγδοήκοντα τὸν ἀριθμὸν οὖσι, τῷ βασιλεῖ προσήχθη δεδεμένος ὀπίσω τὰς χεῖρας. Note that Amm.'s *extractus* suggests that the commander was in hiding when he was found (cf. 24.5.4 *e latebris*), while Zosimus says that he was caught fleeing (ἐν τῷ διαδρᾶναι τὸ φρούριον). This Nabdates, or Anabdates, was later executed, as we learn from Amm. 24.5.4 and Zos. 3.23.4. Baldwin, 1976, 120 correctly notes that his name is missing in *PLRE* I.

As to *serenus imperator et clemens*, it is mentioned in the note ad 21.12.20, q.v. that Amm. more than once depicts Julian as endowed with the imperial virtue of clemency (cf. the note ad 22.10.5 and see for *clementia* in Amm. now also Brandt, 1999, 179 ff.). Amm.'s praise of Julian in this respect is on the whole, as in the present text, clear but modest. Conversely, Libanius in *Or.* 18.239–40 insists that the massacre at 'Maiozamalcha' was not caused by any lack of clemency on the part of the emperor: θήρα τε ἦν πολλὴ τῶν πειρωμένων λαθεῖν καὶ οὐδεὶς ἔχειν αἰχμάλωτον ἐβούλετο μᾶλλον ἢ διαφθείρειν ὥστ᾽ ἀφίεσαν ἄνωθεν, αἱ δὲ αἰχμαὶ κάτωθεν ἀπήντων τοῖς ζῶσι, τοῖς ἡμιθνῆσι, τοῖς τεθνεῶσιν. ἤρκει γὰρ ἡ φορὰ πρὸς θάνατον. 240 τοιαῦτα ἐχόρευσαν μὲν ἐν νυκτὶ τοῖς πολεμικοῖς δαίμοσιν, ἔδειξαν δὲ ἀνίσχοντι τῷ θεῷ. καὶ τοῦτο μόνον ἠπείθησαν τῷ βασιλεῖ. ὁ μὲν γὰρ ἐκέλευε ζωγρεῖν καὶ τὸν εἰλημμένον ἐλεεῖν, οἱ δὲ μεμνημένοι τῶν βελῶν καὶ τοὺς βεβλημένους εἰδότες καὶ τῆς ὀργῆς τὴν δεξιὰν κινούσης παρεμυθοῦντο τὴν ἐπὶ τοῖς πόνοις λύπην τῷ φόνῳ καὶ ἐδέοντο βασιλέως συγγνώμην ἔχειν εἰ δρῶσι πεπονθότες ("There was much hunting out of those who tried to hide. Nobody wanted to take prisoners. They preferred to kill their victims outright and therefore flung them down on to the spears below that welcomed them living, unconscious or dead. The fact that they were thrown down was enough to kill them. 240 Such was the carnival they held during the night to the gods of war and revealed to the Sun God at his rising. In this alone they disobeyed their emperor, for he had given orders to take prisoners alive and show them mercy. The troops, however, remembering the missiles and knowing their losses,

CHAPTER 4.26   139

and impelled to the action by their fury, found in the massacre some
consolation for the rigours they had endured, and they begged the
emperor's pardon for getting their own back", tr. Norman, slightly
adapted).

The expression *praesidiorum magister* seems to be unique; see the
note ad 24.2.21 *Mamersides praesidiorum praefectus.*

Divisa itaque perpensis meritis et laboribus praeda... parvo contentus As
in countless other places, the transition marked by *itaque* should
begin a new section. The rest of §26 and §27 forms a unit dealing
with Julian's exemplary behaviour with regard to the temptations of
wealth and power. In writing this passage, Amm. must have been
thinking of Cic. *Off.* 1.66–73, where Cicero discusses *fortitudo* and
magnanimitas, virtues held in common by philosophers and great
rulers, but much more difficult to practise for the man of action. That
Amm. had this passage in mind is evident from the correspondence
between *ne frangerentur cupiditate, qui se invictos a laboribus ubique
praestiterunt* (§27) and *Off.* 1.68 *Non est autem consentaneum, qui metu
non frangatur, eum frangi cupiditate, nec qui invictum se a labore praestiterit,
vinci a voluptate.* The phrase *parvo contentus* in §26 occurs also in *Off.*
1.70 *si contenti sint et suo et parvo.* For *perpendere* see the note ad 20.9.3.

Amm.'s wording suggests that the division of the booty took
place in an orderly fashion (see also below, the note ad *et tribus
aureis nummis*). The corresponding passage in Zosimus, however,
puts things in a different light: ἐφ' ἁρπαγὴν ὁ στρατὸς τῶν ἀποκειμένων
κτημάτων ἐχώρει· κομισαμένου δὲ ἑκάστου τὸ προσπεσόν etc. (3.22.7).

In Julian's obituary in Book 25 his self-restraint in sexual matters
(see below) and his moderation in eating and sleeping are especially stressed (25.4.2–6; cf. Brandt, 1999, 121 ff.). In his *Mis.* 340
b the emperor himself boasts of sleepless nights and a simple diet:
ἄγρυπνοι νύκτες ἐν στιβάδι ('a pallet'), καὶ τροφὴ παντὸς ἥττων κόρου.
Mamertinus says that Julian was *severe parcus in semet* (*Pan.* 3.12.2).

mutum puerum oblatum sibi suscepit gesticularium The only parallel
for *gesticularius* is Gel. 1.5.3, where the uncouth Torquatus criti-
cizes the orator Hortensius for his unmanly gesticulation: (cum)
*non iam histrionem eum esse diceret, sed gesticulariam Dionysiamque eum
notissimae saltatriculae nomine appellaret*; TLL VI 1958.29–35. In all
probability Amm. found the word in Gellius. In a very interesting article Mary, 1993, 48 n. 56 observes that the word *pantomimus*, which
one would expect here, despite its Greek ring, was an Italian ne-
ologism, and that Zosimus is the first Greek writer to use it. He

140 COMMENTARY

refers to Luc. *Salt.* 67 οἱ Ἰταλιῶται τὸν ὀρχηστὴν παντόμιμον καλοῦσιν. Amm.'s choice of the word *gesticularius* is, according to Mary, a double purism: Amm. rejects *pantomimus*, because it is incorrect Greek, and teaches his Latin readers a lesson in using a perfectly correct Latin form.

multa, quae callebat, nutibus venustissimis explicantem The words *nutibus venustissimis* show that the boy was a pantomime, for which the verb *gesticulari* with its derivatives is the t.t. Cf. the description of a girl playing the role of Juno in Apul. *Met.* 10.31: *procedens quieta et inadfectata gesticulatione nutibus honestis pastori* (Paris) *pollicetur* e.q.s. with Zimmerman's note. Strictly speaking, *nutus* refers to movements of the head, but one gets the impression here that Amm. is thinking of all forms of wordless speech. Quintilian carefully distinguishes between the hands and the head in *Inst.* 11.3.66 *quippe non manus solum, sed nutus etiam declarant nostram voluntatem et in mutis pro sermone sunt.* The expression *multa, quae callebat* is also found in 21.1.6 *per vaticinandi praesagia multa, quae callebat*, q.v. It suggests that the boy had a considerable repertoire. Mary, 1993 has pointed to the importance of Lib. *Or.* 64 Ὑπὲρ τῶν ὀρχηστῶν for a correct appreciation of the role of the pantomime. He embodies the virtue of ἐγκράτεια in his complete mastery over his body (Libanius writes in § 106: Ὥσπερ ... οὐκ ἔστιν ὁμοῦ τό τε σῶμα παχύνειν καὶ τὴν ψυχὴν θεραπεύειν, οὕτως οὐκ ἔστιν ὄρχησιν καὶ πλησμονὴν συνελθεῖν, ἀλλ᾽ ἀνάγκη τὸν θατέρου γλιχόμενον ἀφεστάναι θατέρου). Seen in this light, Julian's acceptance of the young pantomime and his refusal to have anything to do with the beautiful Persian captive women are two sides of the same coin. For *explicare* see TLL V 2.1733.

et tribus aureis nummis Delmaire, 1989, 546 plausibly suggests that the sum of three *aurei nummi* (see for the terms the notes ad 20.4.18 and 24.3.3) was the result of the division of the booty mentioned in the beginning of the section. Seyfarth tries to make sense of V's text, interpreting the abl. as dependent on *contentus* in line with *parvo*, but such a specific continuation of a general indication of value like *parvo* is hard to imagine. Fontaine also keeps V's text, but omits *ut* before *existimabat*. His translation suggests that he takes *tribus nummis* as a kind of abl. qualitatis with *praemium* and *iucundum et gratum* as a predicative accusative. The remedies proposed by Haupt (*tris aureos nummos*) and Horkel (*cum tribus aureis nummis*) are both simple and adequate. As *tris* is not found in V, Horkel's correction seems preferable, especially because it also keeps the ablative in V.

CHAPTER 4.27   141

iucundum, ut existimabat, et gratum If the three gold pieces are indeed the reward for the common soldiers, the adjectives emphasize the modesty of Julian, who graciously accepts being treated as one of the rank and file.

ex virginibus autem, quae speciosae sunt captae… nec contrectare aliquam voluit nec videre The hyperbaton is startling. It will not do to take *speciosae* predicatively ('captured for their beauty'), since beauty is a quality shared by all Persian women. Metrical considerations may be involved, since without the adjective the relative clause would not result in an acceptable cursus.   **4.27**

In 25.4.2 Amm. also refers to Julian's self-restraint in sexual matters (although the text is corrupt, enough of it remains to grasp its general meaning): *ita inviolata castitate enituit, ut post amissam coniugem nihil umquam venerium † augis larens illud advertens.* This feature was noticed by friend and foe alike. Libanius (*Or.* 18.179) puts it thus: Ταυτὶ τοῦ μήκους τῶν νυκτῶν ἀπολέλαυκεν ἡμῖν ὁ βασιλεύς· ἑτέροις δὲ ἐν ταῖς τηλικαύταις τῶν Ἀφροδίτης ἐμέλησεν. ὁ δὲ τοσοῦτον ἀπέσχε τοῦ ζητεῖν εἴ τῳ θυγάτηρ ἢ γυνὴ καλή, ὥστ' εἰ μὴ θεσμῷ γάμων ἐζεύχθη παρὰ τῆς Ἥρας, ἐτελεύτα ἂν λόγῳ μόνον τὰς ἀνθρώπων ἐπιστάμενος μίξεις. νῦν δὲ τὴν μὲν γυναῖκα ἐπένθησεν, ἑτέρας δὲ οὔτε πρότερον οὔθ' ὕστερον ἥψατο φύσει… δυνάμενος σωφρονεῖν ("Such were our emperor's enjoyments during the long winter nights, when other people are usually more interested in matters of sex. But so far was he from enquiring whether any man had a good-looking daughter or wife that, had not Hera once bound him in the rites of marriage, he would have ended his days knowing nothing of sexual intercourse of humans save by report. As it was, he went into mourning for his wife and never touched another woman before or afterwards, for he had a natural bent towards continence", tr. Norman). Julian in *Mis.* 345 c quotes a reproof addressed to him by the Antiochenes: καθεύδεις ὡς ἐπίπαν νύκτωρ μόνος. Cf. also Mamertinus *Pan.* 3.13.3.

In TLL IV 774.47–52 *contrectare* is given an erotic interpretation, which suits the context well. Amm. uses the verb also with other (forbidden) objects: 17.4.12 (Constantius) *hunc* (obeliscum) *nec contrectare ausus est nec movere,* 17.9.5 *non aurum neque argentum petentes, quae olim nec contrectare potuimus nec videre.*

in Perside, ubi feminarum pulchritudo excellit Ἡ δόξα τῶν Περσίδων γυναικῶν is spoken of in Charito 5.3.1. Plut. *Alex.* 21.10 calls the Persian women who were made prisoners of war by Alexander κάλλει καὶ μεγέθει διαφερούσας and ἀλγηδόνες ὀμμάτων ('terrible eyesores').

142 COMMENTARY

Cf. Curt. 3.12.21 *virgines reginas excellentis formae.* Amm. says nothing of the kind in his excursion on Persia and the Persians in 23.6.

Alexandrum imitatus et Africanum, qui haec declinabant, ne frangerentur cupiditate, qui se invictos a laboribus ubique praestiterunt See the note ad § 26 *Divisa itaque* for the Ciceronian background of this sentence.

For Alexander the Great in Amm. see the note ad 21.8.3 and Szidat, 1988. Cf. also Lane Fox, 1997. With *Africanum* Amm. here refers to P. Cornelius Scipio Aemilianus Africanus (Numantinus), pace Viansino, 1985, II, 533. Elsewhere in Amm. he is called Scipio (23.5.20), Aemilianus Scipio (17.11.3, 24.2.16, 25.10.13) or Aemilianus (24.2.17). Cf. for him Astin, 1967. Other Scipiones are mentioned in 14.6.11 (*filia Scipionis*), 15.10.10 (*superioris Africani pater Publius Cornelius Scipio*), 21.14.5 (*superior Scipio*), 22.9.5 (*per Scipionem Nasicam*), 25.9.10 (*Publio Scipioni*) and 31.13.17 (*Scipionum alterum*).

Various authors report that either Alexander or Scipio Africanus showed chivalrous conduct vis-à-vis female prisoners (cf. for Alexander Plut. *Alex.* 21.5 ff., Curt. 3.12.21, 4.10.24, Athenaeus 13.603 c, for Africanus Plb. 10.19.3–7, Liv. 26.49.11–16, 26.50.1–12, D.C. 16.57.43, Flor. *Epit.* 1.22.40, Sil. 15.268–71, V. Max. 4.3.1), but it is in Fron. *Str.* 2.11.5–6 that both heroes are mentioned in one breath. This is also the case in Gel. 7.8.1 ff., as Hertz, 1874, 279 duly observed (cf. Barnes, 1998, 84 with n. 28); compare especially Amm.'s *nec contrectare aliquam voluit nec videre* with Gel. 7.8.2 *facie incluta mulierem vetuit in conspectum suum deduci, ut eam ne oculis quidem suis contingeret.* For Amm.'s use of historical exempla see Blockley, 1994 and Wittchow, 2001.

4.28 *nostrae partis architectus, cuius nomen non suppetit* The *architectus*, "whose exact rank has still to be established" (Le Bohec, 1994, 52), must be a military engineer like the bridge builders mentioned in 25.6.15. In *Dig.* 50.6.7 the *architectus* is listed among the military personnel whose *munerum graviorum condicio* entitled them to *aliquam vacationem.* Cf. Von Domaszewski, 1896 and see TLL II 465.83–466.10 for epigraphical evidence. The intriguing admission of ignorance as to the name of the engineer is reminiscent of 16.12.63, where Amm. mentions among the fallen in the battle of Strasbourg *vacans quidam tribunus, cuius non suppetit nomen.* Are we to think that Amm. had witnessed the incident, but that the name had slipped his mind? Or that the name of the engineer was not mentioned in the source he consulted? Sabbah 170 n. 63 is convinced of the latter, as Amm.'s wording indeed suggests.

CHAPTER 4.28   143

post machinam scorpionis forte assistens For the construction and the handling of the stone throwing *scorpio* or *onager* see the commentary ad 23.4.4–6.

reverberato lapide, quem artifex titubanter aptaverat fundae It is not completely clear what caused the *scorpio* to backfire. The explanations proposed by Müller, 1905, 598 and Brok ad loc. fail to take *reverberato lapide* into account. Marsden, 1971, 253 is more helpful: "On release, the shot ricocheted and came out of the *onager* travelling fairly low down and to the rear instead of to the front and upwards". On the one hand, *reverberato* suggests that the arm of the *scorpio* hit the buffer, but that the loose end of the sling (*funda*, for which see the drawings in Marsden, 1971, 260 and in our commentary on Book 23 following p. 80) failed to fly off and hurled the stone back. On the other, Amm. mentions as the cause of the accident the fact that the marksman had not fitted the stone properly into the sling. It is not clear what the link is between the two details.

Amm. uses *reverberare* in 22.15.7 of the effect of the etesian winds that push the waters of the Nile back: *hinc ui reuerberante uentorum, inde urgente cursu uenarum perennium. Titubare* normally means 'to stagger' or 'to make mistakes'. Both meanings occur in Amm.: 17.5.14 (in a speech) *id experiendo legendoque scientes in proeliis quibusdam raro rem titubasse Romanam, in summa uero bellorum numquam ad deteriora prolapsam* and 19.11.3 *correctione titubantium beniuola*. There is no parallel for the meaning 'sloppily' which is required here.

For *artifex* 'marksman' cf. 23.4.2 *artifex contemplabilis* with the note and 24.4.12 *locabant etiam artifices tormenta muralia*.

obliso pectore supinatus profudit animam The verb *oblidere* is found only here in Amm. It is extremely rare anyway. Pliny uses it in his account of the eruption of the Vesuvius, *Ep.* 6.20.16 *hunc* (pulverem) *identidem adsurgentes excutiebamus; operti alioqui atque etiam oblisi pondere essemus*. The expression *profundere animam* lacks its normal connotation of giving one's life in a cause, as e.g. in Cic. *Phil.* 14.30 *qui pro patria vitam profuderunt* or 23.6.44 *ut iudicetur inter alios omnes beatus, qui in proelio profuderit animam*. Fontaine keeps V's *profundit*, as a historic present would be quite appropriate for this dramatic event. It certainly would be, but following so shortly after a present tense in which the author refers to the time of writing (*suppetit*) and flanked by historical tenses (*aptaverat, noscerentur*) a historic present seems unnatural. See Ehrismann 120–3 for Amm.'s customary practice in this regard.

144   COMMENTARY

adeo, ut ne signa quidem totius corporis noscerentur That is to say that
the engineer was disfigured beyond recognition. A good parallel is
Seneca's description of the boy Astyanax who flung himself from a
tower after the fall of Troy: *signa clari corporis / et ora et illas nobiles
patris notas / confudit imam pondus ad terram datum* (*Tr.* 1112–4).
Cf. also Amm.'s remark about the books of the physiognomists in
15.8.16: *veteribus libris, quorum lectio per corporum signa pandit animarum
interna.*

4.29   *Exin profecto imperatori index nuntiáverat cértus* Bentley conjectured
profecturo, undoubtedly on account of the following pluperfect. Amm.
however, as has been often remarked, e.g. by Ehrismann 124–6,
does not distinguish between perfect and pluperfect as clearly as
do the authors from the classical period. Often, as here, metrical
considerations may play a part. See the notes ad 20.3.3 *scrutatores
causarum*, 20.9.5 *praefectum praetorio* and 24.1.11.

fallaces foveas et obscuras… subsedisse manum insidiatricem Zosimus is
silent on this, as is Libanius, although the latter, elsewhere in his
funeral oration, speaks of the discovery of underground dwellings
of the enemy: καταγείους τε οἰκήσεις ἀνεῦρον (*Or.* 18.231). Jews,
Cassius Dio tells us (69.12.3), had subterranean refuges during their
rebellion under Bar Kochba, while Theophylactus Simocatta *Hist.*
2.7, speaking of the inhabitants of the Persian province of Arzanene,
relates how by using echo-sounding Byzantine soldiers discovered
them in their subterranean pits. The treacherous pitfalls mirror the
character of the Persians, *fallacissima gens* (21.13.4). *Fovea* is used
metaphorically in 30.4.13 to describe corrupt lawcourts: *foveae fallaces
et caecae.* When *subsidere* is used transitively in classical authors, the
object is the person (or the situation) one is lying in wait for: Verg. *A.*
11.268 *devictam Asiam subsedit adulter.* In Amm., however, the object
is the place of the ambush, 'to lie in ambush in', as here *foveas* and
foramen in 15.2.4 *subterraneus serpens foramen subsidens occultum.*

4.30   *compertae fortitudinis pedites* For *compertus* = *spectatus* of persons see the
note ad 22.4.2, of personal qualities cf. 29.5.35 *dux consultissimus ap-
posuit fidei compertae praefectos* and 31.16.2 *compertae fidei… exploratores.*
Apuleius has several instances of similar genitivi qualitatis, e.g. *Met.*
10.8 *unus e curia senior prae ceteris compertae fidi atque auctoritatis.*

amendatos intus prolicere possent As is correctly noted in TLL I 1880.45,
Amm. seems to be unique in that he regularly uses *amendare* in the

CHAPTER 4.30   145

sense of *abdere.* Cf. e.g. 16.12.58 *in secretis se secessibus amendaret* and 20.8.9 *secessi amendatusque... salutem dilatione quaeritabam et latebris.*

fumus angustius penetrans ideoque spissior We must suppose that the smoke was sucked into the *foveae* through the narrow openings (*angustius* being the equivalent of *per angusta foramina*) and for that reason became thick. The adjective *spissus* is rare. The only other instance in Amm. is 19.2.8 *sagittarum creberrima nube auras spissa multitudine obumbrante.* The same effect is described in Sen. *Nat.* 6.14.3 (spiritus) *per aliquam rimam maligne fugit et hoc acrius fertur, quo angustius.*

quosdam vitalibus obstructis necavit Normally *vitalia* refers to the intestines, as in 15.3.10 *extractis vitalibus interiit* and 16.12.52 *tela eorum vitalibus immergebat.* In the description of Valentinian's death in 30.6.3 *vitalique via voceque simul obstructa* means that the emperor choked, which is what happened to the Persians in their underground hiding places.

prodire in perniciem coegit abruptam For *abruptus* 'sudden' cf. 14.5.8 *exitio urguente abrupto* and see TLL I 142.72–80.

ad signa repedavit ocius miles The verb is a fine example of words found in archaic texts, which disappear in the classical period, and turn up again in late Latin, for which see the index in Löfstedt, 1911, s.v. Alt- und Spätlatein. Festus 350.25 says: *repedare recedere,* quoting Pacuvius. It occurs twice in Lucilius (676 and 677); thereafter it is found only in Amm.: 17.2.4, 17.8.5, 19.6.9, 25.1.3, 25.1.18, 26.5.11, 29.5.37 and 31.9.3. For *ocius* see the note ad 20.1.3 *festinaret ocius.*

virtute roboris excisa Romani in pulverem concidit et ruinas Only after this last danger has been averted is the success of the capture of 'Maozamalcha' complete. For *robur* see the note ad 24.1.2 *totius roboris firmamentum.* The pathetic phrase is repeated in 31.8.8 (domus) *quam concidisse vidit in cinerem et ruinas.* Cf. Zos. 3.22.7 τό τε τεῖχος ἄχρις ἐδάφους ('to the ground') προσενεχθεισῶν αὐτῷ πλείστων μηχανῶν κατηνέχθη, καὶ τὰ οἰκήματα πυρί τε καὶ ταῖς τῶν στρατιωτῶν χερσὶ κατελύθησαν. Zosimus adds that hardly a trace of the fortress was left: οὕτω τε εἰς τὸ μὴ γεγενῆσθαί ποτε δοκεῖν περιέστη, while Libanius says that the fortress was destroyed more completely than any other in the district: ἐπαπώλλυτο τὸ φρούριον μάλιστα δὴ τῶν ἐκεῖ φρουρίων ἐκτριβέν (*Or.* 18.241).

146 COMMENTARY

4.31 *Post quae tam gloriosa* It is interesting to compare these sober words of Amm. with Libanius' exuberant comment in *Or.* 18.242: οὕτω δὴ λαμπρὸν καὶ μεῖζον ἀνθρωπείας φύσεως τὸ πεπραγμένον (sc. the capture and destruction of 'Maozamalcha'), ὥσθ' οἱ μὲν ᾑρηκότες οὐδὲν ἔτι αὐτοὺς ἐνόμιζον οἴσειν, τῶν δὲ ἐναντίων συγκατενήνεκτο τὸ φρόνημα τῷ τείχει καὶ ᾤοντο δὴ σφίσι πάντα εἶναι σαθρά. καὶ βασιλεὺς ἀεὶ μὲν ἐργαζόμενος μεγάλα, μικρὰ δὲ πάντα ἡγούμενος οὐκ ἔσχε τοῦτο μὴ νομίσαι πάμμεγα. ἐφθέγξατο γοῦν ὅπερ οὐ πρόσθεν ὡς εἴη τῷ Σύρῳ δεδωκὼς ἀφορμὴν εἰς λόγον, ἐμὲ δὴ λέγων ("So glorious was the event, so far beyond ordinary human endeavour, that the victors began to think that nothing could stop them, and the enemy's morale was brought as low as their walls and they felt utterly insecure. The emperor himself, though ever engaged on mighty tasks and regarding them all as mere trifles, could not but consider this a magnificent feat of arms. At any rate, he passed a remark he had never made before, that he had given the Syrian (me, that is) matter to talk about", tr. Norman).

transitis pontibus... continuatis Because of the number of canals that come together near Ctesiphon the army had to cross one bridge after another. For this use of *continuatus* 'uninterrupted' cf. 27.5.6 *continuatis itineribus longius agentes Greuthungos bellicosam gentem aggressus est.*

ad munimenta gemina venimus aedificiis cavatis exstructa The abl. with *exstructa* may be compared to *diversoriis laetis* in 22.16.14 (Canopus) *amoenus impendio locus et diversoriis laetis exstructus* ("bâti de joyeuses tavernes", Fontaine), q.v. This would mean that the two fortresses were provided with buildings of a certain kind. What kind depends on the adjective that goes with *aedificiis*. V has *cautis*, which cannot be rejected offhand, because Amm. uses *cautus* of places, e.g. in 14.8.13 (castella) *quae... sollicitudo pervigil veterum per opportunos saltus erexit et cautos* ("readily defended defiles" Rolfe). It seems pleonastic, however, to say that a fortress is provided with 'readily defended buildings'. Fontaine proposes *caecis* which is very close to V's *cautis*. The meaning would be "deux fortifications bâties sur des casemates", for which he refers in n. 416 to Var. *L.* 9.58 (cubiculum) *si fenestram non habet, dicitur caecum.* There are no parallels, however, for *exstruere* + abl. in the sense of 'to build upon', and if we interpret *exstruere* as meaning 'to provide with', it is unclear what would be the use of fortresses with windowless buildings. The reading *cavatis*, preferred by all other editors, is attractive in view of the fact that the terrain

CHAPTER 4.31   147

evidently lent itself to subterranean constructions, such as the *foveae* just mentioned. Amm. uses the same participle for passages hewn out of the rock in Amida: 19.5.4 *cavatis fornicibus subterraneis*, and one is also reminded of the reservoirs under the Temple Mount in Jerusalem, mentioned by Tac. *Hist.* 5.12.1 *fons perennis aquae, cavati sub terra montes.*

This must have taken place on May 14, presumably (see the note on chronology). Zosimus is, like Amm., silent about the names of these fortresses: Τῆς δὲ ἐπὶ τὸ πρόσω πορείας ἐχόμενος διῄει μὲν καὶ ἕτερα οὐκ ὀνομαστὰ φρούρια (3.23.1).

Victorem comitem exercitus praevium Victor is now called *dux* (as in 24.4.13, q.v. and 24.6.13), now *comes* (apart from the present text in 24.6.4; see for this title the note ad 20.4.18). His action related here resembles that of 24.4.13, but there is no need to follow the tentative suggestion of Fontaine in n. 417 and assume a doublet. Victor, who was commander of the rearguard in 24.1.2 (q.v.), more often was acting in the front line (cf. 24.6.4). Cf. for his action here Austin-Rankov, 1995, 52. For *praevius* with a genitive cf. 26.10.16 *densitate praevia fulgorum* and see Hagendahl, 1921, 56–7.

a transitu fluminis What *flumen*? According to Brok 144, the Naarmal-cha (which is in his view the canal followed since 24.3.14). According to Paschoud n. 58 it is one of the *amnes* just referred to (*multorum amnium concursu*), i.e. an irrigation canal between Euphrates and Naarmalcha (which is in Paschoud's view the canal followed since 24.2.7). Fontaine n. 417 opts for a non liquet. Matthews 157 offers the best solution: the advance party led by Victor tried to test Persian resistance to the crossing of the Tigris (for Victor's role during the actual crossing of the Tigris see 24.6.4 with the note).

regis filius Two sons of Sapor II (see for him the note ad 20.6.1 *truculentus rex ille Persarum*) are known by name, viz. another Sapor (*PLRE* I, Sapor III), who became king in 383 as the successor of his uncle Artaxerxes II (379–383), and Vararanes (*PLRE* I, Vararanes IV), who succeeded his brother in 388. It is not known which one is meant here (the present text is not cited in *PLRE* I). Besides, Sapor II perhaps had more sons (but in 25.1.11 Amm. speaks only of two: *filiisque regis duobus*). At any rate, Fontaine's "le fils du roi" is not correct (cf. e.g. Rolfe: "a son of the Persian king").

a Ctesiphonte See above, ad 24.2.7.

CHAPTER 5

Introduction

This chapter contains the report of the march from ' Maozamalcha', which had been completely reduced to ruins by the victorious army, to the neighbourhood of Ctesiphon. The most remarkable aspect of this report, the first five sections of which run parallel to Zosimus 3.23.1–24.1, is Julian's repeated loss of composure. On his entrance into Persian territory he had been *celso praeter alios spiritu* (24.1.1), his dangerous adventure at Pirisabora's citadel had merely caused him to be *verecundo rubore suffusus* (24.2.16), only after the Surên's unexpected attack was he *concitus ira immani* (24.3.2), but after the fall of 'Maozamalcha' he showed himself a *serenus imperator et clemens* again (24.4.26). However, in the short time covered in this chapter he repeatedly appears to be unable to control himself. This is implied in the cruel execution of Nabdates (§4), and it is explicitly mentioned no fewer than four times (*iratus et frendens* (§6), *concitus ira immani* (§7), *ira gravi permotus* (§10), *flagrans* (§11)). Obviously, Julian fails to cope with setbacks. It must have been worrying to his staff, the more so since he tended to become more reckless, as is reported very clearly in 24.6.4 *ut propius temeritatem multa crebro auderet*. See for Julian's irascibility in general Brandt, 1999, 169ff., who rightly draws attention to the curious fact that Amm. in his necrology of Julian "eine *cupiditas irascendi* o.ä. mit keinem Wort kritisiert" (171).

Amm.'s report on this phase of the campaign tallies well with Zos. 3.23.1–2, "mais en ordre inverse" (Paschoud ad loc.). Libanius, *Or.* 18.243, however, differs considerably from both versions, as is shown by Sabbah 262–5. **5.1–2**

Pergentes itaque protinus The same combination of adv. and verb occurs in 15.4.1 and 19.8.6, in which cases *protinus* is also slightly pleonastic, as in e.g. Liv. 9.2.9 *cum... protinus pergerent*. **5.1**

ad lucos venimus agrosque pube variorum seminum laetos This was on the 15th of May presumably. There is no parallel for this description of the general surroundings in Libanius or Zosimus. Besides, its wording is remarkable. Lewis-Short seems to be right in interpreting

150 COMMENTARY

pubes here as "fulness, ripeness"; *laetos* should of course be taken in its 'agricultural' sense: 'rich', 'flourishing'. The words evoke a fertile region in which 'all sorts of crops' are in full bloom.

regia Romano more aedificata Amm.'s observation clearly contrasts with Libanius' report that the palace, among other things, showed Persian elegance in its buildings (κάλλος δὲ ἅπαν ἔχοντα Περσικὸν ὅσον τε ἐν οἰκοδομήσεσι καὶ ὅσον ἐν κήποις, *Or.* 18.243). Zosimus' words, however, tally with those of Amm.: βασίλεια εἶδεν (sc. Julian) εἰς τὸν Ῥωμαϊκὸν μεγαλοπρεπῶς ἐξησκημένα τύπον. Zosimus adds that the palace had been built by Romans (3.23.2, quoted in the next note), which is quite possible, since the Sasanian kings had always been prone to take advantage of the technical superiority of captured Romans (see for this Christensen, 1944², 126–7, 213 and 251 and Ball, 2000, 115 ff.; cf. 20.6.7 *residui omnes mandatu Saporis vivi comprehensi ad regiones Persidis ultimas sunt asportati* and the note ad loc.).

quoniam id placuerat, mansit intacta According to Zosimus, the fact that the palace had been built by Romans made it impossible for Julian to destroy it: μαθὼν ταῦτα ὑπὸ Ῥωμαίων ᾠκοδομῆσθαι κατέλιπεν, οὐ συγχωρήσας τοῖς ταξιάρχοις λωβήσασθαί τι τῶν ἐν αὐτοῖς, αἰδοῖ τοῦ Ῥωμαίους λέγεσθαι τοὺς ταῦτα δημιουργήσαντας (3.23.2). Amm. seemingly expresses the same thought in fewer words, *quoniam id placuerat* meaning "quod Romano nempe more aedificata esset" (Wagner), pace Seyfarth, who remarks: "eine Beziehung auf das königliche Jagdschloss…erweist sich durch das *id* als unmöglich" (n. 70) and translates: "da unser Beschluss so lautete" (cf. Hamilton's "in accordance with orders").

As to *mansit intacta,* in Libanius' version the royal palace was burnt down: ταῦτα ἐνεπρήσθη τὰ βασίλεια (*Or.* 18.243). This must be wrong. Libanius relied for his information only on hearsay (cf. ὥς φασιν, ibid.), while Amm., apart from the source he apparently shares with Zosimus, was an eye-witness (cf. Sabbah 263).

5.2 *in hac eadem regione* Sabbah 263 n. 74 energetically defends his rendering "dans cette même direction" instead of merely 'in the same region', with *regio* having "son plein sens de *ligne droite*", as in the phrase *e regione*: palace and park "sont situés à proximité l'un de l'autre, mais indépendants".

extentum spatium et rotundum loricae ambitu circumclausum destinatas regiis voluptatibus continens feras Zosimus and Libanius also mention

CHAPTER 5.2   151

this place and its function as one of the king's hunting grounds (παραγίνεται δὲ καὶ εἰς περίβολον ὃν βασιλέως θήραν ἐκάλουν, Zos. 3.23.1; ἐν οἷς αὐτὸν ἐγύμναζεν ὁ Πέρσης, Lib. *Or.* 18.243). The park, full of trees according to Zosimus (ἦν δὲ τι τειχίον χωρίον ἀπειληφὸς ἔνδον πολύ, δένδρεσι πεφυτευμένον παντοδαποῖς, ibid.), was no doubt one of the parks which Xenophon, borrowing an Oriental word, was the first to call παράδεισοι (*An.* 1.2.7, 2.4.14, *Cyr.* 1.3.14, *HG* 4.1.15–6; cf. Thphr. *HP* 4.4.1, LXX *Ne.* 2.8, Plut. *Art.* 25). However, Musil's (1927, 241) identification of the park mentioned here with that of X. *An.* 2.4.14 is no more than a guess. The fact that there were several of such παράδεισοι in this region makes an attempt to identify the park futile (cf. Brok 145 and Paschoud n. 63).

Hunting, especially the hunting of lions, as a royal pastime had already been in existence for a very long time in the Near East, as is evident from e.g. pictures representing the Assyrian kings Assurnasirpal and Assurbanipal. It may have had ideological overtones in the sense that the killing of lions symbolized the victory over foreign foes. See Heimpel-Trümpelmann, 1976–1980, Magen, 1986, 3, 29–36, plates 1–4 and Galter, 1989, 241–245. For Achaemenid and Sasanian kings Briant, 1996, 242–4, 309–12, 332–5 and Harper, 1978, respectively. See further below, ad 24.6.3 *gentiles picturas… bella.*

With the meaning 'parapet' *lorica* already occurs in Caesar, e.g. *pinnae loricaeque ex cratibus attexuntur* (*Gal.* 5.40.6). Amm.'s other instances are 31.3.7 and 31.15.4. See TLL VII 2.1677.61 ff. Zos. 3.23.1 calls it a τειχίον.

cervicibus iubatis… corpora bestiarum Neither Zosimus nor Libanius is as specific as Amm. about the fauna of the park: ἐν τούτῳ θηρίων παντοίων ἐναποκλειόμενα γένη (Zos. 3.23.1); συῶν δὲ ἀγέλην ἀγρίων ἔτρεφεν ἀπαντικρὺ χωρίον (Lib. *Or.* 18.243). Apart from a long passage (23.15.14–27) in the digression on Egypt, specific wild animals are not often mentioned by Amm. The typically Asiatic tiger only occurs in 23.6.50 (q.v.) and 52. In 18.7.5 Amm. reports that in the reed beds on the borders of Mesopotamia's rivers *leones vagantur innumeri* and in 23.5.8 (q.v.) that near Dura a lion of huge size (*immanissimi corporis leo*) had been presented to Julian by some soldiers; cf. also 24.8.5 *feroces leonum… assultus.*

Boars and bears are rarely depicted and the general impression is that *lecta* are Amm.'s source of information. The present text, however, with its vivid short sketches, is obviously inspired by *visa.* "The periphrastic use of *corpora* with the genitive is popular in dactylic poetry because it eases versification" (Skutsch ad Enn. *Ann.* 88–9 *ter*

152 COMMENTARY

quattuor corpora sancta/avium, the first instance of this usage). It occurs a few times in Vergil (e.g. *G.* 3.369, *A.* 1.192–3), who may have been Amm.'s model here. The only other occurrence of *hispidus*, 'rough', 'shaggy', in Amm. (30.1.15) concerns a path. The adj. can also be used to describe beasts: *taurus ingens fronte torva et hispida* (Prud. *perist.* 10.1021). See Toynbee, 1973, 25–30, 61–9 (lions), 93–100 (bears), 131–6 (boars and pigs).

quas omnes… confoderunt On May 16. Zos. 3.23.2 is somewhat calmer: φεύγοντα παρὰ τῶν στρατιωτῶν τὰ θηρία κατετοξεύετο. See for *diffractis portarum obicibus* the note ad 21.12.13 and cf. Zos. 3.23.2 Τοῦτο Ἰουλιανὸς θεασάμενος διαρρήγνυσθαι κατὰ πολλὰ μέρη τὸ τεῖχος ἐπέταττεν. The 'hunting spears' may have been captured in warehouses of the *paradeisos*, but it could also be that they belonged to the regular outfit of the horsemen, who often had the opportunity of hunting.

5.3 *quo loco pingui satis et cultu, qui… bus Coche, quam Seleuciam nominant* In spite of a variety of scholarly efforts one cannot but conclude that Amm.'s text has been irreparably lost. There are two main problems: 1. Brok 146 rightly argues that one would have expected some phrase parallelling Zos. 3.23.3 ἡ στρατία… εἰς πόλιν ἀφίκετο Μείνας Σαβαθὰ καλουμένην, especially since his text continues with διέστηκε δὲ αὕτη σταδίοις τριάκοντα τῆς πρότερον μὲν Ζωχάσης νῦν δὲ Σελευκείας ὀνομαζομένης. 2. Obviously, διέστηκε is Amm.'s *disparatur*, and Fontaine's emendation *qui⟨nque mili⟩bus… haud longius* comes reasonably near Zosimus' 30 stadia. However, only Petschenig seems to have realized that *disparari* in a topographical sense needs a complement with *a(b)*. See TLL V 1.1393.81 ff. Amm.'s only other example of the abl. without a preposition accompanying the verb is *quod eos fortuna quaedam inclemens et moderato rectore et terris genitalibus dispararet* (20.4.13, q.v.), where *disparare* is used as a synonym of *verba spoliandi*.

Coche quam Seleuciam nominant was situated on the right bank of the Tigris opposite Ctesiphon. In 23.6.23 (q.v.) Amm. called Seleucia on the Tigris *ambitiosum opus Nicatoris Seleuci*. This city, destroyed more than once in the second century A.D. (see for references the note ad 23.6.23), "was refounded around 230 by Ardashīr as Vēh-Ardašīr" (Oppenheimer, 1983, 226). In late antique Greek and Latin sources it was sometimes called Seleucia (e.g. by Procopius, quoted below), sometimes Coche (as in Greg. Naz. *Or.* 5.10; cf. also 24.6.2 *exercitus iter Cochen versus promovit*), which supports Gelenius'

CHAPTER 5.3   153

reading *Coche, quam Seleuciam* in the present text (V has *cohaequans eleuciam*). Zos. 3.23.3 speaks of Zochase, but no doubt refers to the same city (cf. Paschoud n. 65). Arrian, in the tenth book of his *Parthica*, distinguished between the *city* of Seleucia and a *village* called Coche (καὶ βασιλεύς, sc. Trajan, ἐξελαύνει ἐκ Σελευκείας οὐ πρόσω τοῦ ποταμοῦ τοῦ Τίγριδος ἐς κώμην ᾗτινι Χωχὴ ὄνομα, *fr.* 8 FHG), but later that distinction apparently had been blurred. Nevertheless, it would seem that the new city had not totally occupied the area of former Seleucia: near Coche the deserted city of Seleucia was still to be seen (see for this below, the note ad *civitatem desertam... a Caro principe quondam excisam*).

Coche or Seleucia was, pace Gullini, 1966, 30, situated on the right (western) bank of the river, opposite Ctesiphon: ῥεῖ δὲ αὐταῖν μέσος Τίγρης ὁ ποταμὸς (Lib. *Or.* 18.244). Cf. Greg. Naz. *Or.* 5.10 Ποιεῖ δὲ αὐτὴν (= Ctesiphon) ὀχυρωτέραν καὶ φρούριον ἕτερον, ᾧ προσηγορία Κωχή... τοσοῦτον ἑνούμενον ('made one') ὥστε μίαν πόλιν δοκεῖν ἀμφοτέρας, τῷ ποταμῷ μέσῳ διειργομένας and Procop. *Pers.* 2.28.4 πολίσματα δύο Σελεύκιά τε καὶ Κτησιφῶν..., ἄμφω δὲ ταῦτα Τίγρης ποταμὸς διορίζει. Cf. Weissbach, 1922; Gullini, 1966; Fiey, 1967; Matthews 140–2, with map 4 on p. 142.

According to Eutropius 9.18.1 (cf. Festus 24) the emperor Carus took both *Cochen et Ctesiphontem, urbes nobilissimas*. This must have been in 283 A.D.; see further below, the note ad *civitatem desertam... a Caro principe quondam excisam*.

vallatis opere tumultuario castris Amm. may have borrowed the phrase *opere tumultuario* from Livy (6.29.4, 42.63.4, 44.19.9), but he also uses the adj. to denote hasty improvisation in other phrases: *tumultuario studio* (17.1.11, q.v.), *tumultuario praesidio* (26.8.7). See also the note ad *tumultuarie* in 24.2.18.

per aquarum et pabuli opportuna The grammatical analysis of this phrase is difficult. Translators obviously take *per* in an instrumental or causal sense, e.g. "bei einer willkommenen Menge an Wasser und Nahrung" (Seyfarth), "grâce aux facilités en eau et en fourage" (Fontaine). Presumably, the substantivated n. pl. *opportuna* is regarded as meaning something like 'the welcome availability'. This explanation seems to overstep the boundaries of current grammar and semantics. It is more likely that *per* has a topographical sense; cf. *per varia* (16.3.3), *per hirta dumis et aspera* (27.10.12), *per nemorosa et devia* (31.16.2); indeed, *per opportuna* occurs in such a sense in 21.12.7 and 24.1.6. The present phrase could be regarded as a fur-

154   COMMENTARY

ther development of constructions like *per silvarum densa* (24.4.8):
'everywhere in those parts of the surrounding waters and fields that
provided a timely benefit to the campaigners'.

civitatem desertam collustrans a Caro principe quondam excisam Instead of
V's *sacro* Valesius proposed to read *a Vero*, pointing to Amm. 23.6.24
Seleucia... qua per duces Veri Caesaris, ut ante rettulimus, expulsata and
assuming that the *civitas deserta* of the present text is identical with
Seleucia (which in itself is likely, see below). Seyfarth, however, reads
a Caro, following Lindenbrog, who referred i.a. to Eutr. 9.18.1 quoted
in the note ad *quo loco pingui... nominant*. From a palaeographical
point of view *a Caro* is more plausible: dittography of the s would
almost naturally entail *a sacro*. Besides, the name tallies with Zos.
3.23.4 ὁ βασιλεὺς Κάρος. For Carus see *PLRE* I, Carus + Barnes, 1972,
152–3; Alföldy, *Byzantinoslavica* 34 (1973) 240; Criniti, 1974, 141;
Lippold in *Gnomon* 46 (1974) 269. Cf. also Kienast, 1996², 258–9.
For Ammianus' attitudes toward earlier emperors: Gilliam, 1972 and
Stertz, 1980.

    According to Brok 147 the *civitas deserta* (not "the ruins of the
city", as Hamilton would have it, but 'a deserted or abandoned city')
most probably is to be identified with Zosimus' Meinas Sabatha,
which was at a distance of thirty stades from *Coche, quam Seleuciam
nominant*: Ἐντεῦθεν ἡ στρατιὰ φρούριά τινα παραδραμοῦσα εἰς πόλιν
ἀφίκετο Μείνας Σαβαθὰ καλουμένην· διέστηκε δὲ αὕτη σταδίοις τριάκοντα τῆς πρότερον μὲν Ζωχάσης νῦν δὲ Σελευκείας ὀνομαζομένης (3.23.3).
However, in Zosimus' account Meinas Sabatha was taken by force,
whereas in Amm. the emperor only surveyed the *civitas deserta*: καὶ ὁ
μὲν βασιλεὺς πλησίον που (i.e. near Meinas Sabatha) μετὰ τῆς πολλῆς
στρατιᾶς ηὐλίσθη, προηγούμενοι δὲ οἱ κατάσκοποι τὴν πόλιν κατὰ κράτος
αἱροῦσι (ibid.). The suggestion of e.g. Paschoud n. 65 and Oppenheimer, 1983, 227 that not Meinas Sabatha, but Seleucia is meant,
seems therefore preferable, the more so because 1) in Syriac sources
Seleucia is referred to as Sliq Kharawta or 'deserted Seleucia' and
2) Sliq Kharawta served as a place of execution, precisely as the
civitas deserta did in the time of Julian (cf. *corpora vidit suffixa patibulis multa* in this section and *hic et Nabdates vivus exustus est* in the
next). See for the Syriac sources Gullini, 1966, 26; Fiey, 1967, 8;
Matthews 141.

    For *collustrans*, 'surveying a wide space', see the note ad 20.11.5.

*exercitu omni... biduo recreato antegressus cum procursatoribus princeps...
corpora vidit suffixa patibulis* Amm.'s *biduo* (May 17 and 18, presum-

CHAPTER 5.4 155

ably) is paralleled by Zosimus' τῇ δ' ὑστεραίᾳ: τῇ δ' ὑστεραίᾳ τὰ τείχη ταύτης ὁ βασιλεὺς περινοστῶν ἑώρα σώματα προσηρτημένα σταυροῖς ἔμπροσθεν τῶν πυλῶν (3.23.3). For *procursator* see above, ad 24.3.1.

corpora vidit... rettulimus supra As Lactantius notes, *is qui patibulo suspenditur et conspicuus est omnibus et ceteris altior* (*inst.* 4.26.34), so that this punishment provides a terrifying example. When the Persians had finally captured Amida, they wickedly punished the stubborn leaders of its defence: *Aeliano comite et tribunis... patibulis sceleste affixis* (19.9.2, q.v.). Here too, Persian methods were atrocious: as was pointed out in 23.6.81 (q.v.), by their hands *ob noxam unius omnis propinquitas perit.* Although Isidorus of Sevilla (*Etym.* 5.27.34) distinguished between *patibulum* and *crux* (*patibuli minor poena quam crucis, nam patibulum adpensos statim exanimat, crux autem subfixos diu cruciat*), both forms of punishment can be subsumed under the heading 'crucifixion': "all attempts to give a perfect description of *the* crucifixion in archaeological terms are ... in vain; there were too many different possibilities for the executioner" (Hengel, 1977, 25, pointing i.a. to Sen. *Cons. Marc.* 20.3 *Video istic cruces, non unius quidem generis, sed aliter ab aliis fabricatas: capite quidam conversos in terram suspendere, alii per obscena stipitem egerunt, alii brachia patibulo explicuerunt*). Crucifixion was employed by both Greeks and Romans, but Greek and Roman authors normally played down the fact that their own people used it and stressed its barbarian origin (cf. Hengel, 1977, 22–3 with references). For the report on the commander Mamersides' surrender of Pirisabora see 24.2.21 (q.v.).

hic et Nabdates vivus exustus est, quem extractum cum octoginta e latebris **5.4** *expugnatae docui civitatis* Amm. refers to 24.4.26. His wording in the present text, with its emphatic *vivus*, nicely recalls the earlier passage, where *vivus* also has some prominence (*extractus est autem vivus cum satellitibus octoginta Nabdates*). See for a discussion of the harsh penalty the note ad 21.12.20. When the old lady, who had to guard the girl kidnapped by the highwaymen, was fed up with her wailing, she threatened her with such a punishment: *iam faxo lacrimis istis... viva exurare* (Apul. *Met.* 4.25.4), and the miller's wife was also quite clear in her angry verdict on the fuller's wife: *talis oportere vivas exuri feminas* (9.26.3). From this it may be concluded that Nabdates' cruel execution was also caused by Julian's violent anger.

eo, quod inter exordia obsidii coepti clam pollicitus prodere dimicavit acerrime Amm. had not mentioned this in 24.4.26. Zos. 3.23.4 also

156   COMMENTARY

relates the execution of the former commander of 'Maozamalcha',
but he is less specific than Amm. about the motive for it. According
to him Anabdates had misled the Romans for a long time by pretending that he would help them against the Persians (Ἀναβδάτης ὁ
φρούραρχος ... παραγαγὼν μὲν ἐπὶ πολὺ τὸν Ῥωμαίων στρατὸν ὡς δὴ συν-
τελέσων αὐτῷ πρὸς τὸν κατὰ Περσῶν πόλεμον). His dubious behaviour
at 'Maozamalcha' had been condoned by Julian, who thus showed
himself to be a *serenus imperator et clemens* (24.4.26). Now, however,
he had had enough of the man's continuous unreliability and arro-
gance, which even manifested itself in all sorts of abuse of Hormisdas,
for whom Julian in all probability had an important future role in
mind: see the note ad 24.1.2. Interference with this intention was
unacceptable.

ad id proruperat insolentiae, ut Hormisdam laceraret omnibus probris
Amm.'s phrase *ad id proruperat insolentiae* emphasizes the almost physical aggressiveness of (A)nabdates' impertinence. In a transferred
sense the verb can denote the bursting out into actions or emotions: *in externos mores proruperant* (Tac. *Hist.* 2.73). There is no other
comparable example in Amm. The unique *ad id* + gen. seems to be a
variation of phrases like *eo audaciae provectum* (Tac. *Ann.* 4.10.2). The
author needed such a fierce expression to justify Julian's obviously
intense anger, which could only result in a cruel execution. Zosimus'
report is less 'violent' and about (A)nabdates' death he merely notes:
ἀνῃρέθη.

    For *omnibus probris* cf. *probrosis lacerati conviciis* (30.1.16), *lacera-
tique ad ultimum detestatione atque conviciis* (31.6.3), *cum omnibus locis
me vosque maledictis lacerarent* (Sal. *Jug.* 85.26), *laceratusque probris* (Liv.
31.6.5), *probra quis per occultum lacerabatur* (Tac. *Ann.* 4.42.2). From
these phrases it can be seen that *lacerare*, "to tear a reputation to
shreds" (OLD s.v. 5), tends to be used in phrases expressing violent
abuse. In Zosimus' account the *probra* are specified: Hormisdas was,
according to (A)nabdates, a traitor and the cause of the Persian expedition (τότε δὲ ἐξελεγχθεὶς ὡς ἐλοιδορεῖτο παρὰ πλείστοις Ὁρμίσδην
προδότην ἀποκαλῶν καὶ τῆς κατὰ Περσῶν αἴτιον ἐκστρατείας, 3.23.4).

5.5 *Itaque aliquantum progressi tristi percellimur facto* Whereas Amm. often
uses the perf. part. *perculsus*, there are only two other instances in
the *Res Gestae* of the present stem of *percellere*: *nuntio percellitur gravi*
(15.8.18 and 27.8.1). Obviously Amm. wanted to express the general shock of all those taking part in the expedition by using the first
person plur. of the historic present. Petschenig's pleading for the cor-

CHAPTER 5.5 157

rection *fato* in V's third hand is attractive: "Dieses '*factum*' bestand in einer Schlappe der gegen Ktesiphon vorrückenden Römer. Demnach ist mit dem Korrektur des V, der *c* getilgt hat, *fato* zu schreiben, woruf schon der Zusatz *tristi* weist. Vgl. XIIII 11.19 pandente viam fatorum sorte tristissima" (1892, 680). Indeed, Amm.'s other instances of substantivated *factum* are never combined with an adj. However, *ubi felicius acciderit fatum* (26.6.10) might have provided a better parallel to Petschenig's preference. TLL VI 1.359.3–22 provides a list of instances in which *fatum* means "calamitas, malum". Not all of these are fully convincing, but the term *fatum* can indeed point to one particular incident.

Amm. is silent about the capture of numerous prisoners by Arintheus (see for this general the note ad 24.1.2), which Zosimus mentions before he speaks of this incident (Προϊόντος δὲ περαιτέρω τοῦ στρατοῦ, τὰ ἕλη διερευνώμενος Ἀρινθαῖος πολλούς τε ἐν τούτοις εὑρὼν αἰχμαλώτους ἀπήγαγεν, 3.24.1; cf. for Dillemann's suggestion regarding Zosimus' words the note ad 24.7.2 *cuius utilitate*). According to Zosimus the attack brought about the first defeat during Julian's campaign and caused much distress (ὅπερ πρῶτον ἐλάττωμα Ῥωμαίοις συμβὰν ἀθυμίαν ἐνεποίησε τῷ στρατεύματι, 3.24.1).

Although both Amm. (*aliquantum progressi*) and Zosimus (προϊόντος δὲ περαιτέρω τοῦ στρατοῦ) speak of movements of the army, Paschoud n. 67 doubts their reliability in this respect ("il ne faut pas se laisser égarer par les indications des deux historiens qui décrivent une armée qui s'avance, certainement par erreur"). However, it should not be forgotten that Amm. was an eye-witness, as his use of the first person plural (*percellimur*) once again makes clear.

dum enim tres procursatorum cohortes expeditae cum cuneo Persico decertarent See for *procursator* (κατάσκοπος in Zosimus' version, cited below) and *cuneus* the notes ad 24.3.1 and 23.5.8, respectively. *Cohors* here is undoubtedly used of cavalry, as in 24.5.8 and 10 (cf. the note ad 24.4.7). The outcome of the fight (on May 19 presumably), not mentioned by Amm., is related by Zosimus: the Romans were victorious and forced the Persians to flee to a city nearby (ἐνταῦθα πρῶτον οἱ Πέρσαι συστραφέντες ἐπῆλθον τοῖς τοῦ στρατοῦ προτρέχουσι κατασκόποις, ὀξέως δὲ τραπέντες εἰς τὴν πλησίον ἀγαπητῶς συνέφυγον πόλιν, 3.24.1).

profuderat civitas Presumably this *civitas* is identical with the πόλις to which the Persians fled in Zos. 3.24.1 quoted above, but we have no clue as to its site. If, as was discussed ad 24.5.3, the *civitas deserta*

158 COMMENTARY

mentioned there is to be identified with Zosimus' Meinas Sabatha (3.23.3), the suggestion of some scholars as regards the *civitas* of the present text ("perhaps Sabatha", Rolfe; cf. Seyfarth n. 73, Fontaine n. 423 and Paschoud n. 67) has to be rejected. The personified Agens provides a fascinating picture, which is not given its due by translators: the town pours out a stream of defenders.

proruptores alii ex contraria fluminis ripa iumenta nos sequentia cum pabulatoribus paucis licenter palantibus intercipiunt et obtruncant The first instance of this use of *contrarius* seems to be *ad contrariam* (ripam) (Cic. *Phil.* 2.26). Comparable examples in Amm. are *per contrarias ripas* (18.2.10, q.v.), *ripas occupavere contrarias* (25.6.14), *ad contrarias margines* (30.1.10). The terms *pabulator* and *proruptor* occur only here in Amm. The present use of *palari* is well described in TLL X 1.158.8: "spectat ad ordines solutos militum populantium, frumentantium sim." Amm. has a predilection for *licenter* (or *licentius*); see the note ad 20.10.2. Here it implies disapproval of the foragers' irresponsible behaviour.

Zosimus in 3.24.1 no doubt refers to the same incident (κατὰ δὲ τὴν ἀντιπέρας ὄχθην τοῦ ποταμοῦ τοῖς ἐπιτετραμμένοις τὴν τῶν ὑποζυγίων φυλακὴν οἰκέταις, καὶ ὅσοι μετὰ τούτων ἦσαν, ἐπελθόντες οἱ Πέρσαι τοὺς μὲν ἀπέκτειναν τοὺς δὲ ζῶντας ἀπήγαγον), but there is a notable difference between his version and that of Amm. In Amm. the Roman army train is attacked by Persians *ex contraria fluminis ripa*, which implies that the train marched on the same side of the river as the rest of the army. In Zosimus' more unlikely version, however, the latter does not seem to be the case, for he says that the army train was attacked while on the other side of the water (κατὰ δὲ τὴν ἀντιπέρας ὄχθην τοῦ ποταμοῦ). *Fluminis* in Amm. and ποταμοῦ in Zosimus must refer to the Naarmalcha (cf. Paschoud n. 67 and for the indiscriminate use of *flumen*/ποταμός for both river and canal the note ad 24.2.7). Cf. 24.4.7 for an earlier attack on the army train (*Surena hostium dux iumenta adortus*), which was, however, repulsed by *cohortes repulsoriae*.

5.6 The incident described in this section, to be dated to May 20, it would seem, is no more reported by Zosimus and Libanius than the subsequent siege of the stronghold in question (sections 7–12). This, in addition to the fact that the episode is quite similar to that narrated in 24.4.3–5 (cf. Zos. 3.20.2 ff. and Lib. *Or.* 18.236) about Julian risking his life near 'Maozamalcha', has caused suspicion: "Est-on en présence d'un doublet ou d'une interversion dans l'une ou l'autre des traditions sur l'expédition perse?" (Paschoud n. 52,

CHAPTER 5.6   159

concluding: "il est impossible de répondre"). Julian again appears to
be quite headstrong, exposing himself to risks which he had badly
underestimated. As soon as the defenders of the fortification have
spotted him, he gets the full blast and right at his side his *armiger* is
wounded by a direct hit.

unde profectus imperator iratus et frendens   The word *unde* is not very precise. It apparently refers to the spot where the emperor had heard
the bad news about the *pabulatores*. The most remarkable aspect of
Amm.'s report is the complete absence of any unequivocal disapproval of Julian's unworthy behaviour. Seager 35, however, regards
Amm.'s disapproval as beyond doubt. It is true that in Livy's only
instance of *frendere*, viz. *frendens gemensque ac vix lacrimis temperans*
(30.20.1), Hannibal's desperate disappointment at the failure of his
Italian campaign is also expressed in strong terms, but the combination of *frendere* with words indicating despondency softens the
expression. Amm.'s own use of *frendere*, however, speaks another language: *frendebant ut bestiae* (19.5.3) concerns the defenders of Amida,
but in four of the seven instances it is used to describe barbarians,
e.g. *frendentes immania* (16.12.36). A Roman emperor should have
shown more self-control. As to *iratus*, cf. *concitus ira immani* in the
next section and see the note ad 24.3.2.

iamque regionibus Ctesiphontis propinquans celsum castellum offendit et
munitissimum ad quod explorandum ausus accedere   See for Ctesiphon
above, ad 24.2.7. In the next section this *castellum* is called a *muni-*
mentum and a place which was almost inaccessible (*loco...propemodum*
inaccesso). See for reconnaissances like this the note ad 24.2.9 *obequi-*
tans moenia imperator et situm.

obscurior, ut ipse rebatur   TLL IX 2.169.55–6 persuasively lists this
instance of *obscurus* among those in which the adj. means "invisibilis
vel parum visibilis". It is not identical to e.g. Verg. *A.* 2.135 *per noctem*
obscurus or the famous *Ibant obscuri sola sub nocte per umbram* (*A.*
6.268), where *obscurus* is linked with the darkness of night. The
parenthetical clause implies the illusory character of the thought, as
is noted ad 21.7.1.

cum paucis obequitans muros   See the note on *obequitans ordinibus*
(24.1.1).

statimque diversorum missilium nube exagitatus oppetisset tormento mu-

160   COMMENTARY

rali Cf. *sagittarum creberrima nube* (19.2.8), *sagittarum nube diffusa* (26.8.12). This is perhaps reminiscent of Livy: *velut nube iaculorum* (Liv. 21.55.6), *velut nubes levium telorum* (38.26.7). See for *oppetere* with abl. causae TLL IX 2.750.54–62; cf. also the note ad 21.12.13 *oppetebant*. As in 17.1.12 and 18.9.1, *tormentum murale* denotes an instrument of artillery positioned on the walls of a town; in 24.4.12, however, the besiegers' artillery is meant.

vulnerato armigero, qui lateri eius haerebat "The guard holding the emperor's shield was the imperial guard *par excellence*, the emperor's *armiger*, who never left his side" (Frank, 1969, 141). We encounter the first imperial *armigeri* under Augustus (Suet. *Aug.* 49.1; there were also non-imperial body-guards styled *armigeri*, cf. e.g. Liv. 22.6.4 and CIL 6.6190, 6.6229). In Amm. we find them mentioned, apart from in the text under discussion, in 27.5.9, 31.10.3, 31.10.21 and 31.13.8. The word *armiger* is used as an adjective in 23.3.8 and 24.3.2 (*cum armigera manu*).

In the present text Amm. speaks of only one *armiger*, who during the reconnaissance of the *castellum* rode next to Julian (*qui lateri eius haerebat*). However, we can infer from the other passages in Amm. that an emperor was usually escorted by more than one guard. It was probably thanks to a whole bunch of *armigeri* who protected him by their shields (*scutorum densitate contectus*) that Julian could escape the danger which threatened him here.

The *armigeri* in Amm., as Müller, 1905, 601 already observed, must have belonged to one of the *scholae palatinae* (for which see the note ad 20.2.5 *Gentilium Scutariorum*; cf. now also Woods, 1997). One can perhaps go even further than that and define the *schola* more precisely with the help of a passage in 31.10.20: *punito scutario proditore* (Sabbah, 1999 prints *Scutario*, with capital S, which is to be preferred). With these words Amm. refers to an incident he had mentioned in 31.10.3. It is said there that an Aleman, serving in the Roman army and belonging to the imperial *armigeri* (*ex hac natione quidam inter principis armigeros militans*), gave away secrets to some of his compatriots on the other side of the border. In 31.10.20 we learn that this man was punished. Now, however, he is not called *armiger*, but *scutarius*, that is, as always in Amm. (the word occurs 27 times), a member of one of the *scholae Scutariorum*, either the *schola Scutariorum prima* (cf. 22.11.2, q.v., 26.1.4) or the *schola Scutariorum secunda* (cf. 22.11.2, 25.10.9, 26.1.5). By analogy with this the other *armigeri* mentioned by Amm. perhaps also belonged to one of these units of the imperial guard.

CHAPTER 5.7   161

See for *haerere* with dat. Kühner-Stegmann 1.317–8, Austin ad Verg. *A.* 4.73 *haeret lateri* and *lateri paterno haerentem* (Amm. 19.1.7).

scutorum densitate contectus The same phrase occurs in 21.12.18. Cf. also *clipeorum densitate contecti* (24.2.5, q.v.).

evitato magno discrimine Cf. *ex ipso vitae discrimine tandem emersit* (24.4.3, q.v.). See also the note ad 24.2.14 *omnes aleas*.

Qua causa concitus ira immani munimentum disposuit obsidere No ratio-   **5.7**
nal calculation, but pure irritation because of his dangerous accident prompted the decision to lay a siege (on May 21 presumably). As to V's *concitus immani*, the emendation proposed by Müller, 1873, 345 has been followed by Clark and Seyfarth, though with a change in the word order. See also *concitus ira immani* (24.3.2, q.v.). Müller rejected *immane* (V's third hand, accepted by Valesius), "was ohne folgendes *quantum*…falsch ist". Fontaine, however, prints *immane*, which according to him (n. 426) can be interpreted either as an accusativus adverbialis after the 'vergilian' manner (e.g. *A.* 7.510 *spirans immane*) or as an adj. belonging to *munimentum*. The latter strains the imagination, whilst the former does not occur elsewhere in Amm. In any case, in Fontaine's text too, Julian's decision is inspired by emotions. As if to avoid any misunderstanding Amm. repeats this incentive in §11: *flagrans post haec ad eruendum castellum, ubi periclitatus est*. For *disponere* with inf., 'to decide', see the notes ad 16.11.4 and 20.4.9.

prohibitoribus See the note ad 24.2.13.

quodque rex cum ambitiosis copiis passibus citis incedens propediem affore credebatur In the absence of any further details it is impossible to ascertain whether this particular expectation of the besieged, if not merely the fruit of Amm.'s imagination, was already known to the Romans at the time or was only learned afterwards. In 24.7.1 (q.v.) and 24.7.7 (q.v.) there are other hints at the possibility that Sapor (see for him the note ad 20.6.1 *truculentus rex ille Persarum*) was not far away. See also 25.1.2 *radiantes loricae… adesse regis copias indicabant* and for Amm.'s use of *ambitiosus* the note ad 14.7.6. The present instance is most akin to 27.5.3 *militis cum apparatu ambitioso propinquantis*. Cf. for the t.t. *passibus citis* the notes ad 18.6.17 and 21.10.1.

iamque vineis et residuis omnibus, quae poscebat obsidium See for *vinea*   **5.8**
the note ad 24.2.18. Among the *residua* will have been *plutei*, which

162   COMMENTARY

we find mentioned together with *vineae* in 19.5.1 and 20.6.3. This is a very clear instance of *residuus* as a synonym of *reliquus*. See the notes ad 16.12.35 and 20.4.6. Cf. for *poscere* pertaining "ad necessitatem rebus inhaerentem" TLL X 2.78.72 ff.

vigilia secunda praecipiti Here *praeceps* is used as a synonym of *occiduus*, 'drawing to a close'. See the instances in TLL X 2.418.61 ff. The present text could be an imitation of Sal. *Hist* 2.87 *praecipiti iam secunda vigilia simul utrimque pugnam occipiunt.* The second vigil is between approximately 9 p.m. and midnight (when the night is reckoned to begin at about 6 p.m.). The Romans divided the night into four parts of three hours each (the length of an hour varied according to latitude and season): Veg. *mil.* 3.8.17 *in quattuor partes ad clepsydram sunt divisae vigiliae, ut non amplius quam tribus horis nocturnis necesse sit vigilare,* Cens. 23.9. Cf. for the second watch Luc. 5.506–7 *iam castra silebant, / tertia iam vigiles commoverat hora secundos.* More information in Neumann, 1962. In Amm. we find three of the four watches mentioned: *a prima vigilia* (26.1.9), *secunda vigilia* (15.5.18 and the present text), *ad usque vigiliam tertiam* and *adventante vigilia tertia* (18.2.13, q.v., and 31.15.10, respectively).

nox casu tunc lunari splendore nitens Cf. the exact opposite in 31.13.11 *nullo splendore lunari nox fulgens.* As Brok 150 notes, in other passages Amm. also explicitly mentions the presence of (clear) moonlight (26.9.9, 31.3.6) or its absence (14.2.2, 16.12.11, 21.9.6, 29.5.50, 31.13.11) during actions. The present case must be ascribed to personal memory. In May 363, it can be computed (cf. Grumel, 1958, 302 and Grotefend, 1971[11], 137), full moon fell on the 13th and 14th. A moonlit night therefore does not sound unlikely. Clark was worried by the irregular cursus, but obviously not satisfied by Heraeus' *nitescens* either, so that he printed a crux after *nitens.* Baehrens, 1925, 51 proposed the order *lunari nitens splendore.* Blomgren 93, however, mentions V's order in a list of examples of unusual cursus adduced by him to defend V's text in another place. Seyfarth accepts Blomgren's view and Fontaine follows suit, rightly it would seem. Amm.'s predilection for the three regular cursus should not be regarded as an iron law; see the notes ad 21.5.10 *si id necessitas egerit* and 21.7.1 *tamquam venaticiam praedam caperet.*

There is a curious parallel in August. *C.D.* 18.23 in the Latin rendering of the famous acrostichon in *Or. Sib.* 8.217 ff.: μήνης δέ τε φέγγος ὀλεῖται (233) is translated *lunaris splendor obibit.*

CHAPTER 5.9   163

his, qui propugnaculis insistebant For *propugnaculum* 'bulwark' see the note ad 20.6.4.

in unum pondus coacta multitudo Cf. for *pondus* denoting the massive weight of a densely packed throng *trudente pondere plebis immensae* (18.8.8, q.v.), *ne… multitudinis pondere circumveniretur* (24.6.13), *cum omni pondere multitudinis Artogerassam circumsaeptam* (27.12.12).

cohortemque necopinantem adorta nostrorum As can be inferred from § 10, this *cohors* consisted of cavalrymen. Cf. 24.5.5 and 24.4.7, q.v.

tribunus peremptus est periculum propulsare conatus Cf. 24.4.22 *propulsaturi pericula defensores*. As in 24.3.1 *strato tribuno*, Amm. explicitly mentions the death of an officer. It is possible that the fact that he belonged to that category himself prompted him to mention such details. See for *tribunus* the note ad 24.3.1.

pari modo ut antea Persae ex adversa fluminis ripa partem adorti nostrorum **5.9** A comparative conjunction is less common with *par*; see TLL X 1.277.11–17: the nearest parallel is Liv. 23.43.11 *si paria essent, ut quondam fuissent*. With *pari modo ut antea* Amm. refers to the fact that the Persians, as in § 5 (*ex contraria fluminis ripa*), attacked the Romans from the other side of the river, i.e. the Naarmalcha. Dilleman, 1961, 145 (perhaps misled by Clark's punctuation) sees in the words a reference to *patefactis subito portis* in § 5 ("les assiégés font une sortie *pari modo ut antea*") and, in consequence, wrongly identifies the *civitas* of § 5 with the *castellum=munimentum* of the sections 6–11.

et timore simul The adverb emphasizes the disappointing reaction of the Roman soldiers: instead of holding their heads high when confronted by unexpected Persian attacks, fear deprived them of their spirit 'at the same time'.

in maiorem numerum The acc. is remarkable; cf. 31.7.16 *in numero longe minore*. Possibly it is analogous to *in* with acc. "de similitudine habitu modo" (TLL VII 1.757.30 ff.), as e.g. Cic. *Att.* 5.21.10 *maiorem in modum*. Obviously, like the Persians in § 7, Julian's soldiers also thought that Sapor's troops had arrived.

sed ubi… exercitus cantu concitus bucinarum cum minaci murmure festinaret It is doubtful whether Amm. was well informed about the precise forms and functions of the various musical instruments used

164   COMMENTARY

for military purposes (see for the *bucina* and other instruments the
note ad 24.4.15 *clangore Martio*). De Jonge is quite pessimistic in his
note ad 19.6.9: "His interest in and knowledge of these instruments
was probably nil". However, Fontaine n. 428 suggests that the sound
of *bucinae* is correct here, since they are used to signal the nightly
vigiliae. One can refer for this to e.g. Caes. *Civ.* 2.35.6, Liv. 7.35.1,
26.15.6, Fron. *Str.* 1.5.17, Prop. 4.4.63, Sil. 7.154–6, but note that
Veg. *mil.* 3.8.18 speaks against it: *A tubicine omnes vigiliae committun-
tur et finitis horis a cornicine revocantur.* What does strike the reader is
the immediate emotional effect caused by the sound of the instruments; some examples: *tubarum perciti clangore* (19.6.9), *resultantibus
armis et tubis uno parique ardore hinc indeque pugnabatur* (20.11.21),
concrepante sonitu bucinarum partes accensae in clades mutuas (21.12.5),
ubi... signum dedere bucinae concrepantes, immane quo quantoque ardore...
(25.8.2).

The phrase *minaci murmure* also occurs in 24.4.15. In his note
on the present text Fontaine suggests that the *barritus* is meant. But
in view of the description of that particular war cry in 16.12.43 as
a long crescendo this is open to dispute. See the note ad 21.13.15.
In contrast to 24.4.16 *ubi... perurgerent*, in the present text *festinaret*
cannot be regarded as an iterative subjunctive. See the note ad
21.12.17 *ubi... repugnarent.*

eruptores perterriti reverterunt intacti Like the *proruptores* of §5 *eruptores*
are not attested elsewhere. The word *intactus* is more often the last
word in a sentence: *ut... cum potestate rediret intacta* (15.5.21), *mansit
intacta* (24.5.1), *retinetur intactus* (30.1.13). It thus receives a certain
emphasis, which in the present case could either stress the cowardice
of the *eruptores*, who lacked the guts to take real risks, or the failure
of Julian's men to put their opponents out of action.

5.10   *imperator ira gravi permotus* Amm. uses the participles *percitus* and
perculsus far more often, in combination with *ira* five and three times
respectively. On this occasion (cf. §6 *iratus et frendens* and §7 *concitus
ira immani*) Julian's anger is triggered off by the (in his eyes) cowardly
behaviour of his men.

*reliquos ex ea cohorte, qui abiecte sustinuerant impetum grassatorum, ad
pedestrem compegit militiam* Amm. contrasts *reliquos*, 'those who had
survived the attack unscathed', with those who had been killed
or taken prisoner (§9). Mark the constructio ad sensum *ea cohorte
qui... sustinuerant.* Interpreting *ea* in an anaphoric sense is less con-

CHAPTER 5.11   165

vincing, since the noun as such does not occur in the immediately preceding text, but in §8 (*cohortemque*). Cf. for *sustinere*, "to check the advance of" (OLD s.v. 8), 21.13.5 *impetum regis ardentissimi sustinere*; the combination with *impetus* occurs often in Livy, e.g. 25.11.5 *nec sustinuere impetum Romani*. As to *abiecte*, in 15.13.3, 30.8.11 and 31.14.8 it qualifies an adj. or a participle. It is combined with a verb in 15.2.3 *ne se proiceret abiectius cavens* (q.v.), where it denotes baseness. In the present text *abiecte* rather summarizes the lack of courage and spirit described in §9; cf. these renderings: "da pusillanimi" (Caltabiano), "lâchement" (Fontaine). The term is used here to justify Julian's anger. See for *grassatorum*, "de ces brigands" (Fontaine) the note ad 24.3.2. In combination with *in vincula* the verb *compingere* occurs three times: 17.8.5 (q.v.), 26.7.4, 28.1.8; in 26.10.5 it is combined with *in custodiam*. See Leeman-Pinkster ad Cic. *de Orat.* 1.46 for further examples in this vein, from which it appears that *compingere* is used in contexts implying loss of status.

dignitatibus imminutis This is the second time in his narrative of Julian's Persian campaign that Amm. speaks of the emperor resorting to disciplinary measures against a military unit. The first time was in 24.3.2, q.v. (the punishment on that occasion was much more severe). Another example is given in 25.1.8–9.

Reduction in rank and transfer to a lower-ranking unit were not uncommon punishments, as is clear from e.g. Caes. *Civ.* 3.74.1, D.C. 80.3.5, *Dig.* 49.16.3.1 (*militiae mutatio, gradus deiectio*), 5, 9, 15, 16, 21; 49.16.5.1; 49.16.13.4 and 6 (*in deteriorem militiam… dari*). A notorious case of degradation to the infantry is mentioned by Fron. *Str.* 4.1.31 (*Idem*, i.e. consul C. Cotta, *P. Aurelium… virgis caesum in numerum gregalium peditum referri et muneribus fungi iussit*) and V. Max. 2.7.4. See further Watson, 1969, 124–5, Campbell, 1984, 3. ff. and, for the army in late antiquity, Grosse, 1920, 234 ff.; in general Sander, 1960 and Brand, 1968.

flagrans Usually this is in some way defined, e.g. 14.1.3 *eius amore*, **5.11** 14.2.15 *vesania*, 18.4.1 *cupiditate*, 20.7.16 *desiderio capiendae Phaenichae*, 29.6.2 *studio muniendorum limitum*. The absolute use of *flagrans* in the present text emphasizes Julian's fervent excitement in a general way.

ubi periclitatus est This refers to §6. In classical Latin the subjunctive would have been used to express Julian's personal feelings, which obviously are the main factor in the author's eyes.

166   COMMENTARY

nusquam ab antesignanis...exemplo In his speech after the crossing of the Abora, Julian had explicitly announced himself as *imperator et antesignanus* (23.5.19). In this phrase the author's apologetic intentions become fully clear: Julian's rash conduct on the battlefield is given a rational justification. Brandt, 1999, 321 aptly refers to Constantius' words in 15.8.13, e.g. *fixo gradu consiste inter signiferos ipsos*. He next concludes: "In Julians Person verbinden sich also die Qualitäten des Heerführers mit der Tugend des einfachen Soldaten". Here, however, he overlooks the fact that Constantius lays down some essential conditions for a commander's bravery: *audendi in tempore consideratus hortator pugnantes accendens praeeundo cautissime.* Julian did not show himself to be *consideratus* nor did he act *cautissime*; cf. the note ad 24.2.14. See for the possible meanings of *nusquam* the notes ad 20.4.11 and 22.14.2.

spectator probatorque gestorum TLL X 2.1455.73 explains *probator* in these and comparable cases as "qui examinat, iudicat, temptat", which fits the context excellently. Constantius had urged Julian to act as a *verissimus testis affuturus industriis et ignavis* (15.8.13).

quo inter discriminum vertices diu multumque versato "Dopo essere rimasto a lungo nei luoghi dove era più grave e frequente il pericolo" (Caltabiano). The remarkable phrase *inter discriminum vertices* also occurs in 16.12.22 (q.v.) and 25.4.11: it evidently denotes extreme danger. One is tempted to regard *vertex* here as a metaphor borrowed from (the risks caused by) raging water: 'the whirlpool of dangers'; cf. Sen. *Ep.* 82.3 *in istis officiorum verticibus volutari.* Amm. once uses *vertex* in the literal meaning 'eddy': 15.4.4 *spumosis strependo verticibus amnis*; 22.8.40 *praeruptis undarum verticibus* is a different case: see the note ad loc. In all the other 20-odd instances in Amm. *vertex* denotes the highest point: a) the summit of mountains etc., e.g. 17.1.5 *per montium vertices*, 22.8.14 *gemini scopuli in vertices undique porrecti deruptos* (about the Symplegades), b) a person's head, e.g. 16.12.36 *miles scutorum obicibus vertices tegens*, c) high officials, e.g. 19.1.3 *multiplici vertice dignitatum*, d) the top of an (imaginary) list, e.g. 22.16.7 *Alexandria enim vertex omnium est civitatum* (q.v.). Therefore Amm.'s use of *vertex* here appears to suggest a different metaphor: Julian did not merely run risks, but 'the extreme forms' of risks.

varietate munitionum atque telorum et conspiratione oppugnatorum The manifold character (*varietate*) of the instruments is nicely complemented by the unanimity of those using them. The only other oc-

CHAPTER 5.12   167

currence of *munitio* with the meaning "siege-engines" (Hamilton) in Amm. is 20.11.20. As TLL IV 499.54 notes, *conspiratio* here is a synonym of "consensio, concordia etc."; cf. *conspiratione concordi* (14.1.6), *pertinaci conspiratione* (26.9.3), *conspiratio consensusque virtutum* (Cic. *Fin.* 5.66).

idem castellum incenditur captum For anaphoric use of *idem*, which grew steadily in later Latin, see the note ad 20.4.5.

consideratis asperitatibus ante gestarum rerum et impendentium After **5.12** all the emotional reactions reason finally gains the upper hand. The verb *considerare* and its derivative *consideratio* always imply some form of reflection: cf. e.g. *properantes concito quam considerato cursu* (16.12.36), *consideratione gemina* (21.7.3). Remarkably, the Agens is not mentioned; presumably Julian and his staff drew the lucid conclusion that a period of rest was badly needed in between the severe difficulties of the campaign. The noun *asperitas* is used by Amm. of roads etc. (15.10.10 *viarum asperitate*), illness (25.3.19 *longa morborum asperitate*), human behaviour (14.1.1 *asperitate nimia*), circumstances (18.6.22 *ad tolerandam rerum asperitatem*, q.v.). In contrast to *gestarum, impendentium* primarily denotes the future in a purely temporal sense, but the chosen term could also imply some threatening evil; cf. the relevant note ad 20.8.15.

requievit exercitus labore nimio quassatus On May 22, it would seem (see the note on chronology). But cf. Paschoud n. 67: "les périodes de repos de 5, 3 et de 5, 12 sont les mêmes, ou du moins s'enchaînent dans le même camp".

multis victui congruis affatim distributis See for *congruus*, 'suitable for' (or even 'necessary for') and *affatim* the relevant notes ad 20.6.1 and 20.7.16 respectively.

vallum tamen sudibus densis et fossarum altitudine cautius deinde struebatur In his note ad 18.7.6 De Jonge provides much information about the various uses of *sudes*, "small pointed poles". Polybius would have been delighted by the 'densely constructed palisade': in 18.18.5 ff. he compares the Roman usage favourably with that of the Greeks, who offered opportunities which were too easy for invaders. The Romans went to work far more efficiently: τιθέασι γὰρ εὐθέως ἐμπλέκοντες εἰς ἀλλήλους οὕτως ὥστε μήτε τὰς κεραίας εὐχερῶς ἐπιγνῶναι, ποίας εἰσὶν ἐκφύσεως τῶν ἐν τῇ γῇ κατωρυγμένων, μήτε τὰς ἐκφύσεις, ποίων

168 COMMENTARY

κεραιῶν (18.18.12), "for in planting them they so intertwine them that it is not easy to see to which of the branches, the lower ends of which are driven into the ground, the lateral prongs belong, nor to which prongs the branches belong" (transl. W.R. Paton). Moreover the points had been carefully sharpened. Remarkably, Vegetius complains that the proper techniques to fortify a camp had fallen into oblivion: *sed huius rei scientia prorsus intercidit; nemo enim iam diu ductis fossis praefixisque sudibus castra constituit* (*mil.* 1.21.4, cf. also 3.10.14). Whichever grounds Vegetius may have had for this sad remark, in Amm. there are two other cases where such fortifications are explicitly mentioned: shortly after Julian's death a camp was pitched *undique in modum mucronum praeacutis sudibus fixis* (25.6.5), and Valens, when preparing an attack on the Goths, waited near Hadrianopel *vallo sudibus fossaque formato* (31.12.4). See for *fossarum altitudo*, 'deep moats', the note ad 20.11.6. The adverb *cautius* indicates that for the time being reason prevailed: prudent caution in military matters was much appreciated by the author: see the note ad 20.11.1 *caute* and Brandt, 1999, 387.

cum a vicina iam Ctesiphonte repentini excursus et alia formidarentur occulta The memory of the action of one of Sapor's sons was still fresh (*regis filius progressus a Ctesiphonte cum optimatibus et multitudine armata*, 24.4.31; see for Ctesiphon the note ad 24.2.7). Besides, the cunning of the Persians was notorious: *astus gentis et ludificandi varietas timebatur* (24.1.13). Cf. also 24.7.7 *audaces excursus et insolita temptamenta.*

CHAPTER 6

Introduction

This chapter is dominated by two events, the crossing of the Tigris and the battle against the Persian army. Both ended in success, and in a way this is the culmination of the Persian campaign. The victory, however, failed to produce lasting results. The ominous sacrifice to Mars Ultor at the end of the chapter is the prelude to the disastrous end of the expedition.

In sections 1 and 2 we are told how the fleet reached the Tigris by way of a canal, wrongly identified by Amm. with the Naarmalcha. In reality it was 'Trajan's canal', connecting the Naarmalcha with the Tigris. The army, in order to follow the fleet along the canal, crosses the Naarmalcha and marches towards the Tigris.

After a short period of rest (§3), Julian decides, against the advice of his generals, to cross the Tigris with the whole army during the night. This was an extremely hazardous undertaking, characteristic of Julian's style as a military leader, with its mixture of decisiveness and bravura verging on recklessness, which prompts a comparison with the crossing of the Rhône by Sertorius (§4–7). In Amm.'s report the crossing of the Tigris is followed without a break by a full-sized battle lasting until the evening of the next day. It was the only engagement between Romans and Persians during Julian's expedition that offered Ammianus the opportunity for a battle description, in which the following stages may be distinguished. First (§8–10) Amm. presents the battle order of the opposing armies and their outward appearance with a keen eye for visual details, such as the glittering cuirasses of the Persian cavalry and the disciplined approach of the Roman infantry. The account of the actual battle (§11) takes up no more than six lines. The superior tactics of the Roman army and Julian's ubiquitous presence on the battle field are emphasized. Sections 12 and 13 are devoted to the retreat of the Persian army to Ctesiphon, pursued by the Roman soldiers. They are forbidden to enter the city by their commander Victor for eminently sensible reasons. Suggestions in the parallel sources that the greed of the plundering soldiers prevented the capture of Ctesiphon are ignored by Ammianus. In the words of Smith, 1999, 94, the references to the battle of Troy and the Persian Wars (§14) "mark a wish to monu-

170   COMMENTARY

mentalize a campaign in which no full-scale battle was actually ever fought." The fact that the victory in the field did not lead to the capture of Ctesiphon may help to explain why Amm. did not provide a more colourful account of this battle in the style he had adopted for the battle of Strasbourg in 16.12. The high point of the chapter is reached in section 15, where the soldiers praise Julian, because they had suffered minimal losses, whereas the Persians had lost thousands, and Julian rewards his men for their bravery. However, the chapter ends in gloom (§16). When Julian offers ten bulls to Mars, the sacrifice ends in a fiasco, which provokes such anger in Julian that he threatens the god of war never to sacrifice to him again. His death a short time later robbed him of the opportunity to make up for these rash words. The last section marks the change from an until then rather successful campaign to a series of disastrous events which eventually resulted in the death of Julian, the calamitous retreat of the Roman army, and the dishonourable peace treaty Jovian had to conclude with Sapor II.

6.1 *Ventum est* On May, 23 presumably. Amm. has used the impersonal form *ventum est* twice before in his account of the Persian expedition: 24.2.3 *ventum est ad locum Baraxmalcha* and 24.2.9 *ad civitatem Pirisabora ventum est*. The first person plural *venimus* is much more frequent. The most natural interpretation of the latter form would be that Amm. uses it to describe actions in which he was personally involved. If one looks at the context of these phrases, it is remarkable that they are preceded or followed by remarks about activities on the river: 23.5.7 *Zaithan venimus* follows the destruction of a bridge (23.5.5) and the arrival of new ships (23.5.6); 24.1.5 *venimus Duram* comes after an instruction to the fleet; 24.2.1 *ad castra pervenimus nomine Thilutha* is followed by *in medio fluminis sita*; 24.2.2 *cum ad munimentum aliud Achaiachala nomine venissemus* is preceded by *praetermeantes moenia ipsa naves nostras verecunda quiete spectabant*. The next stage, quoted above, Baraxmalcha, opens with an impersonal form, which is followed by *amne transito*, after which Amm. writes *templum…vidimus* and *Ozogardana occupavimus*. There is one first person form in ch. 3 (§10 *nos ituros*) after which Amm. mentions the manipulation of the waterworks by the enemies, and one in 4 (§31 *ad munimenta gemina venimus*) which is preceded by *transitis pontibus multorum amnium concursu continuatis*. All this may be pure coincidence in a report in which rivers, river fortresses and the building of bridges play an important role, but it tallies remarkably well with the suggestion mentioned by Fontaine

CHAPTER 6.1   171

in his Introduction to Books 23–25 (17 n. 1) that Amm. would have been on the fleet until the army reached Ctesiphon. For what it is worth, this chapter opens with an impersonal *ventum est* and switches to a first person account in section 3, after Amm. has described work on what he calls the Naarmalcha and the construction of bridges.

Mommsen, 1909, 428 was far too sceptical on this point: "In dieser Weise, als habe er selbst den Feldzug mitgemacht, erzählt Ammian durchaus, nirgends aber deutet er auch nur an, in welcher Stellung er sich befunden und was ihn persönlich betroffen hat. Vergleicht man damit seine Erzählung der Belagerung von Amida, bei welcher er wirklich im Sattel gesessen hat, so erscheint seine eigene Betheiligung in hohem Grade zweifelhaft".

ad fossile flumen Naarmalcha nomine In 24.2.7 (as was remarked in the note ad loc.) and in 24.6.1 Amm. uses the name Naarmalcha for watercourses which were definitely not one and the same. Brok 151 and Dillemann, 1961, 157 already noted that in the present text Amm. must be mistaken (cf. also Klein, 1914, 46–7). The *fossile flumen* here cannot be the Naarmalcha itself, but must be a canal ('Trajan's canal', see for this name below, ad *Traianus posteaque Severus*) that branched off from the Naarmalcha and joined the Tigris. Zosimus' account is correct: Ἐντεῦθεν ὁρμήσαντες ἦλθον εἴς τινα διώρυχα μεγίστην... εἰς ἣν ἐμβαλὼν ὁ Ναρμαλάχης ποταμὸς εἰς τὸν Τίγριν ἐκδίδωσι (3.24.2; in Paschoud's n. 68 it is i.a remarked that this canal branched off from 'his' Naarmalcha not far eastward from Meinas Zabatha, mentioned in 3.23.3, at the point where it turned off in southerly direction). Lib. *Or.* 18.245 (see Bliembach ad loc.) refers to the same canal when he reports that Julian began to enquire about a navigable channel which would bring him to the Tigris upstream of the two cities (see for these cities, *Coche quam Seleuciam nominant* and Ctesiphon, the note ad 24.5.3): λαβὼν γὰρ αἰχμαλώτους τῶν αὐτοῦ που πλησίον οἰκούντων ἐζήτει διώρυχα ναυσίπορον... ἄγουσαν δὲ τὸν Εὐφράτην ἐπὶ τὸν Τίγρητα ταῖν δυοῖν ἀνωτέρω πόλεων. See further Soz. *HE* 6.1.5 and Greg. Naz. *Or.* 5.9.

The adj. *fossilis* in the sense of "fodiendo effectus" (TLL VI 1213, 60) is without parallel.

quod amnis regum interpretatur For *interpretare* see the note ad 24.2.7 *alia Naarmalcha*. There Amm. had given the translation *fluvius* (regum), which he avoids here, presumably on account of the preceding *flumen*.

172   COMMENTARY

aridum The canal had dried up because the Persians had blocked it with a huge dam of stones (24.6.2: *mole saxorum obruere multorum*). Lib. *Or.* 18.246 reports that an old man informed Julian about the location of the canal: φράζει τοίνυν ὁ πρεσβύτης οὗ τέ ἐστι καὶ ὡς κέκλειται καὶ ὡς ἀναχωσθεῖσα τὸ πρὸς τῷ στόματι σπείροιτο ("The old fellow, then, told where it was situated and revealed that the channel had been closed and that the blockage at its mouth was under cultivation"; transl. Norman).

Traianus posteaque Severus Amm. is the only author who mentions Severus in this respect, but that Trajan excavated the channel is also related by Zosimus, according to whom this information was given by people living in the area: διώρυχα μεγίστην, ἣν ἔλεγον οἱ τῇδε παρὰ Τραιανοῦ διωρύχθαι Πέρσαις ἐπιστρατεύσαντος (3.24.2; see for the campaigns of Trajan and Severus the note ad 23.5.17). Lib. *Or.* 18.245, when relating that Julian derived his information about the channel not only from captives, but also from books (ἐκ βίβλων), adds to this that the channel was the work of a παλαιὸς βασιλεύς. Presumably he referred with these words to Trajan but, as Valesius already suggested, originally the channel must have been the work of a much older king, Seleucus Nicator (cf. Plin *Nat.* 6.122).

Apparently neither Amm. nor Zosimus nor Libanius was aware of the fact that Trajan (if we may believe Cassius Dio 68.28.1), although he planned to excavate the canal, actually did not do so: Τραιανὸς δὲ ἐβουλεύσατο μὲν τὸν Εὐφράτην (= the Naarmalcha, it would seem) κατὰ διώρυχα ἐς τὸν Τίγριν ἐσαγαγεῖν… μαθὼν δὲ ὅτι πολὺ ὑψηλότερος τοῦ Τίγριδός ἐστι, τοῦτο… οὐκ ἔπραξε – this is the reason why it is appropriate to put 'Trajan's canal' between inverted commas.

fodiri in modum canalis… curaverat The passive infinitive *fodiri* is found i.a. in Cato *Agr.* 2.4; TLL VI 991.77–82. For the phrase *in modum* + gen. cf. the note ad 23.4.2, the only other place in Amm. where *canalis* is used, in that case to denote the 'groove' of the ballista.

ut aquis illuc ab Euphrate transfusis naves ad Tigridem commigrarent The verb is a hapax in Amm. Normally it is found with a human or, less frequently, an abstract subject. As to *Euphrate*, Amm. makes the same mistake as Cassius Dio just quoted: the Naarmalcha must be meant.

6.2   *ad omnia* 'In view of all eventualities'. The only other instance of this phrase in Amm. is 29.2.1 *ipsa sortis infimitate ad omnia praeceps*, cf. Sen. *Prov.* 5.8 *nos laeti ad omnia et fortes.*

CHAPTER 6.2173

eadem loca purgari The canal, which had not been used for a long period, was blocked up with earth and other material. Hence the need to clear it out. Cf. Zos. 3.24.2 ταύτην ὁ βασιλεὺς καθῆραι τε ἅμα καὶ ἐρευνᾶν διενοήθη, πόρον... τοῖς πλοίοις ἐπὶ τὸν Τίγρητα παρασκευάζων. The verb *purgare* in its literal sense is found also in 22.12.8 and 30.5.17 *cumque locus aggestis ruderibus neglectus purgatur*. The metaphorical meaning 'to justify' is much more frequent. For the passive infinitive after impersonal expressions see Szantyr 353. It is found in all periods of Latin and is especially frequent in Livy.

mole saxorum In a similar fashion the emperor Hadrian had blocked up the Castalian fount 22.12.8 *quem obstruxisse Caesar dicitur Hadrianus mole saxorum ingenti veritus, ne, ut ipse praecinentibus aquis capessendam rem publicam comperit, etiam alii similia docerentur.*

hacque valle purgata avulsis cataractis This must have taken some time, say May, 24–26. For *vallis* 'river bed' cf. Ov. *Met.* 2.255–6 *ostia septem /* (Nili) *pulverulenta vacant, septem sine flumine valles.* There is a note on *cataractae*, 'weirs' ad 24.1.11.

undarum magnitudine Abl. causae with *secura*: 'safe because of the great mass of water'. V's reading (SBG have *multitudine*) is found also in 24.1.11 *magnitudine... fluentorum*, q.v.

classis This is the first time since 24.2.2 that we hear again of the fleet (cf. the note ad 24.2.7). It was perhaps on May, 27 that the fleet reached the Tigris.

stadiis triginta decursis Since *depellere* is never used in the sense of 'to cover' (a distance), V's *depulsis* is considered corrupt in TLL V 1.563.57–8. Fontaine defends *depulsa* of Vm3 with dubious parallels. The series *secura, depulsa, eiecta* would be inelegant. In view of 24.3.10 *decursis milibus passuum quattuordecim* Valesius' emendation seems just right. For Amm.'s varied use of designations for distances, see the note ad 24.2.3. Thirty stadia is approximately 5.5 km. Paschoud, 1978, 357–8 and n. 68 draws attention to the difference of the level between the point where 'Trajan's canal' split off from the Naarmalcha and where it joined the Tigris. D.C. 68.28.1–2 already noted this, but Amm. and Libanius also implicitly refer to it. Lib. *Or.* 18.247 reports that the cleaned and newly opened canal transported such an enormous amount of water to the Tigris that the latter became swollen to such a degree that the inhabitants of Coche/

174 COMMENTARY

Seleucia and Ctesiphon were struck by panic and feared that their city walls would not hold.

contextis ilico pontibus congressus exercitus iter Cochen versus promovit Cf. 17.10.1 *contextoque navali ponte Rheno transito* and 17.12.4 *flumen Histrum… super navium foros ponte contexto transgressus.* As these examples show, one would expect a verb with the prefix *trans-*. V's *congressus* arouses suspicion anyway, because in Amm. *congredi* and its derivatives are always used of military engagements. Moreover *congressus* can be explained as a form of dittography after *contextis*, so that there is ample reason to accept G's *transgressus. Iter promovere* occurs only here in Amm. and is extremely rare. The only parallels in TLL X 2.1895.55–9 are from Symmachus. The boatbridges were used to cross the Naarmalcha and not, as Zos. 3.24.2 seems to imply, 'Trajan's canal' (ἐρευνᾶν διενοήθη, πόρον τε τοῖς πλοίοις ἐπὶ τὸν Τίγρητα παρασκευάζων, καὶ εἴ πῃ παρείκοι, γεφύρας τῇ τοῦ πολλοῦ στρατοῦ διαβάσει). For Coche see the note ad 24.5.3. Zos. 3.25.1 ff. is mistaken when he reports that the passage met with fierce resistance from the Persians. Zosimus clearly confuses this crossing with that of the Tigris which is described by Amm. in §4 ff. of this chapter. See especially Paschoud n. 69: "Zosime s'est donc rendu ici coupable d'une grosse maladresse en résumant ses sources et a commis un 'saut du même au même' en confondant Canal de Trajan et Tigre".

6.3 *utque lassitudini succederet quies opportuna* Already at the beginning of his military career, Julian demonstrated great care for the well-being of his men: 16.4.4 *efficacissimus Caesar providebat constanti sollicitudine, ut militum diuturno labori quies succederet aliqua licet brevis.*

It is probably during this rest (May, 28–30 presumably) that Julian offered his army various sorts of entertainment (pace Dillemann, 1961, 148, who, because both Amm. and Zosimus are silent about such festivities, finds it difficult to believe in their historicity). Lib. *Or.* 18.249–50 relates that Julian organised horseraces near Ctesiphon. The same information is handed down to us by Soz. *HE* 6.1.6 (κέλησιν ἆθλα προθεὶς ἐπὶ θέαν ἱπποδρομίας τοὺς στρατιώτας ἐκάθισεν) and the *Suda* E 322 (ὁ δὲ Ἰουλιανὸς καὶ ἱππικὸν ἀγῶνα ἔθηκεν). However, cf. Lib. *Or.* 24.37, where we are told that these races took place before the walls of Babylon, and Lib. *Or.* 1.133, about horseraces as well as athletic competitions. Festus 28 speaks of *ludi campestres* (*Cum contra Ctesiphontem in ripa Tigridis et Euphratis iam mixti castra haberet, ludosque campestres, ut hosti sollicitudinem demeret, per diem agi-*

CHAPTER 6.3   175

tasset). It would seem that Eun. *fr.* 27.3 is also relevant: Ὅτι τὸ πρὸ Κτησιφῶντος πεδίον ὀρχήστραν πολέμου πρότερον ἀποδείξας, ὡς ἔλεγεν Ἐπαμινώνδας, Διονύσου σκηνὴν ἐπεδείκνυ Ἰουλιανός, ἀνέσεις τινὰς τοῖς στρατιώταις καὶ ἡδονὰς ποριζόμενος ("having made the plain before Ctesiphon a dance-floor of war, to use Epaminondas' phrase [cf. Plut. *Marc.* 21.2], Julian then put on a Dionysian scene, providing the soldiers with relaxation and enjoyment", tr. Blockley). Cf. further Eun. *fr.* 27.4 Ὁ δὲ Ἰουλιανὸς ἐν Πέρσαις ὢν γυμνικοὺς ἀγῶνας ἦγε.

There is another piece of evidence, viz. a scholiast's note on *Anth. Gr.* 14.148, which, if reliable (it is accepted by e.g. *PLRE* I, Iulianus 29, rejected by e.g. Lippold, 1999–2000, 444; see in general Demandt, 1989, 94 n. 2), would give us a plausible reason for the organisation of horseraces and other festivities in the middle of a war (cf. for other motives Festus, just quoted, and Lib. *Or.* 18.249 ὁ δὲ πρῶτον μὲν ἃ τῶν εὐθυμουμένων ἐστίν, ἐποίησεν ἱππόδρομόν τε λεάνας καὶ ἱππέας ἐπ᾽ ἀγῶνα καλέσας, "his first actions were indicative of confidence: he levelled out a race-track and summoned cavalrymen to a contest", tr. Norman). Speaking of horseraces near Ctesiphon the scholiast says that Julian organised the spectacle on the occasion of his birthday: χρησμὸς δοθεὶς Ἰουλιανῷ τῷ ἀποστάτῃ, ὅτε τὴν γενέθλιον ἡμέραν ἐπιτελῶν ἑαυτοῦ διῆγεν περὶ Κτησιφῶντα ἀγῶνας ἱππικοὺς θεώμενος. The oracle itself has also been transmitted, with some slight modifications, in the *Suda* I 437. It is *fr.* 27.7 in Blockley's edition of Eunapius. Unfortunately however, its introductory phrase, although mentioning Ctesiphon, is silent on Julian's birthday: Ἔστι δὲ καὶ ὁ χρησμὸς ὁ δοθεὶς αὐτῷ, ὅτε περὶ Κτησιφῶντα διῆγεν.

> Γηγενέων ποτὲ φῦλον ἐνήρατο μητιέτα Ζεύς,
> ἔχθιστον μακάρεσσιν Ὀλύμπια δώματ᾽ ἔχουσι.
> Ῥωμαίων βασιλεύς, Ἰουλιανὸς θεοειδής,
> μαρνάμενος Περσῶν πόλιας καὶ τείχεα μακρὰ
> ἀγχεμάχων διέπερσε πυρὶ κρατερῷ τε σιδήρῳ ...

"There is also the oracle which was given to him in the neighbourhood of Ctesiphon:

> Once all-wise Zeus slew the race of the Earth-born
> Most hateful to the blessed gods who live on Olympus.
> The king of the Romans, god-like Julian,
> Warring at close quarters with the cities of the Persians
> And their long walls, has destroyed them with fire
> And strong steel..." (tr. Blockley).

176   COMMENTARY

in agro consedimus opulento For the richness and fertility of this region, see the note ad 24.5.1. Cf. also Eunapius *fr.* 27.5, quoted ad 24.3.14 *ubi formidabatur inedia.* The estate was a παράδεισος, like the one referred to in 24.5.2 *extentum spatium* (q.v.) and may have belonged either to the Sasanian king himself or to a Persian nobleman. It is perhaps to this place that Eutr. 10.16.1 (*castra apud Ctesiphonta stativa aliquamdiu habuit*) and Malalas *Chron.* 13.330 (ὁ βασιλεὺς ἐσκήνωσεν ἐν τῇ πεδιάδι τῆς αὐτῆς πόλεως Κτησιφῶντος) refer. Zos. 3.23.1 gives a description of such an estate.

arbustis et vitibus et cupressorum viriditate laetissimo The phrase specifies *opulento.* As TLL II 430.34–63 suggests, the trees serve to support the grapevines. For the gen. inversus *cupressorum,* which is a constant feature of Amm.'s descriptive passages, see the note ad 20.6.7 and cf. Ambr. *in psalm. 118 serm.* 4.21 on the cypress: *numquam amittit viriditatem suam.* For *laetus* with abl. cf. Verg. *G.* 2.112 *litora myrtetis laetissima.*

diversorium The noun is used in a variety of meanings. Here, as in 23.6.46 *diversoria regum ambitiosa,* it must be a royal hunting-palace. In 22.12.6, q.v., it denotes a military inn and in 30.1.14 *eques mittitur clandestinus ad dextrum itineris latus diversoria paraturus et cibum* it can be no more than a simple sleeping place for the night.

gentiles picturas… bella I.e. the paintings were in the Persian style. Contrast the palace in 24.5.1 *Romano more aedificata.* For *gentilis* cf. 16.10.16 (Hormisdas) *respondit astu gentili* and 31.16.1 *Conversi… ad vulnerum curas artesque medendi gentiles.* Hunting and battle scenes are the major themes in Sasanian art. They were depicted on e.g. (rock) reliefs, (silver) vessels, frescoes and textiles. Especially scenes depicting the king hunting were popular. Ghirsman, 1962, plates on pp. 152, 173, 177–8 (Naqs-i-Rustam), 182–3 (frescoes), 187, 194–8, 207, 208, 212, 213, 249, and overview on 252–3; see also Shepherd, 1983; Harper, 1986.

venatione multiplici The adjective refers to "various kinds of hunting" (Rolfe) rather than to the king's large retinue, as Fontaine's translation suggests ("en chasse nombreuse").

pingitur vel fingitur See the note ad 23.4.12 *qualia nobis pictores ostendunt* and for the jingle cf. the elogium on Valentinian in 30.9.4 *scribens decore venusteque pingens et fingens.*

CHAPTER 6.4   177

praeter varias caedes et bella By remarking that the Persians depicted nothing except slaughter and scenes of war Amm. gives an unfavourable moral evaluation of the Persians. As the encounter with
the Persian army is drawing near, this also serves as a timely reminder
by the author of the savage character of the enemy.

Proinde cunctis ex sententia terminatis Cf. Zos. 3.25.1 Τούτων δὲ ταύτῃ **6.4**
πραττομένων. As TLL X 2.1806.9 notes, *proinde*, 'accordingly', i.e.
'in accordance with what I have told' occurs frequently in Amm.
(and Augustine). For *ex sententia*, 'satisfactorily', cf. 27.7.1 *His ex
sententia rectoris et militum ordinatis* and the note ad 22.10.1. A similar
formula of transition is 16.12.62 *Quibus ita favore superni numinis
terminatis.*

Augustus altius iam contra difficultates omnes incedens This is the first
time in Amm.'s description of the Persian campaign that Julian
is designated as *Augustus*, instead of *princeps* or, more commonly,
imperator. For the different ways in which Amm. refers to Julian
see the notes ad 24.1.1 *impetrabilem principem* and 24.2.21 *salutarem
genium*. In combination with *altius incedens* it emphasizes Julian's
success so far, while at the same time preparing the reader for the
περιπέτεια, as in 23.5.8: *quo omine velut certiore iam spe status prosperioris
elatus exsultantius cedebat* (or *incedebat* rather), *sed incerto flatu fortunae
aliorsum prorupit eventus.*

tantumque a fortuna sperans nondum afflicta One is strongly reminded
of the remark about Constantius in 20.11.32 *ut ipsum Constantium
dimicantem cum Persis fortuna semper sequeretur afflictior*, q.v. For *fortuna*
see the note ad 23.5.19.

ut propius temeritatem multa crebro auderet Several examples of Julian's
recklessness have been collected in the introductions to chs. 4 and
5. Here Amm. expresses his criticism as a professional soldier on
Julian's plan to cross the Tigris and confront the enemy on the other
side of the river. Julian's generals were also against this strategy, as
Amm. mentions in the next section. Lib. *Or.* 18.248, 250 reports that
there was no other option than to cross the Tigris since the army was
shut in by rivers and returning by the same route was impossible
because of the devastation of the land. According to Zos. 3.25.1,
Julian felt provoked by the gathering of the Persian army on the
other bank: ταύτην ὁ βασιλεὺς τὴν παρασκευὴν τῶν πολεμίων βλέπων
ἐπὶ τὸ διαπλέειν ἐπ' αὐτοὺς ἠρεθίζετο.

178 COMMENTARY

validiores naves ex his, quae alimenta portabant et machinas deoneratas octogenis implevit armatis These are the cargo-carriers of which there were 1.000 at the start of the expedition; 23.3.9, q.v. *mille erant onerariae naves commeatus abunde ferentes et tela et obsidionales machinas.* According to Lib. *Or.* 18.250, this unloading took place while the army was enjoying some recreation at the horseraces (for which see the note ad § 3 *utque lassitudini*): ἐν ᾧ δὲ τοῖς δρόμοις τῶν ἵππων ὁ στρατὸς ἐψυχαγωγεῖτο, κεναὶ τῶν φορτίων ἐκ παραγγέλσεως ἦσαν αἱ νῆες. Libanius adds that Julian ordered the cargo ships to be unloaded because in view of the action to come he wanted his troops to embark suddenly, without giving them advance notice (the ostensible reason, however, was that there might be a check on any deficiency of rations): τῷ λόγῳ μὲν ὅπως ὀφθείη τὸ σιτηρέσιον εἴ πῃ παρανάλωται, τὸ δὲ ἔργον ἦν, οὐ προειδότας ἐξαίφνης ἐμβιβάσαι τοὺς στρατιώτας ἐβούλετο. Julian's decision to remove the cargo from the ships also caused Sozomenus to look for its motive: ἐν τούτῳ δὲ τοὺς προεστῶτας τῶν πλοίων ἐκέλευσεν ἀποβαλεῖν τὰ φορτία καὶ τὸ σιτηρέσιον τῆς στρατιᾶς, ὅπως ἐν κινδύνῳ σφᾶς ἰδόντες οἱ στρατιῶται, ὡς ἐπυθόμην, ἀπορίᾳ τῶν ἐπιτηδείων εἰς θράσος τράπωνται καὶ προθυμότερον τοῖς πολεμίοις μαχέσωνται (*HE* 6.1.7).

octogenis We need a distributivum here, so *octogenis* is clearly better than *octingentis*. Rolfe reads *octogenis*, but translates "eight hundred".

quam in tres diviserat partes This detail is lacking in the parallel accounts by Libanius and Zosimus. The strategic reasoning behind the tripartition of the fleet is not quite clear. Possibly Julian wanted to attack the Persian troops at the other side of the river in three phases. It could also be that by dividing his forces he intended to give the impression that his fleet was greater than it actually was. Cf. 21.8.3 and 24.1.2–3 for similar tactics.

unam cum Victore comite For Victor see the note ad 24.1.2. The last time we saw him in action was in 24.4.31 (see further 24.4.13). While Zosimus does not report who was to lead the first attack, Libanius does, though indirectly. In *Or.* 18.250–1 he says, without mentioning names, that the man who should have been in charge was replaced by someone else. This new commander, he adds, would receive a wound in the hand. Since Amm. in § 13 (q.v.) and Zosimus in 3.25.7 explicitly report that Victor was wounded during the battle (albeit in his shoulder, according to Amm.), it does not seem too rash to assume that Libanius here is talking about the same man.

CHAPTER 6.5   179

Now Victor was the commander of one part (*unam*) of the fleet, and Julian of another (*robore firmiore*). One wonders who was in command of the third. Perhaps it was the man of whom Libanius says that he was replaced as commander of the vanguard because of his criticism of Julian's plans to cross the Tigris in arms, and who had under his command the main body of the army: ὑφ' ᾧ δὲ ἦν τῆς δυνάμεως τὸ πλέον (*Or.* 18.250). If so, who was this man? According to Brok 153, Bliembach, 1976, 185 and others the praetorian prefect Salutius must be meant (i.e. *PLRE* I, Secundus 3; see for him the notes ad 22.3.1 and 23.5.6), according to Fontaine n. 435 Nevitta (cf. for him 24.1.2 and 24.4.13), according to Woods, 1998, 247 Lucillianus (see for him 24.1.6). Cf. Paschoud n. 69: "on ose à peine rester neutre dans ce petit jeu".

quiete prima noctis emitti disposuit It was the night of May, 31 presumably (see the note on chronology). As a young commander, Julian had ordered a similar naval action by night on the Rhine: 17.1.4 *Caesar noctis prima quiete navigiis modicis et velocibus octingentos imposuit milites,* on that occasion, too, in the face of opposition of his men: *refragante vetabatur exercitu* (17.1.2). The expression *noctis prima quiete* is also found in 18.3.3. In view of what follows *emitti disposuit* must mean that Julian informed his commanders of his decision that Victor must cross the Tigris. The actual command to start the crossing is given in the next section *sublato vexillo, ut iussum est.* This is the only instance of *emittere* in Amm. for sending out troops. Usually, weapons are the object, such as the fists of the Gallic virago in 15.12.1: *cum illa ... emittere coeperit pugnos ut catapultas tortilibus nervis excussas,* or animals released in the amphitheatre, as in 31.10.19 *centum leones in amphitheatrali circulo simul emissos,* or swimmers at the start of a race: *simul emissi spe citius ripas occupavere contrarias* (25.6.14). Therefore Amm. probably means that Julian 'threw' his crack troops into battle. See TLL V 2.504.28–35 for parallels in other authors.

acri metu territi These are strong words. The commanders do not   **6.5** merely object to Julian's plan, they are terrified. Lib. *Or.* 18.250–1 suggests that all but one of Julian's generals accepted his strategy. The dissident (ὑφ' ᾧ δὲ ἦν τῆς δυνάμεως τὸ πλέον, see the note ad §4) argued that the opposite bank of the river was too high and the enemy too numerous. As to this last argument, Zos. 3.25.1 also mentions the fact that many Persians were assembled on the other side of the river, ready to thwart any attempt of the Romans to cross: ἐπὶ τῆς ἀντικρὺ ὄχθης πλῆθος Περσῶν συνδραμὸν ἱππέων τε καὶ πεζῶν, εἴ τις ἐπιχειρηθείη

180   COMMENTARY

διάβασις, ἐπειρᾶτο κωλύειν. In 24.6.6 Amm. tells us that the banks were high and precipitous (*praealtas ripas et arduas*). The risks involved are eloquently spelled out by Lib. *Or.* 18.252: ὃν οὐκ ἂν ἐν εἰρήνῃ τε καὶ μηδενὸς εἴργοντος μεθ᾽ ἡμέραν εὔζωνοι κρημνὸν ἐθάρρησαν (sc. ἀναβαίνειν), διὰ νυκτὸς ὁπλῖται τοὺς πολεμίους ὑπὲρ κεφάλης ἔχοντες ἀναβεβήκεσαν, echoed by Ruf. Fest. 28.2: *per ardua nitentes, qua difficilis etiam per diem et nullo prohibente fuisset ascensus.* Zos. 3.25.2 says that the bank had a wall along it: ἅμα θριγκόν τινα συμπαρατεινόμενον, εἰς ἔρυμα μὲν παραδείσου βασιλικοῦ τὴν ἀρχὴν ᾠκοδομημένον, τότε δὲ καὶ τείχους πληροῦντα χρείαν ('function'), which is not unlikely. Cf. 24.5.2, where a similar παράδεισος is described as *extentum spatium et rotundum loricae ambitu circumclausum.* There may also have been some type of dykes or mounds; cf. 25.6.8 *riparum aggeribus humana manu instructis.* It is not known where exactly Julian crossed the Tigris.

concordi precatu The noun is a hapax in the *Res Gestae*. Apart from five instances in Statius, it is found only in late authors; TLL X 2.1152.15–50.

destinationem See the note on 20.4.14 *destinatius.*

sublato vexillo For *vexillum* see the notes ad 20.6.3 and 24.3.1. The raising of the flag was the sign to attack.

evolant e conspectu quinque subito naves Amm. may have had in mind Cic. *Ver.* 5.88 *evolarat iam e conspectu fere fugiens quadriremis.* For other examples of *evolare* "de navibus" see TLL V 2.1066.11–15. Zos. 3.25.2 mentions only two ships.

cum ripas iam adventarent The particle seems to indicate that the Persians held their fire until the ships had come within the range of their weapons.

facibus et omni materia, qua alitur ignis Cf. Zos. 3.25.2 τὰς...τῶν βέλων τε καὶ πυρσῶν βολὰς (fireballs). For a technical discussion of firedarts and the incendiary materials that were used see the notes on 23.4.14.

veloci vigore pectoris excitus Inspired (*excitus*) by his quick intelligence and his presence of mind, Julian finds the right answer to this critical situation. Cf. Mary, 1992, 599 n. 28: "Il se peut qu'il y ait là une allusion au passage de l'Iaxarte par Alexandre, face aux Scythes" (Arr. *An.* 4.4.1 ff.). In any case this is a fine tribute to Julian without the reser-

CHAPTER 6.6 181

vation implied in *ut erat in rebus trepidis audax et confidentior* (21.10.1, q.v.). Julian had been called *adolescens vigoris tranquilli* by Constantius, when he presented him as Caesar to the troops (15.8.10). His 'innate energy' had made him dream of the din of battle (16.1.1 *urguente genuino vigore pugnarum fragores... somniabat*). *Vigor animi* or – *ingenii* is more common than *vigor pectoris*. See Börner on Ov. *Met.* 8.254 *sed vigor ingenii quondam velocis*. *Vigor animi* is mentioned as a quality of Theodosius senior in 28.3.1: *Theodosius vero, dux nominis incluti, animi vigore collecto ab Augusta profectus*. The substitution of *pectoris* for *animi* or *ingenii* may emphasize Julian's military qualities. As Valesius saw, V's *frigore* is totally unacceptable. In the words of TLL VI 1334.13–4 *frigus* is used "animantium prae pavore horrentium, inde i.q. timor, metus", as in Ov. *Fast.* 1.98 *et gelidum subito frigore pectus erat*. Characteristically, Libanius presents Julian's decision as divinely inspired: ὁ δ' εἱστήκει βλέπων εἰς οὐρανόν, ὡς δὲ ἔλαβεν ἐκεῖθεν τὸ σύνθημα, δίδωσιν αὐτὸ τοῖς ταξιάρχοις (*Or.* 18.252).

signum sibi datum nostros... erexisse This action of Julian shows his cunning in a seemingly hopeless situation. Note that the bluff could only succeed because it was night and the ships were out of sight (*e conspectu*). The soldiers only saw a blazing fire. Cf. the parallel account in Zos. 3.25.3: Ἐκδειματωθέντος δὲ πλέον τοῦ στρατοῦ, τὴν συμβᾶσαν ὁ βασιλεὺς καταστρατηγήσων διαμαρτίαν ("pour neutraliser par la ruse l'effet de l'échec qui s'était produit", Paschoud) 'περιγεγόνασιν' ἔφη 'τῆς διαβάσεως, καὶ κύριοι τῆς ὄχθης γεγόνασι· τοῦτο γὰρ δηλοῖ τὸ πῦρ τὸ ἀπὸ τῶν πλοίων ἐξαφθέν, ὅπερ αὐτὸς ἐπέσκηψα τοῖς ἐπὶ τῶν νεῶν στρατιώταις σύμβολον τῆς νίκης ποιήσασθαι'. The content of the relative clause ὅπερ... ποιήσασθαι is rendered by *signum sibi datum*, in which *sibi* refers to *nostros*, the subject of the AcI *nostros erexisse*, which depends on *proclamans*. For Amm.'s practice in this respect see the note ad 20.5.4 *cum iactura*. See Szantyr 576 for *quod*-clauses instead of the AcI.

properare citis remigiis adegisset This seems to be a variation of the common expressions *citis passibus*, on which see the note ad 21.10.1, and – *itineribus* (e.g. 26.8.4). On *adigere* see the note ad 21.16.10 *hic etiam*.

et naves incolumes sunt receptae et residuus miles... stabat immobilis As **6.6** Paschoud n. 69 observes, a comparison with Zos. 3.25.4: οὐ μόνον ἐκράτησαν τῆς ὄχθης, ἀλλὰ καὶ τὰ πρότερον περαιωθέντα δύο πλοῖα καταλαβόντες ἡμίφλεκτα τοὺς περιλελειμμένους ἔτι τῶν ἐν αὐτοῖς ὁπλιτῶν

182 COMMENTARY

περιέσωσαν suggests that there is an abridgement in the text of Amm. Indeed, one may surmise that *residuus* and *incolumes recipere* have been suggested to Amm. by words corresponding with περιλελειμμένους and περισῴζειν in Zosimus' source.

saxis Stones were a common weapon in a situation like this which is comparable to a siege; see the note ad 24.2.14.

post concertationem acerrimam For *concertatio* see the note ad 21.11.3. The difficulties of the fight have been enumerated in the note ad § 5 *acri metu.* According to Lib. *Or.* 18.252 the embankment was taken with divine help: οὐκ ἀνθρώπων μᾶλλον ἦν τὸ ἔργον ἢ θεοῦ τινος ταῖς αὐτοῦ χερσὶ μετεωρίζοντος ἕκαστον.

praealtas ripas et arduas supergressus stabat immobilis For the risks involved in this operation see the note ad § 5 *acri metu territi.* According to Brok 154, *praealtas* and *arduas* describe the impression of the soldiers, whereas in reality the embankments of the Tigris were rather flat. Fontaine n. 437 correctly observes that the height of the embankments may be different nowadays from the situation in antiquity. He furthermore notes that Amm. may exaggerate the height and steepness of the embankment to underscore the achievement of the Roman army. This is the only example of *supergradior* in its literal meaning. In the other instances the verb means 'to overstep' (the bounds), as e.g. in 27.6.16 *Valentinianus morem institutum antiquitus supergressus. Stabat* or *mansit immobilis* is one of Amm.'s favourite expressions. See the note ad 23.5.8 *stetit immobilis.*

6.7 *et miratur historia Rhodanum arma et loricam retinente Sertorio transnatatum* A clear case of *et* introducing an exclamatory sentence; TLL V 2.890.51–67. Amm. constantly enhances the colour of his story by comparisons with ancient history. More examples are given in the introduction to chapter 4. This particular episode is related by Plut. *Sert.* 3.1. Sertorius served in 105 B.C. under Caepio against the Cimbri and Teutones. After the defeat of the Romans, Sertorius was put to flight. Although he had lost his horse and had been wounded, he made his way across the Rhône, swimming against a strong current with his shield and breastplate. Nepotian. 3.2.2 goes one better: *Sertorius loricatus, hastam fixam oculo gerens, Rhodanum transnatavit.* See Konrad, 1994, 43–4.

eo momento I.e. during the crossing of the Tigris.

CHAPTER 6.8   183

post signum erectum If, as the wording strongly suggests, this is the same signal as the one mentioned in § 5 *signum ... erexisse proclamans*, Amm. evidently accepts Julian's interpretation of the fire on the ships.

scutis ... proni firmius adhaerentes eaque licet imperite regendo per voraginosum amnem velocitatem comitati sunt navium Fontaine n. 439 thinks that the soldiers who crossed the river on their shields were of German origin, mainly because that is the case in similar situations, described in 16.11.9 (Cornuti) *scutis in modum alveorum suppositis nando ad insulam venere propinquam* and 16.12.57 (licebat videre) *nonnullos* (sc. Alamannos) *clipeis vectos praeruptas undarum occursantium moles obliquatis meatibus declinantes ad ripas ulteriores post multa discrimina pervenire.* In 25.6.13 Jovian ordered the Gauls *mixti cum arctois Germanis* to be the first to cross the Tigris, apparently because they were experienced swimmers. Various other sources report that certain Germanic cavalry units (esp. Batavi) were famous for their ability to swim across rivers with armor, weapons, horses and other equipment; Tac. *Agr.* 18.4; *Hist.* 4.12.3; *Ann.* 2.8.3; D.C. 60.20.2–6; *CIL* 3.3676 = *ILS* 2558, cf. D.C. 69.9.6. However, it is questionable whether Amm. refers here to the German contingents in Julian's army. If they were indeed so experienced in swimming across rivers, it is hard to understand why Amm. says that they were panic-stricken.

The current of the Tigris can be pretty strong. The river, which in this region can become some 200 m. wide, reaches its maximum height in the last weeks of April and the first weeks of May – 14.312 million cubic meters monthly. The Tigris is particularly liable to sudden flooding, and can rise at the rate of 3–4 m per twenty-four hours. See Ionides, 1937, 161; Al-Kashab, 1958, 41 ff.; Fisher, 1978, 363–6.

Presumably nobody is skilled in steering a shield across a river, so *licet imperite* may be taken to mean 'with difficulty', 'as well they could'.

In the following sections (§ 8–12) Ammianus describes the battle **6.8** between Julian's army and the Persians led by the Surên, Pigranes and Narseus, the most important Sasanian generals. This is the first serious confrontation in the open field between Romans and Persians during Julian's campaign after some insignificant skirmishes on the march to Ctesiphon. It is in fact the only major battle of the whole campaign. It took place on June, 1 presumably. Rosen, 1970,

184 COMMENTARY

173 is sceptical with regard to the historicity of this account: "Eine regelrechte Schlacht, in der 2500 Perser und 70 Römer gefallen seien, ja die fast die Ausmasse der Schlacht bei Strassburg gehabt habe, hat es nie gegeben."

Persae obiecerunt instructas catafractorum equitum turmas For *obicere* cf. 22.12.2 (Julianus) *in aetatis flore primaevo obiectus efferatarum gentium armis* and 25.3.18 *ubicumque me velut imperiosa parens consideratis periculis obiecit res publica, steti fundatus.* See for *catafracti* the notes ad 20.7.2 and 24.2.5 and for *turma* the note ad 23.3.4.

ita confertas, ut lamminis cohaerenter aptati corporum flexus splendore praestringerent occursantes obtutus I.e. the "serried bands" (Rolfe) formed as it were a wall or a mirror of gleaming iron. The reading *cohaerenter aptati (quae aptati* V), was proposed by Clark, who tried to account for V's *quae,* starting from 24.2.10 *lamminae singulis membrorum lineamentis cohaerenter aptatae.* It has been accepted by all subsequent editors and may well be correct. The resulting expression is, however, very strained, in that *cohaerenter* goes more naturally with *aptatae* 'adjusted to' than with *aptati* 'provided with'. It should also be noted that *aptati* alone (G) gives perfect sense, but fails to account for V's *quae.* The normal construction is *aptare aliquid alicui rei,* as in 24.2.10 quoted above and 25.1.12 *humanorumque vultuum simulacra* ('masks') *ita capitibus diligenter aptata.* The alternative construction with a complement in the abl., which is chosen here, is also found in 20.4.18 *aptari muliebri mundo,* q.v.

Amm. regularly refers to the closely fitting (iron) armour of the Persian cavalry (24.4.15 *hostem undique lamminis ferreis in modum tenuis plumae contectum;* 24.7.8; 25.1.12), as well as to its gleam and glittering (24.2.5; 24.7.8; 25.1.1).

For the various meanings of *praestringere* see the note ad 21.7.2. *Occursare* and its derivatives are often used of attacking soldiers, as in 19.2.6 *intentaque occursatione nostrorum.* Cf. also Tac. *Ann.* 1.64.1 *barbari...lacessunt, circumgrediuntur, occursant. Occursantes obtutus* is best understood as the equivalent of *occursantium oculos.* For *obtutus* see the note ad 20.3.12 *sed ita.*

operimentis scorteis equorum multitudine omni defensa Like the Sasanian cavalryman his horse was also protected; Mielczarek, 1993, 67. The present passage in Ammianus is the main source for this fact. We have more information on mail clad horses for the Parthian period; *ibid.* 62–3.

CHAPTER 6.8   185

in subsidiis manipuli locati sunt peditum The Persian infantry was lined up behind the cavalry. The infantry consisted of ordinary men, mostly peasant soldiers, who were probably recruited whenever the king gave the order; cf. 29.1.1 *Exacta hieme... Sapor... suppleto numero suorum abundeque firmato erupturos in nostra catafractos et sagittarios et conductam misit plebem.* The infantry was clearly subservient to the cavalry; see 23.6.83 with notes. A maniple in this context means a subdivision of the (Persian) army; see 19.1.10, 7.6; 25.1.16; 29.5.39; 31.7.10 for the same meaning. Whether the maniple still existed as a formal detachment of the Roman army is uncertain. Amm. uses the term several times, suggesting that it is a formal subdivision of a legion: 17.13.25; 21.13.9, q.v.; 23.5.15; 26.2.3; 27.10.10. However, the use of the term in a technical sense probably reflects a general trend in using archaic terms and does not tell us anything about the organisation of the legion in the late Roman period. According to Veg. *mil.* 2.13.7 a *contubernium* in late antiquity is the same as what used to be called a maniple: *Contubernium autem manipulus vocabatur.* See Nicasie, 1998, 52.

contecti scutis oblongis et curvis The effective protection provided by these shields prompts a comparison with the Roman *myrmillones* in 23.6.83 *pedites enim in speciem myrmillonum contecti.*

texta vimine et coriis crudis Whether one prefers *tecta* (V) or *texta* (G), this is a zeugma. *Tecta,* coming so soon after *contecti,* is less attractive than *texta.* In 24.2.10, q.v., Amm. avoids the zeugma by adding *vestitis: obtecti scutis vimine firmissimo textis et crudorum tergorum densitate vestitis.* Compare the description of the *testudo* in 23.4.11 *contegitur coriis bubulis virgarumque recenti textura.*

densius se commovebant The comparative does not have its proper force here. *Dense se* would have been cacophonous.

elephanti Neither Zosimus nor Libanius speaks of elephants. Soz. *HE* 6.1.6, however, does: σὺν πολλῇ δὲ παρασκευῇ ἱππέων καὶ ὁπλιτῶν καὶ ἐλεφάντων τῶν Περσῶν φανέντων ἐπὶ τῆς ὄχθης τοῦ Τίγρητος. The Romans first encountered elephants in the battles with Pyrrhus of Epirus; Plin. *Nat.* 8.6.16 *Elephantos Italia primum vidit Pyrrhi regis bello;* Eutr. 2.11.2; Scullard, 1974, 101 ff. The use of elephants in battles had almost ceased with the decline of the Hellenistic kingdoms; cf. Arr. *Tact.* 19. The Parthians did not use them in warfare but the Sasanians reintroduced and used them regularly in battles and

186 COMMENTARY

sieges; Scullard, 1974, 201–7. Roman soldiers were full of dread for them (Thompson, 1947, 12, n. 3: "The only objects which Ammianus likes less than the Persians are elephants"). Their monstrous size, trumpeting and smell frightened both men and horses; 19.2.3; 19.7.6–7; 25.1.14; 25.3.4; 25.3.11; 25.6.2. Elephants were used as a screen against enemy cavalry, for attacking and penetrating the enemy infantry, and for breaking into a fortified position; Peddie, 1994, 87. Apart from that, they also had a psychological effect. However, in general elephants do not seem to have played an important role in battles. The use of elephants could even have a disadvantage: when they panicked they could turn upon their own troops and crush them, as Caesar witnessed at Thapsus; *B. Afr.* 83. To guard against this happening, the drivers carried knives bound to their hands so that they could kill the beasts by cutting trough their vertebrae; 25.1.15. The place of the elephants in battle lines could apparently vary. In this passage they are placed behind the *catafracti* and the infantry, whereas in 25.6.2 they were in the front line.

Veg. *mil.* 3.24.7–16 describes various ways in which elephants may be resisted in battle. Jul. *Or.* 2.65 b-c is not impressed by the use of elephants in war situations.

gradientium collium specie... propinquantibus exitium intentabant Other comparisons with *specie* + gen. are 16.11.3 *multitudine geminata nostrorum forcipis specie trusi in angustias* and 31.13.2 *collisae in modum rostratarum navium acies trudentesque se vicissim undarum specie.* Cf. the description in 19.2.3 (Segestani) *cum quibus elata in arduum specie elephantorum agmina rugosis horrenda corporibus leniter incedebant. Exitium intentabant* seems reminiscent of Vergil: *Verg. A.* 1.91 *intentant omnia mortem.*

documentis praeteritis Such as the siege of Amida where elephants were present; 19.2.3 *ultra omnem diritatem taetri spectaculi formidanda* and 19.7.6. For *documentum* in Amm. see Sabbah 380 ff.

6.9 *secundum Homericam dispositionem praestituit* A reference to *Il.* 4.297 where it is said that Agamemnon placed the less reliable troops in between the brave and reliable soldiers in the frontline and those in the rear to prevent them from fleeing. Fron. *Str.* 2.3.21 tells the same about Pyrrhus: *Pyrrhus pro Tarentinis apud Asculum, secundum Homericum versum, quo pessimi in medium recipiuntur, dextro cornu Samnites Epirotasque, sinistro Bruttios atque Lucanos cum Sallentinis,*

CHAPTER 6.10 187

in medio acie Tarentinos collocavit, equitatum et elephantos in subsidiis esse iussit. For the positioning of troops and tactics in battle, see Nicasie, 1998, 209–19.

Quintilian *Inst.* 5.12.14 too, speaks about a *Homerica dispositio,* in which the weaker parts of the speech are located in the middle: *ut Homerica dispositione in medio sint infirma.* In the classical period the verb *praestituere* is used almost exclusively for fixing a point in time. In its more general meaning 'to assign', which it has here, it is found in late and Christian authors, TLL X 2.905.32–906.25.

cedentesque deformiter For the adverb cf. Suet. *Nero* 49.3, where in his last hour the emperor mutters to himself *vivo deformiter, turpiter* – οὐ πρέπει Νέρωνι, οὐ πρέπει.

postsignani pone omnes reiecti centurias Apart from Fron. *Str.* 2.3.17, *postsignanus* is found only in Amm. Cf. 16.12.31 *postsignanos in acie locatos extrema* and 18.8.7. For *pone* see the note ad 20.11.22. Pace Brok 182, the use of the term *centuria* is probably an archaism; see the note ad 21.13.9 and Nicasie, 1998, 52.

auxiliis Probably contingents of the *auxilia palatina,* but which exactly cannot be determined; Nicasie, 1998, 53–6; Hoffmann I, 1969, 72. For auxiliaries in Julian's army, see also the notes ad 20.1.3 and 20.4.2.

per prima postremaque discurrens The verb is used of the restless activity of the commander during a battle. Cf. 20.5.5 (Julian about himself) *inter confertissima tela me discurrente,* q.v. and 23.5.25 *eo* (Julian) *ductante perque ordines discurrente.*

contiguae Cf. 17.7.2 *amendato solis splendore nec contigua nec apposita cernebantur;* TLL IV 698.3–4 "saepius apud posteriores, imprimis Amm." **6.10**

cristatis galeis corusci Romani vibrantesque clipeos Amm. combines here the two meanings of *coruscus,* 'quivering' of the crest and 'gleaming' of the helmet. For the former cf. Verg. *A.* 1.164 *silvis scaena coruscis,* "a backdrop of quivering woods" (Austin) and Sil. 2.397/8 *coruscis … cristis,* for the latter 16.10.8 *ordo geminus armatorum clipeatus atque cristatus corusco lumine radians nitidis loricis indutus* and 24.2.5 *corusci galeis.* The soldiers are swinging their shields as they march in step. This is different from the exercises, during which the soldiers

188 COMMENTARY

are taught to protect themselves with their shields as described in
21.2.1, q.v.

velut pedis anapaesti praecinentibus modulis lenius procedebant The ana-
paest is the best metre for exhortation, according to Cic. *Tusc.* 2.37:
nec adhibetur ulla sine anapaestis pedibus hortatio. It is important to
note *velut.* The soldiers advance rhythmically *as if* they were accompanied by music, just as the Gallic soldiers, after their attack
on the Persian camp before Amida, withdrew in an orderly fashion 19.6.9: *velut repedantes sub modulis.* Real music was used during
military training, as is evident from 16.5.10 *cum exercere proludia dis-
ciplinae castrensis philosophus cogeretur ut princeps artemque modulatius
incedendi per pyrricham concinentibus fistulis* (for the pyrricha, which
Jul. *Or.* 1.11 calls a χορείαν τὴν ἐν τοῖς ὅπλοις, see De Jonge's note
ad loc.). Amm.'s wording is taken from V. Max. 2.6.2 *Eiusdem civitatis* (Sparta) *exercitus non ante ad dimicandum descendere solebant quam
tibiae concentu et anapaesti pedis modulo cohortationis calorem animo traxis-
sent.* Gel. 1.11.3–4 reports, on the authority of Thucydides, that
the Spartans did this to maintain calm: *tibicines inter exercitum posi-
ti canere inceptabant. Ea ibi praecentione tranquilla et delectabili atque adeo
venerabili ad quandam quasi militaris musicae disciplinam vis et impetus militum... cohibebatur.* Further on, in §9 Gel. wonders *Quid ille
vult ardentissimus clamor Romanorum, quem in congressibus proeliorum
fieri solitum scriptores annalium memoravere?* He suggests the following
answer: *An tum et gradu clementi* (cf. *lenius procedebant* in Amm.) *et
silentio est opus, cum ad hostem itur in conspectu longinquo procul distan-
tem, cum vero prope ad manus ventum est, tum iam ex propinquo hostis et
impetu propulsandus et clamore terrendus est,* which sounds eminently
plausible.

praepilatis missilibus per procursatores principiis pugnae temptatis The
verb *praepilare* occurs only in Amm., here and in 16.12.36 *Dato... signo
ad pugnandum utrimque magnis concursum est viribus... paulisper praepi-
labantur missilia* e.q.s; TLL X 2.765.81–766.4. One wonders whether
it is based on a misinterpretation of Liv. 26.51.4 (about military
drills) *in modum iustae pugnae concurrerunt praepilatisque missilibus ia-
culati sunt,* where *praepilatus* is an adj. meaning "tipped with a ball
(to prevent penetration)" (OLD).

The normal verb for these opening moves is *lacessere.* Cf. 26.7.15
*cum legiones iam pugnaturae congrederentur, inter reciprocantes missilia
quasi procursatione hostem lacessens solus prorupit.* See also the note ad
24.4.15 *crebris procursationibus* and for *procursatores* the note ad 24.3.1.

CHAPTER 6.11   189

excita undique humus rapido turbine portabatur Whirling clouds of dust
are a recurrent theme in Amm.'s descriptions of battles and of the
approach of the enemy: 16.12.37, 43; 19.1.5; 24.8.5; 31.13.2. Amm.
also speaks metaphorically of *pulvis Martius*: 21.12.22 (with extensive
note); 21.16.3; 27.6.8; 30.9.4. Brok 166–7.

cum undique solito more conclamaretur See the end of the note ad § 10   **6.11**
velut pedis and cf. Caes. *Civ.* 3.92.5 *neque frustra antiquitus institutum
est, ut signa undique concinerent clamoremque universi tollerent; quibus
rebus et hostes terreri et suos incitari existimaverunt.* In 24.5.9 Amm.
mentions that the Roman soldiers attacked the Persians *cum minaci
murmure*. In 16.12.43, q.v., Amm. refers to the battle cry of the
barbarian auxiliaries, which is called the *barritus*; cf. 21.13.15 with
note.

classicum Veg. *mil.* 2.22.1: *Classicum... appellatur, quod bucinatores per
cornu dicunt. Hoc insigne videtur imperii, quia classicum canitur imperatore
praesente.* In *mil.* 3.5.3 Vegetius explains that there were three types of
military signals: *vocalia, semivocalia* and *muta*. The (*signum*) *classicum*
belongs to the second type; *mil.* 3.5.6 *Semivocalia sunt, quae per tubam
aut cornu aut bucinam dantur* (all mentioned by Amm.). That this
signal could only be given by or in the presence of the supreme
commander is also mentioned by Caes. *Civ.* 3.82; Suet. *Jul.* 32,
Vit. 11; Verg. *A.* 7.637; Hor. *Ep.* 2.5. Also Amm. 16.12.45 with De
Jonge's note; 21.5.1, q.v.; 24.8.7, q.v.; 31.5.8. The *classicum* is also
sounded to convene the contio: Liv. 7.36.9; 26.48.13; 28.27.15.
For metaphorical use of the word, see Verg. *G.* 2.539; Tib. 1.1.4;
Luc. 4.186. For the *classicum* the *cornu* was apparently used. This
instrument was made of horn and silver and shaped like the letter
G. Uncoiled it had a length of *c.* 3.30 m (11 feet). From modern
experiments with a facsimile it may be inferred that it produced a
soft but voluminous sound. For the use of musical instruments in the
army see the notes ad 20.7.6 *hinc inde* and 24.4.15. On this subject
consult Wille, 1967 and Peddie, 1994, 19–25.

*sagittarum periculo miles erat immunis, quantum interiora festinatius occu-
pabat* The same tactic has been described in 24.2.5 *et quamvis arcus
validis viribus flecterentur et splendor ferri intermicans Romanorum metum
augeret, ira tamen acuente virtutem clipeorum densitate contecti, ne possint
emittere, coegerunt*, q.v. By closing in on the enemy, the Roman soldiers make it impossible for the Persians to use their bows, which
are effective only at long range. See also 25.1.17 *et ne sagittariorum*

190 COMMENTARY

procursus nostrorum cuneos disiectaret, illatis concitatius signis spiculorum impetum fregit datoque ad decernendum sollemniter signo denseti Romani pedites confertas hostium frontes nisu protruserunt acerrimo. This is well explained by Fontaine in n. 502, who refers i.a. to Iust. 2.9.11: during the battle of Marathon the Athenians showed so much daring *ut, cum mille passus inter duas acies essent, citato cursu ante iactum sagittarum ad hostem venerint.* Veg. *mil.* 3.14.6 says there should be three feet between the lines *ut nec acies interluceat et spatium sit arma tractandi.*

As in 20.6.4 *ad interiora ferocius se proripientes, interiora* means the space between the two parties. See the note ad loc., where the present passage is incorrectly interpreted. *Immunis, quantum festinatius* is the equivalent of *tanto magis immunis, quanto festinatius.* There is a similar construction in 16.10.14 *quidquid viderat primum, id eminere inter alia cuncta sperabat: Iovis Tarpei delubra, quantum terrenis divina praecellunt,* which may be paraphrased 'the temple surpassed (all other buildings) by as much as the divine surpasses what is human.'

pulsos fulcire subsidiis incitareque tardantes Brok 157 aptly compares Constantius' instructions to the new Caesar Julian in 15.8.13 *turbatosque subsidiis fulciens, modeste increpans desides.* See also the note ad 24.5.11.

quasi conturmalis strenuus… et rector Cf. 17.1.2 *omnis operae conturmalem auctoritate magnificum ducem* and see the note ad 23.5.19 *imperator et antesignanus.* Being brother-in-arms with his troops made Julian popular with his soldiers and belonged to his public image.

6.12 *laxata itaque acies prima Persarum* Breaking the ranks of the enemy decides the battle. Cf. 15.4.11 *universos in fugam coegere foedissimam. qui dispersi laxatis ordinibus* e.q.s. and 19.7.4 *Persae pedites sagittas tormentis excussas e muris aegrius evitantes laxarunt aciem.* This military use of *laxare* is found from Caesar onwards; TLL VII 2.1071.83–1072.11.

concito gradu Cf. 29.5.11 *concito gradu Tyndensium gentem et Masinissensium petit* and see the note ad 20.4.12 *alacri gradu;* more examples in TLL IV 37.79–84.

calefactis armis This singular expression is explained in TLL III 145.34 "metonymice pro armatis". This cannot be rejected out of hand, in view of 31.12.13 *miles fervore calefactus aestivo,* but far more attractive is Wagner's suggestion that it is equivalent to *pugna calidiore*

CHAPTER 6.12   191

facta, 'after a heated fight', which Pighi, 1935, 73 lists among his examples of the *sermo castrensis* in Amm. It is not listed as such in either Kempf, 1901 or Heraeus, 1902. Fontaine aptly compares Suet. *Aug.* 71.3 (a letter from Augustus to Tiberius) *lusimus enim per omnis dies forumque aleatorum* (aleatorium?) *calfecimus*, which is translated "I kept the gaming table hotly at work", by Shuckburgh, who compares Cic. *Fam.* 8.6.4 (Caelius) *si Parthi vos nihil calfaciunt, nos frigore frigescimus.*

ad usque diei finem a lucis ortu Zos. 3.25.5 reports that the battle lasted from the middle of the night until noon next day: ἐκ μέσης νυκτὸς διέμεινε μέχρι μέσης ἡμέρας ἡ μάχη. This makes some sense since the Roman troops crossed the Tigris at night while the Persians were awaiting them on the opposite bank. From Lib. *Or.* 18.254 it can also be inferred that the fighting started in the night (ἐν νυκτὶ καὶ σκότῳ, cf. Soz. *HE* 6.1.7 ἐν νυκτὶ), although he has the unlikely story, which is echoed by Soz. *HE* 6.1.8, that the Persians were surprised in their sleep by the Roman attack (cf. Paschoud n. 70 who speaks of "des détails stupides chez Libanios"). See also the note ad 24.6.4. Paschoud has the plausible suggestion that the engagement took place in two phases. Firstly, the night crossing of the Tigris, which will have taken some time and during which some skirmishes between Roman and Persian soldiers took place, and secondly, the actual battle on the following day. The latter may have ended at noon, as Zosimus says, but may also have lasted until the end of the day, as Amm. reports.

eiusque occipitiis pertinacius haerens This expression for following the enemies at their heels is a peculiarity of Ammianus; TLL IX 2.356.53–6. It is found also in 31.7.13 *et sequebantur equites hinc inde fugientium occipitia lacertis ingentibus praecidentes et terga* and 31.15.1 (soldiers fleeing in the dark of night): *occipitiis propriis ferrum arbitrantes haerere.* Cf. also 31.7.12 *haerente iam morte cervicibus.*

Pigrane et Surena et Narseo potissimis ducibus Cf. Zos. 3.25.5 τῆς φυγῆς ἡγησαμένων τῶν στρατηγῶν· ἦσαν δὲ οὗτοι Πιγράξης τε ... καὶ Ἀνάρεος καὶ ὁ σουρήνας αὐτός. Pigranes/Pigraxes is only known from Amm. and Zosimus. For the Surên see the note ad 24.2.4. It is not clear whether Zosimus' Ἀνάρεος is the same as Amm.'s Narseus (*PLRE* I, Narseus) but this is not improbable. Narseus evidently belonged to the inner circle of Sapor II and was one of his confidants. In 17.5.2, q.v., he is mentioned as the envoy who delivered Sapor's letter to

192   COMMENTARY

Constantius: *missoque cum muneribus Narseo quodam legato litteras ad Constantium dedit.* Petr. Patr. *fr.* 17 mentions him as Ναρσῆς. For his name: Justi, 1895, 221–5 and Gignoux, 1986, 134.

Ctesiphontis See the note ad 24.2.7.

(aciem) egit praecipitem aversorum feriens sura et terga During their training at the post, soldiers learned to go for the flank, feet or head, according to Veg. *mil.* 2.23.5 (cum) *latera vel pedes aut caput petere... condiscant.* Enemies fleeing in disorder expose these vulnerable parts: 27.10.15 *pandebant sequentibus poplites et suras et dorsa.* For *aversorum* cf. 25.3.5 *aversorumque Persarum et beluarum suffragines concidebat et dorsa.*

6.13 *perrupissetque civitatis aditus lapsorum agminibus mixtus* In contrast to Amm., Zos. 3.25.6 only reports that the Romans (and Goths) pursued the fleeing Persians and killed many of them; Paschoud n. 71. Zosimus also mentions the booty – mainly gold and silver – which the Romans captured. So does Lib. *Or.* 18.255 who, remarkably enough, adds that they would have gained Ctesiphon had they not wasted time around the Persian dead in search for booty. Ruf. *Fest.* 28.2 again follows Libanius: *apertas Ctesiphontis portas victor miles intrasset, nisi maior praedarum occasio fuisset quam cura victoriae.* Libanius also mentions a failed attack of the Persian cavalry on the following day.

  For *labi* 'to escape' cf. 18.6.12 *lapsoque per fugam domino* and in section 16 below *decimus vero* (taurus), *qui diffractis vinculis lapsus aegre reductus est*; TLL VII 2.788.57 ff.

ni dux Victor nomine manibus erectis prohibuisset et vocibus Cf. for the same gesture 25.3.6 *Iulianus... elatis vociferando manibus aperte demonstrans.* For Victor see the note ad 24.6.4. Zos. 3.25.7 adds the detail that the Roman victory was dampened by Victor's wound inflicted by a catapult: τὸν δὲ ἐπὶ τῇ νίκῃ τοῦ στρατοπέδου παιᾶνα Βίκτωρ ὁ στρατηγὸς ἔδοξέ πως ἐλαττοῦν καταπέλτῃ τρωθείς.

ipse umerum et sagitta praestrictus et timens The reading of V would make *umerum* belong both to *praestrictus* and *timens*, which, pace Blomgren 95, is very difficult to believe. Kellerbauer's suggestion, on the other hand, to place the first *et* before *ipse* is attractive. It gives two reasons for Victor's order, his own wound and his fear that the soldiers might become trapped inside Ctesiphon. The detail about Victor's wound is intriguing. Libanius had reported in *Or.*

CHAPTER 6.14   193

18.250 that, when the commander of the main body (ὑφ᾽ ᾧ δὲ ἦν τῆς δυνάμεως τὸ πλέον) had opposed Julians' plan to cross the Tigris, the emperor had given the command to someone else (unnamed), predicting that he would succeed, but not without a wound (251 ὡς κρατήσει μὲν οὗτος, οὐκ ἄνευ δὲ τραύματος). The emperor moreover, had told him where the wound would be and that it would easily be cured. The fact that Victor's wound is mentioned by Ammianus and Zosimus (who adds the detail that it was inflicted by a *ballista*) without any reference to a former prophecy to that effect by Julian, gives rise to the suspicion that the prophecy was no more than an invention *ex eventu* by Libanius, who is fond of such embellishments.

timens, ne intra moenium ambitus rapidus miles inconsulte repertus Although the singular *ambitus* is more common with *murorum* or *moenia* than the plural, the latter does occur, cf. 19.2.3 *Persae omnes murorum ambitus obsidebant* and 22.16.7 *cum ampla moenia fundaret et pulchra, ... omnes ambitus liniales farina respersit*. Therefore Seyfarth seems right in keeping V's *ambitus*. *Rapidus* is surprising. It must mean something like 'carried away', for which there are no parallels in Amm. Liv. 22.12.12 *ferox rapidusque consiliis* has a similar ring. A simple remedy would be to read *raptus*. For *reperiri* 'to find oneself' see the note ad 22.7.6 *ex negotio*.

multitudinis pondere circumveniretur For *pondus* used of the pressure of an overwhelming number of adversaries see the note ad 20.7.15 *plebis immensae ponderibus*.

Sonent Hectoreas poetae veteres pugnas The style matches the subject   **6.14**
matter: *sonare* has an epic ring, witness Verg. *A.* 12.529–30 *Murranum hic, atavos et avorum antiqua sonantem / nomina*. So has the adj. *Hectoreus*, cf. e.g. Verg. *A.* 3.304 *Hectoreum ad tumulum*.

Thessali ducis I.e. Achilles.

longae loquantur aetates Cf. 21.5.4 *per aetatum examina* with the note.

Sophanem et Aminiam et Callimachum et Cynegirum All four are Athenians known for their heroic deeds in the wars against the Persians at the beginning of the fifth century. Sophanes was known for his heroism during the battle of Plataea (479); Hdt. 9.73–75 (Herodotus also mentions him in 6.92). Aminias was the first to engage an enemy ship and thereby started the battle of Salamis; subsequently he chased the

194 COMMENTARY

ship of queen Artemisia: Hdt. 8.84, 93; Plut. *Them.* 14.2; D.S. 11.27.2, who also calls him ἀδελφὸν Αἰσχύλου τοῦ ποιητοῦ; Ael. *VH* 5.19. The vote of Callimachus, *archon polemarchos* in 490, was decisive when the votes were equally divided between the Athenian *stratègoi* on the question whether or not to give battle against the Persians at Marathon. Callimachus died in this battle; Hdt. 6.109–111, 114. Cynegirus also died in the battle of Marathon; Hdt. 6.114; cf. V. Max. 3.2.22; Iust. 2.9.16–19. Pace Barnes, 1990, 70, who sees an Herodotean imprint on Amm.'s writing, it is highly questionable whether Amm. had direct knowledge of Herodotus' *Histories*; cf. Fornara, 1992. As Brok 158 saw, it is very likely that the present passage is based on the *syncrisis* in Plut. *Arist. et Cato* 2.2, where the same names occur in the same reverse chronological order: Σωφάναι καὶ Ἀμεινίαι καὶ Καλλίμαχοι καὶ Κυναίγειροι.

Medicorum egregia culmina illa bellorum Amm. often uses the terms *Media, Medi* and *Medicus*, which are strictly speaking anachronistic, for Persia (14.8.13; 23.3.5; 25.7.12; 31.2.21), the Persians (23.5.9; 25.4.13) and Persian (22.8.2; 28.1.3; 31.4.7). V's *in graeci aculmina* has been emended in different ways. Fontaine, following Lindenbrog, stays closest to V and reads *in Graecia fulmina* (accepting Lindenbrog's conjecture *fulmina* for *culmina*). He defends *in Graecia* as a contrast to the victory of the Greeks in Asian Troy, but this seems far-fetched. It is difficult to choose between *ingentia* (Haupt) and *egregia* (Heraeus), but Amm. uses *egregius* for eminent leaders, as in 27.2.8 *ductor egregius* and 29.2.9 *egregium illud par consulum*, which is not the case with *ingens*. Lindenbrog's *fulmina* is very attractive in view of i.a. Verg. *A.* 6.842–3 *duo fulmina belli, / Scipiadas*, but TLL IV 1294.74–1295.32 provides solid support for *culmina* 'eminences', especially in late authors. There seem to be no compelling reasons to depart from Seyfarth's text.

inclaruisse virtutem For *inclarescere* see the note ad 24.4.20 *facinoribus speciosis.*

6.15 *calcatasque ruinas hostilium corporum* Even this repulsive detail is found more often in battle descriptions. In 15.4.12, after the victory on the Lentienses *cavendi immemores proterebant barbaram plebem ... calcantes cadaverum strues et perfusi sanie peremptorum* and 31.13.6 during the battle of Adrianople *acervis caesorum aggestis exanimata cadavera sine parsimonia calcabantur.* Cf. Tac. *Hist.* 5.17.1 (Germanos) *cineres ossaque legionum calcantes,* Luc. 9.1044–5 (Caesar) *qui duro membra*

CHAPTER 6.15   195

senatus / calcarat voltu. The periphrasis *ruinas hostilium corporum* ('the
bodies of the slain') is characteristic of Amm.'s ornate style.

iusto sanguine miles etiamtum cruentus Even those who had opposed
Julian at the beginning of the campaign, had not done so because
they thought the campaign was unjustified: 23.5.10 *Etrusci tamen
haruspices... ostendebant signum hoc esse prohibitorium principique aliena
licet iuste invadenti contrarium.* In his speech to the soldiers at the
Abora Julian had insisted that the expedition was a just retribution
for Sapor's wrongdoings and that *aequitati semper solere iungi victoriam*
(23.5.23).

laudes ei perhibebat et gratias Possibly an *acclamatio* confirming the loy-
alty of soldiers to their emperor; cf. the note ad 24.1.1. The soldiers'
thankfulness is in strong contrast with their recent dissatisfaction,
when they nearly mutinied and Julian had to address them to quiet
them down; 24.3.3–7.

ignoratus ubique dux esset an miles With this traditional compliment
cf. the note ad § 11 *quasi conturmalis.* For the risks Julian was prone
to take cf. the note ad 24.2.14 *omnes aleae.*

† *magis tum* The simplest solution for this difficult passage would
be to read, with Fontaine, *dux esset an miles magis* and to take this to
mean 'whether he was a commander or rather a soldier'. But such
a use of *magis* without *quam* is not attested in Amm. and, moreover,
it does not produce an acceptable cursus, so a crux seems still to
be unavoidable. Novák's tentative *magis ⟨aliorum quam suum respiciens
commodum⟩ ita* (1911, 321) suits the context.

*ut caesis Persarum plus minusue duobus milibus et quingentis septua-
ginta caderent soli nostrorum* Zos. 3.25.7 Ἔπεσον δὲ καὶ ἐν τῇ μάχῃ
Περσῶν μὲν πεντακόσιοι καὶ δισχίλιοι, Ῥωμαίων δὲ οὐ πλείους πέντε καὶ
ἑβδομήκοντα. Lib. *Or.* 18.254 and *Ep.* 1402.2 estimates the number of
Persian dead at 6000 (τῆς γῆς τοσοῦτον ἐκέκρυπτο τοῖς τῶν πεπτωκότων
σώμασιν ὅσον ἂν καλύψαιεν ἑξακισχίλιοι νέκροι), but this number is
clearly too high; see Paschoud n. 71 and Rosen, quoted ad §8.
Libanius is silent on the number of victims on the Roman side.

As Szantyr 551 observes, in consecutive clauses imperfect and
perfect subjunctives tend not to be rigidly distinguished. However,
the use of *caderent* after *gesserat* and *caesis Persarum... mille* is remarkable. Ehrismann 28 quotes 14.1.6 *relaturi quae audirent* as a parallel.

196 COMMENTARY

qui appellans plerosque nominatim Cf. 20.4.12 *ex more laudans quos agnoscebat, factorumque fortium singulos monens.* Knowing their soldiers by name is a topos in the description of generals; see the note ad 20.4.12 (*singulos*).

stabili mente The expression is found only here. *Stabilis* is combined with *erectus* in 15.7.2 *praefectum incessebat ut timidum, sed ille stabilis et erectus* e.q.s. and with *fundatus* in 31.3.2 *quamvis manere fundatus et stabilis diu conatus est.*

navalibus donavit coronis et civicis et castrensibus As was noted ad 24.4.24 *obsidionalibus coronis donati,* the giving of crowns and other decorations instead of cash remunerations had become extremely rare in Late Antiquity, but there is no need to assume that Amm. is wrong in mentioning these crowns. One should, however, be aware of the fact that in the course of time most of the crowns lost any connection with the deeds which they were originally designed to commemorate (see the literature cited ad 24.4.24).

The *corona navalis* (e.g. Gel. 5.6.18, Fest. p. 163M, HA *Aur.* 13.2) also named *corona classica* or *rostrata* (e.g. Plin. *Nat.* 16.7), was made of gold and initially awarded to the first man to board an enemy ship in a sea battle, but in late Republican times it could also be awarded to a victorious fleet commander. During the Principate any connection it had with the sea was lost. It then became especially connected with men of consular rank (cf. e.g. CIL 3.1457, 3.4031, 5.531, 5.6977, 6.1377, 10.8291).

The *corona civica* (e.g. Gel. 5.6.13, Fest. p. 191M, Plin. *Nat.* 16.7ff., HA *Aur.* 13.3, *Pr.* 5.2–3, Claud. *carm. min.* 30.181–2; cf. Claud. *Cons. Stil.* 3.72 and Heus, 1982) was one of the most important military decorations, second only to the *corona obsidionalis* (for which see 24.4.24). It had a purely symbolic value – it was made of oak leaves – and was awarded to those men who, in battle, saved the life of a Roman citizen and for the rest of the day held the ground where the exploit had occurred. The decoration was very prestigious and conveyed benefits such as the exemption from public duties for the recipient, for his father and for his paternal grandfather.

The *corona castrensis* (e.g. Gel. 5.6.17, Fest. p. 57M) or *corona vallaris* (e.g. Liv. 10.46.3), made of gold and decorated with a rampart, was originally awarded to the man who first climbed over the rampart of an enemy camp, regardless of his rank. Later only centurions and men of equestrian or consular rank could have this honour conferred upon them.

CHAPTER 6.16   197

Abunde ratus post haec prosperitates similes adventare More than once **6.16**
Amm. tells us that military successes increased the confidence of the
army and Julian: 24.1.12 *affore sibi etiam deinde dei caelestis existimans
curam*, 24.4.14 *quo efferati gaudio milites omnes elatique firmioribus animis
ad certandum signum opperiebantur armati*, 24.6.4 *cunctis ex sententia
terminatis Augustus altius iam contra difficultates omnes incedens*. For the
reader, who knows the outcome of the campaign, these remarks have
a poignant ring.

complures hostias Marti parabat Ultori I.e. the normal ritual before a
sacrifice was followed. Cf. Verg. *A.* 2.132–3 (Sino's speech) *mihi sacra
parari / et salsae fruges et circum tempora vittae*. The horns of the *hostiae*
had probably been gilded. As for *Mars Ultor*, revenge was one of the
motives for Julian's campaign as Amm. 23.5.18 (q.v.) reports; see
also 22.12.1, q.v. Amm. uses *Mars* often as a metonym for warfare
(see the note ad 23.5.20), but in this passage he is a cultic reality;
Rike, 1987, 25–6. This is, however, the first (and only) time that
Amm. mentions Mars Ultor, which is remarkable, considering the
god's importance to Julian and for his campaign. It is also the first
time that Amm. tells us about Julian's sacrifice to the god of war. The
failure of the sacrifice, a clear sign that Mars had abandoned Julian,
obviously filled the emperor with great fear and left little hope for
a successful end to the expedition. Julian's fear of Mars is so deep
that in 25.2.4 he interprets the appearance of a comet as a sign of
the god's wrath: *flagrantissimam facem cadenti similem visam aeris parte
sulcata evanuisse existimavit horroreque perfusus est, ne ita aperte minax
Martis apparuerit sidus*.
    The title *Ultor*, Mars' most common epithet, was given to Mars
by Augustus, in recognition of the victory over Caesar's assassins at
Philippi (42 BC); Suet. *Aug.* 29.2; Ov. *Fast.* 5.569. Although Dio
Cassius (54.8.3) mentions that Augustus dedicated a temple to Mars
Ultor on the Capitol in 20 B.C. this notion is now generally believed
to be entirely imaginary. The only temple Augustus built in honour
of Mars Ultor was the one in his own forum, the *Forum Augustum*; Ov.
Fast. 5.551 ff.; Aug. *Anc.* 21; Suet. *Aug.* 29.1; Richardson, 1992, 161–
2, 245–6 and Spannagel, 1999, 15–21. For Mars, see Latte, 1960,
302–3; Versnel, 1993, 289–313, 319–34.
    Amm. is critical of Julian's excessive sacrificing; see 22.5.2 (q.v.),
22.12.6 with relevant notes and 25.4.17.

ex tauris pulcherrimis… ominosa signa monstravit In general *suovetau-
rilia* (Cato *Agr.* 141.3; Festus p. 204M; Liv. 8.10.14; D.H. 4.22.1) or

198   COMMENTARY

only oxen (Liv. 7.37.1; Plin. *Nat.* 22.5.9; Str. 5.4.12 [250C]) were
sacrificed to Mars. Divination plays an important role in Julian's expedition as well as in Amm.'s description of it; earlier in his work
Amm. had already regularly hinted at the ominous signs indicating
the failure of Julian's expedition; e.g. 23.1.5–7, q.v., 2.3–4, 3.6, 5.4 ff.
and there is an excursus on divination in 21.1.7–14.

nondum aris admoti voluntate sua novem procubuere tristissimi For *admo-*
vere aris as part of the ritual see TLL I 773.79–774.7. As Latte,
1960, 386 observes, "So geschmückt werden die Tiere zum Opfer-
platz geführt. Es galt als böses Omen, wenn sie sich sträubten, wie
umgekehrt die Freiwilligkeit öfter hervorgehoben wird." The bulls
do not resist, but fail to reach the altar, which is a bad *omen*, hence
they are called *tristissimi.* For this meaning of *tristis* see OLD s.v. 5b.

decimus vero, qui diffractis vinculis lapsus aegre reductus est For *lapsus*
'escaped' see the note ad §13 *perrupissetque civitatis.* This was a
particularly bad omen. Liv. 21.63.13 reports such an event before
the battle at the lacus Trasumenus; cf. also Suet. *Jul.* 59 and Luc.
7.165–6 *admotus superis discussa fugit ab ara / taurus.* Zosimus does not
mention the sacrifice to Mars. Libanius has one vague sentence which
probably refers to the incident in *Or.* 18.261 (Julian planned to go
to the rivers of India) ἤδη δὲ τῆς στρατιᾶς ἐπὶ ταῦτα ὡρμημένης ... θεῶν
τις τοῦ μὲν ἀφίστησι, νόστου δὲ κατὰ τὸ ἔπος παρῄνει μεμνῆσθαι. Amm.
seems to have dramatized the event to mark the reversal of Julian's
fortunes.

Iovemque testatus est nulla Marti iam sacra facturum Julian was convinced that Mars was against him, as is also apparent from 25.2.4
quoted above. For the omission of the subject *se* in the AcI see Szantyr 362.

nec resecravit celeri morte praereptus The verb *resecrare* "to set free from
a religious ban" (OLD) is extremely rare. Its meaning is paraphrased
in Fest. p. 280M as follows: *solvere religione, utique cum reus populum*
comitiis oraverat per deos, ut eo periculo liberaretur, magistratus iubebat eum
(sc. populum) *resecrare.* However, its meaning here is probably not as
technical as all that, since, as Valesius saw, it may be a literal rendering
of the Greek verb ἀφοσιοῦσθαι. This verb is far less uncommon
and can be used absolutely with the meaning 'to make atonement'.
Cf. Nepos *Alc.* 6.5 *iidemque illi Eumolpidae sacerdotes rursus resecrare*
sunt coacti, qui eum devoverant ('had pronounced a curse on him').

CHAPTER 6.16 199

The same measure is described in Plut. *Alc.* 33 with the words (ἐψηφίσαντο) τὰς ἀρὰς ἀφοσιώσασθαι πάλιν Εὐμολπίδας. Julian uses the verb in *Mis.* 361 b ἀφοσιούμενοι τὰ πρὸς τοὺς θεοὺς 'making atonement for what you have done to the gods.'

CHAPTER 7

Introduction

The importance of this chapter can hardly be overrated: it describes the turning point in the campaign. Pace Klein, 1986, 290 ("eine Kette strategischer Fehler"), up till the victory reported in ch. 6 this campaign had developed fairly successfully. Julian's expeditionary force had proved competent and versatile, important strongholds had been captured, and, generally speaking, the emperor himself had demonstrated a quite satisfactory control of the situation. Of course, there had been some adversities: no one would have envisaged the enemy merely watching Julian's progress, but the losses sustained were no worse than reasonable calculation beforehand would have led one to expect.

Ctesiphon, however, caused a "Peripetie", as Rosen, 1968, 163 calls it. Julian's undoubted intention to capture this city met with clear negative advice of his military experts. He complied with it, but strongly refused to return home, as at least part of the staff advised. Instead, he decided to march inland and, in line with this, to burn his fleet. The Persians responded with a strategy of scorched earth. The combination of these events had a negative effect on the morale of the men. The loss of the ships and the enemy's strategy made them feel that they were trapped in a hopeless situation.

Amm.'s report of the events in this chapter has met with considerable criticism. The details in his report lack precision and can only be understood by a comparison with other sources, and even that not satisfactorily. This state of affairs is unfortunately worsened by the evident lacuna in the textual tradition between §2 and §3. Some scholars tend to regard the extent of this lacuna as rather large, assuming that Amm.'s original text contained the majority of details known from other sources. As will be explained in the note ad loc., such an assumption quickly leads to speculation. Moreover, it takes insufficient account of the author's main purpose in the chapter. In a fine paper Sabbah, 1992 has shown a method to understand what Amm. is in fact offering the reader. His exposition convincingly points the way to an interpretation of the text which does not expect precise details. According to Sabbah, the report testifies to "la façon dont Ammien vécut la marche cahotée des événements".

202 COMMENTARY

For such an interpretation it is vital to realize that the balance between the historian's consultation of written sources and the memories of an eye-witness in the present chapter has definitely and sharply shifted to the latter direction. This entails that the whole episode is reduced to a handful of vivid memories, the most overwhelming of which is the burning of the ships. Indeed, this is the central and unforgettable event, which was the result of a few basic decisions, viz. to abandon the intention to lay siege to Ctesiphon and to march further inland, an event which was to be the cause of enormous problems. Julian had plausible reasons for his order to set the ships on fire, and Amm. duly registers them, but in this he seemed to be an instrument in the hands of a higher force, which had resolutely taken control of the events: it looked as if Bellona herself effectively brandished her torch and brought about the momentous loss of the fleet. In Amm.'s eyes this was a decisive turn for the worse, indeed the beginning of the end of a worthwhile undertaking led by an emperor, who, for all his momentary fits of rashness, was in full possession of his mental powers. In accepting his staff's advice not to attack Ctesiphon he showed himself a *princeps sollertissimus*, and even in his fatal decision to burn the ships he was not led astray by any lack of reasoning, but even so he ended up in Bellona's destructive path.

Modern scholars are fully justified in their complaints about Amm.'s incomplete report. He could and should have done better. But his report has a sort of 'qualité de ses défauts', in that it conveys the immense disappointment, despondency and even despair felt by a participant engaged in the expedition. In the final sections of the chapter this personal involvement bursts out into a sudden spate of pronouns and verbal forms denoting the first person plural. To Amm. the name Ctesiphon not merely evoked an episode of prime and fatal importance, but above all a bitter personal experience.

7.1 *Digesto itaque consilio cum primatibus super Ctesiphontis obsidio* A similar situation is described in 31.10.15 *diu reputante Gratiano cum optimatibus*. Zos. 3.26.2 does not refer to any council at all. Translators tend to blur the precise meaning of the first words of the present text: Rolfe's "having held council" is a representative example. No doubt the entire section reports the discussion in a council of war, but *digesto... consilio* has a different meaning, as can be witnessed in the parallel cases 14.6.14 and 26.8.1: *digerere* means "animo revolvere" (TLL V 1.1120.33). The immediately preceding section (24.6.16) should be taken into account, in which initially Julian's unbridled optimism about the campaign is clearly worded. Next, however, the

CHAPTER 7.1   203

omina prove to be extremely unfavourable; therefore (*itaque*) this
calls for a consideration (*digesto*) of the strategy (*consilio*) to be followed, in particular concerning (*super*) the siege of Ctesiphon. See
for this city the note ad 24.2.7. HA *Car.* 9.1 refers to a remarkable
conviction: *plerique dicunt vim fati quandam esse, ut Romanus princeps
Ctesiphontem transire non possit.* The late Latin word *primas* means
'highest ranking' (in a specific situation). Some examples in Amm.:
14.7.1 *urbium primatibus,* 15.5.18 *primates... properarunt omnes in regiam* (where they were called by Constantius to give advice), 25.1.16
cum primatibus (i.e. highest ranking officers) ... *imperator.*

itum est in voluntatem quorundam   TLL V 2.647.68 lists this phrase
under the heading "se accommodare, se submittere in aliquid". It
seems far more likely to regard it as a variation of the wellknown
t.t. for voting in the senate: *pedibus in sententiam Tib. Neronis iturum
se dixerat* (Sal. *Cat.* 50.4), *pedibus in sententiam ibat* (Liv. 27.34.7). It
is not clear whether the *voluntas* of the prudent part of the council
should be regarded as identical with or just as the basis of the *sententia
melior* in §2. It is not known which generals were against besieging
Ctesiphon. Victor, who had restrained Roman soldiers from entering
the city in their pursuit of the Persians (24.6.13), may have been one
of them. It appears from 25.5.2 that there were at least two factions
amongst the commanding officers: on the one hand the former
officials of Constantius II, like Arintheus and Victor, and on the
other hand generals like Nevitta and Dagalaifus as well as the chiefs
of the Gauls; the latter were the true supporters of Julian. Refraining
from a siege of Ctesiphon must have been a dramatic decision, since
the capture of the Sasanian capital was no doubt one of the prime
objectives of Julian's campaign.

Some authors report, erroneously no doubt, that Julian did lay
siege to Ctesiphon: Κτησιφῶντα ἐπολιόρκει (Zonaras 13.13.1). Socr.
HE 3.21.4 even adds that the Persian king offered him a part of
his kingdom in exchange for peace: περιστοιχίσας δὲ Κτησιφῶντα τὴν
μεγάλην πόλιν τοσοῦτον ἐπολιόρκει τὸν βασιλέα Περσῶν, ὥστε ἐκεῖνον
πρεσβείαις χρήσασθαι συχναῖς ἱκετεύειν τε ζημιωθῆναι μέρος τι τῆς αὐτοῦ
πατρίδος, εἰ καταλύσας τὸν πόλεμον ἀποχωρήσῃ. A further step is taken
in *Art.pass.* 69, where it is said that Julian in fact took the city: καὶ τὴν
Κτησιφῶντα πόλιν καταλαβὼν ἐδόκει τι μέγα διαπραξάμενος ἔργον ἐφ'
ἕτερα μεταβαίνειν κρείττονα.

facinus audax et importunum esse noscentium id aggredi   Michael, 1874,
22 refers to Cic. *Ver.* 2.74 *incredibili importunitate et audacia.* The

204   COMMENTARY

adjective *importunus*, which already occurs in archaic Latin, is quite aptly used here: a siege of Ctesiphon 'does not suit' the situation at all. For *noscere*, 'to recognize', see the note ad 22.9.3 *recte noscentibus* and cf. Cic. *Leg.* 1.11 *vereor ne istam causam nemo noscat*. Some other examples of Amm.'s use of *aggredi* with the meaning 'to undertake' are *nihil voluntate praeter ea, quae in commune conducunt, aggrediar aut temptabo* (21.5.7), *arduum est opus aggressus* (28.2.2). With *id* Amm. refers to *obsidio*.

civitas situ ipso inexpugnabilis defendebatur Editors rightly reject Gelenius' *inexpugnabili*: it is the city which is 'impregnable' (cf. 25.8.17 *urbem inexpugnabilem*). The adj. should be taken predicatively with *situ ipso* as abl. causae; *defendebatur* probably expresses that the city was being defended actively with manpower and fortifications. As Amm. reported in 24.6.13, it had a circuit of walls (*moenium ambitus*). The best impression of Ctesiphon's defences – together with those of Coche or Seleucia on the west bank of the Tigris, with which it formed one city – can be gained from Greg. Naz. *Or.* 5.10. This contemporary reports that Ctesiphon was a strong fortress with walls made of baked bricks and surrounded by a deep moat. It derived additional strength from a marsh fed by the river. Gregory adds that it was neither possible to take the city by assault nor by siege. It was probably better fortified than in the second and third centuries when Trajan (116), Avidius Cassius (165), Septimius Severus (198) and Carus (283) were able to capture the city. The lack of archaeological evidence (Abdul Khaliq, 2000 is not very relevant) is an obstacle to obtaining precise information, but it would seem that the city reached its greatest territorial expansion in Sasanian times. See Oppenheimer, 1983, 202–6. Apart from the expected massive support from the Persian king's troops, Ctesiphon's mere position defended it 'as a city which could not be captured'.

protinus rex affore credebatur It is remarkable that Amm. makes no mention at all of the whereabouts of Sapor and the main Persian army. The Romans seem to have had no clear idea where precisely they were; they merely surmised the king was in the neighbourhood; see also 24.5.7 *quodque rex cum ambitiosis copiis passibus citis incedens propediem affore credebatur* with the note and 24.7.7 *advenisse iam regis auxilia*. Socr. *HE* 3.21.4 (quoted above in the note ad *itum est*) implies that the king was in Ctesiphon. Malalas, *Chron.* 13.331 says that Sapor had fled to the region of Armenia which was controlled by the Persians: φεύγει ἐπὶ τὴν Περσαρμενίαν, (cf. 332 ἐπὶ τὰ μέρη

CHAPTER 7.2 205

τῶν Περσαρμενίων) which is quite unlikely; for one thing, the term Persarmenia is anachronistic: this part of Armenia came under Persian control only after 363; see Sturm, 1938, 932 and cf. further Blockley, 1984; Blockley, 1987; Seager, 1996 and Greatrex, 2000. A military confrontation in the battlefield between the two armies never took place. The Romans joined battle with divisions of the Sasanian army, commanded i.a. by the Surên, Pigranes and Narseus, as in the battle described in 24.6.12 ff.

vicit sententia melior This is a phrase which Amm. must have copied **7.2** from his predecessors, who used such expressions for decisions of the senate: *vicit tamen sententia ut mitterentur coloni* (Liv. 9.26.5), *haec sententia valuit* (Tac. *Ann.* 13.27.3), or other councils: *postremo vicit sententia plurium* (Liv. 23.6.5, about deliberations at Capua), *ea sententia valuit* (Tac. *Ann.* 6.44.4, about Tiridates' council of war). With *melior* presumably 'the best of two' options in the council is meant. Obviously Amm. agreed with the conclusion. As an experienced officer he must have understood that an attempt to take the city was practically hopeless. Zonaras, who in 13.13.1 reports that Julian did lay siege to Ctesiphon (see the note ad 24.7.1 *itum est*), also knows of a different tradition, viz. that Julian gave up the idea of a siege δι' ὀχυρότητα (13.13.10). Amm. does not explicitly state the contents of the council's advice. It is of course implied that the idea of laying siege to an impregnable city should be abandoned, but which alternative strategy was decided on? This cannot be sufficiently inferred from the immediate tactical measures taken by Julian. Neither can it be concluded that the (majority of the) staff approved of these measures.

cuius utilitate princeps sollertissimus… latebrae texere notissimae It is unfortunate that *approbata… expedita* is only found in Gelenius, but, as they stand, these words do not necessarily raise suspicions. The direct context does not offer any specific element which Gelenius could have used in composing the phrase in question himself. Julian's shrewdness is highlighted on several occasions: *quod ne fieret, consilio sollerti praevidit* (21.8.3), *sollerti remedio turbatis consuluit rebus* (21.12.16, q.v.). He is called *sollertissimus Caesar* in 17.2.3. Here the author probably wants to avoid giving the impression that any irresponsible behaviour on the part of the emperor met with a timely correction by his staff: *sollertissimus* emphasizes that he is fully in command and quite able to appreciate the value of the various opinions within the council of war.

206   COMMENTARY

Julian's precise strategical intentions cannot be gathered from
his orders to Arintheus (see for him the note ad 24.1.2). He has to
supply provisions by plundering the fertile agricultural surroundings
(see for *laetus*, 'rich, flourishing', the note ad 24.5.1, and for a comparable action 24.1.14) and to deal just as energetically (*pari... industria*) with potential threats from scattered enemies who could
hide themselves in "hide-outs known only to themselves amid a network of overgrown paths" (Hamilton), perhaps comparable to the
frutecta squalida vallesque mentioned in 24.1.13. Having only a group
of light-armed infantry (*cum manu peditum expedita*) at his disposal,
he obviously has to refrain from any large-scale actions; Zosimus
does not mention Arintheus' mission, unless the suggestion of Dillemann, 1961, 145 is right that Zos. 3.24.1 (quoted in the note ad
24.5.5 *Itaque aliquantum progressi*) is wrongly placed by its author and
in fact corresponds to the present text. However, this does not seem
very likely, as Paschoud n. 67 rightly notes.

7.3   *hinc opulenta* After these two words there is obviously a lacuna, which
must have contained the words completing the sentence. Presumably
in it was mentioned the richly rewarding success of Arintheus' action.
Thörnell, 1927, 14 is quite sure that *praeda* should be supplemented
to go with *opulenta*. Admittedly, this combination can be found
elsewhere, e.g. Liv. 10.39.4, Apul. *Met.* 9.19.1. Amm., however, uses
the adjective only of persons or houses, towns and regions: e.g.
matronam opulentam (26.8.12), *urbem opulentam* (29.5.18). Judging
from Amm.'s own text, the lacuna was in all probability somewhat
larger. At the end of the chapter he reports that the auxiliary forces
commanded by Procopius, Sebastianus and Arsaces failed to turn up
ob causas impedita praedictas. It is reasonable to presume that *praedictas*
refers to something in the present section which has been lost:
"ubinam praedictas nisi hoc in loco?" (Valesius). The lacuna may
also have contained some information about Julian's staff advising
him to abandon any further projects and to return home. The use of
sed to mark his firm contrary decision would fit this idea, although
it is not strictly necessary: after all in Amm.'s report Julian's sharp
reaction could have manifested itself at the very moment he set out
on his bold march inland. Be this as it may, all further assumptions
about the original contents of the lacuna are speculations based on
the reports of other authors. See for a specific case Di Maio, 1981.

Of course, a full reconstruction of all the proceedings and intentions on the basis of the various reports is the modern historian's
task. Yet it would be imprudent to regard all gaps in Amm.'s selective

CHAPTER 7.3

and fragmentary account as indications of textual lacunae. In that case far more lacunae would have to be assumed. Amm.'s selective account simply differs from that of other writers, who e.g. refer to a request by Sapor for a truce and for a stop to further hostilities, through an envoy he sent to Hormisdas. Julian declined the offer; see Lib. *Or.* 18.257–260.

Socrates, *HE* 3.21.4 has the unlikely report that the Persian king even sent several embassies to Julian, offering to surrender part of his kingdom on condition that Julian left his lands and ended the war. Amm. may also have referred to an attempt by some generals to dissuade Julian from his plan to burn the fleet (Austin, 1979, 97), and especially to the arrival of Persian deserters (see §4 and 5), as well as to another council of war. All these details would provide a further explanation of Julian's actions. See Fontaine n. 456 and Matthews 159 and 503, n. 65, who rightly contests Di Maio's suggestion (1981) that the missing text can be restored from Zon. 13.13.2–9, a passage which does contain a few details reminiscent of Amm., but reports the whole episode within a different framework. All these events may have taken place during the five days which Julian, according to Zos. 3.26.1, spent at Abouzatha, where he arrived two days after the battle near Ctesiphon: Τῇ δὲ ὑστεραίᾳ τὸν Τίγρητα ποταμὸν ὁ βασιλεὺς τὸ στράτευμα ἐπὶ πολλῆς ἀδείας διαβιβάσας, τρίτῃ μετὰ τὴν μάχην ἡμέρα καὶ αὐτὸς μετὰ πάσης τῆς ἀμφ᾽ αὐτὸν δορυφορίας ἐπεραιοῦτο, καὶ πρός τι χωρίον ἐλθὼν (Ἀβουζαθὰ τοῦτο Πέρσαι καλοῦσιν) ἡμέρας ἐν τούτῳ διέμεινε πέντε. See Paschoud n. 72. The Swiss scholar is very sceptical about the reliability of Zosimus' remark ("Je pense donc que le début de ce paragr. est de son invention") and indeed, it is not clear why the Tigris once again should have been crossed. This casts doubts on Zosimus' chronological information too. There is no reason, however, to distrust his remark about the stay at Abouzatha, which presumably is to be dated to the first week of June.

avidae semper ad ulteriora cupiditatis According to Seager, 1997, 265 Amm. uses here "language ... close to that reserved for Sapor". As such, this remark cannot easily be argued with and undoubtedly, *semper* expresses a general trait of Julian's character, yet the translations "ever driven on by his eager ambitions" (Rolfe) and "Julian ... whose ambition was never satisfied" (Hamilton) are too vague. Seyfarth and Fontaine rightly remain closer to the context with their "Julian, der immer voller Begierde nach weiteren Zielen strebte" and "Mais lui, toujours ardemment désireux de pousser plus avant" respectively.

208   COMMENTARY

Indeed, the words indicate Julian's plan to proceed into the interior
of the Persian territory. From a grammatical point of view it is best to
construe *avidae* with *ad ulteriora*. See for *avidus ad* Kühner-Stegmann
1.436–7 and OLD s.v.

What exactly was Julian's strategy after abandoning the intention
to besiege Ctesiphon? Or, put in a broader perspective: what was
Julian trying to achieve with the Persian expedition apart from
getting revenge (23.5.18, q.v.), and what was his main objective?
Was his primary goal to capture Ctesiphon, or did he intend to
defeat Sapor in an open battle in order to bring the Roman-Persian
conflict to a permanent conclusion (Crump, 1975, 57), thereby
safeguarding the eastern part of the Roman empire? Or did he only
choose this latter option, when it became clear to him that it was
impossible to take Ctesiphon? The various sources do not lead to a
clear answer to such questions. As was already stated above, Amm.
leaves the reader almost completely in the dark. Libanius' *Oration*
18 is highly panegyrical and apologetic, echoing the great deeds
of Alexander. He speaks about harming the Persians (*Or.* 18.214,
306) and causing as much damage as possible to them (*Or.* 18.231).
However, he also mentions the hope of overthrowing Persia, adding
its territories to the Roman empire, Roman governors taking the
place of Persian satraps and the introduction of Roman law in the
conquered territories (*Or.* 18.282); see in general Bliembach, 1976,
Benedetti, 1990 and Wolski, 1993; cf. also Scholl, 1994, 134ff. and
Seager, 1997, 262ff. Socrates, like Libanius, describes Julian as a
new Alexander, but he, of course, looks at him from a very different
angle: ὀνειροπολήσας τὴν Ἀλεξάνδρου τοῦ Μακεδόνος δόξαν λαβεῖν
ἢ καὶ μᾶλλον ὑπερβαίνειν... καὶ γὰρ ἐνόμιζε κατὰ τὴν Πυθαγόρου καὶ
Πλάτωνος δόξαν ἐκ μετενσωματώσεως τὴν Ἀλεξάνδρου ἔχειν ψυχήν,
μᾶλλον δὲ αὐτὸς εἶναι Ἀλέξανδρος ἐν ἑτέρῳ σώματι, *HE* 3.21.6–7; cf.
further *Art. pass.* 69. The aim of Julian's strategy cannot be gathered
from Zosimus' report; he does not mention the council of war at
Ctesiphon nor the decision not to lay siege to the Sasanian capital or
the discussions between Julian and his generals about the next steps
to be taken.

It is not difficult to understand that, having decided not to besiege Ctesiphon, Julian rejected the proposal to return home. The
decision to retreat was taken later; Amm. only mentions it in 24.8.5.
Instead, it was decided to invade the inner parts of the Sasanian empire (pace Soz. *HE* 6.1.9: Δόξαν δὲ τῷ βασιλεῖ μηκέτι περαιτέρω χωρεῖν,
ἀλλ᾽ εἰς τὴν ἀρχομένην ἐπανελθεῖν), possibly with the objective to confront Sapor and his army on the battlefield. Apart from by Amm. (see

CHAPTER 7.3   209

mediterraneas vias in the present section and *ad interiora tendebat* in
§6), this decision is mentioned by Zosimus (3.26.2: ἀνιέναι δὲ ἐπὶ τὴν
μεσόγειαν) and Libanius (*Or.* 18.260: ἐπεθύμησε μὲν Ἄρβηλα καὶ ἰδεῖν
καὶ διελθεῖν... καὶ γνώμην δὲ εἶχεν ἐπιβῆναι πάσης ὅση Πέρσαις ὁρίζει τὸ
κράτος, μᾶλλον δὲ καὶ τῆς ὁμόρου, 261: καὶ πρὸς τὴν Ὑρκανίαν ἔτεινε
τὸν λογισμὸν καὶ τοὺς Ἰνδῶν ποταμούς). Cf. also Festus' *in Madaenam*
(i.e. 'into Media'; Ruf. Fest. 28) and Malal. *Chron.* 13.330 βουλόμενος
μετὰ τῆς ἰδίας συγκλήτου καὶ ἕως Βαβυλῶνος εἰσελθεῖν καὶ παραλαβεῖν τὰ
ἐκεῖσε. See Ridley, 1973, 322; Browning, 1976, 208–9; Wirth, 1978,
486–7. It is not clear whether this decision was taken independently
or on the advice of (an) untrustworthy Persian deserter(s). See for
this the note ad *infaustis ductoribus praeviis*; see also below the note
ad *tortique perfugae* (§5).

vetantium dictis Cf. for *vetare*, 'to oppose', *nec enim dissuadere palam
audebat quisquam vel vetare* (21.15.1, q.v.). Zon. 13.13.7 mentions that
many, amongst whom Hormisdas, warned Julian against marching
into the interior of the Persian empire: καὶ ταῦτα πολλῶν λεγόντων
αὐτῷ καὶ αὐτοῦ τοῦ Ὁρμίσδου δόλον εἶναι τὸ πρᾶγμα.

*quod ob inertiam otiique desiderium amitti suaderent prope iam parta regna
Persidis* As in §2, six words only stem from Gelenius' edition: *otiique
desiderium amitti suaderent prope iam.* In this case it is perhaps conceivable that Gelenius devised the text himself, but would he have added
an expression synonymic to *inertiam*? The subjunctive probably expresses that this is Julian's own explicit motive for chiding them. In
any case, *parta regna Persidis* is one of the few clear expressions used by
Amm. about the specific objective(s) of Julian's expedition. Another outspoken one is *abolenda nobis natio molestissima* (23.5.19, q.v.).
Julian's overconfidence in thinking that the Persian kingdom was
now within his grasp was caused by the fact that he had insufficient
knowledge of the strength of Sapor's forces and of the geographical
difficulties.

flumine laeva relicto The Roman army marched to the north of
Ctesiphon, according to Zos. 3.26.3 to Noorda (cf. the note ad 24.7.6
numero potior), thereby becoming further and further removed from
the Tigris and leaving the river to its left; cf. Lib. *Or.* 18.264 Οὕτω
μὲν τοῦ Τίγρητος πίνοντες ἐχώρουν κατ' ἀριστερὰν χεῖρα τὸν ποταμὸν
ἔχοντες and Soz. *HE* 6.1.9. According to Libanius the country there
was more hospitable than before: καὶ διὰ χώρας ἤεσαν τῆς προτέρας
ἀμείνονος (ibid.).

210   COMMENTARY

infaustis ductoribus praeviis mediterraneas vias arripere citato proposuit gradu TLL V 1.2167.81–2168.17 mentions this among a small group of passages in which *ductores* denote people "monstrantes viam", i.e. 'guides'. Amm. has some clear examples: 17.10.2 *ductores viarum praeeuntes alacri gradu*, 17.10.5. The choice of the adjective is remarkable. Some term indicating their unreliability or perfidy would have been easier to understand; *infaustis*, however, immediately expresses that Julian's new strategy is not merely perilous, but doomed. Various sources mention that Julian was persuaded by (an) untrustworthy Persian deserter(s) sent by Sapor to burn the fleet with its provisions and to march inland. They further report that these guides soon led the army into ambushes and deserts where the Romans would be short of supplies and hence an easy prey for the Persian forces. See Greg. Naz. *Or.* 5.11, Ruf. Fest. 28 (*cum a transfuga qui se ad fallendum obiecerat inductus viae in Madaenam compendia sectaretur*; cf. for Festus' source(s) here Blockley, 1973 and Arce, 1974), *epit.* 43.2, Hier. *Chron.* a. 363, Ephr. Syr. *HcJul.* 2.18 ("the bearded ones deceived him, and he did not perceive it, he the goat who avowed that he knew the secrets", transl. Judith M. Lieu), Oros. *hist.* 7.30.6, Soz. *HE* 6.1.9 ff., Philost. *HE* 7.15, Malalas, *Chron.* 13.331, Joh. Lyd. *Mens.* 4.119, *Art. pass.* 69, Zon. 13.13.4–6, Cedrenus, *Hist.* 307 C-D. Remarkably, neither Zosimus nor Libanius mentions this. Gregory of Nazianzus and John Lydus both refer to the story told by Herodotus (3.153–160) about the so-called betrayal of Zopyrus, who mutilated himself by cutting off his nose and deceived the Babylonians on behalf of his king Darius. Without referring to Zopyrus, Malalas *Chron.* 13.331 has a similar story: δόλῳ πέμψας (sc. the Persian king, called Sabborarsacius) δύο συγκλητικοὺς αὐτοῦ καὶ αὐτοὺς κατὰ ἰδίαν βούλησιν ῥινοτομήσας πρὸς Ἰουλιανόν. Amm.'s words in 24.7.5 *tortique perfugae aperte faterentur se fefellisse* can be best understood by assuming that the *perfugae* are the same as the 'guides' in the present section. Since the various sources are not univocal, it is hard to establish the facts. One could imagine that Julian consulted Persians about the route into Persia's interior – pace Ridley, 1973, 322, who considers the entire story about the Persian deserters to be a fable: "the Roman army had no need of Persian guides because of Julian's study of previous campaigns and the presence of Hormisdas" (cf. also Meulder, 1991, 470 who, interestingly, points to Plut. *Crass.* 21.1–22.5, where we are told that at the end of Crassus' ill-fated eastern campaign an Arab chieftain, Ariamnes by name, treacherously lured him away from the river Euphrates and led him into the desert by a route which at first was suitable and easy but which soon became troublesome) – and

CHAPTER 7.4

that, when it appeared that this strategy failed, the Persian advisers were held responsible and were accused of deceit. Amm.'s lack of precision at this point may have been prompted by his desire not to shed an unfavourable light on Julian's strategic decision as such. See Brok 161; Dodgeon-Lieu, 1991, 235–6, 238 ff.

The wording of the weighty phrase *mediterraneas vias arripere citato proposuit gradu* is careful and deserves close attention. In spite of all contrary advice the expedition is to take its route inland not with hesitation, but purposefully. The verb *arripere* implies taking hold of something or setting out on a certain course with determination: *opus arreptum est memorabile* (17.1.10, q.v.), *arripere fidentius principatum* (23.3.2), *ad arripienda quae urgebant* (29.6.11). This determination is further expressed by *citato gradu*, a combination which occurs only here in Amm. and is not often used by other authors; cf. e.g. Liv. 28.14.17, Sen. *Med.* 891. Cf. also *concito gradu* (24.6.12, 29.5.11). The predicate should also be weighed with precision: translators tend to blur its full meaning with either "resolved" (Rolfe), "decise" (Caltabiano) or "se proposa" (Fontaine), "nahm sich vor" (Seyfarth). Amm.'s use of the verb often has the connotation of putting something clearly before people's eyes. This is directly obvious in such concrete phrases as *edictis propositis* (16.12.69, 27.8.10) or *propositarum rerum pretia* (23.6.68), but it is also present in phrases denoting ideas or suggestions: *adverte iustitiam... quam propono* (20.8.11), *ad haec, quae proposuimus* (23.5.18). It may be concluded that *proposuit* does not only denote Julian's personal decision, but also the fact that he did not leave his staff and soldiers in the dark about it: he put it clearly before their eyes. In Zosimus' version such details are absent: Διασκοπῶν δὲ περὶ τῆς ἐπέκεινα πορείας ἄμεινον ἔχειν ᾠήθη μηκέτι συμπαραπέμπειν τῇ ὄχθῃ τοῦ ποταμοῦ τὸν στρατόν, ἀνιέναι δὲ ἐπὶ τὴν μεσόγειαν (3.26.2).

ut tamquam funesta face Bellonae subiectis ignibus exuri cunctas iusserat **7.4** *naves* This is Sabbah's main testimony for his interpretation of the chapter. The ships are burned on Julian's order, but this human action seemed to cause a deadly divine interference. Amm. is convinced of the disastrous implications of Julian's drastic measure, so much so that the assumption that a higher force was at work with destructive purposes is inevitable.

In Sulla's time the Cappadocian goddess Ma had been introduced in Rome and was equated with the Roman war goddess Bellona; "sie ist die Vergöttlichung der zerstörerischen, jeder städtischer Ordnung gegenläufigen Kraft des brutalen Krieges" (F. Graf in *Der*

212   COMMENTARY

Neue Pauly s.v.). In the poetry of Amm.'s contemporary Claudian she figures ten times in this capacity: e.g. *quid dudum inflare moraris / Tartaream, Bellona, tubam?* (*in Eutr.* 2.144–5), which is reminiscent of Amm. 31.13.1, at the start of the rout at Adrianople, (cum) *lituosque Bellona luctuosos inflaret in clades Romanas.* The present text shows Bellona in the same role as in *saeviens per urbem aeternam urebat cuncta Bellona* (28.1.1, marking the beginning of the series of hideous lawsuits at Rome) and *caesorum ultimae dirae... Bellonae accenderant faces* (29.2.20, about the revenge planned by Justice against the murderous cruelties of injustice). However, the goddess' fiery torch now took a more literal shape in the ill-fated burning of the ships: *funestus* spells destruction. Bellona also figures as a destructive force in roughly contemporary Christian polemical poetry: *iurgantesque deos stimulat Bellona flagello* (*Carmen contra paganos* 22, see Bartalucci's note ad loc.), *Miscebat Bellona furens mortalia cuncta / armabatque feras in vulnera mutua dextras* (Prud. *c. Symm.* 1.600-1). There is, however, no evidence that her cult was still practised in fourth-century Rome. In an inscription dated to this period one of her temples is indirectly referred to, but perhaps rather as a relic of the past. See Guarducci, 1952. Nevertheless Rike, 1987, 25–6 rightly abandons the idea that Bellona's appearances in the *Res Gestae* are merely instances of "amplification rhétorique" (Camus, 1967, 144). The phrase *funesta face Bellonae* may be an echo of Verg. *A.* 7.319–22, where both the goddess and *funestae taedae* are mentioned. Consult for Bellona Wissowa, 1912, 348–51; Waszink, 1954; Blázquez, 1986, 92–3; Chioffi-Viscogliosi, 1993, 190–4, and the literature mentioned in the note ad 21.5.1.

    Apart from Julian's untimely death, the burning of the fleet was the event which perhaps made the most lasting impression on the imagination of contemporary and later authors. Generally speaking, the Christian sources blame treacherous Persian advisers for this decision: Ephr. Syr. *HcJul.* 2.18 and 3.15, Greg. Naz. *Or.* 5.11–12, Joh. Lyd. *Mens.* 4.119, Cedrenus, *Hist.* 307 C-D, Zon. 13.13.4–9. Soz. *HE* 6.1.10–12 and Thdt. *HE* 3.25.1, however, while mentioning the burning of the ships, do not blame Persian deserters. Zosimus and Libanius regarded the measure as sound strategy. Zosimus argues that, because the army was going inland, there was no reason to rely on the fleet: ἀνιέναι δὲ ἐπὶ τὴν μεσόγειαν, ὡς οὐδενὸς ὑπολειπομένου πλοίων εἰς χρείαν αὐτοὺς καθιστάντος. ταῦτα δὴ λαβὼν κατὰ νοῦν εἰσηγεῖται βουλὴν τῷ στρατῷ, τὰ πλοῖα ἐμπρῆσαι κελεύων (3.26.2). Lib. *Or.* 18.262–3 argues that it was better to burn the fleet than to leave it to the enemy: apart from this, the current of the Tigris was very strong and it would

CHAPTER 7.4   213

have taken a lot of men to tow the ships upstream. Some modern authors call the burning of the fleet a strategic error of Julian, e.g. Wirth, 1978, 486: "ihre Zerstörung (lässt sich) vom Strategischen her eigentlich nicht rechtfertigen", Bowersock, 1978, 114: "The emperor did a most astonishing thing when he abandoned the idea of besieging Ctesiphon. He ordered nearly all the ships in his fleet to be burned".

Even though the deliberate destruction of the ships seems to have caused considerable unrest among the soldiers, and is often misunderstood in the sources and in secondary literature, the reasoning behind it was basically sound (so e.g. Ridley, 1973, 325–6). The ships, which were used to carry provisions and military equipment like siege engines, would have no function during a march inland. There were no waterways like the Euphrates, the Tigris and the canals, and a fleet was therefore useless. Even in the case of a retreat into Roman territory it would be more of a burden than a help. Upstream neither of the two great rivers was navigable because of the strong current and the northwesterly wind; see De Graeve, 1981, 11–13. Apart from this, many ships of Julian's fleet were probably only suitable for going downstream; see the note ad 23.3.9 and add to the literature cited there De Graeve, 1981, 79 ff., which book, although concerned with the ancient Near East before 500 B.C., can also profitably be used for the period under discussion. The only way to get the ships upriver was by towing them and this would have required a lot of manpower which then would not be available for fighting, as is noted by Lib. *Or.* 18.262 (see the full text below in the note on *ne relicta classis*); cf. Soz. *HE* 6.1.9. Moreover, it would have seriously hampered the marching speed of the army. All in all, Julian's decision seems to have been a wise one. The only problem was that without ships no provisions for a longer period could be carried along (cf. August. *C.D.* 4.29 *naves iussit incendi quibus alimonia portabantur*; 5.21 *naves, quibus victus necessarius portabatur, incendit*) so that the Roman army had to depend on the land: *alimenta affatim opulentis suggerentibus locis* (24.7.6). See for the general prosperity and fertility of Mesopotamia in Sasanian times Adams, 1965, 69–83 and Howard-Johnston, 1995, 198 ff.

The lemma raises one final question: is *iusserat* merely another example of the pluperfect being used instead of the perfect tense to create a regular cursus, or does it express that Julian's order preceded his announcement of the march inland? The latter interpretation would imply both an improbable sequence of events and a difficult link with the narrative of § 5.

214   COMMENTARY

praeter minores duodecim, quas profuturas pangendis pontibus disposuit vehi carpentis The verb *pangere*, which only occurs here in Amm., is very rarely used as a synonym of *conficere*: see TLL XI.209.9–15. Zon. 13.13.7 has the same number (πῦρ ἐνέβαλε ταῖς ναυσὶ καὶ πάσας κατέκαυσε πλὴν δυοκαίδεκα), but Libanius (*Or.* 18.263) reports that fifteen ships were held back for bridging operations (αἱ δὲ ἦσαν πεντεκαίδεκα γεφυρῶν εἵνεκα πεφυλαγμέναι), while Zos. 3.26.3 mentions that eighteen ships of the Roman type and four of Persian shape were spared to be used as ship bridges; see for the various forms of boats used in the ancient Near East De Graeve, 1981, 79ff. These ships were transported on wagons: Καὶ πάντα, πλὴν ὀκτωκαίδεκα Ῥωμαικῶν Περσικῶν δὲ τεσσάρων, ἐδαπανήθη πυρί. ταῦτα γὰρ ἁμάξαις φερόμενα ἠκολούθει, ταῖς ἀνακυπτούσαις ('cropping up') ὡς εἰκὸς ὑπηρετησόμενα χρείαις. Cf. Veg. *mil.* 3.7.7 on the transport of material for the construction of bridges: *Sed commodius repertum est, ut monoxylos* ("single timbers", Milner) *... carpentis secum portet exercitus tabulatis pariter et clavis ferreis praeparatis.* See for the *carpentum*, a two-wheeled carriage, the note ad 23.3.7. It could probably only carry ships of a small type; the same impression can be gained from Vegetius' description. At the beginning of the campaign the fleet consisted of 1100 vessels: 1000 cargo carriers, 50 warships and 50 vessels for making ship bridges; see 23.3.9 with the note ad loc. In all probability Julian preserved several vessels of the last mentioned type. This number was apparently insufficient for bridging operations: *nec contabulandi pontis erat facultas amissis navibus temere* (24.7.8), but sufficient for crossing rivers by letting them go back and forth: *imperator ipse brevibus lembis, quos post exustam classem docuimus remansisse, cum paucis transvectus eadem navigia ultro citroque discurrere statuit, dum omnes conveheremur* (25.8.3); see Paschoud n. 74.

idque putabat utiliter ordinasse This phrase serves two purposes: it expresses that Julian himself was sure that his order was rationally founded and at the same time it implies that it was no more than his own insight, which was not shared by others.

ne relicta classis... navibus et regendis Remarkably, Amm. goes out of his way to describe Julian's motives as accurately as possible. This is presumably to preclude the reader's conclusion that the emperor had gone mad. His brain functioned well enough, but unfortunately it served the fatal plans of higher forces. Libanius offers similar arguments: τὰ πλοῖα δὲ... ἀφεῖτο πυρί, κάλλιον γὰρ ἦν ἢ τοῖς πολεμίοις (*Or.* 18.262). According to the same author, about half of the men

CHAPTER 7.5

would have been needed to tow the boats because of the strong current of the Tigris: ὀξὺς γὰρ καὶ πολὺς ὁ Τίγρης ἐμπίπτων ταῖς πρώραις πολλῶν ἠνάγκαζε δεῖσθαι χειρῶν τὰ πλοῖα καὶ ἔδει τοὺς ἀνέλκοντας ὑπὲρ ἥμισυ τῆς στρατιᾶς γενέσθαι (*Or.* 18.263). He also mentions that the burning of the fleet disposed of all the idlers who, with the excuse of sickness, would lie sleeping in the ships: πρὸς δὲ τούτοις καὶ τὴν εἰς τὸ μαλακίζεσθαι παράκλησιν ἀνῃρήκει τὸ πῦρ. ὁ γὰρ μηδὲν ποιεῖν ἐθέλων ἀρρωστεῖν σκηπτόμενος ἔκειτο καθεύδων ἐν πλοίῳ, πλοίων δὲ οὐκ ὄντων ἅπας ἦν ἐν ὅπλοις (*Or.* 18.263). With *aut certe* Amm. expresses that, whereas the first motive only took into account an eventuality, the second was beyond doubt. See for *regere*, "to guide the course of ships", OLD s.v. 4a.

Amm.'s report in this section fails to provide a truly satisfactory **7.5** explanation of Julian's change of mind concerning the burning of the ships, but suggests that it was brought about by the soldiers' protest and the discovery of the Persian guides' treachery.

Dein cum metuens sibi quisque mussaret Again a carefully worded phrase: every individual soldier was worrying about his own safety at this turning point in the campaign. The verb *muss(it)are* denotes the muttered expression of discontent or protest. Presumably, there was a threat of mutiny. In Zon. 13.13.9 it is also related that after the burning of the ships protests could be heard. According to him many officers blamed the alleged Persian deserters and demanded an enquiry, for which Julian reluctantly gave permission: ἐπεὶ πολλοὶ τῶν ταξιαρχῶν ἐνέδραν καὶ δόλον ἐνίσταντο εἶναι τὰ παρὰ τῶν αὐτομόλων ἐκείνων λεγόμενα, μόλις που κατένευσεν ἐτασθῆναι τοὺς ψευδαυτομόλους.

perspicua veritas The phrase as such ('plain truth', not in need of any further elucidation) may have been borrowed from Cic. *inv.* 1.65 (see also August. *Conf.* 6.11.18, 13.18.23). Its function in the context, however, deserves close attention: Amm. notes that not merely the soldiers' misgivings, but also the clear and unmistakable facts showed the forbidding and menacing perspectives of the march inland.

quod repulsus forsitan ariditate vel altitudine montium ad aquas redire non poterit See for the construction *quod* with ind. fut. the notes ad 20.8.10 and 22.6.3. The words describe the soldiers' anxiety. If the dry and mountainous landscape were to make progress impossible, they would be trapped, since returning to the watery region between

216   COMMENTARY

Euphrates and Tigris would also lead them into a blind alley. Experience had shown that crossing this area without vessels, rafts and boats was impossible. In other accounts the anxiety described by Amm. has come true. According to *Art. pass.* 69 a Persian deserter led the Romans into to the Carmanitan desert (ἐπὶ τὴν Καρμανίτην ἔρημον), where they had to endure hunger and thirst. Thdt. *HE* 3.25.4 speaks of lack of food and water, but not of any deserters; on the contrary, according to him the Romans had no guides at all and therefore lost their way. Soz. *HE* 6.1.11 says that the hardships, caused by a treacherous enemy, lasted three or four days, while Malalas even gives exact details about distance and date of the journey: the army was led for 150 miles through a barren region until it reached, on June 25, the remains of an old town, named Bubio, and of a fortress nearby, Asia: καὶ ἀπήγαγον αὐτὸν εἰς τὴν ἔρημον καὶ ἄνυδρον ἐπὶ μίλια ρν᾽, πλανήσαντες αὐτούς, τῇ εἰκάδι πέμπτῃ τοῦ δαισίου τοῦ καὶ ἰουνίου μηνός. καὶ εὑρὼν ἐκεῖ τείχη παλαιὰ πεπτωκότα πόλεως λεγομένης Βουβίων, καὶ ἄλλο δὲ χωρίον, ἑστώτων μὲν τῶν οἰκημάτων, ἔρημον δὲ ἦν, ὅπερ ἐλέγετο Ἀσία. (*Chron.* 13.331). Malalas' date, at any rate, cannot be right (cf. 24.8.5).

tortique perfugae aperte faterentur se fefellisse In all probability Amm. refers to the 'ill-starred guides' of 24.7.3, pace Bliembach, 1976, 201. Zon. 13.13.9 is similar: οἱ ἐτασθέντες βασάνοις ('when examined under torture') ἐξέφηναν τὸ ἀπόρρητον ('the abominable truth'). See also Soz. *HE* 6.1.12, who speaks of only one man (ὁ μὲν γέρων ὁ αἰχμάλωτος βασανιζόμενος ὡμολόγησεν ὑπὲρ τῶν οἰκείων αὐτομολῆσαι πρὸς θάνατον). Amm. is silent about the subsequent fate of the *perfugae.* Joh. Lyd. *Mens.* 4.119, however, relates that they were killed when their treachery was revealed. In the *Art. pass.* 69 the same story is told, be it that its author speaks of more than one guide. Malalas *Chron.* 13.332 on the other hand reports that, when the Persians had confessed their betrayal, Julian promised not to kill them if they would lead the Roman army out of the desert. Julian interrogated them on the day after they had reached Bubio and Asia, i.e. on June, 26 (the date is wrong; cf. the preceding note): τῇ δὲ ἑξῆς ἡμέρᾳ μηνὶ ἰουνίῳ κϛ᾽ (*Chron.* 13.331). See in general for torture in Amm. Angliviel de la Beaumelle, 1993.

concursu maximo exstingui iussae sunt flammae Most translators take *concursu maximo* with *exstingui,* e.g. "di spegnere le fiamme con il maggior concorso di uomini" (Caltabiano). This may be right: cf. e.g. 19.5.7 *moenia omnium concursu defendebantur.* However, it seems

CHAPTER 7.5

rather strange, that such a phrase is part of an order. In that case one would rather have expected something like *magnis viribus* (24.8.6). Another possibility should therefore be considered, viz. to regard *concursu maximo* as caused by the terrifying aspects of the situation: the men were to march into a difficult country with no apparent means to return, under the guidance of Persian fugitives, whose treacherous intentions had been exposed. A vast crowd gathered (Seyfarth: "da liefen alle zusammen") to make their worries clear to the emperor, who tried to allay them by ordering to quench the fire. Some interpreters (Andreotti, 1930, 267 n. 145; Austin, 1979, 98; Paschoud n. 74) make much of the passive construction without Agens, which in their view could mean that others, e.g. revolting members of Julian's staff, gave the order. Although this cannot be entirely ruled out, it is improbable for linguistic reasons. In the first place, in passive constructions the Agens is absent in the vast majority of instances. This is also the case in Amm.'s handling of the nom. c. inf. with *iubere*, e.g. *navigia iussa sunt colligi* (17.13.16), *transire iussi sunt in Hellespontum* (31.6.2). In such phrases the precise identity of the Agens is either perfectly clear from the context or irrelevant. The main reason for choosing the passive construction is to give prime attention to the Patiens, which is desirable, when it is the topic which the author wants to be the focus in a specific passage. This is precisely the case in the present text, in which the burning of the ships is the event which overshadows all other aspects of the situation described. This is also made apparent by the conspicuous final position of *flammae*, which is directly taken up by *ignis* at the beginning of the next sentence. Since the Agens is beyond doubt Julian (cf. *iusserat, disposuit, putabat* in §4), it is most natural to assume that Amm. does not intend to create the impression that any other person(s) might be the ultimate author of the order to quench the flames. See Risselada, 1991.

duodecim tantummodo naves...discretae sunt Unfortunately Amm. fails to provide clarity about the identity of the twelve ships saved: are they the same as the 'comparatively small' ones of §4 or is the identical number accidental? In the former case the relative clause has a causal flavour: these ships had been 'set apart' from the others in order to preserve them. TLL V 1.1296.80–1 assumes this meaning with "sc. ne igni comburerentur". This measure had saved them from being burnt. If not, the implication is that these *further* twelve ships were now singled out to be preserved, which is the more plausible explanation, as has been shown by Sabbah, 1992, 630–1. His timely

218   COMMENTARY

reference to 25.8.3, *brevibus lembis, quos post exustam classem docuimus remansisse* clinches the matter: "il faut bien que ces navires, désignés par l'expression *breves lembi*, soient distincts des navires-pontons".

7.6   *cum non oporteret* Although he does not give any reasons, Amm. does not hide his own judgment about the momentous fire: it simply should not have been ordered. In §8 he repeats his verdict in one telling word: *temere*. Zon. 13.13.7 reports that especially Hormisdas had been against it: καὶ ταῦτα πολλῶν λεγόντων αὐτῷ καὶ αὐτοῦ τοῦ Ὁρμίσδου δόλον εἶναι τὸ πρᾶγμα, πῦρ ἐνέβαλε ταῖς ναυσί.

consociato fretus exercitu, cum armatorum nulli per diversa distringerentur Presumably, *consociato* contrasts with *distringerentur*: the army now formed a complete unity, since none of the soldiers would have to cope with other tasks. The verb *distringere* is often used as a synonym of *occupare* (see the note ad 22.8.25), but TLL V 1.1151.2–3 rightly lists the present case as an example of the meaning "manente notione in diversas partes distrahendi". Amm.'s other eight instances of *per diversa* all have a local meaning, e.g. 16.2.2 *per diversa palantes*, 29.6.6 *disseminatus rumor ilico per diversa*. Such a sense is feasible here too: the soldiers were not bothered by conflicting claims on their services in places 'widely apart from one another'.

numero potior ad interiora tendebat alimenta affatim opulentis suggerentibus locis According to Brok 160 this does not mean that the Roman army went further into the interior of the Persian empire, but that the march back to Roman territory is meant. This suggestion does not tally with *mediterraneas vias arripere* (§3). The fact that Julian stuck to this strategy seems to be confirmed by Zos. 3.26.3, who reports that after the burning of the fleet the Roman army marched to Noorda (modern Djisr Nahrawan; see Sarre-Herzfeld, 1911–1920, vol. 2, 86), located at the river Douros (modern Diyala, some 40 km north of Ctesiphon): ὀλίγον δ᾽ ἀνωτέρω τοῦ ποταμοῦ τὸ λειπόμενον ἔδει ποιήσασθαι τῆς ὁδοῦ. Νοορδᾷ δὲ τῷ τόπῳ προσσχόντες αὐτοῦ που κατέλυον. If the Romans were retreating, Noorda would not be an obvious town to pass through and they could have taken a route more to the west and along the Tigris; see Fontaine n. 461, Paschoud n. 75.

From Julian's point of view the future looked bright again: he had more men at his disposal and he trusted that the rich surroundings guaranteed ample food supplies as before (24.3.14, 24.5.1 and 12, 24.6.3, 24.7.3). He was soon to be greatly disappointed. The

CHAPTER 7.7–8   219

scorched earth policy of the Persians and the failure to arrive of the
forces led by Sebastianus, Procopius and Arsaces made a further advance impossible and forced Julian to retreat. The march into the
interior is to be dated to June, 9–13 presumably.

Any reader interested in precise information will be especially dis-   **7.7–8**
appointed, if not exasperated, by the contents of these two sections.
Only when comparing the contents with other sources, will (s)he
discover some parallels, which could explain parts of Amm.'s description. The main reason for this is the author's wish to convey
some of the feelings and impressions of those who took part in the
expedition at this crucial phase, rather than to provide exact information. The author's personal memories of this dreadful episode are
accentuated by the ample use of the first person plural: *nos, tenebamur, nobis, aestimaremus* in §7, *praestolabamur* and *nostris* in §8. This
is not a historian's detached and precise report, but the recollection
of the emotions of the time by a participant.

ut inedia nos cruciarent, herbas cum adultis segetibus incenderunt This   **7.7**
strategy was highly efficient and successful, since the Roman army
now depended exclusively on the yield of the country. Both the animals and the men were the victims of the Persian measures: the
herbs were needed *in pastum* (30.3.3) and the crops to feed the
soldiers. The time of year (the first half of June; see the note on
chronology) makes *adultis* understandable. When necessary, the Romans applied such a strategy themselves; see 18.7.3. Zos. 3.26.4 reports that only after crossing the Douros (for which see the note
ad §8) the Roman army was confronted with the scorched earth
strategy and indeed with a united Persian army: ἐπεὶ δὲ τοὺς Πέρσας ἐθεάσαντο τὸν μὲν ἐν τῇ γῇ πάντα χιλὸν κατακαύσαντας, ὡς ἂν τὰ
ὑποζύγια τῶν Ῥωμαιῶν τροφῆς ἀπορίᾳ πιέζοιτο, συστάντας δὲ αὐτοὺς
κατὰ πολλοὺς λόχους ἐκδέχεσθαι τοὺς Ῥωμαίους ὡς δὴ μὴ σφόδρα πολλοὺς διανοουμένους, τότε δὴ συνειλεγμένους εἰς ταὐτὸν θεασάμενοι. Libanius totally ignores the Persian scorched earth policy, Zonaras only mentions its result: ἐνδείᾳ δὲ τῶν ἐπιτηδείων οἱ Ῥωμαῖοι σφοδρῶς
ἐπιέζοντο (13.13.13)

stativis castris, dum flammae senescerent, tenebamur Cf. Veg. *mil.* 3.8.10
*stativa autem castra aestate vel hieme hoste vicino maiore cura ac labore
firmantur.* Cf. for *senescere* denoting loss of power or beauty Cic. *Fam.*
7.26.1 *iam senescentis morbi remissio,* Liv. 29.22.8 *iam senescente invidia
molliebantur irae,* Liv. 30.19.10 *senescere Punicum bellum cernentis,* Plin.

220 COMMENTARY

nat. 9.115 (on pearls) *Alexander polyhistor et Sudines senescere eos putant coloremque expirare.* It is not clear where the camp was pitched. Possibly at Noorda; see Zos. 3.26.3.

insultantesque nobis… insolita temptamenta One can imagine the irritation caused by the Persian provocations which could not be answered adequately or satisfactorily. Moreover, by his boldness the enemy wanted to create at least the fear that his forces had been enlarged considerably. See for the expectation that Sapor's forces would soon arrive 24.5.7 *rex… propediem affore credebatur,* 24.7.1 *rex affore credebatur.* According to Zos. 3.26.3 the Romans captured and killed many Persians during their halt at Noorda: ἔνθα πολλοὶ πανταχόθεν ἡλίσκοντο Πέρσαι καὶ κατεσφάζοντο. Cf. Lib. *Or.* 18.264: διὰ χώρας ᾔεσαν τῆς προτέρας ἀμείνονος ὥστε οἷς εἶχον αἰχμαλώτοις θαρροῦντως προσετίθεσαν. See for *temptamenta* Tac. *Hist.* 2.38.1 *temptamenta civilium bellorum* with Heubner's note. Cf. also 24.5.12 *repentini excursus et alia… occulta.*

7.8 *maerebat tamen ob haec imperator et miles* See the notes ad 20.5.1, 21.4.6, 21.12.12, 22.15.20 for the loss of the adversative force of *tamen.* By the juxtaposition 'general' ('emperor') and 'soldier' Amm. subtly records that Julian too was now at his wits' end concerning the overall situation.

nec contabulandi pontis erat facultas amissis navibus temere Although Amm.'s report suggests, if anything, that the expedition as yet was not that far from Ctesiphon, the allusion to the crossing of a river comes as a surprise. From the context it is not at all clear which river is meant, perhaps either the Douros (an idea which is rejected by Paschoud n. 75) or, as Brok 165 thinks, the Tigris. He may be right, since Zos. 3.26.4 mentions that the Romans had crossed the Douros by way of a pontoon bridge: Ἐλθόντες δὲ εἰς τὸν Δοῦρον ποταμὸν διέβησαν τοῦτον γέφυραν ζεύξαντες. In this case it could mean that the number of ships preserved, either the twenty-four (or twelve) mentioned by Amm. or the twenty-two of Zosimus, was sufficient for crossing the Douros but not for crossing the much wider Tigris. As Mary, 1992 has pointed out, in the *Res Gestae* conspicuous attention is paid to naval bridges and the crossing of rivers; see the note ad 24.6.1 *ventum est.* For Amm. the bridges are an indispensable part of the equipment needed for an expedition. Being deprived of them must therefore have added to the feeling of helplessness.

CHAPTER 7.8   221

nec occurri poterat hostis adventicii motibus No reason is given. Why was it impossible to take the initiative? Does *adventicii* refer to the continuous arrival of fresh forces? Otherwise the adjective, the general sense of which is 'arriving from elsewhere', would be otiose. See the relevant note ad 23.2.1.

quem adesse coruscus nitor indicabat armorum arte pro singulis membris inflexus See for the Persian armour, especially that of the *catafractarii*, the notes ad 24.2.10 and 24.4.15. In 25.1.1 Amm. also refers to the gleam and glitter of this armour: *ubi vero primum dies inclaruit, radiantes loricae limbis circumdatae ferreis et corusci thoraces longe prospecti adesse regis copias indicabant.* The fear inspired by this glitter is mentioned elsewhere: (quamvis) *splendor ferri... Romanorum metum augeret* (24.2.5), *plurimum enim terroris hostibus armorum splendor importat* (Veg. *mil.* 2.14.8), *quoniam fulgor armorum plurimum hostibus terroris importat* (Donatus ad Verg. *A.* 7.626), *plurimum enim terrorem hostibus incutit etiam splendor armorum* (*ib.* 8.402). Cf. Tac. *Ger.* 43.4 *primi in omnibus proeliis oculi vincuntur.* Mark the functional enallage of *inflexus.* Of course, it was the cuirass which closely fitted their limbs, but this showed itself most conspicuously in the glitter.

adminicula, quae praestolabamur The general meaning of *adminiculum* is 'assistance' or 'support' (14.6.23, 14.8.14, 20.4.9, 22.16.18, 26.5.12, 27.5.1, 27.8.2), but here it denotes military reinforcement, as in 28.5.12 *poscentes adminicula sibi dari,* 29.5.14 *reparatis viribus nationum confinium adminicula ductans,* 29.5.37 *dedit hostibus facultatem... adminiculis augeri vel maximis,* 31.7.4 *veriti, ne destitutae adminiculis Galliae vastarentur licenter Rheno perrupto,* 31.8.2 *post quae repetivit Gallias Richomeres ob maiorem proeliorum fremitum, qui spectabatur, inde adminicula perducturus.* In the present text Amm. refers to the troops of Procopius, Sebastianus and Arsaces; see 23.3.5 and the note ad loc. Two of Amm.'s other instances of the comparatively rare verb *praestolari* also denote 'waiting for support' (21.13.6, 31.12.5). In 31.5.6 the *satellites* of Alavivus and Fritigern are waiting for these generals outside the room, where Lupicinus is entertaining them to dinner.

ob causas impedita praedictas See the note ad 24.7.3 *hinc opulenta.* Libanius' arguments in his *Or.* 18.260 that these much needed forces never reached the main army, viz. Arsaces' betrayal and rivalry between Procopius and Sebastianus, are rightly contested by

Brok 165 and Fontaine n. 465. Arsaces, they argue, is praised in 25.7.12 as a faithful friend who had carried out Julian's order to devastate Chiliocomum, and Amm. never speaks reproachfully about Procopius or Sebastianus. The most likely reason for their failing to turn up is the lingering presence of Sapor's army in the Tigris area.

CHAPTER 8

Introduction

The absence of precise details, which characterizes the contents of ch. 7, continues in this chapter. Remarkably, however, §5 contains the only precise date in book 24. The deliberations about the situation which the campaign had run into, must have taken place in the *stativa castra* of 24.7.7, possibly, according to Paschoud n. 75 ad Zos. 3.26.4, at Noorda. Amm., however, refrains from giving any topographical references, apart from mentioning Corduena as the ultimate goal of the northbound march. No individuals who are involved in the actions on the spot are mentioned and even Julian wellnigh disappears from sight after his pronounced presence in sections 1 and 2. The 'we'-style of the last sections of ch. 7 is carried on, especially from §4 onwards: *nostros* (1), *venimus* (2), *nos* (4), *arriperemus* (5), *nobis* (6), *quievimus* (7). The lack of detailed evidence may be disappointing, but what the author does offer makes up for this. His description conveys the intense worries (§1 *anxios milites*) and uncertainties (§4 *cum nihil humani proficerent sensus diu fluctuantes et dubii*, §7 *inter haec ita ambigua*) of soldiers and staff, which the gods refused to relieve, and the forbidding phenomena of the hot season (§3 *muscarum et culicum multitudine referta sunt omnia*, §5 *vis quaedam turbinata pulveris*).

ut solaretur anxios milites The dire straits, in which the campaign had **8.1** ended up, are clearly illustrated by this phrase. On former occasions the soldiers had to be calmed down (20.4.16), spurred on (23.5.16–23) or chided (24.3.4ff.); now they are worried and in need of consolation. Julian, however, proves up to this task with a timely imitation of the famous Spartan king Agesilaus (see below).

captivos graciles suapte natura… et macie iam confectos Cf. Zos. 3.26.3 and Lib. *Or.* 18.264, quoted ad 24.7.7. The slender physique of the Persians in general had been dealt with in 23.6.75 *graciles paene sunt omnes* (q.v.). Amm. does not mention the reason why they were in such bad shape: because they had been treated harshly as prisoners of war or because they had suffered themselves from famine before their capture?

224   COMMENTARY

"en", inquit, "quos Martia ista pectora viros existimant" Generally speaking, one finds both the nom. and acc. in exclamatory phrases with *en*. See Kühner-Stegmann 1.273–4; e.g. *en quattuor aras* (Verg. *Buc.* 5.65), *en Varus eodemque iterum fato vinctae legiones* (Tac. *Ann.* 1.65.4). In Amm., apart from cases in which a (main) clause follows, there are only clear cases of the nom., e.g. *en Persae* (23.5.3). The present instance is slightly more complicated in that the antecedent of *quos* is not expressed and *deformes... taetras* is congruent with *viros*. Brok 165 refers to Fron. *Str.* 1.11.17–18, where two comparable feats are mentioned, of Agesilaus and Gelo respectively. The latter is not reported in other sources, but Agesilaus' teaching by illustration can be found i.a. in Xenophon and Plutarch, as was noted by Valesius. The relevant passages are X. *HG* 3.4.19, *Ag.* 1.28 and Plut. *Ag.* 9, *apopth. Lac.* 13. The anecdote runs as follows: when Agesilaus had put Persian prisoners of war up for sale, he found out that buyers were only after their clothes, τῶν δὲ σωμάτων λευκῶν καὶ ἁπαλῶν παντάπασι διὰ τῆς σκιατροφίας ('effeminate life indoors') γυμνουμένων κατέγελων ὡς ἀχρήστων καὶ μηδενὸς ἀξίων, which triggered off this reaction of the king: 'Οὗτοι μέν' εἶπεν 'οἷς μάχεσθε, ταῦτα δ'ὑπὲρ ὧν μάχεσθε'. Now Julian was certainly interested in history; see the notes ad 21.12.1 *legensque* and 24.2.16 *legerat*, and although Bouffartigue, 1992, 287, 290 and 443 not without reason airs some doubts about Julian's personal acquaintance with Xenophon's and Plutarch's reports on Agesilaus, he may well have come across derivative evidence about this famous personality; we find the anecdote also in Polyaen. 2.1.6 and Ath. 12.550 e. In that case Julian's graphic instruction may have been inspired by the Spartan king's example.

At the beginning of his short career Julian is styled *Martius iuvenis* by Amm. 17.1.1. The use of *pectora* to denote (worthy) persons is poetical: *iuvenes, fortissima frustra / pectora* (Verg. *A.* 2.348–9), *devota morti pectora liberae* (Hor. *Carm.* 4.14.18).

deformes illuvie capellas et taetras According to TLL III 305.58–61, the present text and 17.11.1 are the only two instances of *capella* used "de hominibus". In 17.11.1 Julian himself is styled *capella, non homo*, which obviously has much to do with his 'hairy' appearance. See also the note ad 23.6.75 *caprinis oculis torvi*. The expression *deformes illuvie* is reminiscent of Tac. *Hist.* 4.46.2 (see Heubner ad loc.). The Persian prisoners were unshaven, unkempt and dirty, and in this condition made a poor and far from warriorlike impression.

CHAPTER 8.2   225

utque crebri docuerunt eventus Julian refers to well-known facts. Cf. e.g. the flight of the Persians at Cunaxa (Πρὶν δὲ τόξευμα ἐξικνεῖσθαι ἐκκλίνουσι οἱ βάρβαροι καὶ φεύγουσι, X. *An.* 1.8.19) and Issus (Arr. *An.* 2.10.4).

antequam... in fugam Although far more disparaging, this verdict tallies with the 'pragmatic' information provided in 23.6.80 *magis artifices quam fortes eminusque terribiles*; cf. also 25.1.18 *Persis, quibus saepe languidis in conflictu artius pes pede collatus graviter obsistebat, pugnare fortiter eminus consuetis.*

remotisque captivis This seems to be a euphemism. Zosimus in 3.26.3   **8.2** bluntly says that all Persian prisoners were killed (κατεσφάζοντο).

super rerum summa consultabatur On June 14–15 presumably. Cf. 15.5.27 *ut... de rerum summa consultaretur*; Amm. may have borrowed this expression from earlier Roman historians, e.g. *principes... cum quibus de summa rerum deliberaret* (Liv. 36.6.6), *consilium de summa rerum Beryti habitum* (Tac. *Hist.* 2.81.3).

multis ultro citroque dictitatis Amm. uses the phrase *ultro citroque* quite often, not least in describing deliberations. See the relevant note on the same expression in 21.12.4.

cum reverti debere per loca, quae venimus, plebs vociferaretur imprudens, resistebat intentius princeps One would have expected the deliberations 'on the entire situation' to have taken place in a meeting of the staff, as on earlier occasions (cf. 24.7.1 *Digesto itaque consilio cum primatibus super Ctesiphontis obsidio*, Lib. *Or.* 18.250 ἀγείρας τοὺς ἐν τέλεσι and Soz. *HE* 6.1.7 συγκαλέσας δὲ τοὺς στρατηγοὺς καὶ τοὺς ταξιάρχους), but now a mass meeting appears to be taking place. Another explanation could be that the rank and file waiting outside became impatient and voiced their demands, so that the emperor and his officers had to address them. See for *plebs*, 'the mass of common soldiers', the note ad 20.6.6, where the present text should have been mentioned.

As e.g. Dillemann, 1961, 149 suggests, *fr.* 27.6 of Eunapius probably refers to the deliberations in the present text: καὶ οἱ στρατιῶται οὐκ ἔχοντες ὅπως ἐπαινῶσιν ἀξίως τὰ πραττόμενα, "τοὺς Ἀχαιούς" φασίν "ἔκρινον ἀπὸ τοῦ πύργου", στρατηγικός τις καὶ περιττὸς εἰς φρόνησιν ἕκαστος εἶναι βουλόμενοι. καὶ τοῖς μὲν ὕλη τις ὑπῆν φλυαρίας· ὁ δὲ τῶν ἐξ ἀρχῆς ἐχόμενος λογισμῶν ἐπὶ τὴν οἰκείαν ἀνέστρεφεν ("The soldiers,

226   COMMENTARY

not having the werewithal to give due praise to what was being done,
"Judged the Achaeans", as they say [cf. Hom. *Il.* 3.141 ff.], "from the
town", each wishing to seem a man of strategy and extraordinary
wisdom; and they found evidence to support their foolishness. But
he, holding to the calculations which he had made at the beginning,
turned back towards home territory", tr. Blockley).

Baehrens, 1912, 294 (where the present passage is erroneously quoted as XXVIII 8.2) regards *quae venimus* as an instance of
the "Fehlen der Präposition in einer den Relativsatz einleitenden
Verbindung". A bold case is Tac. *Dial.* 35.2, where Baehrens prefers
mss *in scholas quibus* to the usual ⟨*in*⟩ *quibus*, defended by Gude-
man and Güngerich in their commentaries. However, two cases in
Sen. *Con.* are less extravagant: *nolo per illos reum gradus ducere* ⟨*per*⟩
quos potes tutus evadere (Sen. *Con.* 7.2.8), where Håkanson follows
Baehrens' plea for the ms reading, and *abdicari etiam propter hoc
non possit,* ⟨*propter*⟩ *quod praemium accepit* (Sen. *Con.* 10.2.8), where
Baehrens again wants to leave out the second *propter*, and Håkanson
conjectures *quo.* This is comparable to Hadrianus Valesius' *qua* in
the present text, which has been generally accepted. Nobody seems
to have suggested *per quae.*

See for *intentius,* 'with great energy', the note ad 20.6.1. If the
reader were inclined to assume that Julian resisted a retreat as such,
he would soon become aware that the decision to retreat had already
been taken. Note that the author never states this explicitly. It is,
however, clearly implied in §4, where the gods are not consulted as
to whether the army has to turn back, but along which route.

multis cum eo id nequaquam fieri posse monstrantibus per effusam planitiem
Presumably, the members of the staff mixed with the mass of soldiers
to explain the impracticability of what they were demanding. See
for *effusus,* 'spacious', *effusissimum Adriatici maris traiecit sinum* (Vell.
2.43.1) with Woodman's note, *effusis ac palustribus locis* (Tac. *Ger.*
30.1).

pabulo absumpto … squalentibus ultima This was the result of their own
anabasis to Ctesiphon. The content of Lib. *Or.* 18.248 (already referred to ad 24.6.4) is pertinent here: τὰ δὲ κατόπιν ὠμῶς πεπορθη-
μένα καὶ οὐ διδόντα τὴν αὐτὴν πάλιν ἐλθεῖν ("to the rear lay the area of
savage devastation that offered no hope of return by the same route",
tr. Norman). Cf. Soz. *HE* 6.1.6 (placed by Sozomen before the battle
which is narrated by Amm. in 24.6.8 ff.): τῶν πόλεων καὶ τῶν κωμῶν δι'
ὧν ἦλθον κατηρειμμένων ('fallen in ruins') καὶ τὰ ἐπιτήδεια μὴ ἐχουσῶν.

CHAPTER 8.3 227

quodque liquentibus iam brumae pruinis omne immaduerat solum et ruptis riparum terminis aucti inhorruere torrentes Cf. 15.10.4 *liquente gelu nivibusque solutis*, 17.12.4 *flumen Histrum exundantem pruinarum iam resoluta congerie*, 18.7.9 *Euphratem nivibus tabefactis inflatum*. As Arr. *An.* 7.21.2 observes, the Euphrates flows within its banks in the winter season, when the volume of the water is not large, but begins to rise in early spring, its level being at its highest about the time of the summer solstice. The river then breaks its banks: Ὁ γὰρ Εὐφράτης ποταμὸς ῥέων ἐκ τῶν Ἀρμενίων ὀρῶν χειμῶνος μὲν ὥρᾳ προχωρεῖ κατὰ τὰς ὄχθας, οἷα δὴ οὐ πολλοῦ ὄντος αὐτῷ τοῦ ὕδατος· ἦρος δὲ ὑποφαίνοντος καὶ πολὺ δὴ μάλιστα ὑπὸ τροπὰς ἅστινας τοῦ θέρους ὁ ἥλιος ἐπιστρέφει μέγας τε ἐπέρχεται καὶ ὑπερβάλλει ὑπὲρ τὰς ὄχθας ἐς τὴν γῆν τὴν Ἀσσυρίαν. Cf. Plin. *Nat.* 5.90. Mutatis mutandis the same holds good for the Tigris (cf. 24.6.7 with the relevant note).

ruptis riparum terminis aucti inhorruere torrentes It is difficult to define the genitive *riparum* precisely: gen. explicativus or identitatis are the most likely explanations; *terminis* is not pleonastic, but emphasizes that the torrents' banks formed the natural bounds. TLL VII 1.1601.6–10 lists this as one of the five instances in which *inhorrescere* is used "de aqua fluctuante". Pac. *trag.* 411 *inhorrescit mare* is the earliest of these. The verb expresses that the torrents not merely flooded the plain, but actually raged through it.

per eas terras vapore sideris calescentes muscarum et culicum multitudine **8.3** *referta sunt omnia* Cf. the similar passage in 18.7.5 about the lions in Mesopotamia during the hot season: *vapore sideris et magnitudine culicum agitantur, quorum examinibus per eas terras referta sunt omnia.* See De Jonge's note ad loc. on the poetical associations of *vapore sideris*, "unter dem Gluthauch der Sonne" (Seyfarth). The usual renderings of *musca* and *culex* are 'fly' and 'gnat' respectively, but entomologists may have more precise names. During their campaign in Mesopotamia in 117 Trajan's soldiers also were hindered by flies: καὶ ὁπότε οὖν δειπνοῖεν, μυῖαι τοῖς βρώμασι καὶ τοῖς πώμασι προσιζάνουσαι δυσχερείας ἅπαντα ἐνεπίμπλων (D.C. 68.31.4). See in general for flies and mosquitos in the ancient world Hünemörder, 1998 and 2000 and the literature cited there.

astrorum noctu micantium facies obumbratur Cf. *obumbrata facie caeli* (24.2.17, q.v.). This fine evocative phrase adds to the atmosphere of personal memories in this chapter.

228   COMMENTARY

8.4 *cum nihil humani proficerent sensus diu fluctuantes et dubii* One is reminded of other passages in Amm. expressing the limits of human insight, e.g. *utque solent manum iniectantibus fatis hebetari sensus hominum
et obtundi* (14.11.12), *hominum coniectura peccavit* (21.1.14), which is
a quotation from Cicero (see the note ad loc.), and his haunting
phrase *velut in Cimmeriis tenebris reptabamus* (29.2.4). See for *fluctuantes* the note ad *ancipitique sententia fluctuans* (20.4.9).

exstructis aris caesisque hostiis This precise circumstantial detail may
be another personal memory. Its wording could, however, have been
inspired by *exstructis altaribus caesisque victimis* (Tac. *Hist.* 2.20.2) or
exstructis in campo Martio aris (Tac. *Hist.* 2.95.1); cf. also *ad aram Divo
Iulio exstructam* (Suet. *Aug.* 15). See further 24.6.16 *complures hostias*
with the note.

consulta numinum citabantur Fontaine also accepts V's text. This is
remarkable, since at 19.12.4 Seyfarth and Sabbah both print the
same phrase with *scitabantur*; see De Jonge's note ad loc. See for
consulta, "advice", "Weisungen", Austin and Heubner ad Verg. *A.*
6.151 and Tac. *Hist.* 4.65.4 respectively. In Amm.'s other two instances of *citare* (15.6.1, 29.1.44) the verb means 'to summon' in a
legal sense. See, however, Leeman e.a. ad Cic. *de Orat.* 1.251: "*citare*
scheint Terminus technicus für das Singen von Hymnen zu sein,
worin Götter 'angerufen' werden". Nevertheless, a personal form of
scitari should be preferred, as was advocated in the note ad 22.12.7.
Presumably perturbed by the absence of a clear subject, Clark, following Wagner-Erfurdt, prints *scitabamur*. It might be objected that
Amm. uses the we-style in his role as an ordinary participant of the
campaign and consulting the entrails of the sacrificed animals is the
specific task of the authorities. Moreover, *humani sensus* refers in
the first place to the officials and it can function as Agens of both
proficerent and *scitabantur*, which is perhaps the most likely correction
of V.

*utrum nos per Assyriam reverti censerent an praeter radices montium lenius
gradientes Chiliocomum prope Corduenam situm ex improviso vastare* TLL
III 793.65 lists this as an example of *censere* with (acc.c.) inf. praes.
or perf. as a synonym of *iubere* or *sancire*; cf. e.g. Tac. *Hist.* 1.39.1 *cum
alii in Palatium redire... censerent*, Tert. *Nat.* 2.7 *poetas eliminari Plato
censuit*.

   The dilemma implied in §2–3 is stated here in different terms:
per Assyriam reverti is the wish of the common soldiers (cf. *reverti... per*

CHAPTER 8.5   229

loca, quae venimus in §2; see for *Assyria* the notes ad 23.2.7 and
23.6.14–15), Julian and many others (whose alternative plan is not
yet mentioned in §§2–3; Amm. there only gives their arguments
against the proposal of the *plebs imprudens*) wanted to go through *Chiliocomum prope Corduenam* (see for these regions the notes ad 23.3.5).
In §5 it becomes clear that Julian cum suis won: *sedit... sententia,
ut... Corduenam arriperemus.*

As to the alternative routes, Amm.'s words in 23.3 may help
to clarify the present text. In 23.3.1 Amm. had said that two different royal roads led from Carrhae to Persia, the one on the left
through Adiabene and across the Tigris, the other through Assyria
and along the Euphrates (*unde duae ducentes Persidem viae regiae distin-
guntur, laeva per Adiabenam et Tigridem, dextra per Assyrios et Euphraten*).
Julian himself, in order to go southwards, had taken the western
road (23.3.6), Procopius and Sebastianus (see for them below, ad
§6) the eastern road, which brought them i.a. through Corduena,
Moxoena and Chiliocomum (23.3.5). In the present text it is the
other way around for Julian: in order to go north he takes, with
his army, the royal road east of the Tigris in the direction of Corduena.

lenius gradientes Cf. 15.10.9 (about Hercules) *lenius gradiens*, 18.2.10
leniter incedentes, 18.6.15 *duci lenius gradienti*, 19.2.2 *clementi gradu
incedentes*, 19.2.3 *leniter incedebant*, 24.6.10 *lenius procedebant*. In all
these cases a quiet, 'leisurely', march is meant, and here the phrase
seems to hint at the choice which was going to be made.

quorum neutrum extis inspectis confore dicebatur The gods' verdict was
clear: both courses envisaged by the human mind were doomed
to failure, and there was no workable alternative. See the note ad
21.1.10 for the verbs used with *exta*. The inf. fut. *confore* is a rarity.
There seems to be no other instance besides Ter. *Andr.* 167, where it
is explained as *perfectum iri* by Donatus (Leumann 530 is slightly more
precise with *confectum iri*), and Dict. 2.22. Concerning the present
text Wagner notes: "*Confore*] συντελεσθήσεσθαι".

sedit tamen sententia The use of *sedere* in phrases expressing a firm   **8.5**
decision is Vergilian: e.g. *sedet hoc animo* (A. 2.660, with Austin's
note), *idque pio sedet Aeneae* (A. 5.418), *ubi certa sedet patribus sententia
pugnae* (A. 7.611, with Horsfall's note). Amm. imitates it on nine
occasions. See the note ad 14.1.5 for a short survey of the various
syntactical patterns.

230 COMMENTARY

ut omni spe meliorum succisa Corduenam arriperemus Because these words express the contents of the decision, presumably those who took the decision, viz. the emperor and his staff, are to be regarded as the Agens of *succisa*; *succidere* would then be a strong equivalent of 'to abandon': they decided to abandon all hope of a better outcome of the campaign etc. It is, however, also imaginable that *spe meliorum succisa* is the reason for the decision: 'since all hope had been dashed', comparable to *spe meliorum abolita* (17.9.4). See for *arripere* expressing determination the note ad 24.7.3.

sextum decimum kalendas Iulias I.e. June 16, 363. This is the first time since 23.5.12 *septimum idus Apriles* that Amm. gives a precise date.

promotis iam signis See for *promovere signa* (or *castra*) the relevant note ad 21.5.13.

vis quaedam turbinata pulveris *Vis* meaning 'a (large) quantity' is already usual in classical Latin, cf. e.g. Sal. *Jug.* 75.7 *vis aquae*, Liv. 30.6.9 *magna armorum vis capta*. The adj. *turbinatus* occurs in various descriptions in Plin. *Nat.*, and its meaning 'cone-shaped' is perhaps best represented by 15.58 *turbinatior piris figura*. The modern reader almost immediately visualizes a tornado, but Amm. and his fellow campaigners react differently. It should be noted that *ventorum... turbo exortus* (24.1.11, q.v.) is the only instance in Amm. where *turbo* denotes a storm of whirlwinds. The whirl of dust in 24.6.10 (q.v.) is caused by human action. All Amm.'s other instances of *turbo* are metaphorical.

ut opinari daretur asinorum esse greges agrestium See for *datur* as a synonym of *licet* or *fieri potest* TLL V 1.1689.48ff., Kühner-Stegmann 1.675, Szantyr 345 and the note ad 16.10.11. Amm. has *ut opinari dabatur* in 19.2.13, 26.1.7, 26.10.16, 28.6.24, 31.13.12. The present text is the only instance where the phrase is not used parenthetically. See Olck, 1909, 628–31, Toynbee, 1973, 192–3 and Raepsaet, 1998, 130 on wild asses. As Brok 167 notes, Xenophon had also seen them during the anabasis (*An.* 1.5.2).

feroces leonum... assultus See for lions the note ad 24.5.2.

8.6 *Arsacen ac duces adventare iam nostros rumoribus percitos, quod imperator Ctesiphonta magnis viribus oppugnaret* As in 24.7.8 (*cum Arsace et nostris ducibus*, see the note ad loc.), Amm. does not mention by name the

CHAPTER 8.7   231

two Roman generals in question, viz. Procopius and Sebastianus, who had been ordered in the early days of the Persian campaign to effect a joining of forces with the Armenian king Arsaces, to march with him through Corduena and Moxoena, to lay waste in passing by Chiliocomum and other regions – note that Chiliocomum and Corduena are also mentioned in §4–5 of the present chapter – and finally to meet Julian in Mesopotamia to reinforce him in case of necessity (23.3.5, q.v.). A sustained and full-blown siege of Ctesiphon (see for this city the note ad 24.2.7) would indeed have been a case of necessity. See the notes ad 20.11.5 and 21.7.7 for Amm.'s predeliction for *percitus*.

nonnulli Persas nobis viantibus incubuisse firmabant See for the late Latin verb *viare* the note ad 19.8.10. This is the only instance in Amm. of *incumbere* with dat. as a synonym of "irruere, c. impetu se inferre, aggredi" (TLL VII 1.1074.70 ff.). See for *firmare* as a synonym of *affirmare* the note ad 20.8.15.

inter haec ita ambigua See for this use of *inter* the note ad 17.4.1, **8.7** and for *ita* qualifying an adj. or adv. with reference to a preceding statement the note ad 20.11.5. The same phrase occurs in 19.11.1; cf. also *inter quae ita ambigua* (17.6.1). In both these cases the phrase is used to change the scene to an entirely different part of the world. Here, however, it explains why it was decided to make a halt.

ne quid adversum accideret See the note ad 20.5.6 for this euphemism and the note ad 20.4.15 on the use of an adj. instead of a gen.

revocantibus agmina classicis This is not superfluous, but a deft descriptive touch: the author remembers how in the murky atmosphere the sound of the trumpets signalled the decision to stop the march. Veg. *mil.* 2.2.3 is very helpful to understand the full meaning of the phrase: *Hoc insigne videtur imperii; quia classicum canitur imperatore praesente.* See for *classicum* the note ad 24.6.11.

in valle graminea prope rivum All geographical details are lacking. Possibly the Douros (Diyala), mentioned by Zos. 3.26.4 (cf. Paschoud n. 75), as in 25.1.2 *fluvio brevi.* But see Fontaine n. 472: "il peut s'agir également d'un canal d'irrigation". In the author's memory the spot was a 'locus amoenus'; cf. e.g. Hor. *Epod.* 2.23–5 *libet iacere modo sub antiqua ilice / modo in tenaci gramine: / labuntur altis interim ripis aquae.*

232 COMMENTARY

multiplicato scutorum ordine in orbiculatam figuram In 19.2.2 a multiple row of shields is employed in laying siege to a town. See the note ad 24.4.10 on similar expressions. Here, as in 16.12.62, it functions as a measure to increase the safety of the encampment in order to strengthen the soldiers' confidence. In 31.2.18 Amm. reports that on reaching grassy surroundings, the Halani place their wagons *in orbiculatam figuram.*

metatis tutius quievimus castris Cf. *metatis alibi salubrius castris* (24.4.6, q.v.) and see Vegetius' long chapter on the necessity of accurately choosing and measuring the site for an encampment (Veg. *mil.* 3.8). With *quievimus* Amm. adds a further detail to his impressions of the short breathing space amidst the dangers posed by nature and the enemy.

nec enim ... squalidius videbatur With the particle *enim* indicating consensus (see for this Kroon, 1995, 171–209) Amm. appeals to his readers' understanding: what else could have been done in the dusty darkness? Cf. for *concreto aere* 19.4.8 *concreto spiritu et crassato* (the sticky atmosphere at Amida), 22.8.46 *quod et concrescat aer ex umorum spiramine saepe densetus* (the misty character of the Black Sea). Fontaine's *hic squalidius* is very near to V, but his own explanation in n. 473 ("en cet endroit dont je viens de parler") seems to show the superfluity of *hic.* According to Sabbah 566 n. 77, "le terme *squalor* et les mots de sa famille *squaleo, squalidus, squalide* sont parmi les plus révélateurs de la sensibilité et de l'imagination d'Ammien". However, one should distinguish between the unclear view which Constantius (21.14.2, q.v.) and Julian (25.2.3) respectively had of their *genius* and the restricted eyesight caused by a *crassae caliginis squalor* (17.7.2) during the earthquake at Nicomedia, or the problems described in the present text. The next day it became clear that the *nonnulli* of §6 were right: *ubi vero primum dies inclaruit, radiantes loricae limbis circumdatae ferreis et corusci thoraces longe prospecti adesse regis copias indicabant* (25.1.1).

BIBLIOGRAPHY

This is not an exhaustive or selective list of handbooks, monographs and articles pertaining to the study of Ammianus Marcellinus. It only registers all publications referred to in the commentary after the manner described in section 3 of the *Legenda*. *RE*-articles are cited after the date of the second 'Halbband'.

Abdul Khaliq, H., 'Results of Excavations in Tulul Jumeyʿa in Medaʿin (Ctesiphon)', *Sumer* 44 (1985–1986) 111–138 (Arabic; English translation in *Suppl. to Sumer* 44, 1985–1986 [2000] 15–35).

Adams, R. McC., *Land behind Baghdad. A History of Settlement on the Diyala Plains*, Chicago 1965.

Adams, R. McC., *Heartland of Cities: Surveys and Ancient Settlement and Land Use on the Central Floodplain of the Euphrates*, Chicago-London 1981.

Adkin, N., 'The Younger Pliny and Ammianus Marcellinus', *CQ* 48 (1998) 593–595.

Aldrete, G.S., *Gestures and Acclamations in Ancient Rome*, Baltimore-London 1999.

Alföldi, A., 'Insignien und Tracht der römischen Kaiser', *MDAI(R)* 50 (1935) 3–158 = *Die monarchische Repräsentation im römischen Kaiserreiche*, Darmstadt 1980³, 121–276, cited as Alföldi, 1980³.

Al-Khashab, Wafiq Hussain, *The Water Budget of the Tigris and Euphrates Basin*, Diss. Chicago 1958.

Altheim, F., and R. Stiehl, *Die Araber in der alten Welt*, II, Berlin 1965.

Anderson, G., *Lucian. Theme and Variation in the Second Sophistic*, Leiden 1976.

Andreotti, R., 'L'impresa di Giuliano in Oriente', *Historia* 4 (1930) 236–273.

Angliviel de la Beaumelle, L., 'La torture dans les *Res Gestae* d'Ammien Marcellin', in: M. Christol e.a. (eds.), *Institutions, société et vie politique dans l'empire romain au IVe siècle ap. J.-C.* (Actes de la table ronde autour de l'oeuvre d'André Chastagnol, Paris, 20–21 janvier 1989), Rome 1992, 91–113.

Angliviel de la Beaumelle, L., see also G. Sabbah.

Appel, G., *De Romanorum precationibus* (Religionsgeschichtliche Versuche und Vorarbeiten VII.2), Giessen 1909 (repr. New York 1975).

Arce, J.J., 'El historiador Ammiano Marcellino y la pena de muerte', *HAnt* 4 (1974) 321–344.

Arce, J.J., 'On Festus' Sources for Julian's Persian Expedition', *Athenaeum* 52 (1974) 340–343.

Astin, A.E., *Scipio Aemilianus*, Oxford 1967.

Austin, N.J.E., 'Julian at Ctesiphon: A Fresh Look at Ammianus' Account', *Athenaeum* 50 (1972) 301–309.

Austin, N.J.E., *Ammianus on Warfare. An Investigation into Ammianus' Military*

234 BIBLIOGRAPHY

Knowledge, Brussels 1979.

Austin, N.J.E., and N.B. Rankov, *Exploratio. Military and Political Intelligence in the Roman World from the Second Punic War to the Battle of Adrianople*, London 1995.

Baatz, D., *Bauten und Katapulte des römischen Heeres*, Stuttgart 1994.

Baehrens, W.A., 'Beiträge zur lateinischen Syntax', *Philologus* Suppl. 12 (1912) 233–556.

Baehrens, W.A., 'Bericht über die Literatur zu einigen wichtigen römischen Schriftstellern des 3. und 4. Jahrhunderts aus den Jahren 1910/1–1924, I. Ammianus Marcellinus', *JAW* 203 (1925) 46–90.

Bagnall, R.S., A. Cameron, S.R. Schwartz and K.A. Worp, *Consuls of the Later Roman Empire*, Atlanta 1987.

Baldwin, B., 'Some Addenda to the Prosopography of the Later Roman Empire', *Historia* 25 (1976) 118–121.

Ball, W., *Rome in the East. The Transformation of an Empire*, London-New York 2000.

Barnes, T.D., 'Some Persons in the *Historia Augusta*', *Phoenix* 26 (1972) 140–182.

Barnes, T.D., 'Literary Convention, Nostalgia and Reality in Ammianus Marcellinus', in: G. Clarke e.a. (eds.), *Reading the Past in Late Antiquity*, Rushcutters Bay 1990, 59–92.

Barnes, T.D., *Ammianus Marcellinus and the Representation of Historical Reality*, Ithaca-London 1998.

Barnett, R.D., 'Xenophon and the Wall of Media', *JHS* 83 (1963) 1–26.

Benedetti Martig, I., *Studi sulla guerra persiana nell' Orazione funebre per Giuliano di Libanio*, Florence 1990.

Bennett, J., *Trajan, Optimus Princeps*, London 1997 (repr. 2001).

Benzinger, I., 'Chalkis 14', *RE* 3 (1899) 2090–2091.

Bitter, N., *Kampfschilderungen bei Ammianus Marcellinus*, Bonn 1976.

Bivar, A.D.H., 'The Political History of Iran under the Arsacids', in: E. Yarshater (ed.), *The Cambridge History of Iran* 3.1, Cambridge 1983, 21–99.

Blázquez, J.M., 'Bellona', *LIMC* 3.1 (1986) 92–93.

Bliembach, E., *Libanius, Oratio 18 (Epitaphios). Kommentar (§§ 111–308)*, Diss. Würzburg 1976.

Blockley, R.C., 'Festus' Source on Julian's Persian Expedition', *CPh* 68 (1973) 54–55.

Blockley, R.C., *Ammianus Marcellinus. A Study of his Historiography and Political Thought*, Brussels 1975.

Blockley, R.C., 'The Roman-Persian Peace Treaties of A.D. 299 and 363', *Florilegium* 6 (1984) 28–49.

Blockley, R.C., 'Subsidies and Diplomacy: Rome and Persia in Late Antiquity', *Phoenix* 39 (1985) 62–74.

Blockley, R.C., 'The Division of Armenia between the Romans and the Persians at the End of the Fourth Century A.D.', *Historia* 36 (1987) 222–234.

Blockley, R.C., 'Ammianus Marcellinus's Use of *Exempla*', *Florilegium* 13

BIBLIOGRAPHY 235

(1994) 53–64.

Blomgren, S., *De sermone Ammiani Marcellini quaestiones variae*, Uppsala 1937.

Bouffartigue, J., *L'Empereur Julien et la culture de son temps*, Paris 1992.

Bowersock, G.W., *Julian the Apostate*, Cambridge Mass.-London 1978.

Bowersock, G.W., 'Mavia, Queen of the Saracens', in: G.W. Bowersock, *Studies on the Eastern Roman Empire: social, economic and administrative history, religion, historiography*, Goldbach 1994, 127–140 (=W. Eck, H. Galsterer and H. Wolff [eds.], *Studien zur antiken Sozialgeschichte*. Festschrift Friedrich Vittinghoff, Cologne 1980, 477–495).

Bowersock, G.W., 'La Mésène (Maišân) Antonine', in: T. Fahd (ed.), *L'Arabie préislamique et son environnement historique et culturel*, Leiden 1989, 159–168.

Brand, C.E., *Roman Military Law*, Austin-London 1968.

Brandt, A., *Moralische Werte in den Res gestae des Ammianus Marcellinus* (Hypomnemata 122), Göttingen 1999.

Briant, P., *Histoire de l'empire perse de Cyrus à Alexandre*, 2 vols., Leiden 1996.

Briant, P., 'Katarraktai du Tigre et *muballitum* du Habur', *NABU* (1999) 15–16.

Briscoe, J., *A Commentary on Livy. Books XXXIV–XXXVII*, Oxford 1981.

Brok, M.F.A., *De Perzische expeditie van keizer Julianus volgens Ammianus Marcellinus*, Groningen 1959.

Broughton, T.R.S., *The Magistrates of the Roman Republic*, I, New York 1951; III, Atlanta 1984.

Browning, R., *The Emperor Julian*, Berkeley-Los Angeles 1976.

Buck, D.F., 'Some Distortions in Eunapius' Account of Julian the Apostate', *AHB* 4.5 (1990) 113–115.

Butzer, K.W., 'Environmental Change in the Near East and Human Impact on the Land', in: J.M. Sasson e.a. (eds.), *Civilizations of the Ancient Near East*, I, New York 1995, 123–151.

Caltabiano, M., *Ammiano Marcellino. Storie*, Milan 1989.

Callu, J.P., 'Denier et Nummus (300–354)', in: *Les "dévaluations" à Rome. Époque républicaine et impériale*, Rome 1978, 107–121.

Cameron, A.D.E., 'An Alleged Fragment of Eunapius', *CQ* 13 (1963) 232–236.

Campbell, J.B., *The Emperor and the Roman Army, 31 BC – AD 235*, Oxford 1984 (repr. 1996).

Camus, P.-M., *Ammien Marcellin. Témoin des courants culturels et religieux à la fin du IVe siècle*, Paris 1967.

Cansdale, G., *All the Animals of the Bible Lands*, Grand Rapids 1970.

Češka, J., 'Ad Ammiani Marcellini libros XXII–XXXI a W. Seyfarth novissime editos adnotationes criticae', *Eirene* 12 (1974) 87–110.

Chalmers, W.R., 'An Alleged Doublet in Ammianus Marcellinus', *RhM* 102 (1959) 183–189.

Chalmers, W.R., 'Eunapius, Ammianus Marcellinus, and Zosimus on Julian's Persian Expedition', *CQ* 10 (1960) 152–160 (='Julians Perserzug bei Eunapius, Ammianus Marcellinus und Zosimus', in: R. Klein, ed., *Julian Apostata*, Darmstadt 1978, 270–284).

236 BIBLIOGRAPHY

Chaumont, M.-L., 'Études d'histoire Parthe. V. La route royale des Parthes de Zeugma à Séleucie du Tigre d'après l'itinéraire d'Isidore de Charax', *Syria* 61 (1984) 63–107.

Chesney, F.R., *The Expedition for the Survey of the Rivers Euphrates and Tigris, carried on by Order of the British Government in the Years 1835, 1836, and 1837, preceded by geographical and historical Notices of the Regions situated between the Rivers Nile and Indus*, London 1850 (repr. New York 1969).

Chesney, F.R., *Narrative of the Euphrates Expedition carried on by Order of the British Government during the Years 1835, 1836, and 1837*, London 1868.

Chioffi, L., and A. Viscogliosi, 'Bellona', in E.M. Steinby (ed.), *Lexicon Topographicum Urbis Romae*, I, Rome 1993, 190–194.

Christensen, A., *L'Iran sous les Sassanides*, Copenhagen 1944² (repr. Osnabrück 1971).

Clark, C.U., *Ammiani Marcellini rerum gestarum libri qui supersunt*, Berlin 1910–1915 (repr. 1963).

Coello, T.E., *Unit Sizes in the Late Roman Army*, n. pl. 1995 (Diss. Open University).

Cole, S.W., and H. Gasche, 'Second- and First-Millennium BC Rivers in Northern Babylonia', in: H. Gasche and M. Tanret (eds.), *Changing Watercourses in Babylonia. Towards a Reconstruction of the Ancient Environment in Lower Mesopotamia*, I, Ghent-Chicago 1998, 1–64.

Colledge, M.A.R., *Parthian Art*, Ithaca 1977.

Cornelissen, J.J., 'Ad Ammianum Marcellinum adversaria critica', *Mnemosyne* 14 (1886) 234–304.

Coulston, J.C.N., 'The 'draco' standard', *JRMES* 2 (1991) 101–114.

Crump, G.A., *Ammianus Marcellinus as a Military Historian*, Wiesbaden 1975.

Criniti, N., 'La nuova prosopografia dell' età tardo-imperiale Romana', *NRS* 58 (1974) 135–152.

Daremberg, C., E. Saglio and E. Pottier, *Dictionnaire des antiquités grecques et romaines d'après les textes et les monuments*, Paris 1877–1919 (repr. 1962–1963).

Delmaire, R., *Largesses sacrées et res privata. L'Aerarium impérial et son administration du IVᵉ au VIᵉ siècle*, Rome 1989.

Demandt, A., 'Magister militum', *RE* Suppl. 12 (1970) 553–790.

Demandt, A., *Die Spätantike. Römische Geschichte von Diocletian bis Justinian 284–565 n. Chr.*, Munich 1989.

Demisch, H., *Erhobene Hände. Geschichte einer Gebärde in der bildenden Kunst*, Stuttgart 1984.

Dennis, G.T., 'Byzantine Battle Flags', *ByzF* 8 (1982) 51–59.

Dillemann, L., 'Ammien Marcellin et les pays de l'Euphrate et du Tigre', *Syria* 38 (1961) 87–158.

Di Maio, M., '*Infaustis ductoribus praeviis*: the Antiochene Connection, Part II', *Byzantion* 51 (1981) 502–510.

Dodgeon, M.H., and S.N.C. Lieu, *The Roman Eastern Frontier and the Persian Wars (AD 226–363). A Documentary History*, London-New York 1991 (repr. 1994).

Domaszewski, A. von, 'Architectus', *RE* 2 (1896) 551–552.

BIBLIOGRAPHY

Driel-Murray, C. van, 'New Light on Old Tents', *JRMES* 1 (1990) 109–137.

Duchesne-Guillemin, J., *La religion de l'Iran ancien*, Paris 1962.

Dufraigne, P., 'Quelques remarques sur l'*adventus* chez Ammien Marcellin et les Panégyristes', in: L. Holtz and J.Cl. Fredouille (eds.), *De Tertullien aux Mozarabes*. Mélanges offerts à Jacques Fontaine à l'occasion de son 70e anniversaire par ses élèves, amis et collègues, I, Paris 1992, 497–509.

Ehrismann, H., *De temporum et modorum usu Ammianeo*, Diss. Strasbourg 1886.

Fiebiger, H.O., 'Corona', *RE* 4 (1901) 1636–1643.

Fiebiger, H.O., 'Decimatio', *RE* 4 (1901) 2272.

Fiey, J.M., 'Topography of Al-Mada'in (Seleucia-Ctesiphon area)', *Sumer* 23 (1967) 3–38.

Fisher, W.B., *The Middle East. A Physical, Social and Regional Geography*, London 1950 (1978[7]).

Fletcher, G.B.A., 'Notes on Ammianus Marcellinus', *CQ* 24 (1930) 193–197.

Fletcher, G.B.A., 'Ammianea', *AJPh* 58 (1937) 392–402.

Fontaine, J., *Ammien Marcellin, Histoire, IV (Livres XXIII–XXV)*, 2 vols., Paris 1977.

Forbes, R.J., *Studies in Ancient Technology I: Bitumen and Petroleum in Antiquity. The Origin of Alchemy. Water Supply*, Leiden 1955.

Fornara, C.W., 'Julian's Persian expedition in Ammianus and Zosimus', *JHS* 111 (1991) 1–15.

Fornara, C.W., 'Studies in Ammianus Marcellinus, II: Ammianus' Knowledge and Use of Greek and Latin Literature', *Historia* 41 (1992) 420–438.

Fraenkel, E., 'Das Geschlecht von *dies*', *Glotta* 8 (1917) 24–68.

Frakes, R.M., 'Ammianus Marcellinus and Osroëne', *AHB* 7.4 (1993) 143–147.

Frank, R.I., *Scholae Palatinae. The Palace Guards of the Later Roman Empire*, Rome 1969.

Galter, H.D., 'Paradies und Palmentod. Ökologische Aspekte im Weltbild der Assyrischen Könige', in: B. Scholz, *Der orientalische Mensch und seine Beziehungen zur Umwelt*, Graz 1989, 235–253.

Gasche, H., see S.W. Cole.

Gawlikowski, M., 'La route de l'Euphrate d'Isidore à Julien', in: P.-L. Gatier, B. Helly and J.-P. Rey-Coquais (eds.), *Géographie historique au Proche-Orient (Syrie, Phénicie, Arabie, grecques, romaines, byzantines)*, Paris 1990, 77–98.

Ghirshman, R., *Iran, Parthes et Sassanides*, Paris 1962.

Gignoux, Ph., *Noms propres sassanides en moyen-Perse épigraphique*, Vienna 1986 (=M. Mayrhofer and R. Schmitt [eds.], *Iranisches Personennamenbuch*, II.2).

Gilliam, J.F., 'Ammianus and the Historia Augusta: the Lost Books and the Period 117–285', *BHAC* 1970, Bonn 1972, 125–147.

Gordon, C.D., 'Subsidies in Roman Imperial Defence', *Phoenix* 3 (1949) 60–69.

Graeve, M.-C. de, *The Ships of the Ancient Near East (c. 2000–500 B.C.)*, Louvain 1981.

Greatrex, G.B., 'The Background and Aftermath of the Partition of Armenia in A.D. 387', *AHB* 14.1–2 (2000) 35–48.

238 BIBLIOGRAPHY

Grosse, R., *Römische Militärgeschichte von Gallienus bis zum Beginn der byzantinischen Themenverfassung*, Berlin 1920.

Grotefend, H., *Taschenbuch der Zeitrechnung des deutschen Mittelalters und der Neuzeit*, Hannover 1971[11].

Grumel, V., *La Chronologie*, Paris 1958.

Gschnitzer, F., 'Phylarchos', *RE* Suppl. 11 (1968) 1067–1090.

Guarducci, M., 'Il santuario di Bellona e il Circo Flaminio in un epigramma greco del basso impero', *BCAR* 73 (1949–1950 [1952]) 55–76.

Günther, O., 'Zur Textkritik des Ammianus Marcellinus', *Philologus* 50 (1891) 65–73.

Gullini, G., 'Problems of an Excavation in Northern Babylon', *Mesopotamia* 1 (1966) 7–38.

Hagendahl, H., *Studia Ammianea*, Diss. Uppsala 1921.

Hagendahl, H., *Die Perfektformen auf -ere und -erunt. Ein Beitrag zur Technik der späteren lateinischen Kunstprosa*, Leipzig 1923.

Harper, P.O., *The Royal Hunter. Art of the Sasanian Empire*, New York 1978.

Harper, P.O., 'Art in Iran, V. Sasanian', *Encyclopaedia Iranica* 2 (1986) 585–594.

Hartke, W., 'Eidesleistungen der römischen Kaiser Trajan und Julian auf die Erfüllung grosser Planziele. Zu einer Episode bei Ammianus Marcellinus', *Philologus* 119 (1975) 179–214.

Haupt, M., *Opuscula* II, Leipzig 1876 (repr. Hildesheim 1967).

Heimpel, W., and L. Trümpelmann, 'Jagd', *Reallexikon der Assyriologie* 5 (1976–1980) 234–238.

Hengel, M., *Crucifixion in the ancient world and the folly of the message of the cross*, London-Philadelphia 1977.

Heraeus, W., 'Die römische Soldatensprache', *ALL* 12 (1902) 255–280.

Hertz, M., 'Aulus Gellius und Ammianus Marcellinus', *Hermes* 8 (1874) 257–302.

Herzfeld, E., see F. Sarre.

Heus, W.E., 'Spätrömische coronae militares', in: J. den Boeft and A.H.M. Kessels (eds.), *Actus. Studies in Honour of H.L.W. Nelson*, Utrecht 1982, 109–113.

Hoffmann, D., *Das spätrömische Bewegungsheer und die Notitia Dignitatum*, 2 vols., Düsseldorf 1969–1970.

Hofmann, J.B., 'Das Geschlecht von *dies*', *Philologus* 93 (1938) 265–273.

Hofmann, J.B., and A. Szantyr, *Lateinische Syntax und Stilistik*, Munich 1965 (repr. 1972), cited as Szantyr.

Honigmann, E., 'Ktesiphon', *RE* Suppl. 4 (1924) 1102–1119.

Honigmann, E., and A. Maricq, *Recherches sur les Res Gestae Divi Saporis* (Koninklijke Belgische Academie. Klasse der Letteren en der Morele en Staatkundige Wetenschappen, Verhandelingen, Verzameling in 8°, Tweede reeks, boek XLVII, fasc. 4), Brussels 1952.

Hopkins, C., 'The Parthian Temple', *Berytus* 7 (1942) 1–18.

Howard-Johnston, J., 'The Two Great Powers in Late Antiquity: A Comparison', in: Averil Cameron (ed.), *The Byzantine and Early Islamic Near East* III, *States, Resources and Armies*, Princeton 1995, 157–226.

BIBLIOGRAPHY   239

Hünemörder, C., 'Fliege', *DNP* 4 (1998) 559–560.

Hünemörder, C., 'Mücke', *DNP* 8 (2000) 429–430.

Ionides, M.G., *The Régime of the Rivers Euphrates and Tigris: a general hydraulic Survey of their Basins*, London 1937.

Isaac, B., see A. Oppenheimer.

Jonge, P. de, *Sprachlicher und Historischer Kommentar zu Ammianus Marcellinus* c.q. *Philological and Historical Commentary on Ammianus Marcellinus*, XIV–XIX, Groningen 1935–1982.

Justi, F., *Iranisches Namenbuch*, Marburg 1895 (repr. Hildesheim-New York 1963).

Kaegi, W., 'Constantine's and Julian's Strategies of Strategic Surprise against the Persians', *Athenaeum* 59 (1981) 209–213.

Keller, O., *Die antike Tierwelt*, 2 vols., Hildesheim-New York 1980².

Kellerbauer, A., 'Kritische Kleinigkeiten (zu Ammianus Marcellinus)', *Blätter für das Bayerische Gymnasialschulwesen* 9 (1873) 81–91, 127–141.

Kempf, I.G., *Romanorum sermonis castrensis reliquiae collectae et illustratae*, Leipzig 1901 (=*Jahrb. f. class. Philol.*, Suppl. Bd. 26, 1901, 340–400).

Kennedy, D.L., 'Ana on the Euphrates in the Roman Period', *Iraq* 48 (1986) 103–104.

Kennedy, D.L., and D. Riley, *Rome's Desert Frontier from the Air*, London 1990.

Kienast, D., *Römische Kaisertabelle. Grundzüge einer römischen Kaiserchronologie*, Darmstadt 1996².

Klein, R., 'Julian Apostata. Ein Lebensbild', *Gymnasium* 93 (1986) 273–292.

Klein, W., *Studien zu Ammianus Marcellinus*, Leipzig 1914.

Klotz, A., 'Die Quellen Ammians in der Darstellung von Julians Perserzug', *RhM* 71 (1916) 461–506.

Köves-Zulauf, Th., 'Der Zweikampf des Valerius Corvus und die Alternativen römischen Heldentums', *A&A* 31 (1985) 66–75.

Konrad, C.F., *Plutarch's Sertorius. A Historical Commentary*, Chapel Hill-London 1994.

Kroon, C.H.M., *Discourse Particles in Latin. A Study of nam, enim, autem, vero, and at*, Amsterdam 1995.

Kroon, C.H.M., and P. Rose, 'Atrociter corruptus? The use of 'narrative' tenses in Ammianus Marcellinus' *Res Gestae*', in: R. Risselada, J.R. de Jong and A.M. Bolkestein (eds.), *On Latin*. Linguistic and Literary Studies in Honour of Harm Pinkster, Amsterdam 1996, 71–89.

Kroon, C.H.M., and R. Risselada, 'The Discourse Functions of *iam*', *Estudios de lingüística latina (Actas del IX Coloquio Internacional de Lingüística Latina)*, I, Madrid 1998, 429–445.

Krylová, B., 'Die Partikeln *ergo* und *igitur* bei Ammianus Marcellinus. Ein textologischer Beitrag zur Diskussion um Ammians Sprachkompetenz', in: G. Thome, J. Holzhausen, S. Anzinger (eds.), *Es hat sich viel ereignet, Gutes wie Böses. Lateinische Geschichtsschreibung der Spät- und Nachantike*, Munich 2001, 57–79.

Kühner, R., and C. Stegmann, *Ausführliche Grammatik der lateinischen Sprache* II, *Satzlehre*, 2 vols., Hannover 1955⁴, 1976⁵.

Laere, R. Van, 'Encore le Naarmalcha…', in: J. Quaegebeur (ed.), *Studia*

240 BIBLIOGRAPHY

Paulo Naster oblata, II, *Orientalia Antiqua* (Orientalia Lovaniensia Analecta, 13), Leuven 1982, 269–277.

Lammert, F., 'Veles', *RE* 8A (1958) 624–625.

Lane Fox, R., *Pagans and Christians in the Mediterranean World from the Second Century A.D. to the Conversion of Constantine*, Harmondsworth 1988 (=1986).

Lane Fox, R., 'The Itinerary of Alexander: Constantius to Julian', *CQ* 47 (1997) 239–252.

Latte, K., *Römische Religionsgeschichte*, Munich 1960.

Le Bohec, Y., *The Imperial Roman Army*, London 1994.

Lecker, M., see A. Oppenheimer.

Lehnen, J., *Adventus principis. Untersuchungen zu Sinngehalt und Zeremoniell der Kaiserankunft in den Städten des Imperium Romanum*, Frankfurt am Main 1997.

Lenzen, H.J., 'Architektur der Partherzeit und ihre Brückenstellung zwischen der Architektur des Westens und des Ostens', in: G. Bruns (ed.), *Festschrift für C. Weickert*, Berlin 1955, 121–136.

Leumann, M., *Lateinische Laut- und Formenlehre*, Munich 1977.

Liebeschuetz, W., 'Ammianus, Julian and Divination', in: M. Wissemann (ed.), *Roma Renascens. Beiträge zur Spätantike und Rezeptionsgeschichte* (Festschrift für Ilona Opelt), Frankfurt am Main 1988, 198–213.

Lieu, S.N.C., 'Captives, Refugees and Exiles: A Study of Cross-Frontier Civilian Movements and Contacts between Rome and Persia from Valerian to Jovian', in: Ph. Freeman and D.L. Kennedy (eds.), *The Defence of the Roman and Byzantine East*, 2 vols. (BAR International Series, 297), Oxford 1986, 475–505.

Lieu, S.N.C., see also M.H. Dodgeon.

Lippold, A., 'Iulianus I (Kaiser)', *RAC* Lieferung 148–149/50 (1999–2000) 442–483.

Löfstedt, E., *Philologischer Kommentar zur Peregrinatio Aetheriae. Untersuchungen zur Geschichte der lateinischen Sprache*, Uppsala 1911.

Löfstedt, E., *Syntactica. Studien und Beiträge zur historischen Syntax des Lateins*, I, Lund 1942² (repr. 1956), II, Lund 1933 (repr. 1956).

Lukonin, V.G., 'Political, Social and Administrative Institutions: Taxes and Trade', in: E. Yarshater (ed.), *The Cambridge History of Iran* 3.2, Cambridge 1983, 681–746.

Magen, U., *Assyrische Königsdarstellungen – Aspekte der Herrschaft*, Mainz 1986.

Maricq, A., 'Classica et Orientalia, V: Res Gestae Divi Saporis', *Syria* 35 (1958) 295–360.

Maricq, A., 'Découverte aérienne d'Anbar', in: A. Maricq, *Classica et Orientalia*, Paris 1965, 147–156.

Maricq, A., see also E. Honigmann.

Marsden, E.W., *Greek and Roman Artillery*, 2 vols, Oxford 1969 and 1971.

Mary, L., '"Navales pontes": logistique et symbolique chez Ammien Marcellin', in: L. Holtz and J.Cl. Fredouille (eds.), *De Tertullien aux Mozarabes. Mélanges offerts à Jacques Fontaine à l'occasion de son 70e anniversaire par ses élèves, amis et collègues*, I, Paris 1992, 595–612.

BIBLIOGRAPHY 241

Mary, L., 'Les captives et le pantomime: Deux rencontres de l'empereur Julien (Ammien Marcellin, 24, 4, 25–27)', *REAug* 39 (1993) 37–56.

Matthews, J.F., *The Roman Empire of Ammianus*, London 1989.

Maxfield, V.A., *The Military Decorations of the Roman Army*, London 1981.

Meurig-Davies, E.L.B., 'Notes on Ammianus Marcellinus', *Latomus* 7 (1948) 213–221.

Michalak, M., 'The Origins and Development of Sassanian Heavy Cavalry', *Folia Orientalia* 24 (1987) 73–86.

Mielczarek, M., *Cataphracti and Clibanarii. Studies on the Heavy Armoured Cavalry of the Ancient World*, Lodz 1993.

Mommsen, Th., 'Bemerkungen zu einzelnen Stellen Ammians', *Gesammelte Schriften* 7, Berlin 1909, 426–429.

Müller, A., 'Militaria aus Ammianus Marcellinus', *Philologus* 64 (1905) 573–632.

Müller, C.F.W., 'Zu Ammianus Marcellinus', *Fleckeisens Jbb.* 19 [107] (1873) 341–365.

Münzer, F., 'Fabricius 9', *RE* 6 (1909) 1931–1938.

Münzer, F., 'Manlius 57', *RE* 14 (1930) 1179–1190.

Musil, A., *The Middle Euphrates. A Topographical Itinerary*, New York 1927 (repr. 1978).

Neue, F., *Formenlehre der lateinische Sprache*. Dritte, sehr vermehrte Auflage von C. Wagener, Leipzig 1892–1905 (repr. Hildesheim 1985).

Neumann, A.R., 'Vigiliae', *RE* Suppl. 9 (1962) 1693–1698.

Neusner, J., *Israel's Politics in Sasanian Iran. Jewish Self-Government in Talmudic Times*, Lanham 1986.

Nicasie, M.J., *Twilight of Empire. The Roman Army from the Reign of Diocletian until the Battle of Adrianople*, Amsterdam 1998.

Nicolle, D., *Sassanian Armies. The Iranian Empire early 3rd to mid-7th Centuries AD*, Stockport 1996.

Norman, A.F., 'Magnus in Ammianus, Eunapius, and Zosimus: New Evidence', *CQ* 7 (1957) 129–133.

Norman, A.F., *Libanius. Selected Works*, I, The Julianic Orations, London-Cambridge Mass. 1969.

Northedge, A., 'Ana in the Classical and Islamic Sources', *Sumer* 39 (1983) 235–239.

Novák, R., 'Kritische Nachlese zu Ammianus Marcellinus', *WS* 33 (1911) 293–322.

Oakley, S.P., 'Single Combat in the Roman Republic', *CQ* 35 (1985) 392–410.

Olck, F., 'Esel', *RE* 6 (1909) 626–676.

Oppenheimer, A., in collaboration with B. Isaac and M. Lecker, *Babylonia Judaica in the Talmudic Period*, Wiesbaden 1983.

Partoens, G., '"Deus agricolam confirmat". L'élaboration de la parabole du semeur dans les *Livres contre Symmaque* de Prudence', in: J. den Boeft and M.L. van Poll-van de Lisdonk (eds.), *The Impact of Scripture in Early Christianity* (Supplements to *Vigiliae Christianae*, 44), Leiden 1999, 161–189.

BIBLIOGRAPHY

Paschoud, F., 'Le Naarmalcha: à propos du tracé d'un canal en Mésopotamie moyenne', *Syria* 55 (1978) 345–359.

Paschoud, F., Zosime, *Histoire Nouvelle*, II.1 *(Livre III)*, Paris 1979.

Peddie, J., *The Roman War Machine*, Stroud 1994.

Petschenig, M., 'Zu Ammian', *Philologus* 50 (1891) 64, 498, 544, 565, 730, 742.

Petschenig, M., 'Bemerkungen zum Texte des Ammianus Marcellinus', *Philologus* 50 (1891) 336–354.

Petschenig, M., 'Bemerkungen zum Texte des Ammianus Marcellinus', *Philologus* 51 (1892) 680–691.

Pinkster, H., *Latin Syntax and Semantics*, London-New York 1990.

PLRE I, *The Prosopography of the Later Roman Empire, I, A.D. 260–395*, A.H.M. Jones, J.R. Martindale and J. Morris (eds.), Cambridge 1971.

Potts, D.T., 'Arabia and the Kingdom of Characene', in: D.T. Potts, *Arabia the Blest. Studies in Arabian Archaeology*, Copenhagen 1988, 137–167.

Raepsaet, G., 'Esel', *DNP* 4 (1998) 129–135.

Rankov, N.B. see N.J.E. Austin.

Richardson jr., L., *A New Topographical Dictionary of Ancient Rome*, Baltimore-London 1992.

Ridley, R.T., 'Notes on Julian's Persian expedition (363)', *Historia* 22 (1973) 317–330.

Rike, R.L., *Apex Omnium. Religion in the Res Gestae of Ammianus*, Berkeley-Los Angeles-London 1987.

Riley, D., see D.L. Kennedy.

Risselada, R., 'Passive, Perspective and Textual Cohesion', in: R. Coleman (ed.), *New Studies in Latin Linguistics*, Amsterdam-Philadelphia 1991, 401–414.

Risselada, R., '*Tandem* and *postremo*: two of a kind?', in R. Risselada (ed.), *Latin in Use. Amsterdam Studies in the Pragmatics of Latin*, Amsterdam 1999, 85–116.

Risselada, R., see also C.H.M. Kroon.

Rolfe, J.C., *Ammianus Marcellinus*, with an English translation, 3 vols., London-Cambridge Mass. 1935–1939 (repr. 1971–1972).

Rose, P., see C.H.M. Kroon.

Rosen, K., *Studien zur Darstellungskunst und Glaubwürdigkeit des Ammianus Marcellinus*, Diss. Heidelberg 1968 (repr. Bonn 1970).

Rostovtzeff, M.I., '*Vexillum* and Victory', *JRS* 32 (1942) 92–106.

Sabbah, G., *La méthode d'Ammien Marcellin. Recherches sur la construction du discours historique dans les* Res Gestae, Paris 1978.

Sabbah, G., 'Ammien Marcellin 24, 7: l'incendie de la flotte. Histoire et tragédie', in: L. Holtz and J.C. Fredouille (eds.), *De Tertullien aux Mozarabes. Mélanges offerts à Jacques Fontaine à l'occasion de son 70e anniversaire par ses élèves, amis et collègues*, I, Paris 1992, 627–642.

Sabbah, G., and L. Angliviel de la Beaumelle, *Ammien Marcellin, Histoire*, VI *(Livres XXIX–XXXI)*, Paris 1999.

Sander, E., 'Das römische Militärstrafrecht', *RhM* 103 (1960) 289–319.

BIBLIOGRAPHY

Sarre, F., and E. Herzfeld, *Archaeologische Reise im Euphrat- und Tigris-Gebiet*, 4 vols., Berlin 1911–1920.

Schlumberger, D., *L'Orient hellénisé. L'art grec et ses héritiers dans l'Asie non méditerranéenne*, Paris 1970.

Scholl, R., *Historische Beiträge zu den julianischen reden des Libanios*, Stuttgart 1994.

Scullard, H.H., *The Elephant in the Greek and Roman World*, London 1974.

Seager, R., *Ammianus Marcellinus. Seven Studies in his Language and Thought*, Columbia 1986.

Seager, R., 'Ammianus and the Status of Armenia in the Peace of 363', *Chiron* 26 (1996) 275–284.

Seager, R., 'Perceptions of Eastern Frontier Policy in Ammianus, Libanius, and Julian (337–363)', *CQ* 47 (1997) 253–268.

Seston, W., 'Feldzeichen', *RAC* 7 (1969) 689–711 (= *Scripta Varia. Mélanges d'histoire Romaine, de droit, d'épigraphie et d'histoire du Christianisme*, Rome 1980, 263–281).

Seyfarth, W., *Ammiani Marcellini rerum gestarum libri qui supersunt*, adiuvantibus L. Jacob-Karau et I. Ulmann, 2 vols., Leipzig 1978 (repr. 1999).

Seyfarth, W., *Ammianus Marcellinus. Römische Geschichte. Lateinisch und Deutsch und mit einem Kommentar versehen*, II, Berlin 1983⁵, III, Berlin 1986³.

Shepherd, D., 'Sasanian Art', in: E. Yarshater (ed.), *The Cambridge History of Iran* 3.2, Cambridge 1983, 1055–1112.

Smith, R., 'Telling Tales: Ammianus' Narrative of the Persian Expedition of Julian', in: J.W. Drijvers and E.D. Hunt (eds.), *The Late Roman World and its Historian. Interpreting Ammianus Marcellinus*, London-New York 1999, 89–104.

Southern, P., and K.R. Dixon, *The Late Roman Army*, London 1996.

Spannagel, M., *Exemplaria principis. Untersuchungen zu Entstehung und Ausstattung des Augustusforums*, Heidelberg 1999.

Steiner, P. 'Die dona militaria', *BJ* 114 (1906) 1–98.

Stern, M., *Greek and Latin Authors on Jews and Judaism*, II, Jerusalem 1980.

Stertz, S.A., 'Ammianus Marcellinus' Attitudes toward Earlier Emperors', *Studies in Latin Literature and Roman History*, ed. C. Deroux, II, Brussels 1980, 487–514.

Stiehl, R., see F. Altheim.

Stol, M., and H.J. Nissen, 'Kanal(isation), *Reallexikon der Assyriologie* 5 (1976–1980) 355–368.

Streck, M., 'Diakira', *RE* 5 (1903) 317.

Sturm, J., 'Persarmenia', *RE* 19 (1938) 932–938.

Szantyr, A., see J.B. Hofmann.

Szidat, J., *Historischer Kommentar zu Ammianus Marcellinus Buch XX–XXI, Teil I: Die Erhebung Iulians*, Wiesbaden 1977; *Teil II: Die Verhandlungsphase*, Wiesbaden 1981; *Teil III: Die Konfrontation*, Wiesbaden 1996.

Szidat, J., 'Alexandrum imitatus (Amm. 24,4,27). Die Beziehung Iulians zu Alexander in der Sicht Ammians', in: W. Will and J. Heinrichs (eds.), *Festschrift für Gerhard Wirth zum 60. Geburtstag*, Amsterdam 1988, 1023–1035.

244 BIBLIOGRAPHY

Teitler, H.C., *Notarii and Exceptores. An Inquiry into Role and Significance of Shorthand Writers in the Imperial and Ecclesiastical Bureaucracy of the Roman Empire (from the Early Principate to c. 450 A.D.)*, Amsterdam 1985.

Thörnell, G., *Ad Scriptores Historiae Augustae et Ammianum Marcellinum adnotationes* (Skrifter utg. K. human. Vetenskaps-Samfundet 24, 6), Uppsala-Leipzig 1927.

Thompson, E.A., *The Historical Work of Ammianus Marcellinus*, Cambridge 1947 (repr. Groningen 1969).

Toynbee, J.M.C., *Animals in Roman Life and Art*, London 1973.

Tränkle, H., 'Ammianus Marcellinus als römischer Geschichtsschreiber', *Antike und Abendland* 11 (1962) 21–33.

Trümpelmann, L., see W. Heimpel.

Unger, E., *Babylon: die heilige Stadt nach der Beschreibung der Babylonier*, Berlin 1970².

Veenhof, K.R., 'Militaire strategie en water in het oude Mesopotamië', *Phoenix* (Bulletin uitgegeven door het Voor-Aziatisch Genootschap) 20 (1974 [1975]) 371–380.

Veenhof, K.R., 'Mesopotamië. Het land en het water', in: D. van der Plas, B. Becking and D. Meijer (eds.), *Landbouw en irrigatie in het Oude Nabije Oosten*, Leuven 1993, 63–96.

Verhoeven, K., 'Geomorphological Research in the Mesopotamian Flood Plain', in: H. Gasche and M. Tanret (eds.), *Changing Watercourses in Babylonia. Towards a Reconstruction of the Ancient Environment in Lower Mesopotamia*, I, Ghent-Chicago 1998, 159–245.

Versnel, H.S., *Inconsistencies in Greek and Roman Religion*, II, *Transition and Reversal in Myth and Ritual*, Leiden 1993.

Viansino, J., *Ammiani Marcellini rerum gestarum Lexicon*, 2 vols., Hildesheim-Zürich-New York 1985.

Viscogliosi, A., see L. Chioffi.

Vogler, Ch., 'Les officiers de l'armée romaine dans l'oeuvre d'Ammien Marcellin', in: Y. Le Bohec (ed.), *La hiérarchie (Rangordnung) de l'armée sous le haut-empire*, Paris 1995, 389–404.

Volkmann, H., 'Valerius 137', *RE* 7A (1948) 2413–2418.

Wagner, J.A., *Ammiani Marcellini quae supersunt*, cum notis integris Frid. Lindenbrogii, Henr. et Hadr. Valesiorum et Iac. Gronovii, quibus Thom. Reinesii quasdam et suas adiecit, editionem absolvit Car. Gottl. Aug. Erfurdt, 3 vols., Leipzig 1808 (repr. in 2 vols., Hildesheim 1975).

Walter, F., 'Zu Ammianus Marcellinus', *PhW* 34 (1914) 701–702.

Walter, F., 'Zu lateinischen Schriftstellern', *Philologus* 80 (1925) 437–453.

Waszink, J.H., 'Bellona', *RAC* 2 (1954) 126–129.

Watson, G.R., *The Roman Soldier*, London 1969.

Webster, G., *The Roman Imperial Army of the First and Second Centuries A.D.*, London 1981².

Weissbach, F.H., 'Is', *RE* 9 (1916) 2047–2048.

Weissbach, F.H., 'Koche', *RE* 11 (1922) 943–944.

Weissbach, F.H., 'Μηδίας τεῖχος', *RE* 15 (1931) 68–79.

BIBLIOGRAPHY

245

Weissbach, F.H., 'Naarmalcha', *RE* 16 (1935) 1440–1449.
White, P., 'The Authorship of the Historia Augusta', *JRS* 57 (1967) 115–133.
Wille, G., *Musica Romana. Die Bedeutung der Musik im Leben der Römer*, Amsterdam 1967.
Williams, M.F., 'Four Mutinies: Tacitus *Annals* 1.16–30; 1.31–49 and Ammianus Marcellinus *Res Gestae* 20.4.9–20.5.7; 24.3.1–8', *Phoenix* 51 (1997) 44–74.
Wirth, E., *Agrargeographie des Irak* (Hamburger Geographische Studien, 13), Hamburg 1962.
Wirth, G., 'Julians Perserkrieg. Kriterien einer Katastrophe', in: R. Klein (ed.), *Julian Apostata*, Darmstadt 1978, 455–507.
Wissowa, G., *Religion und Kultus der Römer*, Munich 1902 (1912², repr. 1971).
Wittchow, F., *Exemplarisches Erzählen bei Ammianus Marcellinus. Episode, Exemplum, Anekdote*, Munich-Leipzig 2001.
Wolski, J., 'La politique impérialiste de Rome à l'égard de l'Iran: ses formes et ses effets', in: *Studia z dziejów Grecji i Rzymu* (Festschrift T. Kotula), Wroclaw 1993, 223–228.
Woods, D., 'Ammianus and some *Tribuni Scholarum Palatinarum* c. AD 353–64', *CQ* 47 (1997) 269–291.
Woods, D., 'The Role of the *Comes* Lucillianus during Julian's Persian Expedition', *AC* 67 (1998) 243–248.
Woods, D., 'A Persian at Rome: Ammianus and Eunapius frg. 68', in: J.W. Drijvers and E.D. Hunt (eds.), *The Late Roman World and its Historian. Interpreting Ammianus Marcellinus*, London-New York 1999, 156–165.
Zuckermann, C., 'Sur le dispositif frontalier en Arménie, le *limes* et son évolution, sous le Bas-Empire', *Historia* 47 (1998) 108–128.

INDICES

I. *Lexical (Latin)*

abiecte: 165
abortus: 96
abruptus: 145
absque: 16
abusive: 126
accursus: 104
addicere: 74
adhaerere: 122
adigere: 181
adminiculum: 221
admovere: 198
adventicius: 221
adventus: 64
aegre: 115
aeneator: 129
aequus: 124
affatim: 167
afluere: 26
agger: 62
aggredi: 204
agitare: 62
agmen: 41
alacritas: 2
alius: 20
altitudo: 168
ambiguus: 53
ambitiosus: 161
ambitus: 193
amendare: 144
amplecti: 110
anapaestus: 188
animare: 40
animosus: 116
antesignanus: 25
apparatus: 119
apparitio: 12
appetitus: 113
aptare: 123, 184
architectus: 142
arduus: 3

aries: 53
arripere: 211, 230
artifex: 118, 143
arvum: 90
asper: 85
asperitas: 31, 167
aspirare: 86
assuetus: 13
auctoritas: 86
auxilia: 25
auxilium: 111
aversus: 192
avidus: 208
ballista: 55, 118
barritus: 189
bucina: 120, 164
caecus: 146
canalis: 172
canorus: 132
capella: 224
capreolus: 13
caritas: 19, 87
carpentum: 214
casus: 29
catafract(ari)i: 39
catapulta: 55
cataracta: 23, 91, 173
cautela: 50
cautus: 46, 82, 146, 168
cavatus: 146
cavillatio: 52
celebritas: 114
celsus: 46
censere: 228
centuria: 187
cervus: 13
cibus: 70
cinis: 115
circumfluere: 78
circumluere: 15

248 INDICES

circumvallare: 49
citare: 211, 228
citus: 181
classicum: 120
clemens: 47, 138
clementia: 138
clibanarii: 39
cohors: 157
coire: 97
collustrare: 154
commigrare: 172
compertus: 144
compingere: 165
complanare: 53
concertatio: 182
conferre: 64
confidens: 107
confirmare: 88
conflictus: 119
confore: 229
congeries: 59
congredi: 174
congruus: 167
considerare: 167
consilium: 116, 203
conspiratio: 167
constare: 54
consternere: 108
consultum: 228
consurgere: 24
contentio: 116
continens: 53
continuare: 146
contra sperata: 125
contrarius: 158
contrectare: 141
controversus: 124
conturmalis: 190
convenire: 130
copiosus: 114
cornu: 121
coruscus: 187
crebritas: 114
crustare: 59
crux: 155
culex: 227
culmen: 194

cultus: 19
cuneus: 58, 157
cuniculus: 118
cura: 24
dama: 13
decimatio: 74
decurrere: 90
deformiter: 187
deierare: 87
delenire: 86
densare: 58
densere: 58
depellere: 173
derigere: 55
destinatio: 57
destrictus: 125
detegere: 61
dies: 52, 69
diffundere: 23
digerere: 46, 202
dilabi: 111
dilatare: 11
dirigere: 55
diripere: 79
discedere: 83
discurrere: 187
disparare: 152
disponere: 161
distendere: 128
distinere: 128
distringere: 218
diversorium: 176
diversus: 218
docilitas: 5
documentum: 186
dorcas: 13
ducere: 41
ductor: 210
efferatus: 120
effervescere: 123
effusus: 226
elatus: 24, 106
emittere: 179
en: 78, 224
enim: 117, 232
enite(sc)ere: 135
erectus: 102

INDICES

erumpere: 10
eruptor: 164
et: 104, 182
et quia: 24
evolare: 130, 180
ex: 78
ex animo: 86
ex sententia: 177
excessus: 113
excubare: 125
exculcatores: 6
excursatores: 6, 25, 70
exigere: 3
eximere: 52
exordium: 46
exstruere: 146
exta: 229
extimare: 133
extrahere: 3
exuviae: 107
facies: 61
factum: 157
fatigatio: 127
favor: 24
fecundare: 90
femina: 95
festinare: 72
fetus: 96
fidens (-nter): 121
fides: 61, 96
figere: 104
finire: 127
firmamentum: 7
firmare: 231
firmiter: 65
firmus ad: 120
flagrare: 165
flectere: 123
fodicare: 59
fodina: 128
foederare: 66
fortiter facere: 135
fortitudo: 104, 139
fortuna: 177
fossilis: 171
fovea: 144
frendere: 159

frustra habere: 110
frustrari: 38
funestus: 212
geminare: 123
generare: 95
genius: 66, 133
gens: 104
genticus: 133
gentilis: 176
gesticulari: 140
gesticularius: 139
glans: 59
gradi: 109
gradus: 190
grassator: 72, 165
gravis: 82
hactenus: 31
haerere: 161
Hectoreus: 193
helepolis: 62
hispidus: 152
humilis: 101
iam: 83, 180
ibi tum: 126
ibi tunc: 126
idem: 55
illuvies: 224
immane quantum: 104
immobilis: 182
impeditissimus: 62
imperator: 2
imperatus: 14
imperitus: 183
imperterritus: 82
impetrabilis: 2
impetus: 98
importunus: 204
impunitas: 65
incedere: 98
incessere: 52
inclarescere: 126, 194
incohibilis: 13
increpare: 59
incumbere: 231
incutere: 126
indicium: 64
indignatio: 77

250   INDICES

indutus: 39
inexpugnabilis: 204
infaustus: 210
infigurabilis: 122
inhorrescere: 227
inopinus: 70
insistere: 25, 112
instanter: 124
instituere: 12
insularis: 49
intactus: 164
intentus: 124, 226
inter: 85, 231
interiora: 190
interluvies: 39
interpretare: 171
intersaepire: 53
inultus: 98
ita: 56, 231
itaque: 139
iter: 112
itinerarium: 3
iuramentum: 17
iustus: 116
labi: 192, 198
lacerare: 156
laetus: 150, 206
lanugo: 19
lapis: 11, 33
lapsus: 121
latro: 37
laxare: 190
lenis: 85
levis: 48
librare: 112
licenter: 158
limes: 38
lituus: 120
lorica: 151
luce palam: 127
lux: 53
magnanimitas: 139
magnitudo: 87
maritare: 95
mas: 95
Medicus: 194
medius: 85

mel: 94
metari: 108
miliarium: 33
minae: 54, 63
mitis: 82
modestus: 84
modus: 172
molimen: 109
mollis: 9
momentum: 57
multifidus: 98
multiformis: 55
multimodus: 55
multiplex: 55, 119, 176
munitio: 167
munitor: 64, 127
murmur: 121
musca: 227
muss(it)are: 215
nam: 66
namque: 105
nescius: 26
neutrubi: 57
nihilo minus: 56
nimbus: 57
nimirum: 52
nitidus: 34
nobilis: 80
noscere: 204
nudare: 137
nummus: 76
nusquam: 166
nutus: 140
obequitare: 4, 159
obicere: 51, 184
oblidere: 143
obliquus: 118
oblongus: 118
obnixe: 52
obscurus: 159
obtegere: 51
obtutus: 184
occipitium: 191
occursare: 184
ocius: 16, 145
onager: 143
opera: 64

INDICES

operositas: 62
opimitas: 78
oppetere: 160
opulentus: 206
opus: 64
orbis Romanus: 88
ordinatim: 12
ostendere: 36
otium: 70
pabulator: 158
pacisci: 65
palari: 158
pandere: 63
pangere: 214
papilio: 21
par: 163
pari sorte: 57
parvitas: 77
passus: 33, 161
patibulum: 155
patrare: 29, 113
paucus: 71
pectus: 224
penetrare: 13
per: 153
percellere: 96, 156, 164
percitus: 164, 231
percutere: 96
perfectus: 84
perfungi: 84
pergere: 83
periculum: 91
permittere: 25
perpendere: 63, 139
perpensare: 63
perquam: 11
perrumpere: 19, 23
phylarchus: 38
plebs: 225
pondus: 13, 163, 193
pone: 187
ponere in: 81
pons: 108
ponticulus: 91
poscere: 162
postica: 105
postridie: 32

postsignanus: 187
potestas: 137
praeceps: 162
praecipitare: 105
praedocere: 90
praepilare: 188
praepilatus: 188
praestituere: 187
praestolari: 221
praestringere: 8, 184
praestruere: 3
praetermeare: 31
praevius: 147
precatus: 180
primas: 203
primitiae: 40
princeps: 2, 125
priscus: 75
pristinus: 82
pro(r)sus: 109
pro tempore: 86
probator: 166
procinctus: 40
procursatio: 121
procursator: 70, 155, 157
proditio: 20
profundere: 143
prohibitor: 55, 63
proinde: 177
promovere: 174, 230
proponere: 211
propositum: 124
propugnaculum: 51, 114
propugnatio: 107
prorumpere: 156
proruptor: 158, 164
protervus: 115
protestari: 64
protinus: 149
pubes: 150
purgare: 173
quadratus: 5
quassare: 88
quidam: 30, 129
quies: 32, 64, 79, 179
quisquam: 129
rapidus: 193

ratio: 82
recensere: 134
recipere: 61
redemptare: 79
regere: 82, 215
regio: 150
repedare: 145
reperire: 193
reprimere: 23
repulsorium: 109
repulsorius: 109
resecrare: 198
reserare: 137
residuus: 72, 106, 162
reverberare: 143
robur: 7, 145
sacramentum: 73
sagina: 98
saltus: 58
salubrius: 108
sauciare: 26
saxa manualia: 56
saxa muralia: 56
saxum: 59, 122, 182
scindere: 41
scorpio: 118, 143
se inferre: 115
secernere: 87
secundus: 85
secuto die: 124
sedere: 229
semirutus: 41
senescere: 219
sensim: 7
sequellae: 31
situs: 16
sonare: 3, 193
sortiri: 20
spadicum, spadix: 94
specie + gen.: 186
species: 88
spectatissimus: 84
spiritus: 21
spissus: 145
spolia opima: 106
squalere: 25
squalor: 232

stabilis: 196
subinde: 112
sublica: 128
subsidere: 144
succidere: 230
sudes: 167
suffodere: 60
suggestus: 117
summa res: 3
supercilium: 8, 9
supergradi: 182
superponere: 54
suppliciter: 17
suscipere: 17, 107
suspectus: 24
sustinere: 165
tabernaculum: 21
tamen: 220
tandem: 78, 105
temerarius: 27
temptamentum: 220
tentorium: 104
testudo: 61
tinnitus: 129
titubare: 143
tormentum: 160
tractus: 41
traicere: 108
trames: 118
transgredi: 174
travectus: 108
tribunus: 71
tuba: 120
tum: 127
tumultuare: 77
tumultuarius: 153
tumultuosus: 16
turbinatus: 230
turbo: 21, 230
turma: 70, 112, 184
uber: 93
ulterior: 111
ultro citroque: 225
ululabilis: 16
unum spirare: 78
urere: 116
urg(u)entia: 62

INDICES 253

urgere: 125
usu venire: 11
ut ... ita: 135
uter: 92
utpote: 31
utricularii: 92
utrimque: 129
vallis: 173
vapor: 227
vaporatus: 124
vel: 115

velitares: 25
velites: 25
vertex: 166
vespera: 14
vetare: 209
vexillum: 71
viare: 231
vigor: 180
vinea: 62, 118
vis: 230
vitalia: 145

II. *Lexical (Greek)*

ἀφοσιοῦσθαι: 198
ἄμορφος: 122
δαίμων: 133

κατάσκοπος: 157
παράδεισος: 176
πνεῦμα: 22

III. *Syntax and Style*

abl. gerundii: 106
ad id + gen.: 156
adjective instead of a gen.: 231
adverbs in -im: 7
archaism: 30
asyndeton: 3, 111
brachylogy: 115
comparative: 115
constructio ad sensum: 164
cum ... tum: 17, 122
cursus: 39, 46, 62, 129
dative in -u: 13, 124
die, gen.: 52
dies, gender of –: 33, 69
dum with subj.: 127
enim in eye-witness accounts: 117
exclamatory phrases: 224
fodiri, infin. pass.: 172
gen. identitatis: 7
gen. inversus: 9, 13, 22, 53, 87,
    114, 117, 176
gen. qualitatis: 134
gerundive
    as a substitute for inf. or
        part.fut.pass.: 16, 59
    in -undus: 112
grecism: 21, 31

hyperbaton: 128, 141
idem anaphoric: 167
(im)perfect subj. in consecutive
    clauses: 195
imperfect in past irrealis: 134
in with acc.: 163
iubere with NcI.: 217
omission of se in the AcI: 198
omission of the preposition in a
    relative clause: 226
participle
    attr. use of the future –: 137
    present – anterior to main verb:
        124
    present – in gen. pl.: 12
    accumulation of participles: 3,
        134
passive, use of –: 32
passive infinitive after impersonal
    expressions: 173
perfect and pluperfect in Amm.:
    20, 124, 144
perfect in -ere: 135
perfect tense, use of –: 31
periphrasis: 117
permittere, infinitives after –: 25
personificatio: 137

254 INDICES

pronouns, anaphoric use of –: 31,
   36, 55
pseudo-conditional sentence: 133
ptc. perf. of deponentia used in a
   passive sense: 108
quidam and quisquam: 129
quod + AcI: 31
quod with ind. fut.: 215

quod-clauses instead of the AcI:
   20, 181
sermo castrensis: 191
signum, constructions after –: 120
stylistic variation: 4
sui, sibi, se: 4, 110
tamquam + participle: 115
zeugma: 185

IV. *Geographical Names*

Abora: 4
Abouzatha: 207
Achaiachala: 32, 34, 115, 125
Adiabene: 229
Alexandria: 94
Amida: 50, 99, 155, 186
Anatha: 1, 14, 30, 32, 114
Aquileia: 50
Arabia: 10
Armenia: 10
Asia: 216
Assyria: 4, 41, 229
Babylon: 35, 41, 42
Baraxmalcha: 33
Besouchis: 110
Bithra: 97, 100
Bubio: 216
Cannae: 126
Carmanitan desert: 216
Carrhae: 229
Carthage: 60
Castalia: 173
Cercusium: 13, 24
Chalcis: 1
Chalcis (Coelesyria): 19
Chalcis (Syria): 18
Characene: 94
Charax Spasinu: 94
Chiliocomum: 222, 229, 231
Coche: 102, 152, 153
Corduena: 223, 229, 231
Ctesiphon: 49, 103, 110, 119, 146,
   147, 149, 159, 168, 169, 174,
   183, 192, 203, 231
Cunaxa: 225
Dacia(e): 89

Danubius: 89
D(i)acira: 15, 25, 30, 34
Douros: 218, 220, 231
Drobeta: 89
Dura: 1, 12, 13, 101
Euphrates: 92, 227, 229
Hadrianopel: 168
Hister: 89
Macepracta: 41
Mahoza: 101, 102
Maozamalcha: 50, 102, 110, 117,
   119, 125, 131, 135, 149, 156,
   158
mare magnum: 94
Marses: 43
Masice: 42
Media: 194
Meinas Sabatha: 154
Mesene: 94
Mesichise/Misiche: 49
Mesopotamia: 10
Moxoena: 229, 231
Naarmalcha: 147, 169, 171
Neherda: 45, 100
Nicomedia: 232
Noorda: 209, 218, 223
Osdroene: 6, 10
Ozogardana: 34, 36, 37
Palaestina: 10, 100
Persarmenia: 205
Phatousa: 14
Phissenia: 41, 46, 90
Phoenice: 10
Pirisabora: 36, 46, 48, 49, 61, 69,
   91, 114, 149, 155
Pumbedita: 101

INDICES

255

Radwaniyah canal: 45
Saqlawiyah canal: 45
Seleucia: 45, 65, 102, 152, 153, 173
Sippar: 45
Sliq Kharawta: 154

Sura: 101
Syria: 10
Thilutha: 30, 32, 34, 115, 125
Tigris: 183, 220, 227, 229
Trajan's canal: 169, 171, 174

V. *Names of Persons/Peoples*

Agesilaus: 224
Alavivus: 221
Alexander: 4, 5, 10, 11, 142, 180
Aminias: 193
(A)nabdates: 100, 138, 149,156
Anaximander: 22
Apollodorus of Damascus: 89
Ariamnes: 210
Arinth(a)eus: 1, 6, 8, 84, 157, 203
Arsaces: 206, 219, 221, 231
Artaxerxes II: 147
Assanitae: 38
Assurbanipal: 151
Assurnasirpal: 151
Avidius Cassius: 204
Bar Kochba: 144
Barzimeres: 59
Batavi: 183
Bellona: 202, 211
Callimachus: 194
Carus: 153, 154, 204
Chnodomarius: 134
Constantinus Magnus: 5
Constantius: 177
Corbulo: 73
Cynegirus: 194
Dagalaifus: 1, 6, 7, 9, 84, 116, 118, 128, 203
Darius: 210
Demetrius Poliorcetes: 62
Exsuperius: 130, 135
Fabricius Luscinus: 81, 100, 134
Fritigern: 221
Gelo: 224
Gordianus: 49
Hadrianus: 173
Halani: 232
Hannibal: 11

Hormisdas: 1, 6, 8, 36, 38, 84, 156, 207, 209, 218
Hormisdas II: 8
Iovianus: 8, 131, 135
Iovinus: 8
Lucillianus: 1, 7, 14, 48, 84, 179
Lupicinus: 221
Ma: 211
Magnus: 131, 132, 135
Magnus of Carrhae: 7, 132
Mamersides: 65, 155
Mamertinus: 7
Marcellus: 126
Mauzanitai: 102
Maximianus: 1
Nabdates: 100, 138, 149, 156
Narseus: 183, 191, 205
Nevitta: 1, 6, 7, 12, 118, 128, 179, 203
Pap: 92
Pigranes: 183, 191, 205
Podosaces: 36, 37
Procopius: 206, 219, 221, 229, 231
Pusaeus: 17, 18
Pyrrhus: 5
Quadi: 121
Regulus: 81
Salutius: 179
Sapor I: 15, 18, 49
Sapor II: 8, 18, 37, 49, 147, 161, 191, 207
Sapor III: 147
Saracens: 1
Sarmates: 121
Scipio Aemilianus: 5, 60, 142
Scipio Africanus: 81, 142
Sebastianus: 206, 219, 221, 229, 231

256 INDICES

Secundinus: 1, 6, 10, 84
Seleucus Nicator: 19
Septimius Severus: 204
Sertorius: 182
Sophanes: 193
Superantius: 130
Surena: 36, 37, 70
Theodosius: 88
Theodosius (general): 75
Torquatus: 106, 107

Traianus: 36, 88, 204
Ursulus: 80
Valentinianus: 176
Valerius Publicola: 81, 106
Vararanes: 147
Vespasian: 101
Victor: 1, 6, 8, 9, 48, 84, 100, 116, 119, 147, 169, 192, 203
Zopyrus: 210

VI. *Military Matters*

aeneatores: 120
agmen quadratum: 5
architectus: 142
arcus: 56
aries: 53
armiger: 160
artifex: 118
auxilia: 25, 187
auxiliares: 48
ballista: 55, 118, 123
barritus: 164, 189
bucina: 120, 164
cargo-ships: 178
catafractarii: 39,184, 221
catapulta: 55
cavalry (Persian): 185
centuria: 187
classicum: 189
clibanarii: 39, 121
clipeus: 40
coats of mail: 51
cohors: 157, 163
comes: 147
comes rei militaris: 8
Constantiniani: 75
cornicines: 120
cornu: 189
Cornuti: 183
corona: 135
corona castrensis: 136, 196
corona civica: 135, 136, 196
corona classica : 196
corona graminea: 136
corona muralis: 135

corona navalis: 136, 196
corona obsidionalis: 132, 196
corona rostrata: 196
corona vallaris: 196
cuneus: 58, 157
cuniculus: 118
degradation: 165
draco: 71
dust in battle-scenes: 189
dux: 147
elephants: 185
exculcatores: 6
excursatores: 6, 25, 70
fleet: 12
frontier armies: 10
funditores: 122
helepolis: 62
infantry (Persian): 185
Iovii: 128
Lancearii: 6, 128
liticines: 120
lituus: 120
magister equitum: 8, 9
magister peditum: 8, 9
magister praesidiorum: 139
malleolus: 123
manipulus: 185
Mattiarii: 6, 128
military signals: 189
munitio: 167
music used during military training: 188
musical instruments: 120, 163
numerus: 130

INDICES

257

onager: 143
opus: 64
otium: 70
pabulator: 158
papilio: 21
parma: 40
pluteus: 161
postsignanus: 187
procursator: 70, 155, 157, 188
prohibitor: 161
propugnaculum: 163
sagittarii: 122
Saracen auxiliaries: 1
schola scutariorum clibana-
    riorum: 8
scholae palatinae: 160
scholae Scutariorum: 160
scorpio: 118, 123, 143
scutum: 40
siege

activities of sappers during a –:
    117
engines: 52
stones, use of – in sieges: 57
sudes: 167
Surena: 37, 183, 191, 205
tabernaculum: 21
tactical manuals: 5
testudo: 40
tormentum: 118, 160
tribunus: 18, 71, 132, 163
tuba: 120
tubicines: 120
turma: 70, 112, 184
utricularii: 92
velitares: 25
velites: 7, 25, 48, 104
vexillum: 71, 180
Victores: 128
vinea: 62, 118, 161

VII. *Various Topics*

acclamatio: 2, 24, 195
adventus: 64, 65
aerarium: 79
Alexander: 5
Ammianus
    admission of ignorance: 142
    as an eye-witness: 2, 35, 157
    attitude toward earlier
        emperors: 154
    direct knowledge of Herodotus:
        194
    his bilingualism: 127
    his disposition of the events: 76
    his use of exempla: 81
    personal judgment: 218
    possible service on the fleet: 171
    tendency to avoid t.t.: 118
    use of the first person: 170, 223
anapaestus: 188
Assyria: 4
Augustus: 2
Bar Kokhba: 101
Bellona: 202, 211
bitumen: 34, 35, 54

Caesar: 2
cavalry (Persian): 104
contorniate: 88
cross-references: 76
crucifixion: 155
cursus: 83, 124, 128
deportations: 18
digression: 93
distances, designations of –: 33,
    173
divination: 198
divine interference: 211
donativum: 69, 76
dress of the emperor: 106
Egypt, administration of –: 18
Euphrates
    flooding of the –: 22
    water works in the –: 22
exempla, Amm.'s use of –: 107,
    142
fides Romana: 63
fiscus: 79
fleet, burning of the –: 212
fortuna: 177

258 INDICES

Gauls, character of –: 24
genius: 66, 133
geographic expressions: 34
gesture: 64
hunting: 151
Jews: 100
Julian
    compared with heroes of Rome's
      ancient history: 99
    designated as Augustus: 177
    his care for the well-being of his
      men: 174
    his cautiousness: 1, 5, 104
    his fondness for
      histor(iograph)y: 60
    his 'innate energy': 181
    his loss of composure: 72, 149
    his physical skills: 59
    his self-restraint: 139
    his strategy in provisioning the
      troops: 2
    inspired by heaven: 181
    lofty spirit of –: 4
    policy towards the provincials of
      –: 112
    prominent personal role of –: 91
    recklessness of –: 57, 177
    reliance on speed of –: 72
    shrewdness of –: 205
    speeches of –: 77
    strategy of –: 208, 209
    terms to denote –: 2
limes: 38
lions: 230
Ma: 211
Magnus of Carrhae: 7
Malechus: 37
Mars: 100, 133
Mars (Ultor): 197
Median Wall: 41
Mesopotamia, fertility of –: 213
moonlight: 162
Nevitta: 84

notarius: 131
nummus: 76
ominous signs: 198
orbis: 88
pantomime: 140
peripeteia: 177
Persia, wealth of –: 78
Persians
    characteristics of –: 104
    cunning of –: 24, 168
    their physique: 223
    valour of –: 114
Pharos: 46
phoenix dactylifera: 95
phylarch: 38
Polybius: 5, 60
polygamy: 20
praefectus praesidii: 65
praefectus praesidiorum: 65
primicerius notariorum: 131
Pyrrhus: 5
Res Gestae Divi Saporis, l. 10: 49
Romans, technical superiority of –:
    150
Salamis, battle of –: 193
salt, importance of –: 34
Sapor, peace proposals by –: 207
Sasanian art, themes in –: 176
satellite kings: 79
schola notariorum: 131
ship-bridge: 108
siege, negotiations before the
    actual –: 114
spolia opima: 106
Strasbourg, battle of –: 170
Surena: 70, 109
Talmud Qiddushin 70b: 45
Talmudic sources: 102
temple of Jerusalem, destruction
    of –: 101
torture: 216
Trajan ("the second –"): 88
tribunus honorarius: 18

INDICES

VIII. *Passages referred to (Latin)*

Ambrosius
hex. 3.55: 95
Hymn. 2.15: 85
in psalm. 118 serm.
  4.15.2: 109
  4.21: 176

Anonymus *de machinis bellicis*
  16: 91

Apuleius
Met. 4.3: 16
  4.25.4: 155
  7.22: 32
  9.19.1: 206
  9.26.3: 155
  10.8: 144
  10.28: 64
  10.31: 140
Soc. 127: 133

Augustinus
conf. 6.11.18: 215
  13.18.23: 215
c. acad. 3.1.1: 96
C.D. 4.29: 213
  5.21: 213
  18.23: 162
de catech. rud.
  25: 83

Augustus
Anc. 21: 197

Avienus
ora 249: 90

Bellum Africanum
  83: 186

Caesar
Civ. 1.48.7: 92
  2.35.6: 164
  3.44.6: 98
  3.74.1: 165

  3.82: 189
  3.92.5: 189
Gal. 1.41.1: 2
  1.51.3: 63
  2.1.4: 80
  5.8.1: 86
  5.40.6: 151
  5.49.5: 33
  7.60.2: 120

Carmen contra paganos
  22: 212

Cato
Agr. 02.4: 172
  141.3: 197

Catullus 5: 87
  33.13–4: 88
  62.49: 95
  109.3–4: 86

Cicero
Amic. 52: 78
Att. 5.21.10: 163
de Orat. 1.251: 228
  1.34: 83
  1.46: 165
  1.58: 84
  2.36: 108
  2.12: 69
  2.290: 81
  2.345: 4, 5
Div. 2.69: 23
Fam. 7.26.1: 219
  8.6.4: 191
  9.25: 11
Fin. 5.54: 81
  5.66: 167
inv. 1.65: 215
Leg. 1.11: 204
Mur. 58: 7
N.D. 1.114: 26
Off. 1.66–73: 139
  1.68: 139

	1.70: 139
	2.48: 25
	3.93: 127
Phil.	2.26: 158
	5.26: 125
	14.30: 143
Pis.	96: 79
Q. fr.	1.1.12: 12
	1.1.21–3: 84
Quinct.	81: 90
Rep.	2.23: 129
	6.21: 94
Sul.	19: 115
Tusc.	2.14: 81
	2.37: 188
	2.43: 5
	3.44: 78
	5.62: 84
Ver.	2.74: 203
	3.185: 137
	3.212: 88
	5.88: 180

CIL	3.1457: 196
	3.3676: 183
	3.4031: 196
	5.531: 196
	5.6977: 196
	6.1377: 196
	6.6190: 160
	6.6229: 160
	9.6005: 89
	10.8291: 196
	12.187: 92
	12.4107: 92
	12.700: 92
	14.74: 14
	I 2 p. 20.44: 107

Claudianus
carm. min.
    30.181–2: 196
Cons. Stil.
    3.72: 196
Epith. dict. Hon. Aug. et Mar.
    66–7: 95

III Cons. Hon.
    138–41: 71
in Eutr. II 144–5: 212
in Ruf. 2.355: 51
VI cons. Hon.
    569: 51

Codex Theodosianus
    7.1.11: 19

Curtius Rufus
    3.1.3: 23
    3.10.4: 4
    3.12.21: 142
    4.4.19: 86
    4.10.24: 142
    5.1.25: 54
    7.8.6: 92
    10.6.23: 79

[Ps.] Cyprianus
 sing. cler. 36: 109

Dictys	2.22: 229
Digesta	49.16.3.1: 165
	49.16.3.5: 165
	49.16.3.9: 165
	49.16.3.15: 165
	49.16.3.16: 165
	49.16.3.21: 165
	49.16.6 pr: 73
	49.16.6.3: 75
	50.6.7: 142

Donatus
 Ter. *Ad.*
    363.1: 124
 Verg. A.
    7.626: 221
 Verg. A.
    8.402: 221

Edictum Imperatoris Diocletiani
    3.12 Lauffer: 94

INDICES

261

Ennius
Ann.   88–9 Sk.: 151, 152
           167 Sk.: 125
           298 Sk.: 40
           490 Sk.: 63
scen.   85: 78

Epitome   9.18: 83
           43.2: 210
           48.8: 88

Eutropius 2.11.2: 185
           9.9.1: 37
           9.18.1: 153, 154
           10.16.1: 176

Festus   p. 57M: 196
           p. 163M: 196
           p. 190M: 135, 136
           p. 191M: 196
           p. 204M: 197
           p. 350M: 145

Florus
Epit.   1.8: 107
           1.22: 142
           4.1.2: 79

Frontinus
Str.   1.4: 11
           1.5.17: 164
           1.11.17–18: 224
           2.3.17: 187
           2.3.21: 186, 187
           2.6.10: 11
           2.11.5–6: 142
           4.1.31: 165
           4.1.37: 75

Gellius   1.5.3: 139
           1.11.3–4: 188
           1.11.9: 188
           3.9.9: 94
           5.6.8: 135
           5.6.9: 136
           5.6.13: 196
           5.6.16: 135

5.6.17: 196
5.6.18: 196
5.6.19: 196
7.8.1: 142
7.8.2: 142
9.11.1: 107
9.11.2: 108
9.11.8: 107
9.11.13: 107
9.13: 107, 108

Hegesippus
           3.5.2: 109

Hieronymus
Chron.   a. 363: 210
in Ps.   93: 83

Hirtius
Gal.   8.8.4: 5, 6
           8.9.3: 108

Historia Augusta
A   7.5: 112
AC   14.8: 112
AS   15.3: 112
Aur.   13.2: 196
           13.3: 196
Dd.   1.6–8: 3
Max.   22.4: 91
Pr.   5.1: 137
           5.2–3: 196

Horatius
Carm.   1.2.1: 87
           1.3.1: 89
           2.1.6: 58
           2.1.17: 121
           4.9.17–18: 55
           4.14.18: 224
Ep.   2.5: 189
Epod.   2.23.5: 231
           11.2: 96
S.   2.7.6–7: 125

Isidorus
Etym.   5.27.34: 155

262 INDICES

Iustinus 2.9.11: 190
        2.9.16–19: 194
        41.2.1: 37

Iuvenalis 13.76: 46

Lactantius
  inst. 4.26.34: 155

Livius 1.10.6: 106
       1.16.1: 134
       1.34.9: 54
       2.23.9: 91
       2.39.9: 134
       2.49.2: 33
       2.59.11: 74
       4.24.7: 24
       4.38.4: 51
       5.16.5: 118
       5.19.9: 121
       6.18.6: 127
       6.29.4: 153
       7.7.3: 137
       7.9.6–10.14: 107
       7.10.11: 106, 107
       7.10.14: 137
       7.26.7: 106
       7.26.12: 107
       7.33.4: 2
       7.35.1: 164
       7.36.9: 189
       7.37.1: 198
       8.10.14: 197
       8.25.11: 63
       9.2.9: 149
       9.17.12: 107
       9.26.5: 205
       9.31.9: 123
       9.42.7: 53
       10.39.4: 206
       10.46.3: 196
       21.19.10: 63
       21.27.5: 92
       21.31.4: 110
       21.48.9: 65
       21.55.1: 70
       21.55.6: 160

21.57.3: 91
21.63.13: 198
22.6.4: 51, 160
22.14.11: 69
23.6.5: 205
23.43.11: 163
24.23.4: 53
25.6.23: 126
25.11.5: 165
25.18.3: 125
26.10.3: 4, 49
26.15.6: 164
26.48.4: 137
26.48.13: 189
26.49.11–16: 142
26.50.1–12: 142
26.51.4: 188
27.13.5: 124
27.34.7: 203
27.47.10: 12
28.14.17: 211
28.27.15: 189
29.22.8: 219
30.6.9: 230
30.19.10: 219
30.20.1: 159
30.24.11: 15
31.6.5: 156
31.11.10: 134
31.24.3: 41
31.46.15: 126
33.2.5: 63
35.14.8–12: 11
35.14.9: 11
36.6.6: 225
36.18.2: 7
38.7.10: 51
38.26.7: 160
42.63.4: 153
44.19.9: 153

Lucanus 4.186: 189
       4.776: 57
       5.506–7: 162
       7.165–6: 198
       9.1044–5: 194, 195
       10.152: 81, 82

INDICES

Lucilius 676: 145
677: 145

Lucretius 1.276: 121

Manilius 2.171: 55

Nemesianus
Cyn. 85–8: 71

Nepos
Alc. 6.5: 198

Nepotianus
3.2.2: 182

Notitia Dignitatum
Or. 33.20: 15

Orosius
hist. 5.1.10: 79
7.30.6: 210

Ovidius
Fast. 1.98: 181
1.601–2: 107
5.551: 197
5.569: 197
Met. 1.484: 60
2.255–6: 173
4.89: 93
8.254: 181
8.633: 81
9.116–7: 47
Tr. 3.11.70: 24

Pacuvius
trag. 411: 227

Panegyrici Latini
3.12.2: 139
3.13.3: 141
8.21.1: 18

Persius 3.60: 55

Plautus
Cur. 290: 64
Truc. 7: 82

Plinius Maior
Nat. 3.74: 94
4.75: 108
5.81: 19
5.90: 42, 49, 227
6.120: 43
6.122: 172
6.138: 94
7.111: 60
8.6.16: 185
9.115: 219, 220
9.47: 94
13.126: 124
13.34: 95
13.35: 96
14.102: 94
15.58: 230
16.7: 196
17.134: 97
22.5.9: 198
22.6: 136
22.6–7: 136
22.7: 135
23.52: 94

Plinius Minor
Ep. 6.20.16: 143
10.61.4: 23
Pan. 12.2: 79

Priscianus
Anast. 201–3: 79

Propertius
4.4.63: 164

Prudentius
c. Symm. 1.600–1: 212
perist. 10.1021: 152

INDICES

Quintilianus
Inst. 5.12.14: 187
8.6.35: 126
11.3.66: 140

Rufius Festus
24: 153
28: 174, 175, 209, 210
28.2: 180, 192

Rusticus
synod. I 4 p. 221.10: 122

Sallustius
Cat. 39.4: 124
40.4: 126
50.4: 203
58.21: 98
Hist. 2.19: 58
2.64: 41
2.87: 162
3.37: 92
4.65: 121
4.66: 51
4.85: 128
Jug. 08.2: 137
21.2: 129
25.5: 16
26.1: 65
75.7: 230
85.26: 156
93.2: 15
94.5: 127
106.3: 83

Seneca Maior
Con. 7.2.8: 226
10.2.8: 226

Seneca Minor
Cons. Marc.
20.3: 155
De ira 4.10.6: 61
Ep. 51.1: 69
79.2: 36
82.3: 166
116.8: 61

122.10: 81
Med. 891: 211
Nat. 6.14.3: 145
Ot. 8.5.6: 36
Prov. 5.8: 172
Tr. 1112–4: 144

Sidonius
carm. 5.402–7: 71

Silius Italicus
2.397/8: 187
7.154–6: 164
15.268–271: 142

Sisenna
Hist. 107: 51

Solinus 1.51: 90
9.2: 113
27.1: 124

[Ps.]Solinus
22.13: 39

Statius
Ach. 1.632: 55

Suetonius
Aug. 24.2: 75
29.1: 197
29.2: 197
49.1: 160
71.3: 191
81.2: 88
Cal. 30: 61
44.1: 134
Jul. 25.1: 88
32: 189
57: 92
59: 198
Nero 49.3: 187
Vesp. 6.3: 71
24: 83
Vit. 11: 189

INDICES

265

Symmachus
epist.   1.95.3: 61

Tabula Peutingeriana
         IX.5: 19

Tacitus
Agr.   18.4: 183
Ann.   1.9.2: 107
         1.25.2: 32
         1.63.4: 124, 125
         1.64.1: 115, 184
         1.65.4: 224
         2.5.2: 124
         2.8.3: 183
         2.12.3: 87
         2.32.3: 3
         2.48.3: 81
         2.59.1: 134
         2.69.2: 88
         3.21.1: 74
         3.43.2: 133
         4.6.3: 84
         4.10.2: 156
         4.25.1: 41
         4.36.3: 125
         4.42.2: 156
         6.37.2: 22
         6.42.7: 37
         6.44.4: 205
         12.26.2: 30
         12.37.3: 126
         12.49.2: 86
         13.27.3: 205
         13.36.2–3: 74
         14.44.4: 74
         14.53.5: 135
         14.59.1: 83
         15.37.2: 54
         15.60.3: 31
Dial.   35.2: 226
Ger.   30.1: 226
         42.2: 79
         43.4: 221
Hist.   1.39.1: 228
         1.49.2: 85
         1.62.2: 98

2.15.1: 23
2.20.2: 228
2.38.1: 220
2.73: 156
2.81.3: 225
2.95.1: 228
3.34.3: 79
3.77.2: 98
3.77.3: 25
4.12.2: 15
4.12.3: 183
4.28.3: 125
4.33.1: 40
4.46.2: 224
4.65.4: 228
5.12.1: 147
5.17.1: 194
5.17.3: 59

Terentius
Andr.   167: 229
Eun.   175: 86

Tertullianus
Nat.   2.7: 228

Tibullus   1.1.4: 189
         1.3.45: 95

Valerius Maximus
         1.8.6: 134
         2.6.2: 188
         2.7.4: 165
         2.10.6: 105
         3.2.6: 107
         3.2.22: 194
         3.8.2: 122
         4.3.1: 142
         4.8 ext. 2: 82
         8.2.2: 125
         8.13.1: 107

Varro
L.   7.3: 96
         9.58: 146

INDICES

Vegetius
   mil.   1.3.2: 21
           1.4.1: 19
           1.9: 58
           1.21.4: 168
           1.23.2: 21
           2.2.3: 231
           2.10.2: 21
           2.13.6: 21
           2.13.7: 185
           2.14.8: 221
           2.15.6: 6
           2.17.3: 51
           2.22.1: 189
           2.23.5: 192
           3.5: 71
           3.5.3: 189
           3.5.6: 189
           3.6: 5
           3.6.3: 24
           3.6.22: 10
           3.6.22–23: 24
           3.6.25–26: 25
           3.7.7: 214
           3.8: 232
           3.8.10: 219
           3.8.15: 21
           3.8.17: 162
           3.8.18: 164
           3.10.14: 168
           3.12.6: 40
           3.14.6: 190
           3.16.5: 25
           3.16.7: 25
           3.18.6: 21
           3.24.7–16: 186
           3.26.13: 70
           4.2.2: 113
           4.5.1: 52
           4.8: 55
           4.8.2–4: 59
           4.8.3–4: 57
           4.8.4: 56, 57
           4.29.2: 56
           4.38.3: 50

Velleius   2.129.3: 81
           2.25.1: 64
           2.43.1: 226
           2.66.3: 77

Vergilius
   A.   1.91: 186
           1.164: 187
           1.192–3: 152
           1.505: 61
           1.669: 90
           2.132–3: 197
           2.135: 159
           2.348: 224
           2.443–4: 51
           2.660: 229
           3.102: 108
           3.263: 63
           3.304: 193
           3.637: 54
           4.73: 161
           4.88: 54
           5.418: 229
           6.151: 228
           6.268: 159
           6.842–3: 194
           7.319–22: 212
           7.510: 161
           7.611: 229
           7.637: 189
           8.190: 128, 129
           9.153: 127
           9.400–1: 115
           9.569: 61
           9.694: 72
           10.90: 24
           10.323: 19
           10.698: 61
           10.770: 82
           10.787/8: 115
           10.830–1: 59
           11.268: 144
           11.770–1: 121
           12.377: 51
           12.491–2: 105
           12.529–30: 193

INDICES

Buc.	4.21–2: 95		2.112: 176	
	5.65: 224		2.476: 96	
G.	1.95: 122		2.539: 189	
	1.322: 41		3.369: 152	
	1.430–1: 60		4.70–2: 120	

IX. *Passages referred to (Greek, including Ephraem Syrus)*

Achilles Tatius
 1.17.3–5: 95

Aelianus
 VH 5.19: 194

Aeneas Tacticus
 32.1.9–10: 51
 fr. 1: 11

Aeschylus
 Pers. 105–6: 82

Anthologia Graeca
 14.148: 175

Appianus
 Pun. 117: 60
 Syr. 57: 19

Arrianus
 An. 2.10.4: 225
 2.27.2: 58
 3.30.11: 58
 4.3.3: 58
 4.4.1: 180
 4.23.3: 58
 4.26.4: 58
 5.12.3: 92
 6.10.1: 58
 6.10.3: 58
 6.13.4: 58
 7.7.7: 22, 23
 7.10.2: 58
 7.21.2: 227
 fr. 8 FHG: 153
 Tact. 19: 185
 35.3: 71

Artemii passio
 69: 203, 208–210, 216

Asinius Quadratus
 FHG III, 660: 30

Athenaeus
 12.550 e: 224
 13.603 c: 142

Basilius
 Ep. 152: 9
 269: 8
 Hex. 5.47B: 95

Cedrenus
 Hist. 307 C–D: 210, 212

Charito 5.3.1: 141

Chron. Ps.-Dionysianum
 a. 674 = CSCO 91: 18

Dexippus
 Scyth. *fr.* 29.3: 51

Dio Cassius
 16.57.43: 142
 40.16.1: 37
 40.18.3: 71, 72
 40.21.1: 37
 40.26: 37
 41.35.5: 74
 48.42.2: 74
 49.27.1: 74
 49.38.4: 75
 54.8.3: 197
 60.20.2–6: 183
 66.17.2: 83

INDICES

68.3.1: 84
68.13.1–6: 89
68.27.1: 34, 35, 55
68.28.1: 172
68.28.1–2: 173
68.30.3: 36
68.31.4: 227
69.9.6: 183
69.12.3: 144
69.18.4: 83
80.3.5: 165

Diodorus Siculus
2.12.1: 35
11.27.2: 194
32.8: 60

Dionysius Halicarnassensis
4.22.1: 197
9.50.7: 74
15.1.4: 107

Ephraem Syrus
HcJul. 2.18: 210, 212
3.15: 212

Eunapius
fr. 27.2: 51
27.3: 175
27.4: 175
27.5: 97, 98, 176
27.6: 225
27.7: 175
68: 8

Gregorius Nazianzenus
Ep. 133: 9
Or. 4.11: 212
4.66: 71
5.9: 171
5.10: 152, 153, 204
5.11: 210

Heliodorus
8.5: 22, 23

Herodianus
8.4.4: 91

Herodotus
1.179: 34
1.193: 93, 94
1.193.2: 44
1.193.5: 95
3.153–60: 210
6.109–111: 194
6.114: 194
6.92: 193
8.84: 194
8.93: 194
9.37: 127
9.73–75: 193

Homerus
Il. 1.165–6: 82
3.141: 226
4.297: 186

Isidorus Characenus
1 (= GGM 1 247): 22
1 (= GGM I 249): 15,
30, 34, 43

Josephus
AJ 3.172–3: 51
11.133: 101
18.379: 100

Julianus
Caes. 315 a: 80
329 a: 79
329 c: 88
Ep. 14, 385 c: 75
Ep. ad Ath.
270 c: 80
270 c – 271 a: 80
273 b: 80
280 a-b: 79
286 a: 79
Mis. 340 b: 139
345 c: 141
351 b: 84
361 b: 199

INDICES

Or. 1.11: 188
2.65 b-c: 186
3.98 c-d: 79

Libanius
Ep. 1402: 8
1402.2: 40, 195
Or. 1.133: 174
18.22: 27
18.172: 133
18.179: 141
18.214: 208
18.218: 15, 16, 18
18.219: 30, 31
18.219–221: 25
18.223: 23
18.223–227: 91
18.227: 49, 53
18.228: 53, 56, 62, 65
18.229: 70, 71, 73, 75
18.231: 144, 208
18.234: 92, 93
18.235: 54, 103, 105,
114, 123
18.236: 105, 106, 109,
133, 158
18.237: 108, 116
18.238: 117, 130, 132
18.239: 130, 131, 137,
138
18.239–40: 138
18.241: 145
18.242: 146
18.243: 149–151
18.244: 153
18.245: 5, 171, 172
18.246: 172
18.247: 173
18.248: 177, 226
18.249: 175
18.249–50: 174
18.250: 177–179, 192,
193, 225
18.250–1: 178, 179
18.252: 180–182
18.254: 191, 195
18.255: 192

18.257–260: 207
18.260: 209, 221
18.261: 198, 209
18.262: 213, 214
18.262–3: 212
18.263: 214, 215
18.264: 209, 220, 223
18.282: 208
18.306: 208
24.20: 9
24.37: 174
59.83–84: 18

Lucianus
Hist. Conscr.
29: 71

Lydus
Mag. 1.47: 5
Mens. 4.119: 210, 212, 216

Malalas
Chron. 13.330: 6, 9, 44, 102,
176, 209
13.331: 204, 210, 216
13.332: 204, 216

Menander Rhetor
402.7: 95

Onosander
33: 58

Oracula Sibyllina
8.217: 162

Petrus Patricius
fr. 17: 192

Philo Mechanicus
Bel 95.34: 51

Philo Iudaeus
Leg. ad Gaium
216: 101
245: 101
282: 101

270 INDICES

Philostorgus
  HE   6.15: 210
             8.8: 8, 9

Philostratus
  Im.   1.9.6: 95

Plato
  Symp.   203 a 2: 133
  Tht.   172 e: 127

Plutarchus
  Ag.   9: 224
  Alc.   33: 199
  Alex.   21.5: 142
             21.10: 141
  apopth. Lac.
             13: 224
  Arist. et Cato
             2.2: 194
  Art.   25: 151
  Crass.   21: 37
             21.1–22.5: 210
  Marc.   21.2]: 175
  Mor.   724e: 93
  Pyrrh.   8.2: 11
  Quaest. conv.
             8.4.5: 93
  Sert.   3.1: 182
  Them.   14.2: 194

Polyaenus
             2.1.6: 224

Polybius   5.51.6: 44
           6.38.1: 74
           6.38.2: 74
           6.39.2: 137
           6.39.5: 135
           10.3.7: 58
           10.13.1–2: 58
           10.19.3–7: 142
           10.24.2–3: 58
           10.32.9–11: 58
           10.33.4–5: 58
           18.18.5: 167
           18.18.12: 167–168

           38.19.1: 60
           fr. 19a 1–4 (B.-W.): 60

Priscus   *fr.* 9.3 (Blockley): 79

Procopius
  Aed.   4.6.13: 89
  Pers.   1.19.32–3: 79
             2.28.4: 153

Ptolemaeus
             5.15.18: 19
             5.18.8: 98
             5.19.4: 34
             5.20.2: 43

Socrates
  HE   3.21.4: 203, 207
             3.21.6–7: 208
             6.1.5: 171
             6.1.6: 174, 185,
                226–227
             6.1.7: 178, 191
             6.1.8: 191
             6.1.9: 208, 209, 213
             6.1.10–12: 210, 212
             6.1.11: 216
             6.1.12: 216

Strabo   2.1.26: 41
           5.4.12: 198
           11.14.8: 41
           16.1.9–10: 22
           16.1.26: 44

Suda   E 322: 174
           I 437: 175
           s.v. ἀνασχοῦσα: 131

Themistius
  Or.   1.2 a: 71

Theodotus
  HE   3.25.1: 212
             3.25.4: 216
             4.33: 8, 9

INDICES

Theophrastus
HP 2.8.4: 95
4.4.1: 151

Theophylactus Simocatta
Hist. 2.6: 134
2.7: 144
5.6–7: 101

Thucydides
2.75.5: 51

Vetus Testamentum
Ne. 2.8: 151

Xenophon
Ag. 1.28: 224
An. 1.2.7: 151
1.5.2: 13, 230
1.5.10: 94
1.7.15: 41
1.8.19: 225
2.3.10: 93
2.3.15: 94
2.4.12: 35, 41
2.4.14: 151
3.5.9: 92
Cyr. 1.3.14: 151
5.2.5: 17
HG 3.4.19: 224
4.1.15–6: 151

Zonaras 9.29: 60
13.5: 8
13.10.10: 205
13.13.1: 203
13.13.2–9: 207
13.13.4–6: 210
13.13.4–9: 212
13.13.7: 209, 214, 218
13.13.9: 215, 216
13.13.13: 219

Zosimus 1.56.1: 17
2.27.1–4: 8
3.11.3: 8, 9
3.13.3: 4, 9, 76

3.13.4: 4
3.14.1: 6, 7, 10, 12
3.14.2: 13
3.14.3: 14, 15, 17
3.14.4: 18
3.15.1: 30, 31
3.15.2: 31, 32, 34, 35, 125
3.15.3: 35, 36
3.15.4: 38
3.15.4–6: 36
3.15.5: 37
3.15.6: 38
3.16.1: 41, 47
3.16.1–3: 44
3.16.2: 6, 47
3.16.3: 7, 9
3.17.1: 7, 9
3.17.2: 48
3.17.3: 48, 49, 53, 54
3.17.3–5: 49
3.17.5: 35, 54
3.18.1: 8, 52
3.18.2: 53, 55, 56, 62
3.18.3: 62–64
3.18.4: 65, 66
3.18.4–6: 64
3.18.5–6: 67
3.18.6: 49, 57, 76
3.18.6–19.2: 69
3.19.1: 70, 71
3.19.1–2: 76
3.19.2: 70, 72, 73, 75
3.19.3: 41, 44–46, 90, 91
3.19.4: 91–93, 97, 100
3.20.1: 93
3.20.2: 103, 106, 158
3.20.3: 104, 106, 109
3.20.4: 109
3.20.5: 103, 110, 111, 113
3.21.1: 122
3.21.2: 116, 123
3.21.3: 105, 113, 114, 116
3.21.3–5: 116

272 INDICES

3.21.4: 7, 117–119
3.21.5: 9, 102, 110, 119
3.22.1: 116, 118, 126
3.22.2: 128, 129
3.22.3: 129, 130
3.22.4: 130–132
3.22.5: 132, 133
3.22.6: 137, 138
3.22.7: 139, 145
3.23.1: 147, 151, 176
3.23.1–2: 149
3.23.1–24.1: 149
3.23.2: 150, 152
3.23.3: 152–155, 158
3.23.4: 138, 154–156
3.24.1: 157, 158, 206
3.24.2: 44, 171–174
3.25.1: 174, 177, 179,

180
3.25.2: 180
3.25.3: 181
3.25.4: 181, 182
3.25.5: 191
3.25.6: 192
3.25.7: 9, 178, 192, 195
3.26.1: 207
3.26.2: 202, 209, 211, 212
3.26.3: 209, 214, 218, 220, 223, 225
3.26.4: 219, 220, 223, 231
3.26.5: 6
3.31.1: 8
4.24.3: 9
4.30.5: 9

X. *Passages referred to in Ammianus 14–23 and 25–31*

14.1.1: 40, 80, 167
14.1.3: 165
14.1.5: 229
14.1.6: 105, 167, 195
14.1.9: 127
14.2.2: 132
14.2.3: 124
14.2.4: 53
14.2.7: 25
14.2.10: 122
14.2.12: 87
14.2.15: 9, 90, 165
14.3.4: 16
14.5.2: 88
14.5.5: 124
14.5.6: 84, 112
14.5.8: 145
14.5.9: 29
14.6.9: 13
14.6.10: 50
14.6.10–11: 81
14.6.11: 142
14.6.14: 125
14.6.23: 115
14.6.25: 21
14.7.1: 203

14.7.6: 161
14.8.5: 2
14.8.12: 88
14.8.13: 133, 146
14.8.15: 107
14.9.2: 85
14.9.8: 11
14.10.10: 86
14.11.7: 80
14.11.12: 228
15.1.4: 5
15.2.3: 165
15.2.4: 144
15.3.2: 74
15.3.10: 145
15.4.1: 46, 82, 149
15.4.4: 166
15.4.10: 8
15.4.11: 116, 190
15.4.12: 194
15.5.5: 17
15.5.16: 71
15.5.18: 162, 203
15.5.19: 3
15.5.21: 164
15.5.27: 225

INDICES 273

15.5.30: 66
15.7.2: 117, 196
15.7.5: 74
15.8.5: 22
15.8.13: 84, 166, 190
15.8.14: 128
15.8.15: 86
15.8.16: 144
15.10.1: 117
15.10.4: 227
15.10.5: 105, 115
15.10.9: 229
15.10.10: 142, 167
15.11.3: 49
15.12.1: 179
15.13.4: 107
16.1.1: 181
16.2.2: 218
16.2.6: 70
16.2.8: 127
16.2.10: 118
16.2.11: 5
16.3.1: 41
16.3.3: 112, 153
16.4.4: 174
16.5.10: 188
16.5.14: 66
16.7.1: 73
16.7.4: 134
16.7.5: 134
16.8.7: 80
16.10.2: 106
16.10.3: 108
16.10.6: 115
16.10.7: 71
16.10.8: 51, 121, 187
16.10.11: 230
16.10.14: 190
16.10.16: 8, 176
16.10.21: 112
16.11.1: 3
16.11.3: 186
16.11.4: 161
16.11.6: 40
16.11.9: 183
16.11.12: 26
16.12.7: 120

16.12.8: 32, 58
16.12.11: 70
16.12.12: 71
16.12.13: 66
16.12.16: 26
16.12.18: 116
16.12.22: 166
16.12.23: 104
16.12.24: 134
16.12.27: 24
16.12.29: 13
16.12.33: 120
16.12.35: 162
16.12.36: 120, 159, 166, 167, 188
16.12.39: 71, 107
16.12.43: 164, 189
16.12.44: 122
16.12.45: 189
16.12.47: 5
16.12.48: 105
16.12.49: 112
16.12.52: 145
16.12.57: 183
16.12.58: 145
16.12.61: 115
16.12.62: 177
16.12.63: 3, 142
16.12.64: 88
16.12.69: 211
16.12.70: 115, 116
16.12.9–12: 77
17.1.1: 46, 224
17.1.2: 91, 108, 179, 190
17.1.4: 179
17.1.5: 104, 166
17.1.7: 104
17.1.10: 211
17.1.11: 112, 153
17.2.1: 25, 78
17.2.3: 205
17.4.1: 231
17.4.6: 3
17.4.12: 141
17.4.14: 112
17.4.15: 54
17.5.2: 191, 192
17.5.14: 5, 143

17.6.1: 231
17.6.3: 7
17.7.2: 187, 232
17.7.12: 22, 124
17.7.13: 117
17.8.5: 165
17.9.3: 117
17.9.5: 141
17.10.1: 174
17.10.2: 210
17.10.8: 77
17.11.1: 52, 224
17.11.3: 60
17.12.1: 70
17.12.2: 121
17.12.4: 174, 227
17.12.10: 120
17.12.12: 24
17.13.4: 89
17.13.6: 106
17.13.16: 217
17.13.23: 17, 107, 129
17.13.25: 85
17.13.27: 24
17.13.34: 2
18.1.1: 79
18.2.10: 158, 229
18.2.13: 162
18.2.17: 31
18.2.18: 112
18.3.1: 24
18.3.3: 179
18.3.9: 129
18.4.1: 165
18.4.5: 61
18.5.2: 19
18.5.6: 112
18.6.12: 192
18.6.15: 229
18.6.16: 93
18.6.17: 161
18.6.18: 85
18.6.21: 63
18.6.22: 167
18.7.3: 219
18.7.5: 151, 227
18.7.6: 167

18.7.9: 227
18.8.2: 70
18.8.5: 59
18.8.8: 163
18.9.2: 124
18.10.3: 26
19.1.2: 51
19.1.3: 166
19.1.5: 99
19.1.6: 124
19.1.9: 133
19.2.2: 232
19.2.3: 186, 193
19.2.6: 184
19.2.8: 145, 159, 160
19.2.11: 132
19.2.13: 57
19.2.14: 111
19.3.1: 25
19.5.1: 62
19.5.2: 119
19.5.3: 159
19.5.4: 16, 147
19.5.6: 32, 118, 123
19.5.7: 216
19.6.9: 164, 188
19.6.10: 118, 123
19.7.2: 119, 123
19.7.3: 12, 51, 122
19.7.4: 190
19.7.8: 106
19.8.2: 50, 53
19.8.5: 105
19.8.6: 149
19.8.10: 231
19.8.11: 70
19.9.2: 155
19.11.1: 70, 231
19.11.3: 143
19.11.15: 120
19.12.4: 228
20.1.1: 64
20.1.3.: 40
20.1.3: 130, 187
20.2.3: 17, 107
20.2.5: 26, 70, 160
20.3.1: 50

INDICES

20.3.3: 144
20.3.7: 34
20.3.12: 22, 184
20.4.1: 116
20.4.2: 131, 187
20.4.5: 2, 167
20.4.6: 72, 106, 162
20.4.8: 83, 125
20.4.9: 161, 228
20.4.10: 19, 87
20.4.11: 166
20.4.12: 2, 40, 190, 196
20.4.13: 30, 34, 152
20.4.14: 125, 180
20.4.15: 231
20.4.17: 116
20.4.18: 107, 140, 147, 184
20.4.22: 134
20.5.1: 112, 220
20.5.3: 3, 7
20.5.3–7: 77
20.5.4: 124, 181
20.5.5: 187
20.5.6: 231
20.5.8: 86
20.6.1: 127, 161, 167, 226
20.6.2: 3, 54
20.6.3: 16, 51, 117, 180
20.6.4: 51, 114, 163, 190
20.6.6: 59, 225
20.6.7: 16, 71, 150, 176
20.6.7–8: 18
20.7.1: 101, 113
20.7.2: 39, 40, 51, 184
20.7.6: 26, 57, 120, 122, 189
20.7.7: 70, 124
20.7.10: 56, 123
20.7.13: 107
20.7.15: 101, 193
20.7.16: 165, 167
20.7.17: 113
20.8.1: 119
20.8.9: 80, 145
20.8.10: 20, 215
20.8.11: 211
20.8.14: 106
20.8.15: 167, 231

20.8.19: 121
20.9.1: 124
20.9.2: 77
20.9.3: 139
20.9.5: 144
20.10.2: 158
20.11.1: 168
20.11.5: 77, 79, 154, 231
20.11.6: 52, 104, 168
20.11.7: 57
20.11.8: 117
20.11.9: 24, 51, 52
20.11.10: 91
20.11.12: 62
20.11.20: 167
20.11.21: 112, 164
20.11.22: 105, 187
20.11.24: 14
20.11.29: 11
20.11.31: 116
20.11.32: 177
21.1.3: 62
21.1.6: 140
21.1.7: 22
21.1.7–14: 198
21.1.9: 116
21.1.10: 229
21.1.14: 228
21.2.1: 40, 188
21.2.2: 134
21.2.4: 4, 124
21.3.1: 77
21.4.1: 72, 124
21.4.4: 2
21.4.6: 220
21.4.7: 24
21.5.1: 117, 189, 212
21.5.2–8: 77
21.5.4: 193
21.5.5: 82
21.5.6: 89
21.5.7: 78, 204
21.5.8: 112
21.5.9: 86, 104
21.5.10: 73, 162
21.5.13: 230
21.6.6: 56, 119

276 INDICES

21.7.1: 159, 162
21.7.2: 19, 184
21.7.3: 167
21.7.6: 10, 11
21.7.7: 231
21.8.1: 7, 9
21.8.2: 89
21.8.2–3: 10
21.8.3: 142, 178, 205
21.8.4.: 109
21.10.1: 65, 66, 161, 181
21.10.2: 7, 66
21.10.3: 114
21.10.4: 31
21.10.7: 2, 80
21.10.8: 52, 61, 75
21.11.3: 182
21.12.1: 5, 224
21.12.3: 104
21.12.4: 113, 225
21.12.5: 116, 120, 164
21.12.6: 7, 60, 117, 122
21.12.8: 64, 127
21.12.9: 55, 137
21.12.11: 120
21.12.12: 220
21.12.13: 56, 105, 152, 160
21.12.14: 104
21.12.15: 98
21.12.16: 205
21.12.17: 164
21.12.18: 62
21.12.20: 138, 155
21.12.22: 189
21.12.23: 124
21.13.2: 13, 129
21.13.4: 24
21.13.5: 165
21.13.6: 58
21.13.9: 76, 185, 187
21.13.10: 85
21.13.13: 88
21.13.14: 21
21.13.15: 164, 189
21.13.16: 6, 128
21.14.2: 232
21.14.5: 133, 135, 142

21.15.1: 209
21.15.2: 124, 137
21.16.7: 11
21.16.8: 85
21.16.9: 128
21.16.10: 181
21.16.13: 59
21.16.17: 112
21.16.19: 59
22.1.2: 90, 91
22.2.4: 65
22.3.1: 7, 179
22.3.12: 74
22.4.2: 105, 144
22.5.5: 100
22.6.2: 58
22.6.3: 215
22.6.4: 38
22.7.1: 7
22.7.5: 52
22.7.6: 193
22.7.7: 8, 84
22.7.9: 84
22.8.1: 5
22.8.2: 15
22.8.10: 49
22.8.14: 124, 166
22.8.25: 218
22.8.33: 52
22.8.37: 31, 56
22.8.38: 46
22.8.40: 166
22.8.44: 89
22.8.46: 232
22.9.1: 88
22.9.3: 56, 204
22.9.5: 142
22.9.9: 84, 101
22.9.14: 65, 66
22.10.1: 177
22.10.5: 77, 138
22.10.6: 83
22.11.2: 18, 160
22.11.6: 79
22.12.1: 197
22.12.2: 51, 184
22.12.5: 4

INDICES

22.12.6: 128, 176, 197
22.12.7: 228
22.12.8: 2, 173
22.14.1: 107
22.14.2: 86
22.15.2: 20
22.15.7: 22, 143
22.15.8: 96
22.15.9: 105
22.15.20: 220
22.15.22: 25
22.15.30: 128
22.16.6: 18
22.16.7: 78, 166
22.16.9: 46
22.16.13: 61
22.16.14: 146
22.16.18: 31
22.16.23: 124
23.1.5: 130
23.1.5–7: 198
23.1.6: 105
23.2.1: 221
23.2.3–4: 198
23.2.4: 115
23.2.6: 13
23.2.7: 10, 46, 108, 229
23.3.1: 41, 229
23.3.2: 211
23.3.4: 20, 38, 70, 184
23.3.5: 221, 229, 231
23.3.6: 229
23.3.7: 214
23.3.8: 20, 38, 72
23.3.9: 7, 12, 14, 18, 22, 26, 44,
    71, 178, 213, 214
23.4.2: 55, 97, 118, 122, 123, 143,
    172
23.4.2–3: 55
23.4.2–7: 118
23.4.4: 123
23.4.4–6: 143
23.4.8–9: 53, 126
23.4.9: 137
23.4.10: 62
23.4.10–13: 62, 63
23.4.11: 185

23.4.12: 176
23.4.14: 98, 123, 180
23.5.3: 224
23.5.4: 12, 31, 46
23.5.5: 4, 46, 82
23.5.6: 12, 57, 179
23.5.7: 4, 49, 170
23.5.8: 13, 24, 58, 151, 157, 177,
    182
23.5.10: 195
23.5.11: 19
23.5.12: 124, 230
23.5.15: 76, 78, 110, 120
23.5.16–23: 77
23.5.17: 36, 88, 98, 172
23.5.18: 79, 197, 208, 211
23.5.19.: 25
23.5.19: 78, 82, 88, 166, 177, 190,
    209
23.5.20: 60, 133, 197
23.5.21: 5, 60
23.5.23: 195
23.5.24: 76, 86
23.5.25: 187
23.6.2: 41
23.6.10: 82
23.6.14–15: 229
23.6.15: 41, 114
23.6.23: 35, 41, 42, 54, 94, 110,
    152, 192
23.6.24: 154
23.6.25: 22, 43, 46
23.6.44: 143
23.6.46: 176
23.6.49: 114
23.6.50: 151
23.6.54: 20
23.6.68: 211
23.6.75: 223, 224
23.6.76: 115
23.6.78: 104
23.6.79: 106
23.6.80: 24, 104, 225
23.6.81: 155
23.6.83: 74, 185
23.6.85: 97
23.8.86: 96

25.1.1: 126, 129, 221
25.1.2: 161, 231
25.1.6: 107
25.1.8–9: 75, 165
25.1.12: 51, 184
25.1.13: 56
25.1.16: 203
25.1.17: 189
25.1.18: 225
25.2.3: 232
25.2.4: 198
25.3.2: 10
25.3.5: 192
25.3.6: 192
25.3.8: 4
25.3.10: 127
25.3.13: 136
25.3.16: 135
25.3.18: 184
25.3.19: 83, 167
25.3.21: 29
25.3.23: 80
25.4.2: 141
25.4.2–6: 139
25.4.7: 5
25.4.9: 25
25.4.10: 125
25.4.11: 166
25.4.12: 83
25.4.16: 25
25.4.17: 197
25.4.24: 79
25.5.2: 7, 203
25.5.6: 24
25.5.7: 21, 22
25.6.5: 168
25.6.6: 52
25.6.8: 30, 180
25.6.13: 183
25.6.14: 158, 179
25.6.15: 91
25.7.5: 37
25.7.14: 66
25.8.2: 120, 164
25.8.3: 108, 214, 218
25.8.17: 204
25.8.18: 131

25.9.10: 142
25.10.5: 41
25.10.8: 21
25.10.13: 128
26.1.9: 162
26.2.2: 85
26.6.4: 13
26.6.10: 157
26.6.12: 57
26.6.15: 106
26.6.18: 80
26.7.1: 111
26.7.7: 11
26.7.15: 188
26.7.17: 2
26.8.4: 102
26.8.7: 153
26.8.12: 160, 206
26.8.13: 79
26.9.3: 167
26.10.10: 137
26.10.16: 147
27.2.1: 70
27.2.5: 11, 87
27.2.8: 9, 122, 194
27.3.13: 86
27.5.3: 161
27.5.4: 9
27.5.6: 146
27.6.4: 88
27.6.6: 4
27.6.14: 88
27.6.15: 24
27.6.16: 182
27.7.1: 177
27.7.2: 84
27.7.4: 124
27.8.1: 156
27.8.10: 211
27.9.10: 75
27.10.12: 13, 153
27.10.15: 192
27.12.3: 105
27.12.6: 31, 97
27.12.12: 163
28.1.1: 212
28.1.52: 13

INDICES

28.2.2: 114, 204
28.2.9: 73
28.3.1: 181
28.3.4: 22
28.4.10: 19
28.5.10: 13
28.5.11: 34
28.5.12: 221
28.6.19: 59, 115
28.6.25: 73
29.1.1: 185
29.1.2: 11
29.1.32: 126
29.1.43: 79
29.2.1: 172
29.2.4: 228
29.2.20: 212
29.2.21: 48
29.5.10: 26
29.5.11: 190
29.5.14: 221
29.5.18: 206
29.5.22: 12, 75
29.5.23: 75
29.5.24: 75
29.5.30: 54
29.5.31: 75
29.5.35: 144
29.5.37: 221
29.5.49: 75
29.5.50: 118
29.5.54: 111
29.6.2: 165
29.6.6: 218
29.6.11: 211
29.6.14: 106
30.1.5: 52
30.1.9: 92
30.1.10: 158
30.1.13: 164
30.1.14: 176
30.1.16: 156
30.2.5: 37
30.3.4: 128
30.4.13: 128, 144

30.5.2: 113
30.5.7: 115
30.5.10: 116
30.5.17: 173
30.6.3: 145
30.6.5: 123
30.7.3: 73
30.7.4: 85
30.9.4: 176
30.9.5: 85
31.2.8: 48
31.2.18: 232
31.2.23: 25
31.4.5: 111
31.5.6: 221
31.5.8: 116
31.6.2: 217
31.6.3: 156
31.7.4: 221
31.7.8: 70
31.7.10: 4, 120
31.7.12: 191
31.7.16: 114, 163
31.8.2: 221
31.8.8: 137, 145
31.8.10: 59
31.10.3: 160
31.10.15: 202
31.10.18: 19
31.10.19: 179
31.10.20: 160
31.12.4: 168
31.12.6: 10
31.12.13: 190
31.13.1: 212
31.13.2: 186
31.13.6: 98, 194
31.13.11: 162
31.13.17: 142
31.14.5: 84
31.15.1: 191
31.15.8: 23
31.15.10: 162
31.16.1: 176
31.16.2: 144, 153

Printed in the United States
By Bookmasters